GLOBAL PERSPECTIVES
ON THE UNITED STATES

GLOBAL STUDIES OF THE UNITED STATES

Edited by Jane C. Desmond and Virginia R. Domínguez, IFUSS founders

*The International Forum for U.S. Studies (IFUSS) is a research center for the
transnational study of the United States at the University of Illinois, Urbana-Champaign.*

A list of books in the series appears at the end of this book.

GLOBAL PERSPECTIVES ON THE UNITED STATES

Pro-Americanism, Anti-Americanism, and the Discourses Between

Edited by
VIRGINIA R. DOMÍNGUEZ
AND JANE C. DESMOND

UNIVERSITY OF ILLINOIS PRESS
Urbana, Chicago, and Springfield

Library of Congress Cataloging-in-Publication Data
Names: Dominguez, Virginia R., editor of compilation. | Desmond, Jane,
    editor of compilation.
Title: Global perspectives on the United States : pro-Americanism, anti-
    Americanism, and the discourses between / edited by Virginia R.
    Dominguez and Jane C. Desmond.
Description: Urbana : University of Illinois Press, [2017] | Series: Global
    studies of the United States | Includes bibliographical references and
    index.
Identifiers: LCCN 2016040295| ISBN 9780252040832 (hardback : acid-free
    paper) | ISBN 9780252082337 (paperback : acid-free paper) | ISBN
    9780252099335 (e-book)
Subjects: LCSH: United States—Foreign public opinion. | United States—
    Relations. | Civilization, Modern—American influences. | World
    politics— 1989- | Social history— 1970- | Social change. | BISAC:
    POLITICAL SCIENCE / Public Policy / Cultural Policy. | SOCIAL
    SCIENCE / Popular Culture. | SOCIAL SCIENCE / Sociology /
    General.
Classification: LCC E183.7 .G558 2017 | DDC 327.73—dc23
    LC record available at https://lccn.loc.gov/2016040295

CONTENTS

ACKNOWLEDGMENTS

A book like this has a lot of moving parts and a long history. As early public talks were developed by colleagues into formal chapters, and then responses to the articles, and finally responses to the responses were crafted, the conversations kept evolving along the way, deepening and branching and coming back together. With dozens of parts, and twenty contributors from ten countries, the logistics of keeping that conversation going were daunting. This book would not have taken concrete form without the exceptional dedication of our colleagues who contributed their ideas, writings, and great flexibility and patience over its long period of development. We received hastily typed emails from scholars in transit about to jump on motorcycles while travelling in Vietnam, or while far from their university offices, conducting fieldwork in Kyrgyzstan. Some replied from cities in the throes of political turmoil, responding, miraculously, to queries about footnote details in the midst of much more pressing issues. We thank each and every one of our contributors for their commitment and intellectual and personal generosity in seeing this project through.

We wish to acknowledge too the exceptional commitment of Sophia Balakian, who helped tremendously in the coordination of the project while writing her dissertation, and Anita Kaiser and Dr. David Schrag, Programming Coordinators for the International Forum for U.S. Studies during the projects' development at the University of Illinois at Urbana–Champaign.

Finally, I must acknowledge the unwavering dedication that my co-editor Virginia Domínguez gave to this project. No matter how many times the challenging logistics threatened to overwhelm us, she never gave up on her vision for this unique volume and saw it through to completion with impressive tenacity and attention to detail.

A few of the essays in this book have appeared in part or in different form in earlier renditions, and we are grateful to the authors and publishers for permission to include those materials in these pages. The sources are listed here:

Virginia R. Domínguez, "Approaching 'America': Is there an Anthropology of Pro-Americanism and an Anthropology of Anti-Americanism?" In *Taiwan Journal of Anthropology* 13(1) June 2015: 1–20.

Sabine Broeck, "The Erotics of African American Endurance; or, On the Right Side of History? White (West-)German Public Sentiment between Pornotroping and Civil Rights Solidarity." In *Germans and African Americans: Two Centuries of Exchange*. Ed. Larry A. Greene and Anke Ortlepp. Jackson: University Press of Mississippi.

Manar Shorbagy, "The Egyptian Movement for Change: Misunderstanding Kefayah: Redefining Politics in Egypt." In *Public Culture* 19.1 (2007): 175–96.

Reading "America" Across and Against the Grain of Public Discourse

Jane C. Desmond

Recent political events like the violent rise of ISIS (the so-called Islamic State), the war in Syria, continuing U.S. engagement in Afghanistan, U.S. participation in fighting the pandemic of Ebola in West Africa, Russian military interventions in Ukraine and their effects on U.S.-Europe relations, plans for strengthening the U.S.-India relationship as part of a wider strategy of Asian diplomacy, and, after fifty years of firm disengagement, the striking easing of relations between the United States and Cuba, all signal the continuing interlocking political spheres of action of the United States and so many other parts of the world. Beyond these political events, ever expanding flows of goods, people, and ideas into and out of the United States demand our attention as scholars with expertise on the political entity and cultural imaginary that gets called "America."

In some discussions of these and other events, the terms "Americanization" and "anti-Americanism" serve as a shorthand for complicated political, cultural, and economic processes, easily bandied about on TV news shows. But the multifaceted relations and the calculus of political capital, economic and military might, cultural influence and flows of people and goods, practices and ideas, and the public discourse that frames them, tell a fuller, more complex story that cannot be captured with such terminological shorthand.

In this volume our aim is to create a venue for that complexity to emerge. Developed over several years by scholars based in many national sites and scholarly communities, and working across numerous disciplinary boundaries, this series of essays and commentaries reflects on events, relationships, and their mobilization in public discourse.

The Unique Structure of the Book

Growing out of a series of international conferences sponsored by the International Forum for U.S. Studies: A Center for the Transnational Study of the United States (IFUSS), these essays have been developed over time, critiqued by other conference participants, and then responded to again by yet other scholars—a dialogic process that teases out the complexities and implications of an argument and then ultimately places those in a wider frame. Specifically, the book is organized around pairs of original essays that overlap thematically or regionally in their concerns. Each author then provides a brief commentary on the other's essay, providing a "Second Look" at the material and ideas. Responding to all of this, a third scholar (or scholars) from a different disciplinary background then offers a final commentary for that section—a "Third Look." All of the commentaries are designed not to shut down debate through simple "correctives" but instead to open up debate and enhance understanding by using the original essays as springboards for thought. Through this innovative structure we have tried to capture something of the vigorous intellectual give-and-take that emerged during the course of these conferences.

Ultimately it is the reader who provides the next "look" as she or he becomes part of this cross-disciplinary conversation. We invite our readers to join the dialogue, to read the essays and critiques with and across one another. Doing so will yield further insights not yet articulated on these pages. For example, an emergent theme across several sections of the book reveals the importance of analyzing actions and ideas along generational lines, a theme that none of the essays explicitly foregrounds.

In carrying out these cross-cutting readings, we invite the reader to recognize, and to embrace, the fact that modes of argumentation, and even what counts as "evidence," vary widely not only across disciplines from literature to political science to art history and beyond but also across the globe in different regional and national scholarly communities, each of which frames these issues, and even the practice of academic writing, differently. A book like this should challenge readers as much as it did the contributing authors who strove to craft commentaries across disciplinary limits. We believe that the complexity of these issues demand this multi-cited and emphatically multi- and trans-disciplinary approach. As difficult as it is to achieve in practice, we argue that such efforts are essential to the development of a truly transnational "American Studies."

Of course, at some point the potentially never-ending dialogic exchange and debate has to be fixed on the page. What appears here, then, is that caesura, a "pause" in the imagined dialogue—a snapshot of a moment in history and in analysis that never really stands still. In most cases the moment of pause does not affect the main argument of the original essay. Large-scale processes do not stop immediately when a president changes office or a new treaty is signed. This is especially true for essays concerned with cultural practices and cultural products such as the circulation of films, music, and literature. But in a couple of cases, notably the essays focused on Central Asia and Egypt, oriented more toward political science, the pace of governmental change has been so dramatic and explosive that the pausing after the moment of the Second Look commentary is not sufficient. In those cases an additional commentary or update has been added to incorporate events right up to the moment of publication.

The level of depth and the intensity of multi- and transdisciplinary scholarly analysis presented here is a hallmark of the type of transnational study of the United States that IFUSS has been dedicated to fostering since its founding by Virginia Domínguez and me over twenty years ago. IFUSS fosters scholarly relations across multiple national and regional boundaries by bringing together scholars in a variety of disciplines from all parts of the globe as peers for shared research residencies, faculty seminars, colloquium series, international conferences, and guest teaching opportunities for distinguished scholars. Still the only international research center of its kind in the United States, in the past two decades IFUSS has become widely acknowledged in the United States and abroad as a leader in the development of transnational perspectives on the understanding of the United States in the humanities and social sciences. This book, and the IFUSS series, Global Studies of the United States, of which it is a part, seeks to make those initiatives even more widely available.

The topics we take up here, the production and circulation of discourses that become named as "anti-American" or as "Americanization," have never been more timely than now as the U.S. foreign policy of drone strikes in the Middle East garners ever more critique, and even old Western European allies, like Germany, bristle at recent stunning revelations about U.S. government cyber-spying on their citizens and political leaders. While each of these essays captures a moment in time and sketches a set of relations that is always changing, the frameworks we suggest here—of discursive analysis and multi-perspectival critique—will prove trenchant, we hope, for years to come.

Above all, this book offers a pattern for constructing dialogue across multiple national and regional boundaries; of capturing flux without ossifying it; and of acknowledging that the role of the United States in the world as geopolitical entity, as cultural imaginary, and as economic and military power, demands ongoing scrutiny and analysis across multiple disciplinary platforms in the humanities and social sciences and must engage specialists from around the globe. We hope this book provides an example of one way to go about that essential work together.

The "American" Conundrum—Criticism, Attraction, and Antagonisms

Virginia R. Domínguez, with Sophia Balakian

This book is a daring collaborative effort.[1] Colleagues outside the United States who have dedicated much of their lives to studying the States are often suspect in their home settings for being too sympathetic to the United States, too obsessed, or at least not critical enough of the United States. To touch on the topic of this book in such an international venue and do so without being beholden to critics at home or abroad takes courage and conviction, not to mention the knowledge, thoughtfulness, curiosity, and research that fills this book with riches. After all, to some just looking quickly at this book, our topic will seem to be "anti-Americanism," to others it may look like "pro-Americanism," and to still others it may seem like some version of "Americanization." But we show something more complex and less easy to pin down so simply.

All essays in this volume entail engagements with the U.S. abroad, including perceptions of the United States and of "American" things, people, culture, and politics. All of them also entail analytic methods and choices that treat certain kinds of talk, images, behaviors, and allusions as references to "America" (usually meaning the United States of America). One of our questions, collectively, is what they all add up to. Another key question becomes how to read the data, the material, the information, and the interpretations that arise from any focus on such material. Contributors to this volume do not always agree about what constitutes anti-Americanism or evidence of anti-Americanism. The essays authored by Edward Schatz, Manar Shorbagy, Seyed Mohammad Marandi, and Ira Dworkin, for example, highlight what is at stake in such disagreements. At times of heightened fear in the United States—security concerns, economic concerns, and military concerns—fear in this country of others (including our official allies) may explain much public and press talk of "anti-Americanism." But how accurate is that? How trustworthy is that assessment? And what does it miss in its labeling?

Thinking about criticism, what it is, how it appears, how it manifests itself, and how it is consumed is important. The mix of praise, engagement, puzzlement, consumption, and criticism of the United States that we include in this book is a wonderful example of why criticism is interesting. Little about it is straight-forward. Yes, it often feels hurtful or at least wrong to a person aggrieved, and, yes, the critic often feels a sense of purpose, right, or clarity in going public with pointed criticism. But the more we plunge into discourses (textual, verbal, and visual) about the United States from many quarters in the world, the more we see the field in which criticism of the country mixes with curiosity about it, and sometimes even admiration of it, or at least of some part of U.S. life, political organization, culture, or experience.

Like many of the contributors to this book, we do not mean literary criticism per se here but, rather, criticism in the most quotidian sense of the word—that is, the finding of fault, the assigning of blame. As the *American Heritage Dictionary* (4th ed.) puts it, in its most widespread usage, "criticism" means "the act of criti-cizing, especially adversely," and the most common synonyms of "criticizing" are blaming, reprehending, censuring, condemning, and denouncing. Yes, to criticize can mean "to judge the merits and faults of; [to] analyze and evaluate"—in other words, "merely to evaluate without necessarily finding fault." But as the *American Heritage Dictionary* writers go on to say, "usually the word implies the expression of disapproval."

The verbal, cognitive, discursive, and social arenas of criticism are interesting both with regard to the naming of certain rhetoric, images, feelings, or actions as anti-American or anti-imperial and in its broader presence in contemporary social, cultural, economic, and political life. What is entailed by criticism? What assumptions do we typically make about its meaning, at least in contemporary English? What else beyond what we already think we know about its meaning and usage might be worth pondering and exploring?

Blame, the *American Heritage Dictionary* tells us, "emphasizes the finding of fault *and* the fixing of responsibility [as in] '*People are always blaming their cir-cumstances for what they are*' (George Bernard Shaw)." *Reprehend* "implies sharp disapproval [as in] '*reprehends students who have protested apartheid*' (*New York Times*)." *Censure* "refers to open and strong expression of criticism; often it im-plies a formal reprimand [as in] '*No man can justly censure or condemn another, because indeed no man truly knows another*' (Thomas Browne)." *Condemn* seems to denote "the pronouncement of harshly adverse judgment [as in] '*The wrongs which we seek to condemn and punish have been so calculated, so malignant and so devastating that civilization cannot tolerate their being ignored because it cannot survive their being repeated*' (Robert H. Jackson)." And *denounce* "implies public proclamation of condemnation or repudiation [as in] '*The press denounces the new taxation policies*'" (all emphasis added).

Finding fault, assigning fault, attributing responsibility, implying sharp dis-approval, expressing sharp disapproval, and publicly proclaiming sharp disap-proval—these are references to actions associated with "criticism" and whose references nobody would see as anything but negative. We do not doubt the implied negativity in our impression of any of these verbs.

But it becomes more interesting to think of criticism as "meaningful social behavior" and to track the implications of such a statement in much the same way Michael Silverstein did for "speech" over thirty years ago when he revolutionized much of linguistics and linguistic anthropology in the United States by arguing, contra semanticists, that "speech is meaningful social behavior" (11). For criticism to be seen this way, it must be meaningful. It must be social. And it must be discernible as behavior.

Our queries here—and framing of the essays we include in this book—follow from it. For criticism to be meaningful, it must have meaning for the critic. Therefore, it must be thinkable. It must arise from the verbal or nonverbal experience of the critic, for whom its references and alternatives are clear; it must consist of discursive objects already in play in the critic's daily life and world, and it must make sense within the logics in play in the critic's daily life and world.

For criticism to be social, it must have an intended audience, regardless of how that speech or visual community is construed. It must be legible to others, whether or not they agree with the stated or implied disapproval. It therefore must be in a language spoken or written by others—and by "language" here we mean a set of signs and symbols recognized and at least partly used by others for the purposes of intentional communication, whether or not the majority of the world's language and literature experts recognize its existence. And for criticism to be discernible behavior, it must be recognized as an act and not just as a thing. It must have a doer—that is, a person, an embodied subject of the verb "to criticize." It must be locatable in time and place; it must be something that is an alternative to other behaviors, and it must have some embodied effect at least for the critic and his or her immediate surroundings.

Though much of this might seem too abstract or too formal for a larger discussion on anti-Americanism, pro-Americanism, or Americanization as discourses inside and outside the United States, we think—and hope—that it allows for the kind of analytic clarity that may be essential, and is often lacking, in these days of fear and anger.[2] Let us put it differently. As scholars, teachers, and intellectuals who are periodically asked to address the general public, it has become important to develop a usable system for understanding the many fears in the United States about the rise of something called anti-Americanism that is presumed to be rampant in the rest of the world. We are interested in figuring out how many different kinds of data we really have that get coded as "anti-American" or are interpreted as evidence of "anti-Americanism" (or as "anti-imperialism").

This volume's contributors have located many different types of such data, often focusing on how the data become coded in societies outside of the United States but also (explicitly and implicitly) within the United States. For example, Loes Nas as well as Kate Delaney and Andrzej Antoszek write about Soviet-era political rhetoric in Poland and Georgia, while Giorgio Mariani writes about accusations of anti-Americanism against academic writings that circulate among Italian scholars of the United States. Other contributors, such as Zsófia Bán, Richard Ellis, Sabine Broeck, Kristin Solli, and Ian Condry, have thought about various art forms that index anti-Americanism or Americanization, thus becoming highly visible and audible objects of criticism by political regimes and social movements that align themselves against the United States.

In addition to spoken rhetoric, written critique, and forms of cultural pro-duction, Guillermo Ibarra argues that certain people—through their embodied subjectivities—can themselves serve as data in a given social milieu. He argues that Mexican immigrants in the United States are expected to be (or become) critics of the United States, thereby exuding a kind of anti-Americanism that is especially seen and feared in some sectors of mainstream U.S. society, but he also problematizes this idea. Drawing on his own survey data, Ibarra shows Mexican American immigrants holding favorable sentiments toward their new country (certainly to a larger extent than usually reported) and embodying new forces and forms of Americanism (even pro-Americanism).

It is one of the reasons we want all of us to focus on figuring out how to identify, and carefully relate, other types of data not captured by meta-discourses of fear and blame but that still harbor criticism of a country, its people, its leaders, its policies, its past, or its present. How legible, for example, are the signs of criti-cism if we are not told to look at something as evidence of criticism? And what if we contemplate the possibility that a great deal of named "anti-Americanism" is the result of signposting that participates in particular discourses for, and by, particular speech communities?

Consider the official release on December 13, 2004, of the results of an Ipsos–Public Affairs poll undertaken between November 19 and 27, 2004, at the request of the Associated Press (AP) in eight countries, including the United States. The AP story is available online and was widely picked up off the wire service by newspapers across the United States (and perhaps the world), including in fairly small metropolitan areas like the Cedar Rapids/Iowa City area in Iowa, in which the editors lived at the time, a micro-metro area with a population of about four hundred thousand. Our local paper's headline read, "Poll: Many Europeans Cool toward Bush, Americans," and in smaller print it added, "Americans fare slightly better than their president in polls conducted in several countries" (ICP-C, "Poll"). If readers missed the "orange alert" signs indicating evidence of criticism, the first sentence of the AP text harped on it. "International resentment of the Bush Administration," it said, "has spilled over to include bad feelings for the American people, too—at least in three European countries that opposed U.S. policies in Iraq." The countries named were France, Germany, and Spain. The fact that the same poll showed that 80 percent of those polled in Canada, 69 percent of those polled in Australia, 60 percent of those polled in Britain, and 56 percent of those polled in Italy had "favorable" opinions of Americans was not mentioned at all in the text. These figures appeared on a chart next to the text, but clearly they were not seen as the newsworthy items.

Instead the AP story interpreted the data as signaling that there was a rift that was worsening, that was the "most serious in years," and that was with "long-time allies France and Germany." It added that "relations with Spain have been particularly frosty since Prime Minister José Luis Rodríguez Zapatero withdrew Spanish troops from Iraq" in April 2004. It commented on President Bush's pledge on November 2, 2004, "that he would work 'to deepen our trans-Atlantic ties with the nations of Europe'" and commented, somewhat editorially, that "the president, and Americans generally, have plenty of work to do to win over Europeans" (ibid.).

The only mention of "anti-Americanism" appeared toward the end of the story in a quote by a Belgian, Gilles Corman, identified as director of public affairs for Ipsos-Inra of Belgium. He is reported as having said that "the polling suggests an increasing lack of European understanding of Americans rather than a surge of anti-Americanism" (ibid.). Yet the mere mention of the word "anti-Americanism" made this story *participate* in an existing discourse about anti-Americanism, even though the data showed signs of pro-Americanism *alongside* disapproval of Bush in several countries (in Canada, 80 percent vs. 32 percent approval ratings; in Britain, 60 percent vs. 30 percent approval ratings; in Australia, 69 percent vs. 40 percent approval ratings)—and even in those countries where the majority of those polled reported "unfavorable" opinions of "Americans," there was still a marked distinction in the percentages reporting "favorable" opinions of "Americans" versus "favorable" opinions of President George W. Bush (in France, 41 percent vs. 19 percent; in Germany, 41 percent vs. 17 percent; and in Spain, 35 percent vs. 19 percent).

Was this news story, then, evidence of anti-Americanism, or, probably more accurately, did it report evidence of anti-Americanism? We were told it did not, yet it discursively *participated* in the discourse of anti-Americanism, it put the notion (as a discursive object) in readers' heads, it used language that was understandable and legible at least in particular terms, and it rhetorically addressed the American public. We could ask people to look more closely to see who and where the enemies and friends of "Americans" might be and whether they (and we) have enough information to know, but how many readers online or in print read that actively and suspiciously? How legible—as signs of criticism—would the simple issuing of the approval ratings be without framing and commentary?

Would we not wonder about the variation by country? Or how favorable "favorable" was and how unfavorable "unfavorable" was? Or exactly what questions were asked? Or how these percentages compare to those from five, ten, or twenty years ago? Indeed it is possible to notice some ambiguity by looking carefully at the reported poll results, yet the key message to be consumed was clearly that even "our" old, longtime friends are critical of "us" and can no longer be trusted.

There was no ambiguity there. Criticism was highlighted and it was discursively tied to anti-Americanism, despite the weak disclaimer. The kind of in-depth exploration we see in this book and the exchanges between contributors is quite unusual in this larger field of polling and media commentary.

Hence, it is useful here to remember the statement made earlier about how it becomes more interesting to think of criticism not just as the expression of disapproval but, rather, as "meaningful social behavior." Doing so forces us to highlight references to ideas, behavior, and other phenomena that are probably tacitly known by many but not stressed in the heat of discussions about whether or not something is evidence of anti-Americanism—namely,

(1)   that this poll was meaningful within a discourse and a discourse (or speech) community within which the terms used and fears expressed were thinkable and understandable—and it is evidence of the existence and objects of that discourse, even if it is not evidence of anti-American thoughts, feelings, or actions per se;

(2)   that the release of the story about the results of the poll was a locatable, traceable behavior—a social act aiming to have an effect—and those who produced it, released it, and handled it are part of, and point to, a discourse (speech) community that thereby calls attention to its existence, whether or not it is right to believe that it has proof of the existence of anti-American thoughts, feelings, or actions outside the United States;

(3)   that this news story may be found legible and meaningful by people without regard to citizenship or geographical place of residence. While the majority of readers of U.S. newspapers printing the story were likely to have U.S. citizenship or at least to live within the United States or its overseas territories, basic legibility really only requires knowledge of English up to the eighth- or ninth-grade level. It is not hard to understand that this story reported data the writers saw as critical of "Americans."

Therefore, we really need to differentiate discourse communities—and their discourses of anti-Americanism—by the extent to which they are communities of production, or communities of reproduction and maintenance, of anti-Americanism. Like the contributors of this book, we all need to ask exactly who is *developing* and who is *maintaining* discourses of anti-Americanism and what is involved in doing so. And we need to look closely at the framing practices that often get in the way of clarity and analysis, both in the public at large and in scholarly analysis. Without such clarity and analysis, discourses of "Americanization" (in more recent forms as well as the early twentieth-century sense largely applied to immigrants and their immediate descendants) seem unrelated to discourses of anti-Americanism, and the partial attraction of some aspects of U.S. ideas, discourses, and other social phenomena to people who are otherwise often critical of the United States may also look mistakenly unrelated.

This volume's contributors have identified the production of discourses critical of the U.S. state and society that are both specific and holistic or all-encompassing.

Among the specific forms of critique we include here are Shorbagy's analysis of the Kefaya movement in Egypt and the group's criticisms of the U.S. military and foreign policy, as well as Nas's contribution on South African critique of the Iraq War by high-powered public figures like Nelson Mandela and popular movements. Others have identified broader critiques of an "America" that stands as a symbol for a larger ideological "other"—as in authors dealing with Cold War–era political rhetoric such as Nas's writing on Soviet and post-Soviet Georgia and Schatz's writing on Central Asian Islamist groups that have used "America" as a catch-all symbol to frame grievances and mobilize support.

On the other hand, other contributors have pointed out how discourses of "anti-Americanism" are developed and employed—by politicians, scholars, and social and political movements, to name a few—in ways that advance U.S. cultural and political projects. For example, Giorgio Mariani uses the phrase "anti anti-Americanism" to highlight how discourses of anti-Americanism are spotlighted and maintained to promote a vision of "an America always under siege" that legitimizes actions against "anti-Americans" both within and outside of U.S. borders.

Several contributors have also shown that it is the very ideological instability of the label "anti-American" that enables it to be so easily deployed to discredit and delegitimize forces seen as a threat to U.S. power (or its allies). Mariani makes this point particularly clear in his writing on anti-American discourses on a global level as well as in Italy more specifically. Sabine Broeck, Zsófia Bán, Amy Spellacy, Kristin Solli, Ian Condry, and Kate Delaney and Andrzej Antoszek all point to "America" as a symbol deployed by multiple actors with various political aims. The symbol "America," they each argue in various ways, holds multiple and contested meanings simultaneously, meanings that also change (or can change) through time and with the changing of political regimes and attitudes. Looking at the flip side of the "anti-American" coin, Shorbagy examines how *pro*-American can be equally discursively powerful in discrediting and delegitimizing in her account of the Egyptian political opposition movement Kefaya. In this case the Egyptian regime used accusations of "pro-Americanism" to discredit Kefaya's anti-regime politics.

Reflecting on Solli's and Condry's essays, Michael Titlestad writes, "It is this *use* of aspects of 'American' culture and history—this endless reworking—that . . . gives the lie to any clear sense of 'Americanization' and 'Anti-Americanism.'" Solli writes about the triangulation of discourses of anti-Americanism and Americanization between the United States, Norway, and Europe/the European Union, in which "America" is invoked (either for or against) in a certain vision of Norway and Norwegian identity. Condry, Broeck, Nas, and Ibarra have conceived of the linkages between "pro-" and "anti-Americanism" by teasing apart different "Americas" that emerge in different discourse communities, highlighting how things that often get labeled "anti-American" also coincide with an embrace of what Sabine Broeck calls the "other America"—namely, marginalized communities and countercultural U.S. movements and actors.

In our own work we pay attention to different types of "data" that likewise follow (and support) analyses that examine relations between discourses of "Americanization" and of "anti-Americanism." Material of potential use can vary greatly. Contributors to this book tend to draw on data they approach within their disciplinary background and training, although at least one contributor, Loes Nas, goes way outside her disciplinary training in literature in the work she shares with readers here. Participants use documentary, visual, literary, archival, observational, and aural material, and they apply analytic tools from a range of social science and humanities fields.

The examples used to frame this analysis are of three different analytic types, textual and visual in content but analytically interesting, because of what a discourse community seems to be doing with the material more than with the material itself. The first are examples of how a discourse community that believes in the existence of rampant "anti-Americanism" reproduces and maintains what it sees as evidence of "anti-Americanism" (even when the actual words do not get invoked). The second are examples of visual or verbal criticisms that include criticism of something connected to the United States but that the critic does not frame as "anti-American" and whose audience(s) could read or not read as "anti-American." The third are examples of visual or verbal criticisms that include criticism of something connected to the United States that a discourse community frames as anti-American and that deliberately leaves little room for any other reading. Each of these types works as an example of a behavior intended as a social behavior whose meaningfulness is identifiable and indeed differentiable and specific to that type of social behavior. As a guide to the range of possible analyses of "anti-Americanism," "pro-Americanism," and "Americanization," including those offered in this multiply situated book, the following are both funny and telling, aggravating and usefully complex, and at least serve as a start to what we hope will be lively discussion among readers, between readers and contributors, and among the contributors themselves.

Reproducing "Anti-Americanism" as Belief and Evidence

Consider the travel page in the January/February 2005 issue of *AARP* magazine (the magazine issued by the increasingly powerful American Association of Retired People targeting a population age fifty on up). Its lead article had a headline reading "GOD BLESS AMERICANS: Five Countries Where the U.S. Is Feted—Not Hated" (14). The words "anti-American" and "anti-Americanism" appear nowhere, but the suggestion that the United States is *hated* in many places loomed large. Not only did the word "hated" appear quite visibly and prominently on the page, but the absence of large or even medium-size countries on this list was striking and *legible* as evidence of widespread anti-Americanism. The five places listed were (1) the Northern Mariana Islands, where reportedly "locals even celebrate the Fourth of July (when U.S. troops secured Saipan from the Japanese)"; (2) Grenada, which reportedly "celebrates Thanksgiving on October 25 to mark the American overthrow of the socialist government in 1983"; (3) Belize, which reportedly has "a growing British and American expat population [that] has buoyed the economy of Central America's only English-speaking country"; (4) Andorra, because reportedly "the U.S. is a primary trade partner of this picturesque kingdom in the Pyrenees sandwiched between Spain and France [and since] tourism fuels the local economy, the natives rarely talk politics"; and (5) Luxembourg, because reportedly "the U.S. liberated this tiny country twice—in 1918 and 1944—and the people haven't forgotten." While the article did not say that the rest of the world hates the United States, the silence about other places did imply that one has to look long and hard to find places free of hatred toward the United States.

Or take two journalistic reports of a survey from about the same period of time, this time from early August 2005. The first ("Survey Highlights U.S. Image Abroad") was an AP story but taken from the online edition of the *Manila Times*, August 4, 2005; the second, posted August 9, 2005, was from the Iranian Quran News Agency. It was given the heading "Newly Conducted Poll Shows, Americans Are Not Satisfied with US's Military Solutions to World Issues, 8/6/2005." Consider these relevant passages.

From the *Manila Times*:

Americans rank a negative US image among the country's top global problems, behind only the Iraq War and terrorism, according to a survey Wednesday.

Three-quarters said they worry the US "may be losing the trust and friendship of people in other countries." . . .

Asked to name the most important problem facing the country in its dealings with the rest of the world, 17 percent said the Iraq war, 11 percent said terrorism or security, and 9 percent said a negative US image. Fully 65 percent thought the world has a negative image of the US, and when asked how the country is perceived, one in ten, the largest single group, offered the words "bully" or "bullying." . . .

While nearly two-thirds gave the US a grade of "C" or worse on having good relations with Muslim countries and 74 percent said they worried about growing US *hatred* [emphasis added] in Muslim countries, only 52 percent gave the US a "C" or worse in having good relations with countries in general.

Asked if the US is only concerned with itself and ignores the interests of other countries, only 19 percent said the charge was totally justified and 44 percent said it's not justified at all.

From the Iranian Quran News Agency:

A new survey focuses on the evolution of U.S. public opinion on foreign policy.

The survey, called the Public Agenda Confidence in U.S. Foreign Policy Index, finds Americans anxious about U.S. relations with the Muslim world and puzzled about their nation's image in the international community.

According to the survey, the relationship between Islam and the West dominates the foreign policy issues that concern Americans the most: the war in Iraq,
terrorism, the United States' image abroad.

This article made a point of quoting Daniel Yankelovich, one of the founders of
Public Agenda and a widely known public opinion expert. "Many polls," he was
quoted as saying, "have reported the growing concern about our engagement
in Iraq. What we find particularly interesting in this study is to see that these
concerns about Iraq were definitely set in the public mind in the larger context
of worries about relations with other nations. . . . In particular, there was a deep
concern (about) the growing *hatred* [emphasis added] of the United States in
Muslim countries and a general loss of trust in friendship in other countries."

Notice the absence of references to anti-Americanism in both cases but the
explicit reference to hatred of the United States and to American anxiety about
such hatred. We quote from these news articles from *outside the United States*
in order to reiterate our earlier point about citizenship and place of residence
not being the defining characteristics of anti-Americanism. These articles may
not endorse the view that there is anti-Americanism in their own discourse or
in their own discourse communities, but they nevertheless produce and sustain
the terms of such discourses and thereby key conditions for their reproduction.

Producing Criticism of Something U.S. without Obviously Participating in Discourses of "Anti-Americanism"

Consider, in contrast, examples of criticism of something U.S. that is not obvi-
ously presented or framed as anti-Americanism. The most obvious examples, of
course, could come from the United States itself—from critiques of the dropping
of atomic bombs in Hiroshima and Nagasaki seventy years ago (see, for example,
Baltimore Sun reporter Michael Hill's "Did the Use of the Terrible Atomic Bomb
Bring an Era of Peace?") to critiques of President Bush's "proposal to revamp
Social Security by creating personal investment accounts for young workers" (*Des
Moines Register*). But the issue here isn't really that insiders (i.e., "Americans")
need not be seen as anti-American each and every time they criticize something
about the United States—despite recent right-wing rhetoric suggesting as much.
This type of criticism, we are arguing, also exists *outside* the United States, and it
is often based on data that are ignored or made legible, we think mistakenly, by
those hunting for evidence of anti-Americanism.

Several political cartoons from South Africa make the point beautifully, as discussed in an essay published in Italian in *Acoma* (the Italian journal of American
Studies) in 2007 (Domínguez). That analysis drew on the best-known and widely
circulating political cartoonists in South Africa—"Zapiro" (Jonathan Shapiro) and
the "Madam and Eve" series (Francis, Dugmore, and Rico). On page 115 of *The*

Madam and Eve Collection, published in 1993, the cartoon poked fun at Michael Jackson, presenting him as an outsider to South Africa as well as a superstar but never identifying him as American or making any discernible reference to the United States. It did poke fun at his changing, indeed whitening, physical appearance, and this in the context of 1993 South Africa, the formal end of the apartheid regime and the discussions in South Africa that led to an explicit clause in the 1996 South African constitution that says South Africa is committed to "nonracialism." That this critique intended criticism of Michael Jackson is clear. That the discourse it feeds, or even participates in, is a discourse of anti-Americanism is a big stretch and one for which there is little corroborating evidence.

Two other cartoons that fit in well with the range of textual and visual work included in this book are from Jonathan Shapiro's 2004 collection, *Long Walk to Free Time*. This volume included cartoons that had already appeared in South African newspapers the *Sowetan*, the *Mail & Guardian*, and the *Sunday Times* prior to their inclusion in *Long Walk to Free Time*. "Fahrenheit 9/11 opens in the US" appeared on June 24, 2004, and shows a statue of Michael Moore (a cartoon depiction labeled "by Michael Moore") next to a statue labeled "by Henry Moore." In the background to the left is a recognizable drawing of the U.S. Capitol's dome and a U.S. flag. The United States was named both visually and in writing, and Michael Moore was indexed as American, but was this pro-Americanism (praise for American Michael Moore?), or a critique of the war in Iraq via praise for Michael Moore, or a critique of Michael Moore as someone who might design and build a statue in his own image? To reduce this to evidence of anti-Americanism—or to assume that this would automatically participate in a discourse of anti-Americanism—seems simplistic and off-base.

"Two Months till US Election," September 14, 2004, featured a recognizable George W. Bush putting two terrified children to bed. The children were labeled "voters," Bush holds a book in his right hand titled "9–11 BEDTIME STORIES," and in the cartoon he says to them, "Now goodnight! . . . And never fear while Daddy's here!" Readers encountering this cartoon will not think there is a great relationship between the "father" and the "children" by looking at this, and they may not think much of voters in the United States who are collectively presented here as children. But this looks like anti-Bush commentary and plausibly a critique of U.S. voters, and isn't even this cartoon only anti-American if one assumes that any critique of a U.S. president and of the voters who elected (or tried not to elect) him constitutes anti-Americanism? Do cartoons outside the United States depicting Barack Obama now automatically signal a position vis-à-vis the United States? Does the expectation that Obama will appeal more to people outside the United States than Bush did shape a scholar's expectation that a reading of a political cartoon is favorable?

If one assumes that any critique of a U.S. president is "anti-American," shouldn't a majority of "Americans" have been portrayed as "anti-American" in the latter stages of the Bush administration or even at many points in the Obama administration? The point we are making here is not just temporally relevant or especially relevant during an unpopular U.S. president's administration. According to Gallup, President Obama's highest approval rating came July 22–24, 2009, right after he became president of the United States. It was then 69 percent. But it has also been as low as 38 percent, in fact, several times. The approval ratings for U.S. presidents since 1938 have averaged 54 percent (according to Gallup), which means that close to half of those polled in the United States have disapproved of a sitting president's performance as president (and not just those who did not vote for the winning candidate). There are always policies and events to note and frequently criticize, and it may be more interesting to note and wonder about "high" approval ratings (e.g., President Obama's 69 percent in late January 2009, President Johnson's 65 percent in July 1965, President Eisenhower's 64 percent in July 1957, President Reagan's 63 percent in July 1985, and even President Clinton's 58 percent in July 1997). Whether it is the BP oil spill in the Gulf of Mexico, the continuing U.S. wars in the Middle East (Iraq, Afghanistan, or Syria), the tragedy in Benghazi, or the economic crisis whose slow recovery and long legs have occupied much of Obama's presidency so far, there has been plenty of criticism of the Obama administration (and his approval rating in a Quinnipiac University Polling Institute poll reported by USA Today's David Jackson on July 11, 2013, was a low 44 percent). Bush became easy to critique, but what did those polls really indicate?

Throughout much of 2006 President Bush's character was seriously questioned by both media and people polled. Consider the amazement of people like CNN senior political analyst Bill Schneider, who on May 15, 2006, posted an article on Anderson Cooper's blog about a poll conducted for CNN by Opinion Research Corporation. It was called "Poll: Clinton More Honest than Bush," and it reported that only 41 percent of those polled considered President Bush honest and trustworthy (Schneider 2006), that "less than half of Americans [48 percent] now say they think President Bush is honest," that even at the start of the year (in January) only 53 percent had thought him honest, and that while "a solid majority still see Bush as likable and a strong leader . . . a growing number view the president's confidence as arrogance, up from 49 percent in January to 56 percent now." Those inside and those outside the United States who were not inclined to support his policies or trust his judgment may take some pleasure in reading these quotes, but in the end what are they evidence of?

Likewise, we need to consider the results of the Pew Research Center Global Attitudes Survey, including the most recent surveys from within the years of the Obama administration. For those looking for evidence of "anti-Americanism" there are results in these polls they could use to support their views. But it is clear that the picture is much more complicated than that and that it includes the opposite in quite a few countries—and a much more differentiated picture if one looks closely enough.[3]

Table 1: U.S. "Favorability" Reports by Pew Research Center Global Attitudes/Global Indicators Poll (2015).

Here "favorable" percentages, column (a), are percentages of those polled in each country responding either "very favorable" or "somewhat favorable" when asked questions about their general opinion of the United States. Column (b) consists of the percentage of respondents coded as "confident" vis-à-vis the U.S. president (Bush '03–'08, Obama '09–present)?" and column (c) consists of the percentage of respondents saying yes, they believe that the U.S. government respects the personal freedoms of its people.

	(a)	(b)	(c)
Philippines	92	94	89
Ghana	89	82	79
South Korea	84	88	83
Kenya	84	80	75
United States	83	58	51
Italy	83	77	71
Israel	81	49	79
Ethiopia	81	65	81
Senegal	80	77	65
Burkina Faso	79	65	63
Vietnam	78	71	79
Tanzania	78	78	65
Uganda	76	69	74
Nigeria	76	73	64
South Africa	74	77	63
Poland	74	64	70
France	73	83	52
Brazil	73	63	58
Peru	70	53	56
India	70	74	56
Ukraine	69	51	72
Japan	68	66	76
Chile	68	60	70
Canada	68	76	54
Mexico	66	49	56
United Kingdom	65	76	57
Spain	65	58	50
Australia	63	81	58
Indonesia	62	64	63
Malaysia	54	61	51
Venezuela	51	26	49
Germany	50	73	43
China	44	44	45
Argentina	43	40	41
Lebanon	39	36	81
Turkey	29	45	36
Palestinian Terr.	26	15	63
Pakistan	22	14	44
Russia	15	11	41
Jordan	14	14	53

Source: Pew Research Center, as grouped on the table included in chapter 1, "The American Brand," of the Pew Research Global Attitudes Project.

Table 2: U.S. "Favorability" Reports by Pew Research Center Global Attitudes/Global Indicators Poll (2000, 2003, 2006, 2009, 2012, 2015).

Here "favorable" percentages are percentages of those polled in each country reportedly responding either "very favorable" or "somewhat favorable" when asked a question about their general opinion of the United States.

	2000	2003	2006	2009	2012	2015
France	62	42	39	75	69	73
Germany	78	45	37	64	52	50
Greece	—	—	—	—	35	—
Italy	76	60	—	—	74	83
Poland	86	—	—	67	69	74
Spain	50	38	23	58	58	65
UK	83	70	56	69	60	65
Russia	37	37	46	44	52	15
Ukraine	70	—	—	—	—	69
Turkey	52	15	12	14	15	29
Egypt	—	—	30	27	19	—
Jordan	—	1	15	25	12	14
Lebanon	—	27	—	55	48	39
Pal. Terr.	—	0	—	15	—	26
Tunisia	—	—	—	—	45	—
Israel	—	78	—	71	—	81
Bangladesh	—	—	—	—	—	—[a]
China	—	—	47	47	43	44
India	—	—	—	—	—	70[b]
Indonesia	—	—	30	63	—	62
Japan	77	—	63	59	72	68
Malaysia	—	—	—	—	—	54
Pakistan	23	—	27	16	12	22
Philippines	—	—	—	—	—	92[c]
South Korea	58	46	—	78	—	84
Thailand	—	—	—	—	—	—[d]
Vietnam	—	—	—	—	—	78

	2000	2003	2006	2009	2012	2015
Argentina	50	—	—	38	—	43
Brazil	—	—	—	—	61	73
Chile	—	—	—	—	—	68
Colombia	—	—	—	—	—	—[e]
El Salvador	—	—	—	—	—	—[e]
Mexico	68	—	—	69	56	66
Nicaragua	—	—	—	—	—	—[e]
Peru	74	—	—	—	—	70
Venezuela	—	—	—	—	—	51[f]
Ghana	—	—	—	—	—	89[f]
Kenya	94	—	—	—	—	84
Nigeria	—	—	—	—	—	76
Senegal	—	—	—	—	—	80
South Africa	—	—	—	—	—	74
Tanzania	—	—	—	—	—	78
Uganda	—	—	—	—	—	76

[a] The 2014 table included Bangladesh and reported a favorability rating of 76 percent in its 2014 poll.

[b] India was obviously not included in the poll until 2013. The Pew table shows 56 percent favorability rating for India in 2013 and 55 percent for 2014.

[c] The polling results from the Philippines are pretty consistently high, even if this table risks giving the impression that the 92 percent is just in 2015. Though not polled annually, Pew polls undertaken there show a 90 percent favorability rating in 2002, 85 percent in 2013, and 92 percent in 2014.

[d] Like Bangladesh, Thailand apparently had not been polled by Pew until very recently. In 2014 Pew reported a 73 percent favorability rating, but it was not included in 2015 nor in earlier years.

[e] Colombia, El Salvador, and Nicaragua appear on the 2014 Pew table, where a 64 percent favorability rating shows up for Colombia in 2014, favorability ratings of 79 percent and 80 percent show up for El Salvador in 2013 and 2014, respectively, and a favorability rating of 71 percent shows up for Nicaragua in 2014. However, these countries were not included in the 2015 data nor in earlier Pew polling results.

[f] Venezuela is another interesting case of surprising inattention from Pew until very recently. It does not appear to have been included in these Pew polls until 2013 (where it reported a 53 percent favorability rating) and 2014 (where it reported a 62 percent favorability rating). The pattern is fairly similar when it comes to countries in sub-Saharan Africa, although a number of them seem to have been included in the Pew polls in 2002 and 2007 (a year that also included more Asian and Latin American countries than other years).

Source: Pew Research Center, as grouped on the table included in chapter 1, "The American Brand," of the Pew Research Global Attitudes Project.

Consider the latest results from a spring 2015 Pew Research Center Global Attitudes Survey. The pollsters ask relevant questions, not just one, and the questions produce somewhat different results. One question asks respondents to choose between "very favorable," "somewhat favorable," "somewhat unfavorable," and "very unfavorable" with respect to their opinion of the United States. The full question wording is (in English, though the question is translated into different languages and the interview conducted in many languages other than English) "Please tell me if you have a very favorable, somewhat favorable, somewhat unfavorable or very unfavorable opinion of the United States." A second question asks respondents about their level of confidence in the U.S. president, and the third question asks respondents if the U.S. government respects the personal freedoms of its people. The full wording for each of these two more specific questions is as follows: (1) regarding confidence in the U.S. president—"Now I'm going to read a list of political leaders. For each, tell me how much confidence you have in each leader to do the right thing regarding world affairs—a lot of confidence, some confidence, not too much confidence, or no confidence at all. U.S. President George W. Bush (2002–2008), Barack Obama (2009–Present)"; (2) regarding personal freedoms—"Do you think the government of the United States respects the personal freedoms of its people, or don't you think so?"

The results are often startling to people who expect one extreme or another or a uniformity by region or continent. For example, in the spring 2015 survey, over 75 percent responded "favorable" to the first question in many African countries, plus a few Asian countries and one European country (not several). And only 83 percent in the United States itself responded that they have a "favorable" view of the United States. Higher favorability ratings than in the United States itself were those reported in the Philippines (92 percent), Ghana (89 percent), South Korea (84 percent), and Kenya (84 percent). And while the lowest (under 40 percent) did include primarily Muslim countries, they did not just include primarily Muslim countries, and primarily Muslim countries also appear in the middle range (with Malaysia posting 54 percent and Indonesia 62 percent). The usual named allies of the United States in Western Europe appear neither at the top nor the bottom, and that has actually been a long-standing pattern. France is high now (with a 73 percent favorability report), but it has not been higher than 75 percent even during the late Clinton and Obama years, and it was as low as 37 percent during the early G. W. Bush years). Germany seems even more skeptical. It is now 50 percent, was mostly between 31 percent and 45 percent during the G. W. Bush presidency, and has been mostly declining since the start of the Obama presidency (from a high of 64 percent in 2009 to its present low of 50 percent). And the results from the United Kingdom are in between—from a high of 83 percent late in the Clinton years to percentages mostly in the 1950s and '60s during both the G. W. Bush and the Obama years.

Of course, there is some similarity if one also examines the survey's results as to people's confidence in the U.S. president, but here, too, there are some startling results. For example, the United States itself appears in the middle of the pack here (with only 58 percent answering "favorable"); France shoots up to 83 percent, the United Kingdom to 76 percent, and Germany to 73 percent. But Venezuela's results go down (from 51 percent responding that they have a "favorable" view of the United States to 26 percent of the same people responding that they have confidence in the U.S. president). And at the very bottom of this list is Russia, not an Arab or even a mostly Muslim country.

Of course, polls are data of only a certain kind, but it is the variety in the results and, where appropriate, the consistency over some years that seem worth noting. The polls try to be as systematic as possible across countries, using a variety of languages and very similar time periods in order to produce results that are as comparable as possible. Pew Research Center describes its survey work as follows: "Pew Research Center conducts public opinion surveys around the world on a broad array of subjects ranging from people's assessments of their own lives to their views about the current state of the world and important issues of the day. Nearly 450,000 interviews in 64 countries have been conducted as part of the center's work" (2015). Here we mention polling data because they should be seen (and treated) for what they are—and compared internally, from poll to poll.

For example, changes in polling results are interesting but ought to be seen as changes in polling results. Polls in 2009 (hence, after Barack Obama became president of the United States) were largely unchanged in Poland and Russia but substantially changed (for the better) in Germany (64 percent), Spain (58 percent), France (75 percent), and Great Britain (69 percent) (with no information given about Italy in 2009). By 2012, many had declined again—and in Western Europe—with Germany down to 52 percent, France down to 69 percent, and Great Britain down to 60 percent. Interestingly, the 2009 figures for Spain were exactly the same in 2012 (58 percent), the 2012 data for Russia stood at 52 percent, and the 2012 data for Poland showed a fairly unchanged figure of 69 percent of those polled reporting favorable views toward the United States.

Yet on specific issues Pew Research Center (2013) reported that "in nearly all countries, there is considerable opposition to a major component of the Obama administration's anti-terrorism policy: drone strikes." In nearly all twenty countries polled around the world, "more than half disapprove of U.S. drone attacks targeting extremist leaders and groups in nations such as Pakistan, Yemen and Somalia"—from a disapproval rate of 90 percent in Greece to 76 percent in Spain, 68 percent in Russia, 63 percent in France, 59 percent in Germany, 55 percent in Italy, 51 percent in Poland, and 47 percent in Great Britain. Contrast those percentages to that of the United States, where 28 percent reported disapproval of the drone strikes.

Producing Criticism of Something U.S. and Framing It as "Anti-American"

Producing criticism of something U.S. and *framing* it as "anti-American" *does* obviously exist, and there are clear examples. Some are visual, and some are not. The more visual they are, the more the press seems to include them, as in an AP photo included in the 2007 *Acoma* essay (Domínguez) of protesters in Lahore, Pakistan, from early June 2005, showing large numbers of men on a street with posters in Arabic/Urdu writing and one large banner in English whose visible words include "the wild American army on [des]ecration of Holy Quran." The caption in the local paper at the time, the *Iowa City Press-Citizen*, read: "Pakistani Muslim protestors hold anti-American rally Wednesday to condemn the alleged desecration of Muslims' holy book, the Quran, at the U.S. prison in Guantanamo Bay, Cuba, in Lahore, Pakistan." The protesters' banner was indeed openly critical of a key U.S. institution—the U.S. Army—and the U.S. media readily named it "anti-Americanism."

But it was evident then (and still now) that this kind of discourse of "anti-Americanism" can indeed be both produced and maintained by a U.S.-based discourse community that ironically sees itself as deeply critical of it, embattled with it, and afraid of it. The concern in this case is not with ambiguity. Participants in this speech/discourse community are especially interested in drawing clear lines identifying friends and enemies, inside or outside the United States, and they do so *not* according to expected racial, religious, or ethnic divisions. The battle is ideological and anti-Americanism is something to name and to deploy.

On August 6, 2005, an essay posted on the website of the *National Ledger* was a case in point. It was written by a presumably young woman who identified herself as a nursing student and a born-again Christian. A few paragraphs will suffice here:

> The unceasing efforts of liberals to drag the Bush administration into a mire of criticism can only make the job of the terrorists that much easier. Thus it feeds the enemies within our gates. If the far left in this country continues in this degrading disrespect for our president [Bush] and our troops fighting in Iraq and Afghanistan, all of America may well reap the bad seeds it sows.
>
> By continuing this fight, the far left gives aid and comfort to terrorist cells here in America, every bit as much as the insurgents in Iraq and anyplace else they call home! The left has shown where its "loyalties" lie, and has essentially assumed the role of America's homegrown enemy.
>
> Fatwas are inspired and stimulated by liberal American big mouths speaking seditious lies! Terrorism is all of America's problem, and that includes those who seem to believe they can somehow play games with the proper American response to it without endangering themselves and their families. Wake up, those of you on the left. It also is your own future, your own security, and your nation that is at stake! (Jon)

Concluding Remarks

Criticism and its deployment are evident in this last example. "Anti-Americanism" was the object of discourse and criticism its discursive field, bringing together into its space speech/discourse communities that see themselves as poles apart and as each other's dreaded enemies. In other words, the very criticism (and naming) of something as anti-American sentiment, bias, or action is part of the discursive field itself, and it makes the "American" more visible and palpable and likely to be the target of criticism. That this is unintentional the great majority of the time seems clear. That it participates in, rather than clarifies, public, national, or sectional sentiment and critique is also clear.

But what is perhaps less clear is how these thinking and talking spaces are linked discursively, visually, or even cognitively, and what the consequences are of seeing them as linked. This book goes a long way toward taking those thinking and talking spaces as worthy of close study and often surprising in what they reveal. Such spaces also individually and collectively allow us to spot many of the consequences—good and bad—of seeing them as linked. Indeed, if we accept the logic that these spaces are linked, we must contemplate the possibility that all are forms of "anti-Americanism." But might we not also need to contemplate the possibility that all of them simultaneously are forms of "pro-Americanism" or "Americanization" or, at least, forms insistent on spotlighting "America"? And if we accept the point that these thinking and talking spaces, though linked, are really analytically different, does this require us to jettison the view that we know "anti-Americanism," "pro-Americanism," or "Americanization" when we see it?

We hope, then, that one point made here is very clear: that the marking of *certain* discursive or visual phenomena as "anti-American" (and not as anti something else) creates analytic problems of vision and recognition that are consequential, especially in the current social, political, religious, and economic climate in which the world finds itself in 2017. This introduction has also tried to show that identifying *only some* phenomena as "anti-American" (when other forms are clearly part of a related or overlapping speech/discursive community) creates analytic problems of vision and recognition as well, problems that are equally consequential.

In one case, for example, a conclusion could be that "anti-Americanism" exists only outside the United States or even that it is characteristic of contemporary Europe. Such a conclusion exacerbates a nationalist U.S. binary pitting "us" and "them" that presents the United States as ideologically unified and in opposition to a presumably ideologically unified place called Europe. That big differences exist by country and time period becomes elided in such a view.

In a second case, a different conclusion could well be that "anti-Americanism" exists but is limited to certain types of protests and does not extend to all things associated with the United States. Here what is subject to scathing critique is something other than a territorially (or even legally) defined society or state. It could be generalized, of course, to something called "American culture," "American tradition," "American individualism," "American corporatism," or even "American militarism," but all of these are really thought of as aspects of something larger, not everything and anything connected with the United States. This means that the critics may themselves be U.S. citizens living in the United States and that what is criticized is an object of discourse shared by a multinational collection of people producing and reproducing a discursive community not rooted in a "us vs. them" nationalist binary.

Organization of the Book

The book consists of six parts. Readers will note that each part consists of essays of different lengths and that some are called "Second Looks" and some even "Third Looks." In conceiving of the book, we wanted to maintain the openness, dynamism, and variety in the IFUSS conferences we have sponsored (first at the University of Iowa and, more recently, at the University of Illinois at Urbana-Champaign). As noted at the outset, the main essays included here had their origins in the original IFUSS conferences on "discourses of 'Americanization' and 'anti-Americanism.'" But there was also much discussion then and since then, and we have wanted to capture much of that dynamism, the agreements, disagreements, and suggestions that have followed. Transcription of those conversations and debates can go only so far in writing, given how difficult it is to turn conversations that make sense in person into exchanges that make sense in print.

Hence, our decision to elicit Second Looks commenting on individual papers and Third Looks commenting on sets of papers, as organized here. Where possible, we sought Second Looks from paired authors and Third Looks from the editors themselves and other scholars deeply involved with the overall intellectual, geopolitical, and ethical project that is, and remains, the central mission and mainstay of the International Forum for U.S. Studies. These Second and Third Look essays often articulate different interpretations of the data offered by contributors whose papers those authors examine, or they are extensions of ideas or interpretations to other parts of the world or other time periods. In some cases they articulate possibilities suggested by the materials included in each section, possibilities for which they are provocations to think with more than unassailable conclusions from the data offered here, and in some cases they articulate real differences of interpretation or understanding or even of framing of the issues.

For example, a Third Look (that I, Virginia R. Domínguez, wrote) draws upon Spellacy's and Ibarra's essays to think, perhaps unexpectedly, about pro-Americanism in Panama and among Mexican immigrants in the United States and to simultaneously consider the peculiar lack of interest in, and engagement with, Latin America in the contemporary United States. In a different move, Sophia Balakian extends Broeck and Mariani's rich conversation to consider "anti-American" as a name that reproduces U.S. power. And fellow volume editor Jane Desmond uses the complex amalgam of "Americanisms" and "anti-Americanism" in Nas's essay and in Delaney and Antoszek's essay to "reverse the vector of analysis," highlighting particular ways in which U.S. cultural products are made meaningful and perform political work in particular non-U.S. contexts. Likewise, Ana Mauad, inspired by Bán and Ellis's essays dealing with the arts, thinks about cultural change and the possibility of "the world as imagined community."

Mohammad Marandi's Third Look may be the most pointed. In it he takes a pointed stance in his reading of Ed Schatz's and Manar Shorbagy's essays, each nuanced but offering potentially conflicting visions of anti-Americanism. Marandi's Third Look, siding more with one than the other, demonstrates the kinds of stakes involved in the topic with which this volume deals and the kinds of debate that both the topic and the book's organization invite. Ira Dworkin makes a point of commenting on all of them and bringing many of the issues to the present moment (as of 2015). In yet a different but useful move, Michael Titlestad's meditation ("Dreaming America") on Solli's and Condry's pieces takes up the complexity of "America" as a sign for which meanings, as he puts it, "can remain elusive even as we sense their profound significance, [where] things can mean at once themselves and their opposite." More than anything else, we offer this volume to be shared with many others, to expand and sustain careful analysis of engagement with the United States, whatever that engagement is called, at any one time or any one place or in conjunction with any explicit or implicit agenda.

Notes

1. Many of these essays have been developed over the past few years as scholars have pursued their research. A number of them had early incarnations as work presented at conferences put on by the International Forum for U.S. Studies at the University of Iowa in 2005 and 2006, conferences that stimulated further research by both the editors and the other participants in those conferences. Clearly intellectual engagement with these issues has continued since moving IFUSS to the University of Illinois in 2007. Some early participants (e.g., Zsófia Bán, Sabine Broeck, Ian Condry, Kate Delaney, Richard Ellis, Guillermo Ibarra, Giorgio Mariani, Loes Nas, Manar Shorbagy, Kristin Solli, Ed Schatz, and Amy Spellacy) became formal authors. Others (e.g., Jane Desmond, Virginia R. Domínguez, Ana Mauad, and Michael Titlestad) became engaged commentators. And still other scholars (Sophia Balakian, Ira Dworkin, and Mohammad Marandi) joined later in the project of creating this book.

2. Scholarly work on related issues is often either more abstract, as in Jean Baudrillard's *Amerique*, or more committed to the view that U.S. corporate, neoliberal capitalism with its global market orientation constitutes the problem and explains it. Good work on that issue exists and has even proliferated in recent years. Consider, for example, Walter LaFeber's 2002 book, *Michael Jordan and the New Global Capitalism*, and Saskia Sassen's *Globalization and Its Discontents: Essays on the New Mobility of People and Money*. But we are not at all convinced that we can understand much about what gets casually called

"anti-Americanism" by making our frame of understanding "globalization" with or without its discontents.

We are more inclined to favor work whose findings are less predictable, such as James L. Watson's *Golden Arches East: McDonald's in East Asia*, or whose content does not clearly suggest a single conclusion, such as Richard Pells's *Not Like Us: How Europeans Have Loved, Hated, and Transformed American Culture since World War II*. A 2004 book edited by Andrew Ross and Kristin Ross, published by New York University Press, and using *Anti-Americanism* itself as its title is a step in the broader kind of direction we seek to foster. However, its seventeen essays, all but one by faculty members at New York University, often address the topic as if "anti-Americanism" were a *fact* to be explained and described, and many of the explanations center on U.S. political and economic actions in the world over a period of time. We do not sense that the question of what is, what counts as "anti-Americanism," and what gets taken to be "anti-Americanism" is this book's real focus, although some authors (Mary Nolan and Mary Louise Pratt, for example) clearly recognize the analytic problem and at times highlight it.

3. Many people will assume that Western Europe, home to countries functioning for years as official U.S. allies, is where one gets the most favorable images of the United States and of U.S. presidents. But "Western Europe" is not that simple. First, it is more variable in its polling results than Americans are likely to anticipate; second, it does not represent a great deal of Europe; and, third, it often holds strongly different views toward specific U.S. policies than are found in the United States itself. For example, late in President George W. Bush's second term, the Pew Research Center reported that only 31 percent of Germans polled, 33 percent of Spaniards polled, 42 percent of those polled in France, and 53 percent of those polled in Great Britain and Italy reported favorable views of the United States. Even in the former Warsaw Pact countries, the variety was significant: 46 percent of Russians polled and 45 percent of Czechs polled reported having favorable views of the United States unlike the 68 percent of Poles polled who did.

Works Cited

AARP. "God Bless Americans: Five Countries Where the U.S. Is Feted—Not Hated." Jan./ Feb. 2005: 14.

American Heritage Dictionary. "Criticism." 4th ed. Boston: Houghton Mifflin, 2001.

Baudrillard, Jean. *Amerique*. Paris: Bernard Grasset, 1986.

Des Moines Register. "Poll: Iowans Reject Bush's Account Plans. April 24, 2005: 10A.

Domínguez, Virginia. "Nemici poco chiari, amici poco chiari." *Acoma* 33. Inverno (2007): 53–65.

Francis, S., H. Dugmore, and Rico [Schacherl]. *The Madam and Eve Collection*. 2nd ed. David Philip, 1998.

Gallup Poll, "Presidential Approval Ratings—Barack Obama." June 29, 2016. http://www .gallup.com/poll/116479/barack-obama-presidential-job-approval.aspx.

Hill, Michael. "Did the Use of the Terrible Atomic Bomb Bring an Era of Peace?" *Iowa City Press-Citizen*. Aug. 7, 2005: 11A.

Iowa City Press-Citizen. "Pakistani Muslim Protestors Hold Anti-American Rally Wednesday to Condemn the Alleged Desecration of Muslims' Holy Book, the Quran, at the U.S. Prison in Guantanamo Bay, Cuba, in Lahore, Pakistan." June 9, 2005: 5B.

———. "Poll: Many Europeans Cool toward Bush, Americans." Dec. 14, 2004: 8.

Iranian Quran News Agency. "Newly Conducted Poll Shows, Americans Are Not Satisfied with US's Military Solutions to World Issues." Aug. 6, 2006.

Jackson, David. "Poll: Obama Approval Rating 'under Water.'" *USA Today.* July 11, 2013. http://www.usatoday.com/story/theoval/2013/07/11/obama-quinnipiac-approval-rating-syria-afghanistan/2507965.

Jon, Marie. "Consider America's Enemies." *National Ledger.* Aug. 6, 2005.

LaFeber, Walter. *Michael Jordan and the New Global Capitalism.* New York: W. W. Norton, 2002.

Manila Times. "Survey Highlights U.S. Image Abroad." Aug. 4, 2005.

Pells, Richard. *Not Like Us: How Europeans Have Loved, Hated, and Transformed American Culture since World War II.* New York: Basic Books, 1997.

Pew Research Center. Global Attitudes & Trends. Survey Data for 2009, 2012, 2013, 2014. www.pewglobal.org/category/datasets.

———. Spring 2015 Survey. http://www.pewglobal.org/2015/06/23/spring-2015-survey.

Ross, Andrew, and Kristin Ross. *Anti-Americanism.* New York: New York University Press, 2004.

Sassen, Saskia. *Globalization and Its Discontents: Essays on the New Mobility of People and Money.* New York: Free Press, 1998.

Schneider, Bill. "Poll: Clinton More Honest than Bush." CNN.com. http://www.cnn.com/CNN/Programs/anderson.cooper.360/blog/2006/05/poll-clinton-more-honest-than-bush.html.

Shapiro, Jonathan. *Long Walk to Free Time.* Cape Town: Double Storey, 2004.

Silverstein, Michael. "Shifters, Linguistic Categories, and Cultural Description." In Keith H. Basso and Henry A. Selby, eds. *Meaning in Anthropology.* Albuquerque: University of New Mexico Press, 1976.

Watson, James L. *Golden Arches East: McDonald's in East Asia.* Stanford, CA: Stanford University Press, 1997.

PART I

Whose "America"?
Whose "Anti-Americanism"?

CHAPTER 1

Internationalizing African American Studies, Too

White (West-) German Responses to the Civil Rights Movement

Sabine Broeck

Editors' Note: As this book was in production at the press, a series of egregious events in the United States unfolded, with police killings of several African American men, including Michael Brown in Ferguson, Missouri, and Philando Castile in Minneapolis, Minnesota, among others. The day after Castile's death, five Dallas, Texas, police officers were killed by snipers at a peaceful protest against police use of lethal force against black men. The Black Lives Matter movement has gained national momentum in calling attention to this ongoing crisis. These events give extra urgency to the arguments, debates, and commentaries in this section of the book, which assess trajectories developing over time.

While no academic press publication can respond to immediately unfolding events given the time it takes to bring a book to physical form, we felt that the urgency of this moment was such that we invited Professor Broeck to add an addendum to her piece as the book was in press. What follows are her additional reflections.

*   *   *

Prologue: July 8, 2016; written the day after what the liberal press has come to call "extrajudicial" killings of two defenseless, unarmed black men in two days, bringing the helplessly cynical count of antiblack killings up to 136 between January and July 2016. (See British newspaper the *Guardian*'s project "The Counted.")

The article to follow is going to press at another moment of rage and grief for the communities, families, friends, and loved ones of the dead, who are left with the enormity of never-ending "wake work" (I borrow the term from Christina Sharpe, "In the Wake") and for mourning and agitation in African American Studies and Black Diaspora Studies in the United States and elsewhere. The ideas were originally developed as a presentation at an IFUSS conference on "'America' in the World" in 2005–2006. The work was later developed into article form (2010) as part of a larger networked research project of European and U.S. African American Studies scholars about the impact of African American liberation movements and cultures on Europe, and in my case, Germany, in the Cold War decades after World War II. Even though it is thus marked by its own historicity as a piece that was embedded in a political, social, and cultural transnational environment altogether different from today, we decided to leave it in the collection to document a paradigmatic moment of crossover cooperation between African American Studies out of Germany, American Studies in the United States, and emerging internationalized American Studies. This critical crossover mirrors the interaction between African American, white American, and German actors and institutions and discourses the article seeks to discuss. However, neither its gist, its tone, nor its upbeat resolution may be borne out by the present escalation of gratuitous antiblack violence, to use a term Afro-pessimists like Frank Wilderson and Saidiya Hartman have introduced. This massive and lethal violence has called forth the Black Lives Matter movement, and many correlated nodes of struggle, on the North American continent. In Europe, black life has become ever more precarious, at risk, and under threat because of, for instance, the rising toll of militant racism in Britain after the Brexit vote (to have Britain leave the European Union) in the summer of 2016, and in Italy with street lynchings of black refugees,[1] with shattering numbers of so-called collateral deaths by drowning of African migrants in the Mediterranean, and in Germany, with an acceleration of armed and violent fascist attacks on "refugee homes" for black- or brown-skinned refugee populations (see Broeck, "Legacies of Enslavism"). Afro-Europeans have been building political, social, and cultural networks to intervene in national and European discourses and legislature as well as many scattered smaller initiatives located all over the continent.[2] To wit, the first British Black Studies degree program was founded at the University of Birmingham in 2016! This is to say that all kinds of possible collaborations between African American struggles and studies, and European actors, black or white, will have to be recast in the face of both the radicalization of black struggle in the United States and Canada on one side and a growing militant articulation of Afro-Europeanness on the other side of the Atlantic, both inside and outside academia. Thus, this addendum serves to mark my white agony: in the face of internationally networked, pervasive, and effective antiblack violence, to speak quasi harmlessly of the more or less benevolent, if racist, white German appropriations of blackness, as this article does, seems a woefully inadequate response to the demands of the historical moment. One may read it, therefore, as a document of evolving, groping, but rather immature coming to terms with ongoing black fungibility, to use Hartman's term—including the medially spectacular, titillating value of pornographic antiblack killings on mobile phone video clips—as an undertaking that, at the point of its articulation, had not fully understood that we still and again live in the afterlife of slavery, as Hartman has argued so forcefully. This agony has to stand without finding closure, and, consequently, the demanding bar for transnational crossover research has been raised in both political and scholarly terms.

*   *   *

This article functions on two levels: on one level it is a case study of moments of cultural and political crossover contacts between African American liberation and the West German public in the Cold War period. On the other level, reading this case study within the frame of the emerging discourses of transnational studies offers first parameters for a framework of internationalizing African American Studies, and thus for a recentering of African American Studies within the recent scholarly push for internationalized American Studies.

Over the past two years, scholars interested in issues of a comprehensively understood Black Atlantic may have witnessed new developments in African American Studies programs within and outside the United States. In cooperation with European literature, transnational history departments, Pan-African and Black Atlantic Studies, African Americanists have begun to pursue a pronounced interest in Black European Studies, as one could most easily witness in a series of conferences to address issues of blackness in Europe in the year 2006 (Northwestern, Amherst, Berlin) where African American Studies made important contributions, or even (co)hosted the events. A focus on Black and European Studies includes a broad range of issues and questions, ranging from the African American expatriate experience in Paris through the convergences of African American with Pan-African and Antillean activities in Europe, to interactions between African American, African, and Caribbean philosophies (across the English-speaking as well as the francophone world) both widely studied and received in Europe (Frantz Fanon studies being the most prominent example). It also includes studies of the complex relationship between European-based philosophy and the challenge of race and racialization of modern societies, which deal with European influences on African American Weltanschauung, and, though to a lesser degree, vice versa. Within European African American Studies, organized most expressly in the Collegium for African American Research/CAAR, there have been concentrated efforts dating as far back as 2000 (conferences in La Laguna, Cagliari, Tour, Münster, Madrid, Bremen, Paris, Atlanta, and Liverpool; see www.caar-web.org) to redirect interest toward the European negotiations with African American culture, history, and politics, encompassing questions that address the constitution of European modernity in the slave trade, as well as twentieth-century "crossovers" between African American agency and Europe. Thus, a focus on the "*histoires croisées*" has emerged, setting free a surge of critical energy. This energy has played itself out independently of, but at the same time—at least in Europe—intimately connected to, the transnational turn in contemporary state-of-the-art American Studies. At European universities the disciplinary trajectories of American Studies have framed African American Studies scholarship. In most cases until today, those two scholarly fields remain institutionally interdependent and tied to each other, if only because of massive underfunding and lack of institutional interest and support to build research and teaching bases in independent black studies.

American Studies in Europe, as well as in the United States, has been witnessing and producing scholarly skepticism vis-à-vis the concept of hegemonic area studies that in too many cases leads to either a sophisticated form of ventriloquism in departments on the European side or a form of parochialism on the U.S. side.

In this essay I explore and demonstrate what happens when these two tendencies purposefully converge, producing, as I would venture to say, rich mutual benefit: the transnational turn in American Studies has helped African Americanists to go beyond a U.S. territorial and epistemological fixation that used to ignore the multifold international and transcultural contact zones of African American agency in a global sense. And it may help American Studies—particularly when seen in international perspective—to reconsider and reconceptualize African American Studies as a crucial focus of well-deserved scholarly attention. It also might enable American Studies scholars to see African American epistemological, cultural, and political impact on world cultures and histories as one of the most important moments of what one could call "subversive Americanization." Beyond all the discussions about McDonald's, shopping malls, and Hollywood's hegemony, a vista opens up on a veritably cosmopolitan culture of crossover contact between African American agents, products, and sign systems (rap's bearing on youth cultures globally being only the most immediately visible tip of the iceberg!), on many forms and instances of transnational, transcultural *zivilgesellschaftliche* alliances, cooperations, and mutual influences that the present time of polarization between the U.S. hegemon and so many parts of the rest of the world might ask for a conceptualization of alternative relations. Both African American as well as American Studies (and audiences beyond those disciplines) might find it in their vital interest to take notice of those points of "crossover," particularly during the early Cold War period, political cosmopolitanism of the global resistance against Vietnam, international alliances against racism, and the cooperation of women's and democratic grassroots movements. In all of these points African Americans played vital roles, had established paradigms that the 1980s and 1990s seem to have discarded all too easily in biases (even in the realm of scholarship) against naïve political do-gooder-ness and often trashed political correctness, and in the freshly discovered lure of post-structuralism promising a respite from what looked to many like a defeat of 1960s and early 1970s political interventions. This has recently found its criticism (fired by the collective memory of a generational tide of people being able to look back on their own pasts, who often arrived in the academy by way of detours through activism), which shows itself, among other features, in the resurgence of African American scholarship on black power, the continuities of civil rights struggles, black militancy, and contemporary campaigns against racism, poverty, and the prison complex. This new scholarship in particular might still benefit from establishing crossover connections. Black power's grace (and possible weaknesses) might be assessed and redeemed not only in studies of the ongoing struggles in U.S. inner-city ghettos but also by way of studying its impact on European elites now designing the European commonwealth, most of them of the generation politicized in the students' movement and other grassroots campaigns—one way or another—by way of contact with African American liberation.

In the following case study, I address a few moments of crossover contact in Europe, focused on one particular historical and cultural moment, in one particular location—the Cold War period in West Germany. I hope not only to contribute valuable insights into the processes of mutual negotiations, conflicts, alliances, and contradictions between the white West German public and African American liberation but also to lay some groundwork for an inquiry into the complexly knotted epistemological and ideological processes of recognitions and mis-cognitions along racial and racist lines within the intellectual history of Europe.

Case Study: The Civil Rights Movement in Germany during the Cold War Period

The interaction between white Germans and African American culture and politics for a long historical phase—roughly encompassing the 1950s, 1960s, 1970s, and to a certain extent the 1980s—was characterized by practices and discourses of white adoration of black endurance and black moral power, along with a rather sentimental use of black suffering and resistance to conceptualize and formulate specifically local, political, and cultural desires. These practices and discourses either went openly hand in hand with, or in rather unacknowledged fashion underlay, explicitly political campaigns and activities that did indeed serve to champion the cause of, first, the civil rights movement, and, later, black power, in Germany. In addition I want to point to the equally strong political enthusiasm the 1960s and 1970s generations mustered in their interest in, their romanticizing fascination for, and sometimes even their support of the plight of Native Americans. The relation white Germans at the time entertained to the United States of America was characterized by a high degree of political and cultural ambivalence; it bifurcated into a militant and outspoken rejection of the U.S. state apparatus and its economic, military, and cultural hegemony. It also emphasized the declarations of elective affinity with representatives of what used to be called the "other America," which entailed everything ranging from the civil rights movement, early American white feminism, Native American struggle, the early ecological protests, Bob Dylan, Woodstock, blues and jazz cultures, the radical student organizations, and, of course, most emphatically, the anti–Vietnam War movement. It involved everybody, that is, who could be regarded as not implicated in the capitalist ruthlessness of U.S. politics and could be considered, culturally or politically, an ally against U.S. imperialism of the State Department, Hollywood, and the mainstream middle-class American way of life, which became a target of leftist and liberal criticism in the 1960s globally, at the same time that its seductions were manifestly successful. This paradox has occupied European Americanists for decades. My contention, however, is that the political potential for civil alliances over and against some of the more ruthlessly capitalist visions of Hollywood and the State Department that became visible in and for the "1968 plus" generation has not been adequately assessed with an eye to recovering its electricity and impetus for today's challenging global political situation.

What also has been missing from the accounts has been a framework of critical race studies for the 1968 generation. My hypothesis here, which will have to be tested in a wider ranging project, is that—mostly because of the naïveté and ignorance those white young intellectuals honed about their own investments in whiteness—race and racialization were not purposefully targeted issues in those days. Whereas white Germans would celebrate their solidarity with people like Martin Luther King Jr. or Malcolm X—depending on their political loyalties—in the German campaigns they were framed as victims of the morally, culturally, and politically corrupt, and, of course, racist, "bad" U.S. American "system." But this solidarity did not involve an examination of their own position as white and privileged in the transatlantic and global scheme of hegemony.

In the following case study, I address some selected facets of this ambivalent crossover relationship between African American liberation and white (West) Germany, which deserves, of course, much further scrutiny. In Cold War West Germany no strong African American, African, or black European presence existed that might have reined in or at least counterpointed the white romanticism of the German public. At the same time, white West German practices and discourses regarding the civil rights struggle remained largely unconnected to black knowledge about the historical, cultural, and political facets of slavery, the slave trade and black resistance to it, and, more importantly, to knowledge of how Europe or even Germany might have been implicated in that history. Which is to say, not only is Sander Gilman's coinage "blackness without blacks" appropriate, but one could even turn it around to descriptive effect. "Blacks without blackness" could quite succinctly capture the relationship between the German "scènes engagés" and representatives of African America: a willful, and sometimes self-serving identification without any context of blackness. African Americans had been and were the victims of the United States' betrayal of democracy, or, in more radical books, of its imperialism; thus, siding with them warranted the reward of seeing oneself a priori on the right side of history. In more intellectual versions of this equation, one "knew" about systemic and endemic racism, but only just so; slavery existed as an unexamined given—its paradigmatic American evil a foil before which one's own righteousness could freely unfold.

The German discursive interest in the African American plight, which across the divides of generation, gender, and political priorities, has been cast in terms that U.S.-American abolitionism prefigured over a century ago—that is, to claim that liberal and progressive West German interaction with African Americans has largely been characterized by a "*Stellvertreter*"—abolitionism. German progressives did not devise a critical epistemology that could have taken into account German antiblack racism, Germany's role in the history of the slave trade and colonialism, actual German implications in an international black diaspora, and a self-critical reading of white hegemony. Here I look at the cultural environment of African American "bodies" in Germany. I say "bodies" advisedly, because my contention is that it was a distinct fascination with the black embodiment of suffering, rather than an actual acquaintance with African American knowledge, that led the liberal West German public into identification with spokespeople like Martin Luther King Jr., James Baldwin, or Alice Walker, for that matter, with various degrees of emotional charge. Campaigns of political solidarity with black liberation were thus often predicated on rather vague kinds of emotional, self-cast "elective affinity"; one aligned oneself with humanity suffering at the hands of white U.S.-American bigotry. This characterizes the practices of intellectuals, church groups, and liberal media, as well as the rather preposterous self-blackening slogans of the radical student movement a few years later.

That kind of imaginary ersatz suffering with oppressed and pained black bodies did valuable work in German postwar intellectual and public cultures:

1. It allowed German progressive intellectuals a fascination with the "other America," as it was called, while positioning themselves at an intellectually and aesthetically productive skeptical angle vis-à-vis the United States.
2. It helped the liberal—church and otherwise 1950s—German public, in a convenient circumvention of a disturbingly close memory of the Shoah, to turn a critical lens on "the hypocritical Americans."
3. By using African American masculinity for a negative foil, even though "black men clearly inhabit their bodies more sensuously," as in the feminist best seller *Häutungen* of 1975, it defined white radical feminists' very own collective voice against overpowering male leftist mental hegemony: sexism is more fundamental than racism—and capitalism!—as author Verena Stephan proclaimed, under massive applause from the newly burgeoning white women's movement. It is a slogan that might, for the historically minded ear, recall not only a faint echo of the late nineteenth-century U.S. women's movement's emancipatory desire for themselves, which also took them beyond antiracism for decades to come.
4. It served—as in the case of best-seller stardom for *The Color Purple*—women who identified as white German women to satisfy both their aesthetic desire and their political need for an articulation of embodiment.

Some of these primarily self-serving receptive gestures had long-term effects in shaping the political and ethical consciousness of the Cold War intellectual generations, which resurfaces in mostly unacknowledged ways in the political vocabulary of Europe's democratic elites and in the professional choices of those students and young academics who formed the marginal subdiscipline of African American Studies on the fringes of the also rather embattled American Studies departments or subdepartments. It did not necessarily bring forth, however, a sustained and widespread interest in antiracist cooperation beyond the particular receptive moment or in acknowledging African Americans, let alone other black people living in Germany, as agents of a dialogue that might have an impact on the world larger than attracting and echoing the respectively involved egos.

Appealing to my readers' memory or imagination, I now ask you to "click" back a few decades. I want to remind you that 1952 was the year of the first UNESCO (United Nations Educational, Scientific, and Cultural Organization) declaration against racism. Seen in light of this declaration, the liberal German postwar discourses on the "negro" and "race"—as opposed to the rampant racism also very much active at the time—were characterized by a strange form of productive amnesia, not to say bigotry. As noted in disgust by Americans, Germans immediately after their liberation, in the face of the Shoah, could be quite adamant in their moralistic rejection of racism as America's evil; it was not such a rare experience in Germany to meet people who performed as negrophiliacs while at the same time being more or less openly anti-Semitic. This public sentiment resulted in official U.S.-American answers like a brochure on "Der Neger im amerikanischen Leben," printed and distributed for the U.S. Archiv Dienst Frankfurt in the early 1950s.

At best these admonitions reproduced classical Yankee ideology to teach the Germans that, yes, slavery was horrible but must be understood within its time and that in having destroyed the "old" South and its system in the Civil War, the North may legitimately lay claim to a moral superiority that outshines any and all occasional lapses into racism in Northern cities. These were the debates that prefigured the mass enthusiasm for the civil rights movement a decade later. Figureheads of African American culture who were associated with that movement, such as Sidney Poitier, Harry Belafonte, Sammy Davis Jr., even jazz icon Ella Fitzgerald, and, above all, Martin Luther King Jr. as spiritual leader, arrived at a kind of public notoriety that went much beyond their coveted status as political/religious spokespeople or as artists within their respective music and movie taste communities. This widespread pro–civil rights sentiment in those decades functioned like a self-realignment of the liberal German public with state-of-the-art international humanism in the UNESCO vein. It had the added benefit of keeping the same circles afloat in a legitimately outspoken critique of U.S. policies—serving purposes that oscillated between downright anti-Americanism and militant anti-imperialist skepticism. These discourses—and that is my point—strikingly recall the abolitionist "urtext," mirroring the proclamations of Uncle Tom's Cabin down to details.

Uncle Tom's Cabin—in German, Onkel Tom's Hütte—has an awesome publication history in Germany; the first edition registered in the online catalog of Die Deutsche Bibliothek (sort of the equivalent to the Library of Congress), certainly by no means the first edition available in German, is from 1908 in Berlin. The catalog documents hundreds of thousands of sold copies in at least a hundred different editions, published annually in new editions, and all through the 1930s, oddly and disturbingly so; those numbers are complemented by versions as plays, as radio plays, as children's books, on disc, cassette, CD and digital versions. In the postwar years, the first edition is with Kiepenheuer and Witsch, one of the larger German publishers, in 1948; followed by two editions, the second one of twenty-five thousand copies, by Neubau Verlag, Munich, in the same year. In the 1950s and '60s the sales do not abate. In 1966 Fischer Verlag brings out a new edition of sixty thousand, and so it continues in like dimensions until 2006, with an announcement in the Deutsche Bibliothek catalog of a new edition, not yet available. For generations, thus, Harriet Beecher Stowe, with all her antislavery goodwill, has been laying down the gospel truth about "the race" in her astute pronouncements of white benevolent empathy coupled with racist fantasies of black jungle sensuality, emotionality, and lack of civilized entrenchment. Even in feminist responses to *The Color Purple* its elements reverberate: the persistent white fascination with the heady magic mix of black spirituality and sensuality, with the "Deep South" appeal of poverty, endurance, and righteousness, works as a static, frozen abolitionist cluster of reception across and against at least two centuries of black self-articulation.

This rather willful politics of abolitionist reception functioned well not only in intellectual discourses but also in the realm of liberal mass media production. A visit to the archives of the German magazine *Stern* enabled me to peruse a few decades of journalistic engagement with African American people and issues. The magazine is a politically respected, glossy, high-end biweekly that is quite catholic in its political and cultural "tastes," characterized by its singular combination of print and photo essays, and has been in business since the late 1940s. I chose *Stern* because to my mind its moral preoccupations, topical selections, and political loyalties best capture the zeitgeist of the enlightened, more or less intellectually educated segments of the German public in the Cold War decades. The magazine faithfully covered and accompanied the crucial political, social, and cultural controversies of those decades with a keen eye for marketable publicity, as well as—to the extent possible for a such a publication—with a liberal ethos.

The 1960s had seen the African American civil rights movement come alive in Germany in ways that matched—sometimes maybe even outdid—its home popularity among white people. In 1964 Martin Luther King Jr., the movement's most cherished living symbol, gave a speech in Berlin for an audience of over sixty thousand; his sermons, speeches, and essays (in German translation) circulated widely in repeated editions of thousands of copies. The Bertelsmann Lesering, a well-established commercial German book club, selected *Why We Can't Wait* (*Warum wir nicht warten können*) for its paying members in 1964. James Baldwin's novels, too, found a wide readership; the Hans Wollschläger translation of *Another Country* sold fifty-seven thousand copies in the first year edition and was reedited four times until 1988; the same translation sold in the German Democratic Republic (GDR), to similar success, by the way. *The Fire*

Next Time (Hundert Jahre Freiheit ohne Gleichberechtigung: Eine Warnung an die Weißen), signaling the threatening transition to black militancy, sold forty thousand copies between 1964 and 1968. The abolitionist drive manifested itself most visibly in features like German translations published complete with white German authorization, thus obviously copying an American nineteenth-century modus of white authorization of African American slave narratives and other texts without any apparent reason for this kind of framing: *Freiheit! Der Aufbruch der Neger Nordamerikas:. Die Thesen der Gewaltlosigkeit exemplarisch ausgesprochen von dem großen Negerführer selbst und in den aktuellen Zusammenhang gestellt durch einen historischen Überblick "Amerika und seine schwarzen Bürger" von Hans Dollinger* (Freedom! North America's Negroes on the Move: The Theses of Non-Violence Spoken by the Great Negro Leader Himself, Put in Historical Context by an Essay by Hans Dollinger, "America and Its Black Citizens") is the cover title of a paperback edition by Heine Verlag, 1968. The *Stern* articles of the 1960s and 1970s should be read within this mental environment of a German public deeply disturbed by and moved to emulate the civic lessons of the civil rights movement's nonviolence campaigns: church groups and neighborhood streets were renamed after Martin Luther King Jr., teaching his "I Have a Dream" speech became canonical in high schools, grassroots activities were designed according to civil rights movement examples, and adults and teenagers eventually mourned King's death in wild outrage.

This empathy, again, was tenable only within an abolitionist framework; its fragility became visible at the precise moment when militant, radical black self-articulation and violent resistance appeared on the 1960s scene. White empathy, even at the German distance, seismographically caught the signs of a threat to white cultural and political hegemony and showed its Janus face of white contempt and racist ignorance. An erosion of discursive control becomes visible in the bizarre and quite helpless narrative strategies of containment with which the *Stern* covered post-1968 and early 1970s black militancy. It also shows up in *Stern*'s ambivalent fascination with Muhammad Ali (or Cassius Clay in his earlier years), whose grandiose but unpredictable performance in and out of the boxing ring merited several high-class photo essays by star *Stern* reporters like Eva Windmöller. Commentary ranges from anxious pity for "*Die armen Neger*" ("the poor n——") to the baffled and self-deconstructive phrasing in one of Windmöller's articles about a Cassius Clay who does not pay attention to white women (meaning also he did not court them!). It is hard to miss the disappointment of white benevolence and the shift to a racist leave-taking from a claim on white solidarity, which would have to be predicated on African American terms, in those passages.

After a number of morally outraged articles about the racist discrimination against "the poor Negroes," between 1963 and 1968 a series of articles appeared that tried to discursively prepare the readers for a social explosion in the United

States and at the same time keep themselves at a safe intellectual distance from that explosion. Titles in the series included "America's Negroes at the End of Their Patience," "Hatred Tears America Apart," and "City in Fear" and culminated in a big photo story about the death of Martin Luther King Jr., in which terrible snapshots of the assassination were accompanied by captions such as "The murder will give the signal for the cruelest Negro riot in the US," which was presented as the gravest problem. In the same issue, a reporter observed the riots, his benevolence collapsing because, "No, they did not mourn, they ran amok. They were not organized, and they were not interested in political organization. They only wanted to enjoy those hours, those singularly ecstatic, trancelike hours, rob, steal, plunder, loot, in the face of the police burn, call officers out of their names, humiliate the established order, and be the masters of Harlem." (All translation of *Stern* articles are mine; articles in print archive of *Stern*.)

Abolitionist goodwill slides into contempt as soon as the object of its empathy does not behave within the rules of the game, which even white subjects, at such a remove as the *Stern* was in 1968 from ghettos burning in the United States, implicate themselves in without prompt. It seems as if a pre-patterned narrative script for "how to read Negroes" is always already in place, even for liberal Germans who are not at all in the center of attack, or even concern, irreverent of specific time, location, actors, reasons, explications, or interests.

My next, and last, example is the *Stern* reportage about Angela Davis, who figures in a series of articles between 1970 to 1972 as the incomprehensible amazon. She is mostly severed of her biography except for the juicy pieces of her German studies with the Frankfurt School, which appears, too, mostly by way of stunned remarks about "how she could read so much, and so well," and "how she taught herself German by reading German plays, with a dictionary." In the articles Davis is always "beautiful," "the young woman with the ample afro-head, the sensuous lips, and the nicely curved neck"; she is "slender," humbly but tastefully dressed, displaying a "fantastical grace, this harmony of brain and body, intellect and sensuality"—attractive, in other words, as a female can be if it weren't for her "extraordinary sharp intelligence" and, even more so, for her utter impracticality: "she could not keep her room tidy, and kept losing her purse," plus, significantly, she "did not have an idea of time." She was courageous but nervous; intellectually trained but disorganized, and—one learns for good measure—traumatized by racism, which is what made her, in Oskar Negt's words, the "incarnation of a revolutionary," complete, if one wants to follow the *Stern*, with "suede leather mini skirt, silk blouse, silver ear loops, and a coral necklace." If she committed a crime, which remains unclear in the articles for a long time, it may just be one of "female passion," because she fell in love with George Jackson, to some audiences' eager delight and other people's racist anger.

Angela Davis—cast as an overdemanding strange crossbreed of Harriet Beecher Stowe's slovenly mammy, the courageous Eliza, and a hitherto unconceptualized extravagant jungle fighter—came onto the German scene with a vengeance of her own. As the previously absented black woman who did not figure in the triangular representational orbit of white men, white women, and black men—which must be seen as an essential constellation of abolitionist attachments—she burst into our imagination from the wings, as it were. She had to be either unmade as a woman (revolutionary, super-intellectual, a fighter, a black sister) or "overmade" as a sexy female, appearing as the "elegant Negress" (*Stern*) which, given all the previous stories about "poor Negroes," analphabetic women and children, or tasteless, cheaply dressed females, seems to have been quite an over-the-top oxymoron for white audiences at the time. Liberal Germans troped African Americans as an overwhelming yet powerless presence and its assumed visceral, charismatic energies.

Apart from arresting readers with its unabashed exoticism and reckless racist presumptions, what are the theoretical implications this material invites one to trace? Further, why would an in-depth reading of those instances—forty to fifty years after the fact—still be useful and productive? The latter question may immediately be answered with a nod toward the German media campaign surrounding Hurricane Katrina and the plight of black neighborhoods of New Orleans in August 2005. It was quite amazing to see how both the double-faced trope of "the poor Negroes" in tandem with its perfect match, the "negro out of control"—give or take a few variations in vocabulary—were put in recirculation at a moment's notice. Even the liberal and progressive German public has been largely ill equipped to formulate a response to the racist disaster beyond pity. Thus, the need for creating and disseminating epistemology within and beyond institutions of high education seems, still and again, a pressing urgency. How, then, to create interventions on the scenes of theory and advance those insights in, for example, German humanities departments, is a challenge to live up to.

This article's excursion into theory, then, uses Hortense Spillers's work as a base of some Germanized speculations, beginning with a longer passage quoted from "Mama's Baby, Papa's Maybe," one of her groundbreaking essays, originally published in 1987. Spillers describes the black body's "meaning and uses" for white discourses as follows: (1) the captive body is the source of an irresistible, destructive sensuality; (2) at the same time—in stunning contradiction—it is reduced to a thing, to being for the captor; (3) in this distance from a subject position, the captured sexualities provide a physical and biological expression of "otherness"; (4) as a category of "otherness," the captive body translates into a potential for what Spillers refers to as "pornotroping" and embodies sheer physical powerlessness that slides into a more general "powerlessness," resonating through various centers of human and social meaning" (206).

In keeping with this argument, Spillers provocatively marks the abolitionist script as one of "the ubertas, of the appetites generally" (177), and speaks of a white "metaphysical desire" for abolitionism's "most coveted body" (178). These passages refer not only to sexually charged scenarios between black and white individuals nor exclusively to clearly pornographic representations of African American bodies in white representations. The notion of pornotroping entails human nego-tiations on various mundane levels; said troping obscenely overwrites the black person with his or her assumed bodily "gestalt": an overwhelming yet powerless presence and its assumed visceral, charismatic energies. This pornotroping as the key element of white abolitionist responses to and assumptions of blackness, then, works as a protean palimpsest—an ever changing same configuration. And the pornotropic casting of African Americans has traveled to white Germany excessively well and has shaped the reception of and negotiation with figures as different as Martin Luther King Jr. and Angela Davis, neither of whom—on the surface—act as sexualized objects. My contention is that whereas Angela Davis was cast as the political brain in a magnetic sexy physique, as the visceral female "material," an individual mobile incarnation of castration fears or omnipotent fantasies for white audiences far into the leftist intellectual scene, Martin Luther King Jr. functioned as the larger-than-life metaphor for African American suf-fering, endurance, and overcoming, with pornotropic desire focusing on him precisely because of his ability to simultaneously embody and transcend the as-sumed existential pain of being black. Both Davis and King, in their respective functions, became "Überkörper"—an act of troping that could crystallize both white longing and white guilt in the affective affinity displayed toward them.

The point needs to be stressed of how well abolitionism has traveled to the Ger-man context—without there having been a clear focus or discursive need for it—and survived even, and especially so, into a social and cultural realm characterized by a lack of an agenda: setting black presence. A nineteenth-century local narrative configuration has actually set the parameters not only for national discourse (as Baldwin and others have amply observed) but also for international discourses. After more than 150 years of active service, it still holds sway over our transatlantic symbolic order of race relations. The dissemination of abolitionist sentiment as one particular feature of U.S.-Americanization, in recurring waves of discursive constel-lations, certainly deserves further examination. The fact of it appears banal to the point of invisibility, since it has been taken for granted over so many generations, but I argue that it is not. Just imagine for a moment how different race relations could be if white people in the transatlantic realm—for example, Germans—had decided to create their own tropes to come to terms with the black diaspora. That this did not happen, I suspect, is due to an extremely persistent hold that the legacy of the slave trade and slavery has had not only on New World peoples but also on white European modernity and postmodernity. In order to surpass abolitionist pornotroping as the hegemonic representation of African Americans as well as other black peoples, German intellectual Weltanschauung needed to first come to grips with their pervasive denial of slavery's constitutive function for the Enlightenment. The palimpsest that slavery and abolition wrote in the nineteenth century not only fixed a segregated symbolic pertaining to the place of black people within it, but even more so—as it turns out today—it inscribed white people within an extremely limited array of subject positions.

Looking at abolitionism thus becomes important all over again, not so much because of whatever more or less racist things it had to say about its script's black characters, which has been thoroughly deconstructed for centuries, but because of its fixation of white subject positions in Western modern collective memory and imagination. As long as white people in Germany create no scripts for themselves other than accepting the choice between the die-hard racist; the benevolent, emphatic, self-reflexive good white man; the white plantation bitch; the stern moralizing and authoritarian do-gooder; or, as the feminine role of choice, sweet little Eva, who may desire the black person in all presumptuous innocence, be it as mother, sister, lover, redeemer, or omnipotent healer of wounds, their "readings" of and, more importantly, their relations with African Americans and other black people will not step beyond the prototypical "peep at Uncle Tom" that Spillers scathingly interrupts with her argument.

One of the most notable features—at least speaking for Germany—in the reception and integration of civil rights discourses on this side of the Atlantic has been the appropriation aspect of it: various African American civil rights approaches, ideas, texts, and agents became absorbed into respective German discourses more or less eagerly, whereas any consciousness of the European connection to the slave trade remains completely absent. The discourse in Europe around civil rights at this particular point, too, focuses on Europe as a haven for universal rights—enlightenment, in this context, still figures as a promise not yet fully delivered. Metaphors of critique are always already ones of descent, decadence, ruin, apocalypse of modernity, betrayal, all of which were wrought on Europe by the Germans in and with the Shoah. The very fact that European modernity was steeped in the slave trade and our notions of "freedom" and "rights" are necessarily predicated on the absence of other peoples' rights (in ways that Europe and particularly its metropolises have not in the least owned up to). So, historically speaking, the acts of appropriation of civil rights discourses could be investigated as largely a series of narcissistic gestures that claimed a connection to the African American movements in solidarity and emphatic interest, all the while remaining strategically innocent of Europe's own constitution by and implications in the history of the African diaspora to the New World.

Epilogue: Repercussions of the Civil Rights Movement in Europe

The challenge of establishing civil rights beyond national, ethnic, or religious borders has become, and will remain, a tantamount issue for contemporary Europe. New and sometimes fraught discourses around civil rights—for example, the debate at the crossroads of (white) women's rights and religious freedom—have emerged. The connections of these new challenges, based as much on demographic change as on the postmodern and postcolonial fragmentation of older unitary and hegemonic conceptions of citizenship and belonging, to the older, Cold War discourses on civil rights has been left largely unexamined. Urgent questions need to be asked: To what extent can we observe a retinue of the post-1960s African American civil rights movement's impact in those European discourses, in various national (and East-West differentiated) incarnations, as well as in the formulations of Pan-European intellectuals? How does the memory of these 1960s and 1970s contact zones become revived and reformulated by the present radical mingling of ethnic, marginal white and black subcultures in the *banlieues* of Europe, facilitated more by hip-hop than by classical political rhetoric? How does this memory figure on the various political, cultural, and individual constellations of transatlantic relations? How has it influenced former national configurations of civil rights discourses, and what has happened to these discourses after the end of the Cold War period, and even more dramatically, after the post-9/11 impact on Europeanization discourses? How do we integrate a knowledge of those long-term transatlantic crossover processes into the most recent discourses of civic life in and of Europe that repeatedly—what with all the obligatory nods toward multiethnicity and diversity—casts and recasts itself as white, devoid of colonial history and slavery, and absolutely untouched by blackness in the political sense?

Notes

1. For the last recorded case at this moment, see http://enar-eu.org/Racist-murder-in-Italy-is-a-wake-up-call-for-a-European-BlackLivesMatter.

2. See "Demand Catalogue by People of African Descent & Black Europeans," Feb. 13–16, 2014 (http://isdonline.de/wp-content/uploads/2014/04/Demand-Catalog-PAD-BE_full-length.pdf); and "Shadow Reports on Racism in Europe," European Network Against Racism, (http://www.enar-eu.org/Shadow-Reports-on-racism-in-Europe-203).

Works Cited

Broeck, Sabine. "Legacies of Enslavism and White Abjectorship." In Sabine Broeck, Carsten Junker, ed. *Postcoloniality—Decoloniality—Black Critique: Joints and Fissures.* Frankfurt: Campus Verlag, 2014. 109–29.

Guardian. "Inside 'The Counted': How Guardian US Has Tracked Police Killings Nationwide." April 11, 2016. https://www.theguardian.com/membership/2016/apr/11/inside-the-counted-guardian-us-police-killings.

Hartman, Saidiya. *Scenes of Subjection: Terror, Slavery, and Self-Making in Nineteenth-Century America.* Oxford: Oxford UP, 2014.

Sharpe, Christina. "In the Wake." *On Blackness and Being.* Durham, NC: Duke UP, 2016.

Spillers, Hortense J. "Mama's Baby, Papa's Maybe: An American Grammar Book." *Diacritics* 17.2 (1987): 64–81.

Wilderson, Frank. *Red, White, and Black: Cinema and the Structure of U.S. Antagonisms.* Durham, NC: Duke UP, 2010.

CHAPTER 2

What We Talk about When We Talk about Anti-Americanism

An Italian Perspective

Giorgio Mariani

The title of my essay is not only meant as a nod to writer Raymond Carver, who attended the world-famous writing workshop at the University of Iowa, and therefore as a symbolic way to express my gratitude to those who have been so kind as to invite me to take part in this symposium.[1] There is a further reason for my title. Ever since, prompted by a set of historical and political circumstances, I began to read and write about the issue of anti-Americanism (and therefore, more or less explicitly, on the related topics of Americanism and Americaniza-tion), I have been wondering about this strange term. The conclusion I have reached is that "anti-Americanism" is no easier to define than a crucial yet also very slippery concept, like "love." I have seen so many different issues discussed under the rubric of anti-Americanism that my impression is that what we talk about when we talk about anti-Americanism depends on such a diverse array of historical, political, and ideological factors that no univocal answer to the question posed by my title is possible. Just as "love," in the Carver story to which my title refers, appears at times under the guise of what we would more read-ily recognize as "hate," anti-Americanism is, to resort to a Melvillean image, an equally "ungraspable phantom." In fact, most analysts of anti-Americanism are fond of pointing out that those who hate America are quite often more or less secretly in love with her.

Yet, while the similarities between Carver's "love" and "anti-Americanism" could probably be pursued in interesting ways, here I wish to stress where the analogy invoked by my title breaks down. Although there are, of course, vari-ous ideologies of love, and it may well be true that any expression of love has an ideological dimension to it, one does not expect from the feeling of love the same kind of consistency associated with ideological beliefs. Ideologies, like love, may be contradictory, yet only to a point. You may love someone and, in a fit of rage, slap that person. But you cannot be against the death penalty and simultaneously wish to put to death those who are in favor of capital punishment. By suggesting that there is a certain metaphorical resemblance between Carver's "love" and "anti-Americanism," my point is therefore not simply to insist that anti-Americanism is a hard-to-pin-down concept but that it is used to accommodate so many different and widely divergent views of "America" (that is, the United States of America) that it simply makes no sense to refer to it as if it were a political ideology comparable to, say, liberalism, socialism, conservatism, and so forth.

Since this is a key point, I would like to take a little more time in order to clarify what I am not saying. I am not saying—how could I?—that critiques of the United States do not exist. What I am disputing is that such critiques can be considered as part of an ideological formation—that is, a corpus of beliefs endowed with at least a modicum of consistency—called "anti-Americanism." On the other hand, there can be no doubt that labels such as "anti-Americanism" or "anti-American" are indeed used as weapons in a variety of ideological struggles. Anti-Americanism, therefore, is an ideological category in so far as we have a great number of books, essays, and articles identifying different critiques of various aspects of American politics or culture as being expressions of something called "anti-Americanism."

Yet that is not—at least not for me—a good enough reason to conclude that anti-Americanism is a sort of platonic, essential object that social and cultural historians may transparently apprehend in their analytical operations. To paraphrase a well-known passage in Michel Foucault's *Archeology of Knowledge*, anti-Americanism is an object that can be defined only by relating it to the rules that enable it to form as an object of a discourse and then constitute the conditions of its historical appearance (47–48). Along similar lines, roughly twenty years ago Terry Eagleton launched a critical attack on the concept of literature by arguing that "any belief that the study of literature is the study of a stable, well-definable entity, as entomology is the study of insects, can be abandoned as a chimera. . . . Literature, in the sense of a set of works of assured and unalterable value, distinguished by certain shared inherent properties, does not exist" (10–11). Anti-Americanism must be subjected to the same kind of deconstructive operation performed by Eagleton, and others, on the notion of literature. Any belief that discussions and analyses of anti-Americanism refer to a stable, well-definable ideological formation is simply empirically false. Anti-Americanism, in the sense of a set of critiques of the social, cultural, and political reality of the United States of America sharing some common analytical principles and a reasonable number of ideological features, does not exist. That is why whenever I use the terms "anti-American" and "anti-Americanism" I will be referring to particular, historically specific constructions of these labels and not to a sort of timeless essence as the one you can find in such landmark denunciations of "anti-Americanism" as, for example, Paul Hollander's *Anti-Americanism: Critiques at Home and Abroad.*

While I believe that a genealogical investigation of so-called anti-Americanism is urgently needed in order to displace the many idealistic accounts that group critiques of America from the Revolution to the present—as if a common, unbroken thread ran from the eighteenth-century aristocratic dislike of democracy to, say, Jean Baudrillard's musings on American hyper-reality—that is not what I can reasonably try to do in a relatively brief essay. My goal is much more modest. What I will do is focus on how the category of anti-Americanism is currently used in political and cultural debates in Italy, though I will also insist that, to the best of my knowledge, the Italian situation is by no means unique. At any rate, while I will also briefly mention some specific Italian critiques—as well as Italian appreciations—of the United States, the main object of my analysis is not so much the ungraspable phantom of Italian anti-Americanism, in the sense of the by now centuries-long history of Italian critiques of America, as it is the rules according to which the latter category is presently deployed in order to characterize and delegitimize, or even demonize, a variety of political positions. More specifically, the point I would like to make is that, especially in the wake of 9/11, anyone wishing to be accepted as a reliable commentator on the United States by the public sphere must first of all subject him- or herself to a ritual repudiation of "anti-Americanism."

Let me put this in more Foucauldian language. All discursive formations posit rules for the construction of a statement that can be considered *dans le vrai*—within the truth. It is not enough to speak the truth; if your truth is to count as such, you must speak according to those "enunciative modalities" that will qualify your viewpoint as a legitimate one. Nowadays in Italy—and, I suspect, elsewhere and certainly in Western Europe—no utterance on American political or sociocultural life is permitted to appear without a preliminary certification of its status vis-à-vis the discourse of anti-Americanism. In other words, no statement can exist independently of what Foucault calls "authorities of delimitation," the repressive force underlying, in our case, current discursive practices on America (41–42).[2] Only a statement free of the charge of anti-Americanism will be considered *dans le vrai*. This, of course, does not mean that what is labeled as anti-Americanism is not allowed to appear in public discourse. To rephrase in global terms what Andrew Ross has recently argued in connection to internal critiques of the United States, the contempt reserved in public debates for anti-Americans "does not make them persona non grata." On the contrary, anti-Americanism is an integral component of the hegemonic global discourse on America, just as necessary to it, as Ross writes, "as the blasphemer or heretic is to the theological scourge" (281).

In support of my thesis, I would like to offer a parallel discussion of two recent books on the United States. The first text is by an Italian scholar, Sergio Fabbrini, a political scientist whose name may be familiar to both Italian and non-Italian readers, since not only has much of his work appeared also in English but, besides

holding a chair at the University of Torino, he is also recurrent visiting professor at Berkeley.[3] The text I will discuss is titled *L'America e i suoi critici. Vizi e
virtù dell'iperpotenza Americana*—that is, "America and Its Critics: The Virtues
and Vices of the American Hyper-power."[4] The second book is titled *America
Embattled: 9/11, Anti-Americanism, and the Global Order*, and its author is Richard Crockatt, professor of American History at the University of East Anglia.[5]
Though these two books cover to a large extent a different territory—the first one
focuses on the institutional features of U.S. society while the second is mainly
devoted to the so-called war on terrorism and its global implications—they are
both conceived as assessments of, and responses to, what their authors perceive
as a new and alarming wave of "anti-Americanism."

I have chosen these two texts because, though personally I do not agree with
many of the arguments they present, their authors are open-minded scholars
whose views could be broadly described as liberal. I insist on this point because
whereas elsewhere—in collaboration with my colleague Alessandro Portelli—I
have focused on how the heresy of anti-Americanism is constructed by intellectuals whose ideological affiliations are with the political right, here I want to
engage a form of liberal discourse that is unquestionably much more balanced
and nuanced (Mariani and Portelli 84–95). Unlike the defenders of what Portelli and I have described as "mythic pro-Americanism"—a sort of Italian-style,
warmed-over, good old American exceptionalism—scholars of a totally different
caliber like Fabbrini and Crockatt are ready to concede that the United States is
not beyond the pale of criticism. Indeed, they both express on more than one
occasion their dislike of the most unattractive features of Americanism. Crockatt,
for example, commenting on the McCarthy era, complains that "the concept of
un-American activity . . . suggests the quasi-theological character of American
nationalism," and though this is hardly news for any student of American literature who has bothered to read Sacvan Bercovitch's work, it is a welcome—at least
to me—reminder of the often not so benign or neutral character of Americanism.
In the opening pages of Fabbrini's book, after noting that "anti-Americanism
has become an ideology, and so has the opposite concept of Americanism," the
author argues that it is a serious mistake to turn America into an ideology, no
matter whether "positive" or "negative" (*America e i suoi critici* 9–10).[6] Since the
United States is a democracy, an "open society," its social and political reality
must be by definition a contradictory one, a mixture of "vices" and "virtues," as
implied by the title of Fabbrini's book. To the ideological vision of both pro- and
anti-Americans, Fabbrini opposes an "empirical" approach destined to refute
both the exaggerated praise of America expressed by its lovers and the excessive
critiques directed at her by America-haters.

From a rhetorical perspective what I find interesting about Crockatt's and Fabbrini's work is that they both begin their arguments by juxtaposing their reasonable and supposedly ideology-free voices to those of a public opinion too often

biased one way or the other, though it is mainly against what they consider as anti-American stereotypes that the two scholars choose to set their own discourse. The two texts, in other words, are both ideologically and rhetorically founded upon a rejection of the "irrationalism" of anti-Americanism so that whatever critical remarks on U.S. foreign or internal policies, their history, and their culture may be uttered by the two scholars in the course of their analyses, such observations will not be confused by the reader with the vulgar and misinformed allegations of more or less rabid anti-Americans.

Now, what is paradoxical about both books is that their authors confess from the outset their doubts about the tenability of anti-Americanism as an analytical category. Crockatt writes, "It is necessary to put quotation marks around the term 'anti-American' because, like all essentially political terms, it proves difficult once you start peeling back the layers of meaning" (43). Fabbrini is perhaps even more explicit in his criticism of the notion of anti-Americanism: "Anti-Americanism is a concept so often used politically and yet so vague analytically. . . . [It . . .] is a concept so charged with exasperated emotional traits that its critical analysis is rather difficult" (Fabbrini 9). Yet, rather than rejecting such a problematic category, or proposing to redefine it in more rigorous terms so that, for example, one can distinguish between what Theodore Zeldin describes as the "hysterics" bent on either loving or hating "a whole nation" and those who criticize given aspects of a country, both authors go on to employ it as if all their provisos had never been uttered (Zeldin 35).[7] Thus, though anti-Americanism is for Crockatt a "contested concept whose range of reference is wide and shifting" and at times may indeed be used "as a political weapon to discredit an opponent rather than anything approaching a term of analysis," he believes that we should not deny its existence but rather "accept that it assumes many different forms, depending on historical contexts and political agendas" (46).

Similarly, Fabbrini claims on the one hand that since anti-Americanism is an ideology, he won't have anything to do with it as such, preferring to focus on its "empirical side"—that is, on the specific critiques that are leveled at the United States in order to measure their degree of fairness. Yet, on the other hand Fabbrini constantly resorts to the labels "anti-American" or "anti-Americanism" in his book any time he wishes to characterize any criticism of the United States but his own. In other words, after denouncing the ideological character of anti-Americanism and indeed complaining, just like Crockatt, that anti-Americanism is employed in political debates "to de-legitimize any criticism of America" (Fabbrini 9), he proceeds to valorize whatever he has to say on the United States through a systematic juxtaposition of his reasonable views to those not of other critics of America but to those of anti-Americans. Analogously, after noting that "anti-Americanism and pro-Americanism can exist in the same culture, indeed in the same individual," so that, for example, the same Baudelaire who was alarmed about the increasing Americanization of the world was also an almost unconditional admirer of American literature, Crockatt does not come to the conclusion that Baudelaire cannot be described as an anti-American—far from it. Baudelaire and all other critics of America remain, in Crockatt's eyes, anti-American because "anti-Americanism is no simple unitary phenomenon" (57).

Lest I be misunderstood, I want to stress not only that many of the views put forward in the two books under discussion are indeed reasonable but also that I share the authors' impatience with regard to certain attacks on the United States and Americanization that I too find misplaced, misinformed, and at times outright grotesque. Yet I cannot help but being disturbed by the pretense the two authors make of speaking to us from some Archimedean position untainted by ideology when in fact the rhetorical maneuvers they perform in their own texts are ideological through and through. For example, both Crockatt and Fabbrini feel a need to begin their studies of contemporary critiques of the United States by offering us brief sketches of the long history of anti-Americanism. Thus in *America Embattled* not only do we read, for example, of Chateaubriand's and de Tocqueville's revulsion at the leveling effects of American democracy, but we are also treated to the list of important things that America lacked compiled by an intellectual figure one would not normally associate with anti-Americanism. It is that famous list compiled by Henry James in his book on Hawthorne, which, as many will remember, begins, "No State, in the European sense of the word . . . no Oxford, nor Eton, nor Harrow; no literature, no novels, no museums" (460). One cannot help but wonder what is the use, in a book that is devoted for the most part to analyzing the threat of global terrorism, of informing us that America has been criticized by the likes of Henry James, de Tocqueville, Baudelaire, Chateaubriand, and others.

Obviously I do not believe even for a second that Crockatt is implying that Henry James may have been an inspiration for Islamic terrorists. Yet it is precisely for this reason that I need to question the usefulness of mentioning de Tocqueville's or James's critiques of America only three pages before moving on to an analysis of "varieties of anti-Americanism and September 11" (Crockatt 55). Whether intentionally or not, despite all of his reservations regarding the category of anti-Americanism, Crockatt resorts to "enunciative modalities" typical of *anti* anti-Americanism discourse, thereby projecting an America that is always under siege both inside and outside, as if there were something truly exceptional about the United States and one could not tell similar stories about the external as well as internal criticism leveled at any other nation in the world. I know, for example, that one could write a multivolume history of "anti-Italianism," grouping together, on the one hand, all the foreign stereotypes on Italians from the Renaissance onward and, on the other, all the impassionate invectives against the mother country uttered by Italians themselves since the days of Dante Alighieri. Yet, except during the Fascist era—when opponents of the regime were indeed stigmatized as "anti-Italians"—the category of anti-Italianism has simply never existed.[8] Moreover, I can't imagine an Italian protesting against, say, the stereotype of the Italian mafioso feeling the need to complain that since the Elizabethan Age Italy was considered a land of murder and intrigue. Yet, notwithstanding the fact that Crockatt would no doubt agree that James's views are no more helpful in understanding the Mullah Omar's hatred of America than is John Webster's depiction of Italian corruption useful in making sense of current myths about the Sicilian mob, he simply cannot resist the urge to follow a discursive tradition according to which all critiques of America, no matter where they come from or what they say, must be comprised under the rubric of anti-Americanism.

While Crockatt's brief history of anti-Americanism is global, Fabbrini's is essentially peninsular, as he focuses mainly on Italian critiques of the United States. According to Fabbrini, all the three major Italian cultural and political traditions of the twentieth century are heavily tainted with "anti-Americanism." With the exception of a few isolated intellectuals, the left, especially the radical left, "never liked America" (Fabbrini 13). But of course also the right, and in particular the Fascist right, never liked America either, though Fabbrini admits that once the war was over and America became the bastion of anticommunism, both conservatives and post-Fascists alike revised their previous condemnations of U.S. modernity.[9] Finally, Italian Catholicism has never been too fond of America, not only because the latter is a largely Protestant country but also because of its immense wealth and power. "The pauperist vision of Italian Catholicism," Fabbrini writes, "does not allow one to see the virtues of America, but only its vices" (Fabbrini 26).

Though Fabbrini's review of Italian forms of anti-Americanism takes up only a dozen or so pages, it bears a striking resemblance to the longer, though certainly no more reliable or objective analysis of Italian anti-Americanism to be found in the book *Maledetti Americani* (Damned Americans), by Massimo Teodori, the current dean of Italian mythic pro-Americanists, a man who is on record for having justified the use of any weapon—including weapons of mass destruction like the white phosphorous used by the U.S. troops in Fallujah—to root out terrorism.[10] What is paradoxical is that in a footnote Fabbrini rightly criticizes Teodori's Manichean vision, according to which the United States can do no wrong and its opponents, instead, are always wrong (Fabbrini 34–35). Yet, in what is to me a virtual textbook example of how a discursive formation can overwhelm the subject responsible for discourse, Fabbrini's account of Italian anti-Americanism runs parallel rather than counter to Teodori's. Of the three political-cultural traditions they analyze, both writers choose to emphasize only those utterances that can be taken as instances of anti-Americanism, disregarding all the evidence that would greatly complicate their theses. In other words, even a liberal thinker like Fabbrini ends up committing the same sin he imputes to anti-Americans. The latter, he feels, never judge America as they would judge another country—that is, by criticizing this or that aspect of its foreign or internal policies. According to Fabbrini, critiques of America are marked by their "holistic" character; they are attacks en bloc on the country (Fabbrini 28). Yet his own views of the three traditions of Italian anti-Americanism are themselves "holistic" in that Fabbrini chooses to ignore all the hard evidence that would show, beyond any shadow of doubt, that neither the Italian left, nor Fascism, nor Italian Catholicism have ever been organically and "holistically" opposed to America.

The left, for example, loved American literature, not only during the Fascist period, when writers/critics Cesare Pavese and Elio Vittorini translated and introduced classic American writers like Melville, Whitman, Hawthorne, Twain, and many others, but also during the McCarthy era and the Vietnam War—one need only think of Fernanda Pivano's translations and her countless articles and reviews.[11] Moreover, Agostino Lombardo, the man who held the first chair ever in American literature at an Italian university, and who worked hard to promote it both inside and outside the academy, though never a Marxist, was for most of his life a member of the Italian Communist Party.[12] On the opposite end of the political spectrum, one must remember that Mussolini was a great admirer of Franklin D. Roosevelt's economic policies and that even during the war Fascists had a wide variety of opinions on American society (Migone). Finally, no matter how strong Catholic reservations against American Protestantism may have been, the Italian Christian Democratic Party was responsible for establishing an iron alliance between the United States and Italy that lasted half a century and always insisted that Americans were Italians' best friends.[13]

Before coming to a conclusion, I want to spend a few more words on Mussolini, given that there is a tendency on the part of Italian students of anti-Americanism to imply that since the Duce criticized America, all anti-Americans are "objectively" fascist. In 1931 Cyril Clemens, Mark Twain's nephew, was in Rome and paid the Duce a visit. Visibly excited about the occasion, he greeted the dictator with these words: "We love you in America." Mussolini replied "in excellent English" that he was an "old and great admirer" of Mark Twain, whose work he had read, including those books that had never been translated into Italian. At the end of the meeting Cyril Clemens handed Mussolini a plate with a dedication to "the great educator" (Clemens 2, 4–5). This episode of mutual admiration does not uncover a pro-American Mussolini. It is more correct to say that even Mussolini displayed a variety of attitudes toward the United States and that these attitudes changed over time in light of shifting political circumstances, which also included the way the United States related to him. It is well known that when Clemens visited with the Duce, a large part of the American ruling classes did like Mussolini, who was considered the strong man needed to keep in line the Italians, a people definitely not at home with democracy.

All of this tells us, once again, that political feelings are often guided by pragmatic and at times outright opportunistic considerations. One has every right to consider this rather common behavior morally reprehensible, yet one must also have the intellectual honesty to acknowledge that the messy historical record of the relations between Fascist culture and the United States (or the Italian left and the United States, or Italian Catholicism and American Protestant culture) can in no way be meaningfully interpreted according to the category of anti- (or pro-) Americanism. How can one put in the same analytical toolbox, for example, the Catholic critique of America as a "materialist" society with that of a Marxist left that is materialist by definition? How can one consider as belonging to the same "tradition" the left and liberal critiques of the history of racial segregation in the United States and the posters of the Italian neo-Fascist group Forza Nuova, with their slogan, "*Non ci piace lo zio Sam e nemmeno lo zio Tom*"—that is, "We don't like Uncle Sam, yet we also don't like Uncle Tom"? How can one apply the same label of "anti-American" to both lovers and haters of the African American presence in U.S. society and culture? How can critiques of America that have absolutely nothing in common, and are based on totally incompatible cultural and philosophical premises, be constructed as being part of the same discourse of anti-Americanism?

The answer to these questions, I believe, has something to do with what Amy Kaplan has described as "the tenacious grasp of American Exceptionalism" and Eric Foner has stigmatized as the temptation "to reproduce traditional American exceptionalism on a global scale" (Kaplan 153–59; Foner). But in order to have a better picture of the situation, let me first take a brief philological detour. If you look up the word "Americanism" in a pre–World War II British, German, French, or Italian dictionary, you will find that besides describing words or expressions characteristic of American English, the term was used to refer to an inordinate admiration of the United States. In those days Europeans were much more worried about Americanism than they were about opposition to it, something that is currently taken as a sign of Europe's traditional legacy of anti-Americanism. Yet from a philological perspective it makes perfect sense that anti-Americanism would be perceived by Europeans as a healthy attitude—as an understandable criticism of those who blindly and naïvely loved America. The situation changed after the war, when in most dictionaries the old meaning of the term "Americanism" fell from first or second place to third or fourth place, and the new term "anti-Americanism" made its appearance. What is worth emphasizing in this regard is that if today I open my standard Garzanti Italian dictionary, of the several words bearing the "anti-" prefix I will find—words like "anti-communism," "anti-Fascism," and so on—only the word *antiamericanismo* refers to a specific people and a specific country. The same, I have discovered, is true of the classic Larousse: the famous French dictionary lists thirty words with the prefix "anti-," yet only *antiamericanisme* refers to the dislike of a particular nationality (Dubin 547).

It was only with the advent of the Cold War, therefore, that the term "anti-Americanism" installed itself in European dictionaries as well as in the language of global politics. Its rise was indeed parallel to that of its twin brother, "anti-Sovietism." This goes a long way, I think, in explaining why, at rock bottom, the discourse of anti-Americanism functions the way it does. It is a discursive formation marked by what Richard Hofstadter has described as the "paranoid style" in American politics (3–40). By labeling all critiques of the United States as "anti-American," and by showing no interest whatsoever in discriminating between fair or unfair criticism, or between the different ideological standpoints from which a given critical argument is deployed, the discourse of anti-Americanism inevitably gives credit to, and constantly reinforces, the idea that a multifarious international network is busy plotting against what inevitably ends up standing out as the world's best hope. So there is something truly paradoxical about both Crockatt's and Fabbrini's lamentation that America tends to invite "all-or-nothing," "holistic" responses. It is the paranoid structure of the discourse of anti-Americanism—a discourse that has always been imbricated with McCarthy-style denunciations of "un-Americanism"—that constructs critiques of America along an all-or-nothing divide. Rather than dismantling the paranoid style of the language of anti-Americanism, even enlightened, intelligent writers like Fabbrini, Crockatt, and many others whose work—given enough time—I could also have analyzed, actually contribute to the very mythology they claim to consider with detached, objective scholarly eyes.

I began this essay by arguing that if one pays some attention to the variety of historical, cultural, and political issues discussed under the rubric of "anti-Americanism," the latter term quickly loses any analytical credibility. As I am sure readers will have by now realized, mine is a plea for getting rid of this term altogether, though I am perfectly aware that (1) this is unlikely to happen, no matter how many deconstructions of the term one may offer, and (2) one would need to propose new terms for discussing both internal and external critiques of the United States, and I have none to propose except the commonsensical observation that even describing a statement as, say, a "criticism of the U.S. government" rather than an instance of anti-Americanism would make a great deal of difference.[14] At any rate, once we take a close look at what we talk about when we talk about anti-Americanism, we realize that it is *how* we talk about it that ultimately makes a difference. As Virginia Domínguez has shown, it is the way we "frame" utterances of so-called anti-Americanism that we need to interrogate.[15] From my European, and specifically Italian, observation post, I can only conclude that giving in to the discourse of anti-Americanism (and anti anti-Americanism) would be the death of independent critical inquiry. Contemporary denunciations of anti-Americanism comprise yet another instance of what John Collins and Ross Glover have intelligently described as "collateral language" (1–13). Like "surgical strike," "collateral damage," or "terrorism," "anti-Americanism" contributes to "America's new war" by occluding certain realities and reframing them in ways that are acceptable to the interests of the global hegemon. Just as it is more convenient to regret as "collateral damage" the family of eleven (including five children and three women) torn to pieces by U.S. missiles in Balad, 90 kilometers north of Baghdad, on March 16, as troops hunted down an "al Qaeda militant," rather than flatly regret that eleven innocent lives were lost in order to kill a suspect, so it is much easier to rave about "anti-Americanism" as if it were a pathology rather than attend to what so-called anti-Americans have to say or, God forbid, wonder whether there may be some reasons for what they say (Democracy Now).[16]

But the implications of the term "anti-Americanism" in the field of "collateral language" are deeper than its being an example of rhetorical manipulation. I have already mentioned that no honest analyst of anti-Americanism can do without the qualification that the very term used for analysis is contradictory, hard to-define, ambiguous. My impression is that just like "terrorism," as John Collins has shown, is a concept that not only cannot be precisely defined but also must be left undefined, since any explicit definition of the word could then be used to accuse the United States and its allies of resorting to terrorist tactics, thus threatening the illusion of American innocence, so the meaning of the words "anti-American" and "anti-Americanism" must remain enveloped in that "sheer cloudy vagueness" that George Orwell associated with political language as such (Collins 155–75; Orwell 256). If, for example, the use of the term "anti-American" were to be restricted to those "hysterical" manifestations of blanket hatred of everything American—if, that is, we should take at their word those who claim that anti-Americanism must be interpreted as being homologous to anti-Semitism—it would not be the effective political weapon that it currently is.[17] Instead, it must remain a vague and undefined term so as to be deployed against any target one sees fit—even against Henry James, if need be. Didn't James, after all, once observe that Americans are "the most addicted to the belief that the other nations of the earth are in a conspiracy to under-value them"? (543).

Lest you think I am exaggerating the spiritually and culturally deadly effects fostered by the mentality that sustains the discourse of anti anti-Americanism, I conclude with a brief allegorical, though unfortunately true, story. In December 2002, Habibullah and Dilawar, two Afghani suspects, were taken into custody by U.S. forces at the Bagram Air Base and so savagely beaten that five days later they were both dead. One of them, according to the medical examiner, was "pulpified." Even though fifteen soldiers were charged in the Bagram abuse, the sentences have ranged from letters of reprimand to five months in jail, and no one above the rank of captain has been brought to trial. The commander of the unit, Capt. Christopher M. Beiring—against whom all charges were dropped as of January 6, 2006, and who was simply issued a reprimand—asked on 60 Minutes by Scott Pelley whether he, in retrospect, had any sympathy for Habibullah and Dilawar, replied with these words: "Sure, I have some sympathy. I wish they were born Americans."

Now, if you happen to believe that human beings should be treated with justice whether they were born American or not, I think it would be a good idea to constantly keep in mind that most denunciations of anti-Americanism are no innocent intellectual exercises. The discourse of anti anti-Americanism is part and parcel of a strategy devoted to reinforcing the myth of American uniqueness and supremacy so effectively and brutally reflected in Captain Beiring's words. Needless to say, I have no magical antidote to this rhetoric of global consensus, but I want to end with the same question posed more than a decade ago by Sacvan Bercovitch: "What if the country [that is, the United States] were to be recognized for what it was, not a beacon to mankind, as [John] Winthrop announced in his *Arabella* address of 1630; not the political Messiah annually proclaimed through the mid-nineteenth-century in July Fourth addresses—not even (in Studs Terkel's reformulation) a covenanted people robbed by un-American predators of their sacred trust—but simply *goy b'goyim*, just one more nation in the wilderness of this world?" If we wish to move beyond current notions of anti- (or pro-) Americanism, this question would seem to be one of the places to start.[18]

Notes

1. My title obviously echoes Carver's famous short story "What We Talk about When We Talk about Love," in *What We Talk about When We Talk about Love: Stories* (New York: Knopf, 1981). I am grateful to IFUSS directors Jane Desmond and Virginia Domínguez for their kind invitation to take part in the second symposium, "'America' in the World: Discourses of 'Americanization' and 'Anti-Americanism.'" Many thanks also to Zsófia Bán for her gracious and insightful comments in response to an earlier draft of my essay.

2. For the notion of the discursive formation as "repressive force" I am indebted to Frank Lentricchia, *After the New Criticism* (Chicago: U of Chicago P, 1980), 195.

3. Among the many books and articles published in English by Professor Fabbrini, I will mention only two items related to the subject at hand: "The Domestic Sources of European Anti-Americanism," *Government and Opposition* 37.1 (2002): 3–14; and "Layers of Anti-Americanism: Americanization, American Unilateralism and Anti-Americanism in European Perspective," *European Journal of American Culture* 23.2 (2004): 79–94.

4. Sergio Fabbrini, *L'America e i suoi critici: Vizi e virtù dell'iperpotenza Americana* (Bologna: Il Mulino, 2005). Brief sections of this book appear in the articles mentioned in note 3.

5. Richard Crockatt, *America Embattled: 9/11, Anti-Americanism, and the Global Order* (London: Routledge, 2003).

6. *America e i suoi critici*, 9, 10. Here and elsewhere, all translations from the Italian are mine.

7. Unfortunately, even a thinker as brilliant and original as Zeldin not only fails to make such a distinction but also goes on to argue that "to hate or love half a nation is still too simple; still too hysterical." One wonders what percentage of "hate or love" of "a nation" may be considered as being "non pathological" and, more importantly, where "hate" ends and legitimate criticism begins.

8. I must note, however, that during the spring 2006 general elections, Silvio Berlusconi once or twice accused the center-left coalition of being unpatriotic and "anti-Italian." Yet the fact that the term has not taken hold proves it is meaninglessness to most Italians.

9. For an account of Italian critiques of the United States during the 1930s, see Michela Nacci, *L'antiamericanismo in Italia negli anni Trenta* (Torino: Boringhieri, 1989). Nacci's study is in many ways an excellent one, but it tends to downplay or simply ignore the degree to which some Fascists—including Mussolini himself—expressed admiration for the United States.

10. Teodori's views on Fallujah were expressed on the television program *Primo piano*, a sort of Italian equivalent of *Nightline*.

11. See, among their many works, Cesare Pavese, *American Literature: Essays and Opinions*, trans. Edwin Fussell (Berkeley: U of California P, 1970); Elio Vittorini, ed., *Americana: Raccolta di narratori* (1943; Milano: Bompiani, 1968); and Fernanda Pivano, *La balena bianca e altri miti* (Milano: Mondadori, 1961), *America rossa e nera* (Firenze: Vallecchi, 1964), and *Beat hippie yippie: Dall'underground alla controcultura* (Roma: Arcana, 1972).

12. Many of Lombardo's essays on American literature can be found in *Realismo e simbolismo: Saggi di letteratura americana contemporanea* (Roma: Edizioni di Storia e Letteratura, 1957), and in *La ricerca del vero: Saggi sulla tradizione letteraria americana* (Roma: Edizioni di Storia e Letteratura, 1961).

13. On the relationship between the Christian Democratic Party and the United States, see Mario del Pero, *L'alleato scomodo: Gli USA e la DC negli anni del centrismo, 1948–1955* (Roma: Carocci, 2001).

14. My invitation to get rid of the term "anti-Americanism" may well be another losing battle akin to the one many have been fighting against the use of the term "America" as a synonym for "United States." My experience is that only enlightened academics bother to distinguish between the two terms, while in everyday language—both in the United States and elsewhere, with the exception, I guess, of Central and South America—"America" is the United States. All this notwithstanding, I believe we must continue to engage in such apparently endless terminological/ideological skirmishes.

15. Virginia Domínguez, "Unclear Enemies, Unclear Friends," paper presented at "'Anti-Americanism and Anti-Imperialism': Critiques from Inside and Outside the U.S.," a panel of the Second World Congress of the International American Studies Association, University of Ottawa, August 18–20, 2005. A revised Italian translation of this essay appears in *Ácoma: Rivista Internazionale di Studi Nord-Americani* 33 (Winter 2007): 53–65.

16. On the Balad massacre, see "Another Civilian Massacre? U.S. Launches Investigation after Iraqi Police Accuse U.S. Troops of Murdering 11 Men, Women, and Children Last Week," *Democracy Now!* March 23, 2006, http://www.democracynow.org/2006/3/23/another_civilian_massacre_u_s_launches.

17. For an example of such wrongheaded attempts at establishing a continuity between anti-Americanism and anti-Semitism, see Dan Diner, *America in the Eyes of the Germans: An Essay on Anti-Americanism* (Princeton, NJ: Princeton UP, 1996), 20–21. This book features a preface by Sander Gilman, who underscores "Diner's image of the Jew as American and the American as the Jew" as one of the praiseworthy features of the text. The point, of course, is not that such an image may be absent from German culture, but to conclude that because some people may be both anti-American and anti-Semitic, all anti-Americans are therefore anti-Semitic is a form of sheer intellectual dishonesty akin to considering any critique of Israel an expression of anti-Semitism. Already thirty years ago Marcus Cunliffe had not only argued that the comparison between anti-Semitism and anti-Americanism was "far-fetched" but had also denounced how "to accept the parallel is

to be forced into believing that any criticism of the United States is evil and unfounded." See Cunliffe, "The Anatomy of Anti-Americanism," in *Anti-Americanism in Europe*, ed. Rob Kroes and Maarten van Rossem (Amsterdam: Free UP, 1986), 20–36.

18. As I reread these sentences I cannot help but think that the United States is, from several points of view, unlike any other nation. I hope it is clear that I am not suggesting we should stop worrying about the circumstances that make the United States an "exceptional" country. The challenge is to apprehend such exceptional status without falling into a more or less explicit endorsement of the ideology of exceptionalism.

Works Cited

60 Minutes. "The Court-Martial of Willie Brand." March 2, 2006. http://www.cbsnews.com/news/the-court-martial-of-willie-brand.

Carver, Raymond. "What We Talk about When We Talk about Love." *What We Talk about When We Talk about Love: Stories.* New York: Knopf, 1981.

Clemens, Cyril. *Mark Twain and Mussolini.* Webster Groves, MS: International Mark Twain Society, 1934.

Collins, John, and Ross Glover, eds. *Collateral Language: A User's Guide to America's New War.* New York: New York UP, 2002.

Crockatt, Richard. *America Embattled: 9/11, Anti-Americanism, and the Global Order.* London: Routledge, 2003.

Cunliffe, Marcus. "The Anatomy of Anti-Americanism." In *Anti-Americanism in Europe.* Eds. Rob Kroes and Maarten van Rossem. Amsterdam: Free UP, 1986. 20–36.

del Pero, Mario. *L'alleato scomodo: Gli USA e la DC negli anni del centrismo, 1948–1955.* Roma: Carocci, 2001.

Democracy Now. "Another Civilian Massacre? U.S. Launches Investigation after Iraqi Police Accuse U.S. Troops of Murdering 11 Men, Women, and Children Last Week." March 23, 2006. http://www.democracynow.org/2006/3/23/another_civilian_massacre_u_s_launches.

Diner, Dan. *America in the Eyes of the Germans: An Essay on Anti-Americanism.* Princeton, NJ: Princeton UP, 1996.

Domínguez, Virginia. "Unclear Enemies, Unclear Friends." Paper presented at "'Anti-Americanism and Anti-Imperialism': Critiques from Inside and Outside the U.S." Panel of the Second World Congress of the International American Studies Association, University of Ottawa, August 18–20, 2005. Revised Italian translation in *Ácoma: Rivista Internazionale di Studi Nord-Americani* 33 (Winter 2007): 53–65

Dubin, Boris. "L'antiamericanismo nella cultura europea, 1945–1991." *L'antiamericanismo in Italia e in Europa nel secondo dopoguerra.* Eds. P. Cravero and G. Quagliarello. Soveria Mannelli, CZ, 2004.

Eagleton, Terry. *Literary Theory: An Introduction.* Minneapolis: U of Minnesota P, 1983.

Fabbrini, Sergio. *L'America e i suoi critici: Vizi e virtù dell'iperpotenza Americana.* Bologna: Il Mulino, 2005.

———. "The Domestic Sources of European Anti-Americanism." *Government and Opposition* 37.1 (2002): 3–14

———. "Layers of Anti-Americanism: Americanization, American Unilateralism, and Anti-Americanism in European Perspective." *European Journal of American Culture* 23.2 (2004): 79–94.

Foner, Eric. "Rethinking American History in a Post-9/11 World." *History News Network.* September 12, 2004. http://hnn.us/articles/6961.html.

Foucault, Michel. *The Archaeology of Knowledge.* Trans. A. M. Sheridan Smith. New York: Harper & Row, 1976.

Hofstadter, Richard. *The Paranoid Style in American Politics, and Other Essays.* Cambridge, MA: Harvard UP, 1965.

Hollander, Paul. *Anti-Americanism: Critiques at Home and Abroad, 1965–1990.* New York: Oxford UP, 1992.

James, Henry. *Hawthorne* (1879). *The Shock of Recognition.* Ed. Edmund Wilson. New York: Farrar, Straus, and Cudahy, 1955.

Kaplan, Amy. "The Tenacious Grasp of American Exceptionalism." *Comparative American Studies* 2.2 (2004): 153–59.

Lentricchia, Frank. *After the New Criticism.* Chicago: U of Chicago P, 1980.

Lombardo, Agostino. *Realismo e simbolismo: Saggi di letteratura americana contemporanea.* Roma: Edizioni di Storia e Letteratura, 1957.

———. *La ricerca del vero: Saggi sulla tradizione letteraria americana.* Roma: Edizioni di Storia e Letteratura, 1961.

Mariani, Giorgio, and Alessandro Portelli. "Mythic Pro-Americanism: An Italian Odyssey." *Americas' Worlds and the World's Americas / Les mondes des Amériques et les Amériques du monde.* Eds. Amaryll Chanady, George Handley, and Patrick Imbert. Ottawa: Legas, 2006.

Migone, Giangiacomo. *Gli Stati Uniti e il fascismo: alle origini dell'egemonia americana in Italia.* Milano: Feltrinelli, 1980.

Nacci, Michela. *L'antiamericanismo in Italia negli anni Trenta.* Torino: Boringhieri, 1989.

Pavese, Cesare. *American Literature: Essays and Opinions.* Trans. Edwin Fussell. Berkeley: University of California Press, 1970.

Orwell, George. "Politics and the English Language." *Nineteen Eighty Four: Text, Sources, Criticism.* Ed. Irving Howe. New York: Harcourt, 1982.

Pivano, Fernanda. *America rossa e nera.* Firenze: Vallecchi, 1964.

———. *La balena bianca e altri miti.* Milano: Mondadori, 1961.

———. *Beat hippie yippie: Dall'underground alla controcultura.* Roma: Arcana, 1972.

Ross, Andrew. "The Domestic Front." *Anti-Americanism.* Eds. Andrew Ross and Kristin Ross. New York: New York UP, 2004.

Teodori, Massimo. *Maledetti americani: Destra, sinistra e cattolici: Storia del pregiudizio antiamericano.* Milano: Mondadori, 2002.

Vittorini, Elio, ed. *Americana: Raccolta di narratori, 1943.* Milano: Bompiani, 1968.

Zeldin, Theodore. "The Pathology of Anti-Americanism." *The Rise and Fall of Anti-Americanism: A Century of French Perception.* Eds. Denis Lacorne, Jacques Rupnik, Marie-France Toinet. Trans. Gerry Turner. London: Palgrave, 1990.

Sabine Broeck on Giorgio Mariani

I hear a tone of exasperation and agony in your article, which has my empathy; I share your fed-up-ness with the constant replays and repetitions of tired, over-used, and hypocritical discursive games between liberals and conservatives with respect to so-called anti-Americanism. Those games have been going on, as you so eloquently evoke, in all of Europe, with different foci and in modulations, but certainly for the hundreds of years America in the form of the United States has existed. And except for occasionally witty polemics by conservatives in Europe who manage to hit the mark rhetorically, if not ethically, if they brandish some particularly extreme and vain incarnation of political correctness (easy target!), or for controversies about the nature of modern societies in which Europeans have had to be taught a lesson or two by the advanced party, I don't see any in-sights to be gained for the public at large or for a more scholarly pursuit in this metaphoric game. In your article you arrive at a similar conclusion, albeit in a strangely subdued way.

Am I wrong to hear something of a shyness or a reticence to radically distance your arguments from those games? Does it not sound as if you come to an alter-native only as an afterthought, between the lines, and strangely sideways?

Why the defensiveness? Why not proudly claim anti-Americanism, not as a critique of anything and everything American as such, but as an act of defiance against Americanism, against identitarian pressure of exceptionalism and na-tionalism?

Since words are slippery, we might as well restress the sign and reclaim it, as it were, from allegedly haunting America to haunting Americanism. Why, I wonder, do we even bother to keep engaging a liberal conservative show-fight that uses Americanism as a point to either downright defend practices that are abominable anywhere—racism, sexism, imperialism—or at least to obscure and evade them, for fear of a disassociation of the power located in Americanism, in nationalism and its prerogatives?

Why not proudly turn the other cheek, proudly boast a love of the other Amer-ica, of moments, events, discourses, and practices like the Wobblies, the Doors, Janis Joplin, Malcolm X, Shulamith Firestone, Emma Goldman, Alice Walker, Toni Morrison, to name just a rather random few—you get the drift? We love them not because they are American, but because of how they redefine the intellectual landscape of Western modernity, of which lately the United States has happened to be the motor, the support system, and rear guard rescuer, all at once? But we would not claim exceptionalism for either Walker or Morrison, as there are so many others on a global scope who have contributed to de-innocenting the modern Western cultural, political, and social realm, and they know and cherish that as well.

Taking up the controversy of pro- and anti-Americanism on its own terms, even in an article as thoughtful and self-reflective as this one, runs the risk of reinscribing the transatlantic divide with a discursive ruse that is patently ridiculous for political but also academic reasons. Of course, globalization has always already pitted nation-states in fierce competition, but why would one buy into a maneuver that has served the respective nationalistic powers on both sides of the so-called folie à deux, or crazy marriage? (Interestingly, all of these metaphors are as sexually fraught as they are gendered—that alone should be reason enough to forego the debate in both of its versions of anti- and pro-Europeanism, as well as anti- and pro-Americanism.

I suggest, in contrast, to focus on queering this message, refusing the narcissistic investments on both sides in continuing to rewrite the history of a happy binary mésalliance. Subversive movements and discourses like black Atlantic and black power, among others, strategically resist being absorbed by and drawn into such hegemonic blackmailing. There is no need from within Americanism to resist anti-Americanism in the sense of antimodern, anti-Semitic, anti-multicultural, anti-America sentiment, because they feed on one another, so we should not support a game that is being staged to detract the antinationalists on all sides.

By embracing anti-Americanism as a stance that always already postulates a difference within, a nonidentity of America with Americanism, we create a polemic platform to criticize imperial politics within and without America, a stance of fugitive justice that will not be located within identification with a nation, exceptional or not, that needs to be obtained in America, in Europe, and elsewhere.

I see a correlation between subversive Americanization, the name I used provocatively, and anti-Americanism. I see black power and other un-American activities spreading anti-Americanism productively. It has been the student movements internationally spreading from the United States through France to Germany that have taught Germans an alternative to their parents' generation's sense of nationhood as the only available paradigm of belonging, no matter how desperately compromised; it has been black power that helped teach the Britons to understand the black Atlantic as a paradigm ever so much more useful and productive and human than empire; it has been the U.S. women's movement that, by way of a detour of Virginia Woolf, brought us more consciousness of gender in Europe. All in all, I can think of no other country after the 1960s that taught us so much. It was an emerging white American female middle class that taught Italians, French, Germans, Scandinavians, and other Europeans all they needed to know about patriarchy's international reign. For such anti-Americanism I have been and will be grateful.

For American Studies scholars, that is where focus and solidarity lie most promisingly. We need to look at how the specific cultural, political, and social conditions and frameworks that make and contain and expand the United States have created a certain kind of modernity, counter-modernity, and postmodernity under the name of, and within, the always permeable limits of America that carry the radical germs of overcoming national exceptionalism of any kind.

Giorgio Mariani on Sabine Broeck

Of the several important points raised in Sabine Broeck's essay, there are three that strike me as especially significant from my perspective as an Italian Americanist who very much shares her desire to resituate African American and, more generally, American Studies within an international framework. To begin with, I cannot help but notice the many similarities between, on the one hand, the German response to the civil rights movement—and to African American politics and culture—and, on the other, the Italian response. Since the end of World War II, most Italians have been ready to sympathize with the plight of the "poor American negroes" without ever feeling much of a need to reexamine their country's shameful and indeed recent colonial legacy, not to mention the Fascist regime's 1938 adoption of racial laws that not only targeted Italy's own Jewish population but also affected the lives of African subjects in the Italian colonies of Libya, Ethiopia, Eritrea, and Somalia. Just as Germans at the end of the war could sympathize with American blacks without interrogating their own tradition of anti-Semitism—as if in one stroke they could cleanse themselves of the latter by vindictively turning back the accusation of racism against the war's victors—in Italy both the socialist and communist left, as well as the hegemonic Catholic center, were ready to imaginatively take sides with the nonviolent Christian ethics of a Martin Luther King Jr. without any mention of Italy's own involvement in the scramble for Africa. If anything, Italian sympathy with the plight of African Americans overseas should be seen as consistent with a strategy of denial vis-à-vis its colonial past, based on the myth of the supposed "benevolent" Italian rule of its African territories.

In 1968 what Broeck interestingly refers to as "subversive Americanization" became operative on the Italian scene, and emphatic, radical "declarations of elective affinity" with representatives of the "other America" (*l'altra America*) were de rigueur, at least on the left. It was in these years that American Studies began to carve itself a niche in the Italian academy, mainly in the shape of chairs of American literature and American history. On the positive side, it is worth pointing out that from the very beginning Italian American Studies was quite responsive to the multicultural/multiethnic reality of the United States. African American Studies and Native American Studies are perhaps a case in point. When in 1980 I enrolled in the English PhD program at Rutgers University, I was rather surprised that not one single course in either field was being offered at the graduate level, whereas at the University of Rome I had taken courses in both African American and American Indian literature and had gone on to write an undergraduate thesis on American Indian newspapers.[1] It took not only Rutgers but many other U.S. universities quite a few more years to revise their notions of what was "representative" in American literature. Unfortunately—and this is the negative part—all the passionate work that was done on the issue of black liberation in the United States did not encourage a seriously critical self-examination of European, and especially Italian, involvement in racism and colonial pillage. In other words, it took a while for Italian—and more generally European—African American Studies to situate itself in a larger, more properly global perspective that would examine U.S. discourses on race along with their European counterparts.

Italian resistance to acknowledging the country's colonial and racist legacy has continued to this day. In fact, as my colleague Alessandro Portelli has eloquently demonstrated, "The combination of denial and supposed kindness that emerges from the stories of Italian colonialism is the template for the specific patterns of the discourse on race today." Now that sizable numbers of African immigrants reside in Italy, what Broeck refers to as "abolitionist goodwill" tends, as she also indicates, to evaporate whenever "the object of empathy does not behave within the rules of the game." I write these lines only a few weeks after the riots in the small southern town of Rosarno (Calabria), where, after two African field workers had been injured by pellet fire, hundreds of them reacted by taking to the streets and attacking some residents and their property. The locals responded by going on a literal "hunt for the negro," running over immigrants with cars and bulldozers, shooting them with pellet fire, and beating them up with the assistance of local mobsters who control the fruit-picking market. Italian civil and police authorities considered mass expulsion based on skin color the only way to bring "peace" in the area, and the African workers there were deported to other locations.

I must add, however, that anti-immigrant and, specifically, anti-African feelings do not target only poor, exploited migrant workers. The Italian soccer player Mario Balotelli, who happens to be both black *and* Italian (and who is not an immigrant either, having been adopted as a small baby by an Italian family), is regularly booed in stadiums throughout the country by people shouting at him that "there are no Italian negroes" (*non ci sono negri Italiani*). Meanwhile, the xenophobic Northern League, which holds key positions in the Berlusconi government, conducted the latest electoral campaign by printing thousands of posters portraying a Plains Indian donning his obligatory war bonnet, with the caption, "They were not able to regulate immigration. They now live in reservations"—as if it were "immigration," and not colonization and genocide, that put the American Indians in reservations! By claiming that Italians are potential victims of immigrants, the image of the "Red" Indian is used by the league to promote a hatred of mostly black and Muslim foreign workers, who would threaten "our" white and Christian civilization.

I mention these episodes neither to suggest that the whole country has gone from sentimental admiration of the likes of Martin Luther King Jr. or, more recently, Nelson Mandela to embracing virulent racism, nor to imply that Italian Americanists have miserably failed in educating their fellow citizens, as if they really had much power to do so. My point is simply to concur with Broeck's assumption that nowadays the teaching and studying of U.S. history and culture, especially of "black matters," has become a more complicated and challenging business than it was in the early days of Italian American Studies. Now that the oppressed blacks are no longer over the ocean, thousands of miles away, global "elective affinities" must always be qualified in terms of a reevaluation of one's local position. This means, however, that new opportunities for the internationalizing of both U.S. and European American Studies begin to emerge, effectively dismantling the rigid academic borders of area studies and opening up novel and exciting fields of inquiry. As a traditionally insular and culturally homogeneous country like Italy becomes more multicultural, and therefore more "like America," the critical displacement recommended by Bakhtinian aesthetics is no longer simply a useful methodological stance but a material-physical condition as well.

The second point in Broeck's essay that I believe deserves to be underscored is probably implicit in what I have said so far. The "international turn" in American Studies has been hailed—most notably, perhaps, in Shelley Fisher Fishkin's address at the 2004 American Studies Association Convention—as a liberating opening up of the field to a variety of stimulating perspectives from both inside and especially outside the United States: "Today American studies scholars increasingly recognize that understanding requires looking beyond the nation's borders, and understanding how the nation is seen from vantage points beyond its borders." As is often invoked, however, the notion of a "turn" that follows chronologically a number of other such turns like "the linguistic turn," "the historicist turn," and others gives the impression that this is a recent and largely U.S.-generated phenomenon. Broeck's narrative shows, on the contrary, the obvious though nevertheless often overlooked fact that non-U.S. Americanists have always practiced "international" American Studies in several ways. They could simply not help but do so, given that they were rooted in different social, institutional, and historical contexts and that they were always simultaneously addressing two publics: the home one, of course (their students, the readers of their books and articles, their fellow academics, the larger public some of them were able to reach by contributing to magazines and newspapers on U.S.-related issues), but also the American one, whether the latter was interested in what they had to say or not.

However—and this is my final point—Broeck's example of the German response to the civil rights movement also demonstrates that to operate within a transnational framework is not ipso facto to have gained a liberating perspective granting us access to necessarily pleasant, edifying truths. A transnational perspective—we must be very clear on this—can be the source of both blindness and insight. Unless we construct the transnational as a province in the somewhat rarefied world of pure critical theory, where scholars politely compare notes, the transnational must be grasped as also being the space where mystifications, gross ideological distortions, and egregious misunderstandings may *also* take place. Sympathy for the black or native victims of U.S. racism can go hand in hand with the denial of one's own country's racist legacy, and this is as much a transnational phenomenon as the "subversive," liberating influence that African American (or American Indian, Chicano, etc.) struggles have had in the construction of European American Studies. In sum, the transnational, as much as the global, is a category that deserves to be mobilized precisely *because of*, and certainly not in spite of, its contradictory status. As Shelley Fisher Fishkin has noted, "Conversation and collaboration across borders is only one dimension of making American studies more transnational." Another dimension is that of attending to the transnational movements of peoples, cultures, and ideas "on the ground," where, as always, both knowledge and ethics must grapple with the inescapably messy nature of human history.

Note

1. For some important observations on the formation and development of Italian American Studies in a comparative context, see Donatella Izzo, "Outside Where? Comparing Notes on Comparative American Studies and American Comparative Studies," in *American Studies: An Anthology*, ed. Janice Radway, Barry Shank, Penny Von Eschen, and Kevin Gaines (Oxford, UK: Blackwell, 2009), 588–604.

Works Cited

Fisher Fishkin, Shelley. "Crossroads of Cultures: The Transnational Turn in American Studies—Presidential Address to the American Studies Association, November 12, 2004." *American Quarterly* 57.1 (2005): 17–57.

Izzo, Donatella. "Outside Where? Comparing Notes on Comparative American Studies and American Comparative Studies." *American Studies: An Anthology*. Ed. Janice Radway, Barry Shank, Penny Von Eschen and Kevin Gaines. Oxford, UK: Blackwell, 2009.

Portelli, Allesandro. "The Problem of the Color Blind: Notes on the Discourse on Race in Italy." *CrossRoutes: The Meanings of "Race" for the 21st Century*. Ed. Paola Boi and Sabine Broeck. Munich: Forum for European Contributions in African American Studies (FORECAAST), 2003. 29–39.

Sophia Balakian on Broeck and Mariani

Sticks and Stones
Discourses of Anti-Americanism as Name-Calling

Merriam-Webster defines "name-calling" as "the use of offensive names especially to win an argument or to induce rejection or condemnation (as of a person or project) without objective consideration of the facts." It strikes me that Sabine Broeck and Giorgio Mariani have, implicitly and explicitly, framed discourses of anti-Americanism as a form of name-calling. Perhaps every social group or context has some form of name-calling. I associate the word first with children, on a playground out of earshot of adult supervisors, who are perhaps best known—at least in the United States—for "the use of offensive names . . . to induce rejection or condemnation." I also think of a long list of names in U.S. English used to condemn women and girls that speak to broader social, specifically gendered patterns and values, as well as racist and homophobic names that are used in a variety of contexts—publicly and privately—by children, adolescents, and adults.

Still, name-calling is discursively marked as something childish—not serious—despite the recent emphasis psychologists and educators have placed on the individual and collective wounds inflicted by name-calling as a part of bullying and social stigma. I think that Mariani and Broeck demonstrate that name-calling, or something close to it, takes place on a global and transnational level and within both cultural and state-centered politics as well. How might thinking about the term "anti-American" as a form of name-calling shift the way we think about discourses of Americanization and anti-Americanism? And does framing it this way spotlight certain aspects of these two essays?

The essays by Broeck and Mariani highlight the complex, shifting, and polysemic nature of the two terms taken up by this volume: "anti-Americanism" and "Americanization." Their writing demonstrates the multiple and sometimes contradictory layers—historical, political, and discursive—that intermingle as these terms travel and are deployed and critiqued. Moreover, both demonstrate, as does Virginia Domínguez in her introduction to this book, that "anti-Americanism" and "Americanization" act as mutually constitutive discourses and processes, despite the appearance of their divergent or mutually exclusive objects.

In Broeck's essay the interlocking of "anti-Americanism" and "Americaniza-tion" unfolds in liberal West Germany's "militant and outspoken rejection" of hegemonic U.S. politics and cultural symbols and the country's simultaneous "romanticizing fascination" and purported solidarity with African Americans. Not only was West German anti-Americanism during the period of the 1950s through the 1970s and '80s linked to transnational flows of icons and ideas con-nected to the U.S. civil rights movement into Europe, but Germany's narratives of African American political struggle were built upon the same racializing tropes as nineteenth-century U.S. abolitionism. German "anti-Americanism," in other words, rested upon Americanizing processes twice over—one based on German affinity for the "Other America" and another based on an unexamined adoption of U.S. racial ideologies that fetishized the black embodiment of suffering.

In a different European context, Giorgio Mariani examines discourses of anti-Americanism in contemporary Italian scholarship. Mariani is interested in how positioning oneself vis-à-vis anti-Americanism has become a prerequisite for engaging in scholarly discourse on the United States. In the two works he exam-ines, he argues that the authors use the term "anti-Americanism" in order to dif-ferentiate their own critiques of the United States from "vulgar and misinformed allegations of more or less rabid anti-Americans." Yet, Mariani argues, these works nonetheless "contribute to the very mythology they claim to consider with de-tached, objective scholarly eyes." The very power of "anti-Americanism," Mariani argues, is its amorphous quality, which enables it to delegitimize (and legitimize) a range of actors, processes, and other objects with no stable ideological basis. He critiques histories of "anti-Americanism" that imagine an ideologically con-sistent thread running through "anti-Americanists" in various places and times: "How can one apply the same label of 'anti-American,'" he asks, "to both lovers and haters of the African American presence in U.S. society and culture?"—in other words, to ideas and movements "based on totally incompatible cultural and philosophical premises"? For Mariani, this is a source of the discourse's danger, its ability—to return to *Merriam-Webster*—"to induce rejection or condemnation (as of a person or project) without objective consideration of the facts."

In different ways both Mariani and Broeck point to dangers in discourses of "anti-Americanism." For Mariani, the term is a product of American exceptionalism and, quoting Richard Hofstadter, the "paranoid style in American politics": "Giving in to the discourse of anti-Americanism (and anti anti-Americanism)," he writes, "would be the death of independent critical inquiry." While Mariani highlights the ways "anti-Americanism" augments U.S. hegemony through its capacity to dismiss critique, Broeck's essay (perhaps more implicitly) holds a different vision of its deleterious effects. The evil of the U.S. hegemon in West German liberal imagina-tion enabled German society to deflect culpability for racializing violence in its own past outward such that discourses of "anti-Americanism" aided the denial of Europe's role in the slave trade and the racializing violence of the Holocaust. For both, the all-encompassing, Manichean nature of "anti-Americanism"—either as a "name" or as a self-ascribed position—threatens open and critical dialogue about the United States and other societies.

Taking the essays together, the two authors present differing views about what should be done with "anti-Americanism" as an unwieldy, problematic, and pernicious term and standpoint. Should we appropriate the term, as Broeck suggests—claim and champion it as synonymous with (or akin to) countercultural production of the United States? Or, as Mariani suggests, should we do away with it altogether—if that were possible? To add to this debate, I would ask if we might name the subversive forces Broeck points to not as "anti-American" at all. Rather, might we envision them, as Broeck suggests later in her reply to Mariani, "under the name of and within the always permeable limits of 'America' which carry the radical germs of overcoming national exceptionalism of any kind"? In other words, perhaps, as I think Broeck begins to do, and as I suspect Mariani might be inclined, we might reposition the "other" or "subversive America" as firmly within "America's" core while not ignoring questions of power that differently position various ideas, movements, symbols, and bodies within the United States and within "America" as it travels abroad.

And what does the existence of this "name" tell us more generally? On the one hand, as Mariani notes, "anti-American" is the only name of its kind referring to opposition to not an ideology or even a religious group (as in "anti-Semitic" or "anti-Islamic"), but to a nation—at least in Italian and French. Yet on the other hand, Mariani and Broeck critique American exceptionalism. Mariani concludes by asking us to consider "America" simply as "*goy b'goyim,* just one more nation in the wilderness of this world." How do we negotiate this contrast? Ultimately, by positioning discourses of anti-Americanism as a form of "name-calling"—as I think both authors implicitly do—they shift the emphasis away from the idea that "America" is exceptionally hated and spotlight the idea that "America" is exceptionally powerful.

PART II

Histories of Engagements: Two Case Studies Looking at Domestic Consumption and Their Contexts

CHAPTER 3

Americanization and Anti-Americanism in Poland
A Case Study, 1945–2006

Kate Delaney and Andrzej Antoszek

The topic of American exceptionalism has long been debated, but a case can also be made for Polish exceptionalism. Certainly with regard to both Americanization and anti-Americanism, Poland has followed a path that differs from that of other European nations—both East and West. These differences can be observed in both the Cold War and post–Cold War eras (1945–1989 and 1989–present); in both eras Poland's experience in adapting American cultural influences as well as Polish views about the United States can be distinguished from those of most of its European counterparts. During the Cold War, Poland was more open to American cultural influence than many of its neighbors, and in the years since the end of the Polish People's Republic, Poland has shown itself to be one of the least anti-American countries in Europe—East or West.

There are many reasons for Poland's particular position, including the role of the Catholic Church in that country and the large Polish immigrant population in the United States. It is well known that the ten-million-plus Americans of Polish descent have long been regarded as an electoral prize by American politicians and that Polish American organizations influence U.S. policy toward Poland. Less attention has been paid to the effects of the long-standing and continuing emigration of Poles to the United States on Poland itself. The Poles in the United States have not only helped to transmit American culture to their relatives, friends, and contacts in Poland but have also served as an important brake on the development of anti-Americanism in Poland.

In the period between 1945 and 1989 one can distinguish two dimensions to the reception of American culture in Poland. American cultural products were valued not only for their "aesthetic" character but also for being tools with which to fight the regime. American products were perceived as symbols of anticommunism, which destined them for success in Poland, regardless of their aesthetic merits. In this way the adoption of American cultural products played a different role in Poland than in Western European countries. Another important consideration in looking at Americanization in the Cold War years is that Poles (and other Eastern Bloc citizens) did not always distinguish American cultural products from those of the United Kingdom, Canada, France, or Australia but often regarded them all as "Western." So the term "Americanization" must be used with caution.

This chapter examines how American culture entered Poland in the years after 1945 and up until the Bush era in 2006, how it was received, and how it was adapted by Polish publics. Of course, this involves looking at the resistance to American culture and a discussion of anti-Americanism in Poland. The essay is organized largely chronologically and within periods looks at various cultural media. Culture became an important weapon in the Cold War, and government-sponsored activities to promote U.S. culture in Poland feature prominently in this essay.

In the immediate post–World War II years, cultural relations between Poland and the United States were limited and remained so until after Stalin's death. One visible sign of this cultural freeze was a drastic curtailment of teaching the English language at Polish universities. After the 1947 elections, through which the communists consolidated their control in Poland, English departments that had recently been opened at the new universities in Łódźand Wrocław and reopened in Poznań and at the Jagiellonian University in Kraków were closed, leaving only two English departments open at Polish universities: one in Warsaw, which was intended to train interpreters and translators to fulfill government needs, and the other at the Catholic University in Lublin, which maintained resistance to ideological pressures. The formalization of censorship and other restrictions on publication meant that American literature in this period was largely represented by translations of the works of Howard Fast and other proletarian writers as well as reissues of works by John Steinbeck, Jack London, Theodore Dreiser, Sinclair Lewis, and Mark Twain (Foeller-Pituch 206).[1]

With many other channels of cultural communication between Poland and the United States blocked during these early postwar years, international broadcasting played an important role in disseminating American culture. In 1952 the Polish section of Radio Free Europe (RFE) was established in Munich. The Polish program, like those of its sister stations broadcasting to other East European countries, was to serve as a surrogate home service staffed with émigré broadcasters providing news and opinions about developments in Poland as well as broader cultural and information programs. Publicly RFE was not a government-funded station but a private organization under the National Committee for a Free Europe, which solicited donations from the public through the Crusade for Freedom, an organization especially incorporated for this purpose. In fact the stations were funded by Congress through the CIA until 1971. The Polish government reacted to RFE not only by jamming its broadcasts but also by conducting a publicity campaign against it.

The Voice of America (VOA) Polish service, begun in 1942, was the open, public, government foreign broadcast service. In addition to news bulletins and editorials in support of U.S. government policy and attacking communism, VOA carried various cultural features. One of the most popular VOA programs was Willis Conover's *Music USA Jazz Hour*, broadcast six nights a week starting on January 6, 1955. When Conover died in 1996, the *New York Times* noted that "at the peak of the cold war it was estimated that Conover had 30 million regular listeners in Eastern Europe and the Soviet Union" (Thomas 35). Countless Polish jazz fans have expressed their appreciation for Conover's program, which kept them connected to current developments in jazz ("America's classical music") throughout the Cold War. Indeed it is almost impossible to find a memoir by a Polish jazz artist or fan that does not begin with a tribute to the influence of Willis Conover and VOA and an account of the excitement of huddling around a shortwave radio to catch the broadcasts. When Conover first visited Poland in 1959, he was given an exuberant hero's welcome with cheering crowds, young girls bearing flowers, and a band. The VOA as well as the Radio Free Europe Polish service introduced programs of pop and rock-and-roll music in the 1960s, and Polish state radio responded by broadcasting its own rock music program on a shortwave band close to that of RFE (Ryback 867–87). Popular music thus entered Poland with little official resistance after 1956 and was readily adopted and adapted by Polish listeners.

The "thaw" in U.S.–Polish relations can be dated from October of 1956 when, after the workers' demonstrations in Poznań in June of that year, Władysław Gomułka became first secretary of the United Workers' Party and initiated a policy of increased liberalization. Cardinal Wyszyński was released, restrictions on the church were eased, censorship was relaxed in comparison to the Stalinist period, emigration policy was loosened, the jamming of foreign broadcasts ceased, and in general contacts with the West increased. Indeed, contacts grew so rapidly in the three years following Gomułka's assumption of power that Jan Błoński could even refer to the "invasion of Americans" (39).[2] The U.S. government had identified Poland as "a model for other regimes to emulate in pursuing independence from Moscow" and elaborated a program of cultural contacts, including the distribution of U.S. publications, films, and exhibits; the establishment of a United States Information Service (USIS) library; as well as exchange programs to bring Polish scholars, technical experts, and cultural leaders to the United States and send their American counterparts to Poland (Hixson 111).

Implementation of this program of increased contacts was tied directly to Poland's need for economic aid. Starting in 1957 the Polish government was allowed to purchase U.S. agricultural commodities (wheat and cotton) under Public Law 480. Payment was made in zlotys, which the U.S. government would use to finance (among other things) cultural and educational exchange programs (Kaplan 155). Under the Information Media Guarantee Program, Poland was given the right to buy in zlotys U.S. media products, including films, books, authors' rights, stage-production rights, musical recordings, newspapers and periodicals, and

TV series (Stehle 239). The spread of U.S. cultural products in Poland was thus directly related to the policy of economic aid ("peaceful engagement") instituted after 1956. The United States also signed agreements providing loans and credits to the new Polish government and in 1957 sent to Poznań a trade fair exhibit housed in a Buckminster Fuller dome. The American Pavilion displayed to the Poles not only machinery but also the latest examples of American consumer culture, including cars, a model home, and women's fashions, all of which attracted eager crowds of Polish fairgoers (Haddow 63). Jeans were the hit of the 1958 Poznań fair (147), and like elsewhere in the Eastern Bloc, they became the symbol of the West.

The "thaw" also meant that restrictions on music and popular culture were eased. Jazz, which had been suppressed during Stalin's lifetime, flourished. Jazz festivals were organized in Sopot in 1956 and 1957. In 1958 Warsaw created the Jazz Jamboree, a festival that over the years attracted to Poland many of the top names in American jazz, including Duke Ellington, Miles Davis, Dizzy Gillespie, Thelonious Monk, Charlie Mingus, Sarah Vaughan, Herbie Hancock, Ray Charles, and Keith Jarrett.

Political relations also entered a new era. In 1959 Vice President Nixon visited Warsaw from August 2 to 5, and on August 29 of that year the United States reopened its consulate in Poznań. The year also saw the beginnings of the Fulbright program in Poland. English departments were restored at the universities that had had them prior to the 1947 closures, and a new department was opened at Maria Curie-Skłodowska University in Lublin. At Warsaw University, Margaret Schlauch, an American expatriate who had become head of the university's English department, helped promote the teaching of American literature (Richmond 54–55). With the relaxation in censorship more American authors appeared in Polish translation, including William Faulkner, Ernest Hemingway, Thomas Wolfe, and Norman Mailer. Best sellers in this period included *The Snows of Kilimanjaro; For Whom the Bell Tolls; The Grapes of Wrath; East of Eden; Absalom, Absalom!* and *Light in August* (Durczak 140). Books by Hemingway, Faulkner, and Thornton Wilder took the top three places in a 1959 survey of Polish writers, who were asked to name which among the new novels they had read that year had most impressed them. In a similar survey in 1960, works by Faulkner, Wilder, and Steinbeck topped the poll.[3] Seeking to account for the enduring popularity of these writers, Błoński remarks, "Polish readers see Hemingway as a marvelous upholder of human liberty" (45). He also notes parallels between Faulkner's South and Polish society: "The Polish South died in the Warsaw insurrection of 1944. But the vanquished are not always defeated, as Faulkner's work testifies" (48).

Over the 1960s the Polish government reasserted some of the censorship controls that had been loosened after 1956. *New York Times* correspondent David Halberstam was ordered out of Poland in December 1965 for writing "slanderous articles about Poland." With the 1968 repression of universities and trials of dissidents, much of the freedom of expression that had been gained in 1956 was lost.[4] However, cultural exchange was allowed to continue. Under the President's Special International Program for Cultural Presentations, the U.S. State Department sent American performing artists, including major ballet companies and symphony orchestras as well as jazz groups and college and university bands and vocal groups, on tour to Poland. Arts exhibits accompanied by Polish-speaking guides were also sent. The touring *Family of Man* photography exhibition attracted a quarter of a million Polish visitors. Arthur Miller, Saul Bellow, and John Steinbeck were among the American writers who visited Poland in the 1960s, a decade in which Miller's plays were staged in Poland as well as those by Tennessee Williams and Edward Albee. Translations appeared of works of a new generation of American authors, including John Updike, J. D. Salinger, Truman Capote, James Baldwin, Phillip Roth, and Bernard Malamud (Durczak 140).

A new warming in U.S.–Polish relations gained impetus in 1972 as part of the broader East-West thaw known as *détente*. In May 1972 Richard Nixon returned to Poland, this time as the first U.S. president to visit that country. This visit was followed by an agreement to establish a U.S. consulate in Kraków and by the signing of a science and technology agreement. Subsequently, presidents Ford and Carter also visited Poland, and Poland's leader Edward Gierek went to the United States. In 1976 policy changed at Radio Free Europe, and new guidelines were issued in keeping with the new era of détente. This increasing warmth in political relations was matched by greater cultural contact. The major American Bicentennial Exhibition "The World of Franklin and Jefferson" was shown in Warsaw in 1975. However, the information about the American bicentennial itself was subject to censorship guidelines and could only be reported through the intermediary of the official Polish news agency PAP (Polska Agencja Prasowa), although "mentions of and references to the anniversary are also permissible in publications popularizing the role of Poles in the revolution, history and modern life in the United States and in historical articles that contrast the progressive nature of these past events with current U.S. socioeconomic problems" (Leftwich 135). In 1976, however, after three years of negotiations, an agreement was signed by Warsaw University and Indiana University to create reciprocal centers—an American Studies center in Warsaw and a Polish Studies center in Bloomington. The American Studies center in Warsaw housed a research library, hosted American students and professors, organized seminars and lectures, and published the journal *American Studies*. The center and journal were the first of their kind among the Warsaw Pact countries, benefiting not only from the relatively relaxed restrictions on Polish academic freedom but also from the support of the Polish American community who endorsed such efforts in their homeland. Seminars organized by the American Studies center as well as by English departments at Polish universities brought noted American writers, including Robert Coover, Susan Sontag, John Ashbery, Ken Kesey, and Joyce Carol Oates, to Poland.

Polish journals such as *Literatura na Świecie* (Literature throughout the World, established in 1971) and *Przekrój* (Profile) published Polish translations of American fiction, poetry, and essays. Among the writers whose works appeared in Polish translation in the 1970s were Robert Coover, Thomas Pynchon, Ken Kesey, John Barth, Sylvia Plath, Kurt Vonnegut, Donald Barthelme, and Joseph Heller. One critic attributes the runaway success of Heller's *Catch-22* to the resonance many Polish readers found between their own situation in 1975 and that of the novel's protagonist Yossarian. "As someone who rebelled against authority and tried to fight a senseless system, he was particularly attractive to Poles, many of whom were involved with their own private struggle with an absurd system they could not accept" (Heller). This book, along with Vonnegut's *Slaughterhouse Five*, opened a generation gap, with older reviewers condemning the mocking of World War II and younger reviewers and readers championing these novels (Durczak 142). Works of American literature, once translated into Polish, circulated beyond Poland's borders into other Slavic-language countries. Readers in Warsaw Pact countries with stricter censorship than Poland often first encountered many American authors in Polish translation. Joseph Brodsky said he taught himself Polish in order to read *Literatura na Świecie* (Liponski 35): "In those days [the 1960s] the bulk of Western literature, and of news about cultural events in the West, was not available in the Soviet Union. Poland was even at that point the happiest and most cheerful barrack in the Soviet camp. People there were much better informed and they were publishing all sorts of magazines and translating everything into Polish." Lithuanian poet Tomas Venclova had a similar experience: "I was one of a large number of people in the USSR who learned Polish for obtaining information on the West and Western culture. We had no access to Western books and newspapers, yet we could subscribe to Polish newspapers and magazines, which from 1956 on became appreciably more informative than Soviet publications" (Richmond, *Cultural Exchange* 201). Thus Poland served as both a translator and transmitter of American culture, making American works accessible to others in the Eastern Bloc.

American films were also more available in Poland than in neighboring countries through most of this period. From 1945 to1967, there were 336 American films imported for exhibition in Poland (Gadomska 18). Polish authorities tried to keep an ideological balance by importing equal numbers of films from the West and from the Eastern Bloc and by giving greater and more enthusiastic press coverage to films from the East, but American films ran longer and played to larger audiences than did those from the East. For example, "although only 5 per cent of the (old and new) films shown in 1960 were American, they accounted for 16 per cent of the total cinema-audience." In that year 29 U.S. and 64 Russian films were imported into Poland (Stehle 209–10). Due to the scarce funds available to Polish state distributors, the release dates of American films in Poland almost never coincided with their release dates in the West. This, however, did not prevent Polish cinemagoers from enjoying movies made even before the war.

The most popular American film in Poland before 1989 (third in the overall rankings) was Bruce Lee's martial arts film *Enter the Dragon* (*Wejście smoka*). Steven Spielberg's *Raiders of the Lost Ark* (*Poszukiwacze zaginionej arki*) ranked nineteenth on the list of most popular films in the 1951–1988 era (Gadomska 18–19). Not all major American films were allowed into Poland before 1989. Films considered anti-Soviet or biased against communist governments were prohibited. As Gierek sought more economic aid and trade ties from the West, he wanted to reassure the Russians of Poland's continuing ideological reliability. Thus, *Doctor Zhivago* was not shown in Polish cinemas before 1989,[5] nor were James Bond films, Ken Russell's *The Devils,* and Fred Zinneman's *The Men* (aka *Battle Stripe*). However, the total number of films—both foreign and Polish—that were prohibited or removed from distribution was relatively small, confirming the observations that Poland enjoyed greater cultural freedom than other countries of the Soviet Bloc. In 1970, for example, censors watched 859 feature films, 247 medium-length films, and 205 shorts, out of which only 6 were held back (Pawlicki 104). Decisions regarding the exhibition and prohibition of films involving the Vietnam War show the nuances of Polish censorship. *Apocalypse Now* (*Czas Apokalipsy*), with its portrayal of drugged, violent Americans, was publicly exhibited in Poland, but both *Rambo* (American hero killing "evil" Vietnamese) and *The Deer Hunter* (*Łowca jeleni*) ("evil" Vietnamese torturing Americans) were not, although the latter circulated in underground film clubs. *Apocalypse Now* was playing when martial law was declared in December 1981, and Chris Niedenthal's unforgettable photograph of the period shows a tank in front of Warsaw's Moskwa cinema with the words *Czas Apokalipsy* (The Time of Apocalypse) on the marquee.

American feature films and TV series were popular on Polish state television. Movie premiers of *The Great Escape* and *The Graduate* as well as the *Dynasty* TV series attracted millions of television viewers. *Roots* was shown in Poland, not for its portrayal of social changes but for its critique of slavery and inequality in the Land of the Free. Westerns like *Bonanza* and family entertainment like *Disneyland* also played on Polish state TV.

The imposition of martial law in December 1981 reversed the thaw in bilateral relations and provoked a sharp and immediate response from the Reagan administration. Economic sanctions were placed on Poland, and President Reagan proclaimed January 30 as a "day of solidarity with the Polish people." Radio Free Europe reversed its détente-era policy and was now collecting and broadcasting Polish samizdat.

In spite of the economic sanctions imposed by the United States against Poland, and notwithstanding the tight surveillance kept on the U.S. embassy and its diplomats during the martial law period, other academic and cultural exchanges were able to continue to operate. American lecturers and scholars came to Poland under the Fulbright program as well as under other exchange programs such as IREX (International Research and Exchanges Board) (founded in 1968 to conduct academic exchange programs with the Soviet Union and Eastern Europe). Polish scholars still had access to American books and periodicals at the American Studies center in Warsaw (Baldyga 571), and in Poznań foreigners who could enter the library at the American consulate checked out books on behalf of Polish students and scholars who were prevented from entering (Liponski 42). The teaching of American literature continued at the universities as did the publication of *Literatura na Świecie*. The 1980s also saw the creation of several new foundations, public and private, that operated in the international cultural field.

After the Round Table talks, the Solidarity election victory, and the installation of Tadeusz Mazowiecki as prime minister, the U.S. Congress passed legislation establishing Support for East European Democracy (SEED) in November 1989. SEED promoted the development of a free market economic system by establishing "enterprise funds" to finance private enterprise activities, by providing agricultural and technical assistance, and by providing currency stabilization loans. This act also specifically included support for the expansion of educational and cultural exchange activities in Poland. It called for the establishment of a binational Fulbright Commission in Poland and the creation of a cultural center. In March 1990 an agreement was signed by the U.S. government and the government of Poland to establish the Office of Polish–U.S. Educational Exchanges, the first independent binational Fulbright office set up in a former Warsaw Pact country.

The early years of the post–Cold War era were marked by a burst of activity in cultural exchanges funded by Congress as well as by private sources. The U.S. embassy opened a cultural center in a palace near Warsaw's Old Town in 1993. The center included a spacious library, an active English-teaching program, and exhibit space where U.S. art could be shown to the Polish public. Lectures and performances were also held there. However, the initial congressional euphoria over the downfall of the communist system could not be sustained, and budget cuts led to the closure of this center in 1996. The U.S. embassy would continue to sponsor cultural exhibits and performances in Poland but would do so in cooperation with local institutions or by renting halls. Exhibits by James Turrell, Tony Oursler, David Hammons, and Jenny Holtzer were among the visual arts projects supported by the embassy, and Steve Reich's orchestra, Trisha Brown's dance group, and the Pilobolus Dance company were among the performers receiving embassy support for performances in Poland in the 1990s. In 2006 the U.S. government cosponsored with various Polish institutions a series of events focusing on African American culture. Zachęta, the leading Polish art gallery in Warsaw, hosted "Black Alphabet—conTEXTS of Contemporary African-American Art." The exhibit was preceded by the "Bridges across Nations: African-American Culture in the 21st Century," a conference organized jointly in February 2006 by universities from Lublin and Warsaw whose goal was to ponder the nature and character of the relations between African American and European cultures.

Corporate sponsorship of culture became an increasingly common feature in Poland in the 1990s, as it had earlier in the West, for largely the same reason: government support for the arts was no longer sufficient to maintain the arts institutions and programs, especially as costs rose under free market conditions. A major exhibition of works by Andy Warhol and concerts by the Philadelphia Orchestra were among the prestigious cultural events that were largely underwritten by corporate sponsorship. Many other American performers, especially of jazz, rock, or various forms of popular music, toured Poland under purely commercial auspices. In the 1990s the roles of both the Polish and U.S. governments in the cultural field in Poland declined in relation to the growing importance of corporate sponsorship, private foundations, and commercial activities.

U.S. culture found new channels by which to enter Poland. Among the changes introduced by the postcommunist government was the establishment of teacher-training colleges, three-year post-secondary institutions designed to prepare English teachers for the new curriculum in which English would replace Russian as the principal second language to be studied by Polish schoolchildren. The American as well as the British and Canadian governments supported this effort, providing materials, training workshops, and scholarships for study abroad, and posting ESL (English as a Second Language) specialists in the new institutions. U.S. Peace Corps volunteers were also assigned to these colleges and to high schools to give instruction in English. The teaching of English carried a cultural component that added to the curriculum works by American authors, American documents such as the Declaration of Independence, and American music and films. The year 1990 saw the founding of a Polish Association for American Studies, which, among other activities, organizes annual conferences on American culture attended both by Polish and international American Studies scholars.

The lifting of censorship after 1989 unleashed an outpouring of new publications. Between 1979 and 1987 on average 20 American novels were published in Polish translation each year. In 1990 this figure zoomed to 116. It eventually peaked at 530 titles in 1994 before returning to 250 in 1997 (Lyra 32). Previously banned works of American literature became available, both in the original English and in Polish translation. American periodicals became ubiquitous on Polish newsstands, including Polish editions of *Time*, *Newsweek*, *Playboy*, *Cosmopolitan*, and *National Geographic*. Among scholars and critics, American ethnic fiction, including works by African American, Asian American, Native American, and Latina/Latino authors, received increasing attention. Toni Morrison was the leading subject for masters' theses in American literature in this decade. In 1996 the number of MA degrees granted in American literature/American Studies (two hundred) by Polish universities surpassed the number of MAs granted on British subjects by Polish universities in the same year.[6]

The importation of American films also accelerated after 1989—more than two hundred U.S. films are now distributed in Poland each year (Gadomska 18). Steven Spielberg's *Jurassic Park* (*Park Jurajski*) was the most popular film in the 1990–1995 period and was accompanied by elaborate merchandising of T-shirts, toys, and other tie-in products (22). In the 1990s, in addition to the mass influx of commercial films, we can also point to examples of more ambitious cinema being welcomed in Poland, probably best illustrated by David Lynch's movies. In 1991 an entire issue of *Film na świecie* (*Film in the World*) magazine was dedicated to Lynch. Several Polish films of the 1990s, like Władysław Pasikowski's *Psy* (*Dogs*; 1992), and Juliusz Machulski's *Kiler* (1997), can be seen as Polish adaptations of popular American film genres. *Psy*, according to reviewer Tadeusz Miczka, a movie "more American than Polish," tells the story of a retired officer for the Ministry of Public Security (Urząd Bezpieczeństwa) who goes on to work in the police force and has to solve a weapons-smuggling case, in which his former colleagues are involved.[7] Full of obscenities, shooting, and blood, the movie turned Bogusław Linda into the chief "thug" of Polish cinema. In the final scene of the movie, Franz—"much like Clint Eastwood's Dirty Harry"—promises to be *fucking* back, and indeed, like Stallone's Rambo or Schwarzenegger's Terminator, back he was in the sequel to the movie, *Psy II*.[8] *Kiler*, a production of the "Polish Hollywood" (the Hollywood with less means, glamour, and, obviously, power, hence only one 'l' in the film's title!) is a fast-moving crime comedy with major characters played by the biggest stars of Polish cinema.[9] A self-reflexive meta-narrative that is somewhat shameless about borrowing (or stealing) from various American films—from *Some Like It Hot* to *Midnight Run* to *Pulp Fiction*—*Kiler* marks the beginning of purely commercial cinema in Poland, where profit margins are far more important than "ambitious marginality."

Some movies reject popular American poetics in favor of a less represented but nevertheless important voice of previously suppressed and marginalized representations and are tributes to contemporary urban/project dwellers culture, an environment that, like Los Angeles' city of Compton or certain neighborhoods of New York's Bronx, has always existed on the fringes of social and cultural life. Sylwester Latkowski's *Blokersi* (Blockers; 2001) is the first docudrama showing the lives of young, poor project dwellers in Poland whose prospects for employment and a better future are hindered by the fact that they neither have education nor can afford it, which creates the familiar problems of violence, alcohol abuse, and crime. To hip-hop music performed by Poland's best old-school rappers, DJ Volt, Paktafonika, and Grammatik, the story is narrated by rapper Peja, once a famous Polish thug and now an exemplary provider for his family. The film offers insight into the development of hip-hop culture in Poland, shows the lifestyles and ways of local hip-hop communities and role models, and presents the situation confronting many youngsters living in the forgotten areas of the new Polish landscape. Another film, *Krew z nosa* (Nose Bleed; 2004), echoes the tensions from *Boyz N the Hood* and *Menace II Society* and presents the somewhat naïve hopes of the main character, Pablo, that he can escape the bleak apartment houses by becoming a hip-hop performer. *Oda do radości* (Ode to Joy; 2006) discusses the tensions between hip-hop identity and business/corporate culture models (vulture capitalism) and the value of independent cultural representations and channels.

The year 1989 also marks the end of Polish state television's monopoly and the beginning of various cable "televisions," where the enthusiasm of their founders sometimes exceeded their professionalism and compliance with the law; by the mid-1990s most of the private stations had been taken over by foreign companies with large capital. Polish cable television, profit-oriented from the word go, tried to meet its market targets by catering to less demanding and entertainment-seeking audiences, filling its schedules with popular American programs and movies.

The development of Poland's biggest cable television network, Polska Telewizja Kablowa, illustrates the trajectory that the more important players on the market followed. Set up in 1989 by David Chase, a businessman with Polish roots, the network managed to persuade Lech Wałęsa to become its first customer. In 1999 it was taken over for half a billion dollars by United Pan-Europe Communications (UPC), and by 2004 it had over 1.2 million customers. Its campaign to launch HBO in Poland in 1997 played explicitly on the Polish desire to have the latest American products: "*To co kocha Ameryka teraz w Polsce. HBO 1997*" ("Now you can get in Poland what America loves: HBO 1997").[10]

Another major cultural field in which America has exerted considerable influence on Poland has been music. The 2002 collection *Jazz in Poland—Anthology*, tracing the development of jazz in Poland between 1950 and 2000, demonstrates how close the links between American and Polish jazz have been and how the progress of the genre in Poland corresponded to the forming of Polish-U.S. relationships (Borkowski). The anthology presents the contributions of many artists and propagators of jazz in Poland, including Glenn Miller, Louis Armstrong, Duke Ellington, John Coltrane, and, of course, Willis Conover. There have been many exchanges between the two cultures with Polish and American artists producing music together, such as those carried out by the trumpet player Tomasz Stańko working with Miles Davis or the sax player Michał Urbaniak and Urszula Dudziak, who have worked with Lester Bowie, Bobby McFerrin, and Lauren Newton. Other American musicians popular in Poland have included Ella Fitzgerald, Count Basie, Elvis Presley, Bill Haley, Bing Crosby, Perry Como, Doris Day, Connie Francis, Rosemary Clooney, Bob Dylan, and Joan Baez. Obviously one should not forget the whole gamut of American pop and rock groups—from older groups like the Beach Boys or the Supremes to the more recent phenomena of Nirvana or Red Hot Chili Peppers—who found ardent followers and inspired imitators in Poland, including famous Polish musicians and performers like Czesław Niemen,[11] rock groups like Niebiesko-Czarni or Czerwone Guitary, or more contemporary and still active groups like Kult, Lady Pank, Budka Suflera, and others who have transformed Anglo-American popular music into Polish rock/punk culture.[12]

Like many other countries, Poland has also adopted and adapted hip-hop culture—a phenomenon with both Americanization and anti-American aspects. Perceived as anarchic and therefore appealing to the contesters of the new market economy, American rap—the father of Polish hip-hop—was rapidly "domesticated" to produce the Polish rapper. Such African American notions as "brothers," "the 'hood," and "black pride" were translated into indigenous forms. The influence of American rap music can be seen in the clothing styles various Polish groups have adopted (baggy trousers, oversized shirts, baseball caps worn backward), the themes they touch upon in their music (the loneliness of poor project dwellers or long-distance school commuters), and in the vocabulary used to express these problems. A great number of words and phrases used by American rappers in their productions, including "the yard," "homies," "yo," and "bitches," have been translated into Polish, creating some rather comic borrowings: *podwórko, kolesie, trzym się,* and *foki.*

In addition to various narratives inspired by American literature and culture—for instance, Marek Hłasko's stories reminiscent of Jack Kerouac's or Charles Bukowski's accounts; Waldemar Łysiak's road novels, including *Asfaltowy Saloon* (Asphalt Saloon); and Edward Redliński's "muck-raking" naturalistic stories of Poles working illegally in New York (*Szczuropolacy* [Ratpolacks])—Polish mainstream literature has recently produced a few books that can be attributed to and influenced by African American culture. Dorota Masłowska's novel *Wojna polsko ruska pod flagą biało czerwoną* (Snow White and Russian Red), set in the Polish *blokowisko* (projects), reminds the reader of Claude Brown's *Manchild in the Promised Land,* Paul Beatty's *Tuff,* or Nathan McCall's *Makes Me Wanna Holler.* Masłowska's characters speak a language that smashes both the syntax and the beauty of the Polish tongue but restores the air of authenticity so often lost in contemporary cultural productions. Masłowska's work makes one realize how the borders between poor black ghetto dwellers and their Polish counterparts are blurring.[13] Her second novel, *Paw królowej* (The Queen's Puke), has the form of a hip-hop narrative with lots of "samples and travesties" (Masłowska 153).[14] As in her first novel, the language here reads like the best hip-hop verbal acrobatics, with rhymes, rhythm, slang, colloquialisms, stream of consciousness, irony, and self-conscious and self-reflexive insertions, pushing the Polish language to its extremes and rediscovering its beauty and power. The novel is set in the projects of the Praga District in Warsaw, presenting, again, the cul-de-sac of the new Polish reality.

Not unrelated to the hip-hop phenomenon has been the Polish adoption of basketball. While football ("soccer" to Americans) remains the number one sport, the National Basketball Association (NBA) has become particularly popular in Poland since the 1980s, when videotapes of NBA games like the 1984/1985 playoff games between the Los Angeles Lakers and the Boston Celtics were shared by owners of the first VCR machines. With live transmissions beginning in the early 1990s, the popularity of the game rose considerably, especially since Polish and other Eastern European basketball stars have joined NBA teams. The NBA is an excellent example of how what begins as "Americanization" can bounce back and lead to "internationalization" of an American institution. Players from every continent now compete in the NBA. The 2005 all-star teams featured players from China, Canada, Lithuania, Argentina, Germany, and the Virgin Islands.

American culture in Poland is expressed not only in the visual and performing arts, in language and literature, and in sports but also in the ways of organizing political campaigns, in business and media practices, and in the creation of nongovernmental organizations (NGOs). In the decade or so after the fall of communism, American multinational companies operating in Poland have become the most desired employers for young people leaving universities. Job fairs organized by the AIESEC (*Association internationale des étudiants en sciences économiques et commerciales*; an organization of students in economics and management) at Warsaw University have drawn such companies as Arthur Andersen, Price Waterhouse, Procter and Gamble, and Mars (formerly Masterfoods) Polska (Grzeszczyk 131). A survey carried out by AIESEC in 2002 revealed the top ten "most desirable" employers on the Polish market to include PricewaterhouseCoopers (the winner), Masterfoods Polska (2), Ernst & Young (6), and Procter and Gamble (10). According to the survey, the promises that America corporate culture holds for Polish students are twofold: working in a highly professional environment and earning a lot of money. Academic programs granting MBAs and diplomas in public relations have sprung up, often under U.S. university auspices.[15] New academic programs in gender and queer studies have also grown out of links with their American counterparts. Since 1991 the Network of East-West Women has been active in supporting the growth of women's movements in Poland and other Eastern European countries. In 1998 Polish universities established an accreditation commission (University Accreditation Commission) that drew on American practice.

In 1999 Poland became a member of the North Atlantic Treaty Organization (NATO) and was on the way to joining the European Union.[16] By the year 2000 Poland had "graduated" from the SEED program, the Peace Corps was bringing its Polish program to an end, RFE had moved to Prague and was no longer broadcasting in Polish, and the VOA Polish Service was greatly reduced. The U.S. consulate in Poznań closed at the end of 1995. Official U.S. cultural activities in Poland became comparable to those in other European Union countries: modest grants in support of exhibits and performances, educational and cultural exchange visits, and support for American Studies conferences. The transmission of U.S. culture to Poland was increasingly carried out through commercial channels and resembled the transmission to other European markets. If the "Americanization" of Poland came increasingly to resemble Americanization in other parts of Europe by the beginning of the twenty-first century, in relation to "anti-Americanism" Poland remains an exceptional case.

Entire books have been written about anti-Americanism in France. The story of anti-Americanism in Poland needs only a few paragraphs. In the early twentieth century the United States benefited from the goodwill Poles felt with regard to

Woodrow Wilson's role in securing an independent Poland through the Treaty of Versailles and over Herbert Hoover's actions with the post–World War I relief efforts in Poland. Poland was an ally of the United States during the Second World War, although some resentment lingers over FDR's role at Yalta. During the Cold War the Polish Peoples Republic (PRL) government was allied with the USSR and opposed to the United States while many in the Polish population cherished the opposite views.

In the early 1950s the Polish government carried out a program of crude anti-American propaganda, displayed in banners, posters, and other art forms. The United States was typically represented by a wild, gun-toting cowboy or fat, greedy banker, wearing stars and stripes along with dollar signs. American products such as Coca-Cola were demonized (one banner proclaimed, "The enemy is tempting you with Coca-Cola"), and even an infestation of potato beetles was blamed on the United States. During the 1960s and '70s the Polish government's official policy was often in open opposition to the United States, adhering to the Moscow line during the Bay of Pigs operation, the Berlin crisis, and the Vietnam War, and criticizing race relations, poverty, and violence in the United States. Opponents of the regime, on the other hand, tended to idealize the West, on the principle that the enemy of "my enemy is my friend."

The "normalization" of U.S.-Polish relations after 1989 was followed by an initial period of uncritical acclaim and insatiable consumption of anything "made in the USA." Soon, however, voices were raised in Poland warning of the "McDonaldization" of the country and "a loss of economic independence because the share of foreign capital in Polish market was too large" as well as expressing fears of "the degradation of Polish culture due to widespread and uncritical imitating of Western patterns."[17] Similar concerns were raised by respondents in Ewa Grzeszczyk's study of success who saw the "dark side" of adopting American patterns: "They are flooding us with everything. Our whole business was learning from whom, from Americans, Cartoon Network, marketing . . ., all these schools and training programs coming to Poland. Also, films, a flood of American pop culture, music . . . America is pushing its way here" (263). One character in Edward Redliński's play *Cud na Greenpoincie* (A Miracle in Greenpoint) complains, "Poland is already America. A worse America. American prices, Polish salaries."[18] Redliński himself said, "America was flooding the whole world. This is an irreversible process: whoever does not give in to Americanization will feel like strangers in their own country."[19] After the over-idealization of everything American during the Cold War, this reaction is perhaps not unexpected. America could hardly live up to the high expectations held by many Poles.

Many of the outbursts of anti-Americanism in post–Cold War Poland can be grouped under the heading of a reaction against modernity. Such antimodern statements are exemplified by "Rynek bez Big Maca" (*Rynek* [Market Square] without Big Mac), a letter from a group of Kraków intellectuals to Polish authorities in 1994, asking them to prevent McDonald's from building its restaurant in the heart of Poland's "cultural capital," and by the Polish Roman Catholic hierarchy's criticism of "American postmodernism" (a term used to denote moral relativism, feminism, and homosexuality). Nationalist groups have been gaining force in Poland in recent years. The publications and broadcasts of the right-wing Catholic radio station Radio Maryja (founded in 1991) are marked by xenophobia that also includes an anti-American strain. Liga Polskich Rodzin (League of Polish Families [LPR]), the political party founded in 2001 by elements connected to Radio Maryja, came in second in the 2004 European parliamentary elections after running on a nationalist, anti-American/anti-EU platform. The antiglobalization forces exemplified by Andrzej Lepper's Samoobrona (Self-defense) party have also made a strong showing in recent elections. Together these populist/nationalist political forces reflect a rejection of an "America" that is seen as representing globalization, modernization, secularization, and commercialization and thus a threat to Polish culture. These parties also accuse "America" of being responsible for a growth of crime and insecurity and a decline in moral values in Poland.

Frequent complaints against the U.S. visa policies can be found in the Polish press. Newspaper editorials have urged the authorities to introduce visas for Americans as a direct response to the U.S. policy of charging Poles high fees for their visa applications, regardless of whether the visa is issued or not. Since Poland has been a loyal member of the "Coalition of the Willing," there have been many calls in the press for Poland to be added to the list of countries in the "visa waiver" program along with resentment that in this respect Poland is treated less favorably than countries that did not participate in the Iraq War. Expectations of "rewards" for participation in the second Iraq War were high, and the actual returns have been disappointing.

In spite of such complaints, however, overall relations between the two countries remain close. Indeed, in any comparative study of European anti-Americanism, Poland would rank at the bottom—that is, among the least anti-American countries in Europe, as evidenced in survey after survey. In response to a survey conducted for the German Marshall Fund in 2003, only 34 percent of Poles polled (as compared with 38 percent of Britons, 50 percent of Germans and Italians, and 70 percent of French) said they found it "undesirable" for the United States to exert strong leadership in world affairs (Crampton 8). Poland was not only a member of the "Coalition of the Willing" during the Iraq War, but its forces have assumed responsibility for a region of the occupied country.[20] In a comparative trends survey carried out by the Pew Research Center for the People and the Press, those holding positive views of the United States represented a greater proportion of the respondents in Poland than in any other European country, although this percentage declined from 86 percent in 1999–2000 to 79 percent in 2002 to 50 percent in March 2003, the decline in 2003 traceable to opposition to U.S. foreign policy, particularly concerning Iraq.[21] But that 50 percent score put the Poles well ahead of the Germans (25 percent), the French (31 percent), the Italians (34 percent), and even the British (48 percent) in their favorable views of the United States. In admiration of U.S. popular culture, Poland was outranked only by Great Britain. In a 2002 survey 76 percent of Britons and 70 percent of Poles agreed they liked American popular culture. Only 22 percent of Poles professed not to like it,[22] confirming their status as the least anti-American in both political and cultural realms.

In a study carried out by the BBC World Service in November–December 2004, Poland was one of only three out of the twenty-one countries surveyed that saw George W. Bush's reelection as positive for peace and security in the world (the other two countries were India and the Philippines). Fifty-two percent of Poles surveyed saw the United States as having a positive influence in the world. Poland was the only European country in which more than 50 percent saw the U.S. influence as positive. In Germany the figure was 27 percent, in France 38 percent, in Great Britain 44 percent, in Italy 49 percent, and in Russia 16 percent. The differences between Poland and other members of the European Union seem to be increasing. A 2006 BBC World Service poll showed that since 2004 the percentage of respondents expressing a negative view of the United States rose in France from 54 percent to 65 percent, in Great Britain from 50 percent to 57 percent, and in Italy from 40 percent to 46 percent. In Poland, on the other hand, *positive* attitudes toward the United States rose from 52 percent to 62 percent over the same period.[23] The 2005 parliamentary and presidential elections in Poland were won by the Law and Justice party. "This new government announced that its foreign policy would focus on relations with the United States" (Geremek 55), and the new president made good on his promise by visiting Washington within two months of assuming office. Adam Michnik's 2003 comments remain true. Calling anti-Americanism a "European illness," Michnik diagnosed the Polish variety as having only "the severity of a light head cold," compared to the "very dangerous illness" infecting other parts of Europe (133–34). In a symposium on the American image, former Polish foreign minister Bronislaw Geremek could confidently summarize U.S.-Polish relations in 2006 as "Among Friends" (55).

Notes

This essay is dedicated to the memory of Andrzej Antoszek, whose untimely death during the production of this book robbed Poland of one of the leading scholars of his generation. We thank co-author Kate Delaney and Andrzej Antoszek's family for their assistance in bringing this work into print.

1. Although Główny Urząd Kontroli Prasy, Publikacji i Widowisk (Main Bureau of Press, Publications, and Shows Control) was *officially* established by the decree of Krajowa Rada Narodowa (National State Council) on July 5, 1946, censorship had existed in Poland since 1944, when a special censorship unit was set up in the PKWN's (Polish Committee for National Liberation) Public Safety Department. This action violated the provisions of the March 1921 constitution, whose article 105 prohibited the introduction of censorship and licensing regulations for publishers. The censor's interventions in newspapers, books, and other printed materials were usually marked by special codes informing the reader that the

text had been censored. In the case of films, movies considered "ideologically improper" or "dangerous" were stopped from being distributed at all, or "shelved" by censorship officers for many years, something that happened to Krzysztof Kieślowski's *Przypadek* (Blind Chance; made in 1981 and officially released in 1987) and Ryszard Bugajski's *Przesłuchanie* (Interrogation; 1982–1989). Censorship in Poland was finally abolished in 1990 by the Press Law Bill. For more information on censorship, sometimes referred to as "the greatest poet of People's Republic of Poland," see Jane Leftwich, ed. *Czarna Księga Cenzury PRL* (PRP's Black Book of Censorship) (London: Aneks, 1977), or Aleksander Pawlicki's *Kompletna szarość: Cenzura w latach 1965–1972: Instytucje i ludzie* (Complete Grayness: Censorship between 1965–1972: Institutions and People) (Warsaw: Wydawnictwo TRIO, 2001). For censorship in the 1980s, see Alexander Remmer, "A Note of Post-Publication Censorship in Poland 1980–1987, *Soviet Studies* 41.3 (1989): 415–25.

2. This "invasion of Americans" was balanced by the more than fifteen hundred Poles who traveled to the United States on cultural and scientific exchange programs between January 1, 1958, and June 30, 1962. See Emilia Wilder, "America as Seen by Polish Exchange Scholars," *Public Opinion Quarterly* 28.2 (1964): 243–56.

3. Błoński, "Americans in Poland," *Kenyon Review* 23.1 (1961): 32.

4. Other interesting and surprising examples of censorship's intervention in Poland at that time offered by Pawlicki include removing any positive references to the hippie movement in the United States from newspapers, magazines, and books and presenting the movement as an excellent illustration of the collapse of moral values in the West.

5. The book was also prohibited.

6. Ronnie D. Carter, "Paradigm Shifts in Polish Academic Writing on American Literature, Arts, and Culture," paper presented at Warsaw University, June 14, 1997.

7. http://www.arts.uwaterloo.ca/FINE/juhde/micz952.htm.

8. http://www.warsawvoice.pl/old/v520/Buzzoo.html.

9. Figura is an interesting figure herself and an example of transmissions and translations merging into one. She played in Radosław Piwowarski's *Pociąg do Hollywood* (Train to Hollywood), a comedy about a girl living in a train car and working in a buffet but dreaming, at the same time, of making a career like that of Marilyn Monroe in Hollywood. The girl keeps writing letters to American director Billy Wilder hoping against hope she may get an invitation from him one day. The real Figura actually did go to Hollywood and played a minor role in Robert Altman's *Prêt-a-Porter*.

10. Gadomska, "The Theatrical Distribution of American Films in Poland After 1989," 25.

11. During the 1969 Sopot Festival, Niemen met Alan Freeman, Radio Luxembourg's famous DJ, who then played Niemen's "Przyjdź w taką noc" on the radio.

12. As far as Polish rock music is concerned, the word "transform" stands dangerously close to the word "plagiarize." In the case of many groups it is not difficult to recognize their musical "fascinations"—Lady Pank being in love with the Police, TSA with AC/DC, and RSC with Kansas.

13. One has to remember that Masłowska was only eighteen when her first novel was published; she is, in a sense, a product of the culture she writes about.

14. Dorota Masłowska, *Paw królowej* (The Queen's Peacock) (Warszawa: Lampa i Iskra Boża, 2005), 153. Translations by Andrzej Antoszek.

15. Among the oldest and most prestigious of such programs are the Executive MBA Program run by Warsaw University's International Management Center and School of Management and the University of Illinois at Urbana–Champaign and the Warsaw Executive MBA offered by SGH (Warsaw School of Economics) in Warsaw and the University of Minnesota.

16. Poland became a member of the European Union on May 1, 2004.

17. Karolina Zawieska, *Poland in Europe; SWOT Anlayses,* http://sj5.swot.wizytowka.pl, accessed in 2015.

18. Kot, "Za szynką," 83, accessed in 2015.

19. Ibid.

20. The scale of the changes in the Polish–U.S. relationship may also be illustrated by a somewhat comic situation. The Polish premiere of Michael Moore's *Fahrenheit 9/11* (originally scheduled for July 16, 2004) was postponed, giving rise to speculation that political pressure had been brought to bear because of the film's questioning of the foreign policy of Poland's ally, the United States, and by extension the policies of President Aleksander Kwaśniewski regarding Iraq. It seemed as if Poland was now using censorship to placate the United States as previously it had aimed to placate the USSR. However, when Marcin Piasecki, director of Kino Świat International, the Polish distributor of the movie, later announced that the film would open July 23, one week later than originally scheduled, his announcement provoked suspicions that the postponement and talk of political influence had been a means to increase public interest in the film—censorship in the interest of increasing profits. See http://film.onet.pl.

21. Support among the Polish public for the Iraq War continued to decline while opposition to the war grew. In April 2004 an opinion poll found only 29 percent of Poles supported the role (down 7 percent from the proceeding November), while opposition had increased to 66 percent (up 6 percent). http://www.cbos.com.pl/SPISKOM.POL/2004/K_076_04.PDF, accessed in 2015.

22. Pew Research Center for the People and the Press, "What the World Thinks in 2002," December 4, 2002, http://people-press.org/reports/display.php3?ReportID=165.

23. "Global Poll Finds Iran Viewed Negatively, Feb. 3, 2006, World Public Opinion.org, http://www.worldpublicopinion.org/pipa/articles/views_on_countriesregions_bt/168.php?nid=&id=&pnt=168&lb=brglm#US.

Works Cited

Bałdyga, Leonard J. "The 20th Anniversary of the American Studies Center at the University of Warsaw: An Historic Overview." *Pochwała Historii Powszechnej.* Ed. Zbigniew Kwiecień. Warsaw: Inst. Historyczny Uniw. Warszawskiego, 1996.

Błoński, Jan. "Americans in Poland." *Kenyon Review* 23.1 (1961): 32–51.

Borkowski, Jan. *Jazz in Poland—Anthology.* Warszawa: Polskie Radio S.A., 2002.

Carter, Ronnie D. "Paradigm Shifts in Polish Academic Writing on American Literature, Arts, and Culture." Paper presented at Warsaw University, June 14, 1997.

Crampton, Thomas. "Europeans' Doubt over U.S. Policy Rises." *International Herald Tribune,* Sept. 4, 2003: 8.

Durczak, Jerzy. "Mixed Blessings of Freedom: American Literature in Poland Under and After Communism." *American Studies* 40.2 (1999): 140.

Foeller-Pituch, Elżbieta. "Catching Up: The Polish Critical Response to American Literature." *As Others Read Us: International Perspectives on American Literature.* Ed. Huck Gutman. Amherst: U of Massachusetts P, 1991.

Gadomska, Agnieszka. "The Theatrical Distribution of American Films in Poland after 1989." *Is Poland Being Americanized?* Ed. Cynthia Dominik. Warsaw: American Studies Center Warsaw University, 1998.

Geremek, Bronislaw. "Among Friends." *American Interest* 1.4 (2006): 55.

Grzeszczyk, Ewa. *Sukces: amerykańskie wzory—polskie realia.* Warszawa: Wydawnictwo Instytutu Filozofii i Socjologii PAN [Polish Academy of Sciences], 2003.

Haddow, Robert H. *Pavilions of Plenty: Exhibiting American Culture Abroad in the 1950s* Washington, DC: Smithsonian Institution Press, 1997.

Heller, Joseph. 1961. *Catch-22.* New York: Simon and Schuster.

Hixson, Walter L. *Parting the Curtain: Propaganda, Culture, and the Cold War, 1945–1961.* New York: St. Martin's, 1997.

Husarska, Anna. "A Talk with Joseph Brodsky." *New Leader*, Dec. 14, 1987.

Kaplan, Stephen S. "United States Aid to Poland, 1957–1964: Concerns, Objectives, and Obstacles." *Western Political Quarterly* 28.1 (1975): 147–66.

Kot, Wiesław. "'Za szynką' rozmowa z Edwardem Redlińskim" (Interview with Edward Redliński), *Wprost* 10.03 (1996): 83–84.

Leftwich, Jane, ed. *Czarna Księga Cenzury PRL* [PRP's Black Book of Censorship]. London: Aneks, 1977.

Liponski, Wojciech. "Western Teachers and East European Students." *Polish-Anglo Saxon Studies* 6–7 (1997): 35.

Lyra, Franciszek. "Is Poland Being Americanized? American Literature in Poland, 1989–1997." *Is Poland Being Americanized?* Ed. Cynthia Dominik. Warsaw: American Studies Center, Warsaw University, 1998.

Masłowska, Dorota. *Paw królowej* [The Queen's Peacock]. Warszawa: Lampa i Iskra Boża, 2005. 153.

Michnik, Adam. "What Europe Means for Poland." *Journal of Democracy* 14.4 (2003): 133–34.

Pawlicki, Aleksander. *Kompletna szarość; Cenzura w latach 1965–1972: Instytucje i ludzie.* [Complete Grayness; Censorship between 1965–1972. Institutions and People]. Warsaw: Wydawnictwo TRIO, 2001.

Pew Research Center for People and the Press. "What the World Thinks in 2002." http://people-press.org/reports/display.php3?ReportID=165, 2002.

Public Opinion Research Center. http://www.cbos.com.pl/SPISKOM.POL/2004/K_076_04.PDF, 2004.

Richmond, Yale. *Cultural Exchange and the Cold War: Raising the Iron Curtain.* University Park: Pennsylvania State UP, 2003.

———. "Margaret Schlauch and American Studies in Poland." *Polish Review* 44.1 (1999): 54–55.

Ryback, Timothy W. *Rock around the Bloc: A History of Rock Music in Eastern Europe and the Soviet Union.* New York: Oxford UP, 1990.

Stehle, Hansjakob. *The Independent Satellite: Society and Politics in Poland since 1945.* London: Pall Mall Press, 1965.

Thomas, Robert McG., Jr. "Willis Conover, 75, Voice of America Disc Jockey." *New York Times*, May 19, 1966: 35.

Wilder, Emilia. "America as Seen by Polish Exchange Scholars." *Public Opinion Quarterly* 28.2 (1964): 243–56.

World Public Opinion. "Views of the United States' Influence." http://www.worldpublicopinion.org/pipa/articles/views_on_countriesregions_bt/168.php?nid=&id=&pnt=168&lb=brglm#US, 2005.

Zawieska, Karolina. *Poland in Europe; SWOT Anlayses.* http://sj5.swot.wizytowka.pl.

CHAPTER 4

Americanization and Anti-American Attitudes in South Africa and Georgia

A Historical Snapshot from 2005

Loes Nas

Let me start out with a disclaimer: being a native from the Netherlands, I can claim to be only a "hands-on expert" of South Africa and the country of Georgia, part of the former Soviet Union. I happened to have lived in both countries for a considerable period of time, fifteen years in South Africa and three and a half years off and on in Georgia. Having moved between the two countries during the past few years, I would like to make a few observations, albeit as an outsider, on processes of Americanization and anti-American attitudes in these countries.

On comparing these processes in the two countries, I was initially struck by the parallels between the two, not in the form of two parallel lines, but rather in the form of the intersecting lines of an *X*. That is, generally speaking, one could argue that South Africa is moving from being pro-American to being increasingly anti-American and that Georgia is moving from being anti-American, or perhaps it is better to say anti-Western, to being pro-American. The major point of reference between the two countries, the vertex of the *X*, is that both are emerging democracies. Nelson Mandela was released in 1990 and South Africa only became a democratic state in 1994, whereas Georgia became independent from the Soviet Union in 1991. In South Africa this transition was smooth; Georgia, however, suffered two civil wars after independence and only held its first free and fair democratic elections in January 2004. This was after the so-called Rose Revolution in November 2003, when a young U.S.-trained Georgian, who had practiced as a lawyer in New York, ousted President Eduard Shevardnadze in a very exciting two-day velvet revolution that was broadcast live on CNN. So here we have two young developing countries, both emerging democracies. I would like to offer some preliminary observations about the different and overlapping ways that they define themselves in opposition to or alignment with the United States.

I would like to begin by arguing that most of the early contacts after slavery between Southern Africa and the Americas tended to be pro-American. Robbie

Fry, for instance, traces the influence of African American music on contemporary South African music in an interesting article in *Black Praxis*. Already, as early as the 1870s, he writes, we find African American troupes, such as the Virginia Jubilee Singers, beginning to tour South Africa. Their shows included spirituals in addition to traditional minstrel songs. These black troupes were an instant success with both black and white audiences. The spirituals were of special interest to the black population because lyrics usually involved themes of longing for freedom and justice or dealt with the horrors of the black social situation. Oppressed South Africans understood these issues and ideas. To the black population these singers signified that blacks were capable of being more than servants for white colonizers.

The initial influence of the Jubilee Singers in South Africa can be seen in the many choirs that began to spring up throughout the country. Other groups, such as South African "coon troupes," started to imitate the minstrel routine. The long-lasting influence that these two genres of American music had on the popular music of South Africa can be seen most profoundly in the choral music known as *isicathamiya*, one of the musical styles used by the group Ladysmith Black Mambazo. I do not have to go into the influence of American jazz on the South African music scene, as Michael Titlestad has already brilliantly done so. Other U.S. influences were in the sphere of literature. For instance, in the third chapter of *The African Image*, titled "Roots," the writer Ezekia Mphahlele has shown the essential importance of the Harlem Renaissance for the Sophiatown Renaissance, writes Ntongela Masilela. The literary legacies of Langston Hughes, Claude McKay, Countee Cullen, and others were an inspiration for the writers of the Sophiatown Renaissance. Masilela writes:

> In his autobiography of 1984, *Afrika My Music*, Mphahlele makes clear that his first publication, a collections of short stories called *Man Must Live* (1946), could not have been conceivable without his having read Richard Wright's collection of short stories, *Uncle Tom's Children*, published in 1936. . . . It is clear that the founding of the Sophiatown Renaissance as a literary school and as a historical phenomenon, was simultaneous with Mphahlele's discovery of Langston Hughes and the Harlem Renaissance.

The other black South African literature of the 1950s that rallied for intellectual space, Masilela continues, was the District Six Renaissance writing, consisting in the main of three so-called Coloured writers: James Mathews, Richard Rive, and Alex La Guma. They were preoccupied with making a fundamental critique of apartheid in the short story form or in the poetic mode. Richard Rive's short story "The Bench," relating defiance of apartheid laws, was selected by Langston Hughes for the first prize in a competition held by *Drum* magazine in the late 1950s (Rive). As in music, African American influence served as a tool in the construction of black and Coloured South African identity. The two slides from Cloete Breytenbach, brother of the famous author Breyten Breytenbach and infamous general Jannie Breytenbach, that were taken on Richmond Street in District Six in 1960 clearly illustrate early Americanization, with the weathered billboard ("Drink Coca-Cola"), the clothing (jeans, sneakers, zoot suit), and the automobile.

African American influence on segments of the South African population was evident in some of the research projects I had my second-year American Studies students involved in during the 2000s. The more affluent part of South African society is saturated with U.S. lifestyle and symbols. In a survey of all the programs shown on South African television, my students found that about 70 percent were of U.S. origin.[1]

When we started this research project, my students had to find their own research topics. They were instructed to research examples of Americanization in their direct environment. Apart from the obvious examples, such as the chain of Spur restaurants, which use the image of a Native American as their logo; the omnipresent Chicago Bull caps and T-shirts; MTV and American programs on TV, three groups came up with other interesting topics. The first had to do with the gangs operating on the Cape Flats; the second with a squatter camp in the vicinity of Cape Town, named after Marcus Garvey; and the third with the establishment of the Metropolitan Church in Cape Town.

The U.S. flag has been adopted by gangsters living on the Cape Flats as a symbol of their independence. In a fashion similar to that of the Hell's Angels, they wear the Stars and Stripes on their back. The gangsters have organized themselves in gangs named after B-rated American movies, such as the *Hard Livings*, the *Clever Kids*, and the *Americans*. In February 2004 one of the most prominent gangsters, Rashied Staggie, intervened when community representatives wanted to paint over two giant murals of Tupac Shakur at Beatrix Court in Manenberg that had been there since 1997. They wanted more suitable murals, such as of the national soccer team, also known as Bafana Bafana. However, Staggie stopped the removal of the murals, because he "had not been consulted."

This landmark was the scene of bloody turf wars in the 1990s between the Cape gangs and had since come to symbolize the problems facing the people living in Manenberg. Staggie wanted to keep the murals, associating their removal with "more hurt than good," and even wanted to have them touched up. Tupac was a role model for gangsters, and the murals paid homage to the slain American rapper and the fight between East Coast and West Coast American gangs (Smith). The students did not get very far in their research. It was too dangerous and uncomfortable for the students from the Cape Flats, as this was exactly the world they were trying to escape through education.

Close to Philippi, one of the informal settlements near Cape Town, another group of students discovered a squatter camp that was named after Marcus Garvey. It was established ten years earlier by a Rasta lobby group headed by Brother

Ruben, who was originally from Pondoland but had lived in the townships of Cape Town for twenty years. On being interviewed he acknowledged being a Garveyite, which is why the community was named after the leader of the Back to Africa movement in the 1920s. Most of the community is self-sustaining through home manufacturing and, more recently, tourism.

The last unexpected example the students came up with was the Metropolitan Church, originating in California. Urban gay blacks mix with gays of other races at the church. In 1999 the gay Christian community in Cape Town became affiliated with the Universal Fellowship of Metropolitan Community Churches. Initially the church had priests from the United States, but more recently a local priest was ordained. They meet every Sunday in Zonnebloem, the former District Six.

What all of these examples signify to me is a leaning from marginalized black South Africans (gangsters, Rastafarians, gays) toward perceived U.S. values and ideas of freedom that have thus become instrumental in processes of construct-ing local identities. This stands in sharp contrast to what has happened on the political scene, where recently, especially since the war in Iraq, there has been a lot of criticism of the United States. Four examples illustrate this point as we move from the pro-American side of the X to the anti-American one.

Although former president Mandela liked to be photographed in the presence of U.S. celebrities such as Michael Jackson, Bill Cosby, Naomi Campbell, and Morgan Freeman, in the early 2000s he was on the warpath against the United States, making some strong statements about U.S. foreign policy. In January 2003, before the outbreak of the Iraq War, Mandela, in a *BBC World News* article, referred to the U.S. stance on Iraq as "arrogant," noting that it would lead to "a holocaust." "Why does the United States behave so arrogantly?" Mandela asked. "Their friend Israel has got weapons of mass destruction but because it's their ally, they won't ask the United Nations to get rid of them." "They just want the oil," Mandela went on. "We must expose this as much as possible." Mandela added that both George Bush and Tony Blair were undermining the United Nations (BBC, "Mandela Condemns").

"Is this because the secretary general of the United Nations [Ghanaian Kofi Annan] is now a black man? They never did that when secretary generals were white," he said. Mandela has consistently voiced strong opposition against a pos-sible war on Iraq—in line with more diplomatic statements issued by the South African government. In an earlier interview with *BBC World News*, Mandela had made it clear that the only member of the Bush team he respects is Colin Powell. He called Dick Cheney a "dinosaur" and an "arch-conservative" who does not want Bush "to belong to the modern age." Mandela recalled that Cheney had been opposed to his release from prison (BBC, "US Threatens").

Other evidence of growing anti-U.S. sentiments during this period included the South African Broadcasting Corporation making known plans to cancel its contract with CNN in favor of Al Jazeera, the Arab news service. This caused a massive public outcry and the plans were dropped. A compromise was found by having a permanent correspondent in Baghdad.

The growing anti-U.S. sentiment was obvious not only in South Africa's support of Cuba and the Palestinians but also in the harboring of dictator Jean Bertrand Aristide, who had to flee Haiti in April 2004. What exactly happened is not quite clear, but according to one South African diplomat, Aristide was forced out of Haiti in what the diplomat referred to as another U.S. coup, also alleging that Aristide had been threatened by U.S. officials and taken to Africa against his will (*Democracy Now*).

Anti-U.S. sentiments were expressed in a spontaneous anti–Iraq War demonstration held across from the public library in the middle of Johannesburg. Children carried posters attacking Bush and Blair and banners that read, "Stop the war in Iraq." They marched and chanted, "We want peace! We want peace!" Their signs had a strong message and likened them to the children who would be killed in Iraq.

Then we come to the other arm of the *X*: Georgia. Having argued that South Africa moved from being pro-American to anti-American, I would like to turn to Georgia, where we see a movement in the opposite direction—that is, from being staunchly anti-American to fiercely pro-American. I realize, of course, that this picture is very simplistic, too black and white, and must indeed be more nuanced. But broadly speaking, it is true to say that under Communist Party rule, which had Georgia in its grip since the beginning of the 1920s until perestroika hit the Southern Caucasus in the late 1980s, the official policy was anti-Western, and more specifically anti-U.S. Before and during the Cold War, the United States signified evil incarnate to the Soviet Union and had to be (officially) condemned and fought on all fronts.

In the various interviews I conducted with a number of Georgians, I quickly found out that in spite of this anti-U.S. or anti-Western policy during the major part of the twentieth century, Georgia had been looking west from very early on. Georgia has cultural traditions that go back to the fifth century BC, and in spite of the many occupations in the course of history by the Turks, Persians, Islamic fundamentalists, and communists, had always felt an alliance with the Western world. European ideas and values first came to Georgia through the Byzantine Empire; through Christianity; and later, until the end of the nineteenth century, through Russia, which for Georgia symbolized access to Western ideas at the time. It is therefore quite ironic that in the twentieth century this access route to the West was cut off because of the Russian Revolution. The Soviet Union adopted an anti-Western stance, and this also became official policy in the Southern Caucasus. During the cruel Stalinist period (incidentally, Stalin was a native of Georgia), millions of people were displaced and large-scale murders of entire population groups took place. Despite communist propaganda and the KGB trying to control the Georgian mentality, an anticommunist stance developed underground.

Listening to jazz music was done in secret in the 1950s and '60s and came to be seen as an act of resistance to the ruling party. The same held for abstract expressionist painting, in the style of Willem de Kooning and Jasper Johns, as the only officially approved style was socialist-realistic, glorifying the working masses. Strangely enough, American literature was available in Russian translation, but these translations might have been doctored. One of my interviewees, Peter Mamradze, who grew up in the 1960s and '70s, said there was even a big split among young intellectuals at the time: you were either part of the Faulkner camp or the Hemingway camp, pointing to the level of intellectual debate at the time. During this period an "ideal vision of the West" came into being under the intellectuals, whereas the population in general, through Soviet propaganda, remained anti-Western. But whatever trickled down from the West, the problems it faced seemed minor compared to those problems experienced in the Soviet Union, as the shops in the West always seemed to be full.

The first contacts between Georgia and the West, if we are to believe one of Georgia's most famous sculptors (known inter alia for his giant statue of Peter the Great aboard a ship in the middle of the Moskva River in Moscow and many monumental statues in Tbilisi), date back to the end of the fifteenth century. On doing research in Spanish archives for his ship sculpture, Zurab Tsereteli alleges to have found evidence that one of the sailors on board the ship was actually Georgian. The second point of contact, as I was told by Georgian film director Irakli Makharadze, was the U.S. Civil War, where the death of three Georgian soldiers who fought on the side of the Union was documented. The third point of contact was at the end of the nineteenth century: Buffalo Bill's Wild West show, when a number of Georgian trick riders, at the time known as Russian Cossacks, performed horse-riding tricks in this circus.

According to David Losaberidze of the Caucasus Institute for Peace, Democracy, and Development, when perestroika came, the rather naïve idea had taken hold in Georgia that the West would be waiting for it. The only remaining problem was how to deal with Russia. Things took a different turn, however, when Georgia became an independent republic in 1991. Zviad Ghamsakhurdia, a former professor of literature, became the first president of this fledgling state. Ghamsakhurdia was a staunch nationalist, wanting to turn neither east nor west, as anything coming from outside of Georgia was considered both evil and non-nationalistic. The West was bad in his eyes, as it supported the criminal clans that had taken root in Georgia. Russia was no option either. A bloody civil war ensued, leading to the secession of a number of provinces, only one of which has since returned to the fold. There are still two renegade provinces that seceded and aligned themselves with Russia. After two years, Ghamsakhurdia died under mysterious circumstances and was succeeded by Eduard Shevardnadze. In Russia's eyes he was a Western-leaning politician who was instrumental in bringing about perestroika during his years as minister of foreign affairs in the Soviet Union.

Russian president Vladimir Putin indeed referred, in an article in *Civil Georgia*, to both former president Shevardnadze and then current president Mikheil Saakashvili, who in November 2003 ousted Shevardnadze, as consistently pro-Western politicians. "For Moscow nothing has changed since the 2003 Rose Revolution in Georgia," he said, as "ex-President Shevardnadze and current President Mikheil Saakashvili are both pro-Western politicians" (*Civil Georgia*, "Putin"). His comments followed a question regarding the creation of a "pro-western ring" around Russia, referring to Georgia and Ukraine, where peaceful power transitions occurred through protest rallies.[2] Officially speaking, this process of looking or leaning toward the West only started after the breakup of the Soviet Union at the beginning of the 1990s. As a successor to Ghamsakhurdia, Shevardnadze tried to introduce democracy, which, after an initially hopeful start, failed dismally, sinking the country into a quagmire of dilapidated infrastructure, high unemployment, and endemic corruption. Georgia became a failing state, at the time number six on Transparency International's list of most corrupt countries in the world.

On November 23, 2003, after weeks of demonstrations over stolen elections, Saakashvili stormed Parliament and ousted President Shevardnadze, who resigned the next day. Six weeks later Saakashvili was elected president with a genuine landslide victory of 96 percent, ironically reminiscent of the high-percentage fraudulent victories in Soviet times. Saakashvili, a U.S.-trained lawyer (attending Columbia Law School and George Washington University), made it clear right from the start that he wanted Georgia to be integrated in the European Union and the Atlantic alliance, much to the chagrin of Russia, of course, which saw this as another example of a reduction in its sphere of influence.

In a statement issued on February 22, Saakashvili praised former U.S. president George W. Bush's address to the European leaders in Brussels in which the latter called for more assistance to Georgia and Ukraine. He noted that "making special emphasis on Georgia and Ukraine in the context of relations with the European Union and NATO creates a new foreign political reality for Georgia" (*Civil Georgia*, "Saakashvili"). In a news broadcast of Imedi TV, one of the commercial networks in Georgia, Saakashvili commented on Bush's February 24, 2005, speech in Bratislava:

> There is a lot of poverty in Georgia, but Georgia has a unique chance it never had before. President Bush, the leader of the free world, today spoke in Bratislava. It was a very important address for him and for Europe. He delivered it in Slovakia's main square. He mentioned Georgia four times in what was a very brief address. We may be used to this, and I know that some people will say, big deal, so what. They will start saying tomorrow that really does not mean anything. As president of this country, I can say that never in its history has Georgia had so much support as it has now on this cold Feb[ruary] day and generally during this period. Never in our history have big and most influential states been so

interested in Georgia being successful. Never before has our country had such a good chance to unite and get up on its feet by peaceful means. (Imedi TV)

This serves to show that at the official level Georgia's government has switched alliances, away from Russia toward the West. The Kremlin has up to now remained a principal sponsor of stalemated conflicts in Abkhazia, South Ossetia, and the Trans-Dniester Republic, all of which have become lawless regions within the sovereign states of Georgia and Moldava, respectively. Because Russia clumsily interfered with the internal politics of Ukraine and Georgia, the people and political leadership of these countries have moved sharply westward. (Chivers)

Georgia, strategically located at the underbelly of Russia, next to Turkey, just above Iraq and Iran, is located at the crossroads of East and West and thus plays an important geopolitical role in U.S. politics. It is therefore no wonder that in the past ten years or so Georgia has been the recipient of large-scale military assistance. The budget for this Sustainment and Stability Operations Program (SSOP) amounts in 2005 to $60.5 million. It comprises inter alia training of Georgian troops for coalition support, to wit, Iraq. At present some 850 Georgian soldiers serve in Iraq. This is the second large-scale U.S.-funded military assistance program for Georgia. The United States already allocated $64 million to help Georgia in training about 2,400 troops under the Georgia Train-and-Equip Program (GTEP) in 2002–2004. Apart from this military assistance there is also an extensive USAID (United States Agency for International Development) program, assisting Georgia in diverse fields such as agriculture, good governance, human rights, education, scholarships, hydroelectrics, and energy.

During this period the names of President Saakashvili and President Victor Yushchenko of the Ukraine were put forward by a number of U.S. senators, among them Hillary Clinton, as nominees for the Nobel Peace Prize for having succeeded with "bloodless revolutions." President Bush also hailed the accomplishments of both Ukraine and Georgia in a speech in Brussels:

As a free government takes hold in [Ukraine], and as the government of President Yushchenko pursues vital reforms, Ukraine should be welcomed by the Europe Atlantic family. . . . We must support new democracies, so members of our alliance must continue to reach out to Georgia, for last year, a peaceful protest overturned a stolen election and unleashed the forces of democratic change. ("Transcript of Bush Remarks")

A few days later, Bush also remarked:

Victory in this struggle will not come easily or quickly, but we have reason to hope. Iraqis have demonstrated their courage and their determination to live in freedom, and that has inspired the world. It is the same determination we saw in Kiev's Independent Square, in Tbilisi's Freedom Square. ("Transcript: Bush Addresses")

He went on to hail the Rose Revolution as an enormously important event, noting:

> In recent times, we have witnessed landmark events in the history of liberty, a Rose Revolution in Georgia, an Orange Revolution in Ukraine, and now, a Purple Revolution in Iraq. . . . We must be equally determined and also patient. The advance of freedom is the concentrated work of generations. It took almost a decade after the Velvet Revolution [in 1989 that defeated communism in then Czechoslovakia] for democracy to fully take root in this country. And the democratic revolutions that swept this region over 15 years ago are now reaching Georgia and Ukraine. In 10 days, Moldova has the opportunity to place its democratic credentials beyond doubt as its people head to the polls. And inevitably, the people of Belarus will someday proudly belong to the country of democracies. (Bush "Transcript: Bush Addresses")

So from being the villain, the United States has turned into a hero. At one level Georgia has adopted a pro-Western, pro-U.S. stance, yet there are also some anti-U.S. voices to be heard, although these are not very loud in the public domain, and often for reasons other than anti-Americanism. There was an incident, for example, where a local man by the name of Guram Sharadze tore up posters at a U.S.-sponsored exhibition of posters of Rafaelo Olbinsky. This action was not really anti-American but, rather, intended to draw attention for his personal political aims. Then there was a controversial Member of Parliament, Irina Sarisvilli-Chanturia, who thought it expedient to attack the government for sending troops to Iraq in support of the United States, whereas earlier, under Shevardnadze, she had approved it.

More disturbing are the anti-U.S., or rather anti-Western, voices coming from the Georgian Orthodox Church. Their stance is nationalistic and thus anti-Western. In the view of Rowena Cross, head of public affairs at the U.S. embassy in Tbilisi, however, "anti-Western" should be read as "anti-change." The Orthodox Church is not adapting to the changing world and fears it is losing ground to proselytizing churches, such as the Baptists, Lutherans, Catholics, the World of Faith, the Pentecostal Union, and the Jehovah's Witnesses, that have recently become active in Georgia. The Orthodox Church focuses on rituals rather than charity, for instance, and for this reason, in a country with enormous unemployment and little faith in government structures, there is fertile ground for these new churches entering Georgia. A defrocked Orthodox priest, Father Basil Mkalavshvili, even went as far as to have Jehovah's Witnesses beaten up and was convicted in court.

There are also examples of what I would call self-censorship rather than anti-Americanism. In the mid-2000s American diplomat Richard Holbrooke visited Georgia, which prompted a critical article about his visit in a church publication. The Liberty Institute, a local human rights advocacy NGO, referred to this incident as anti-American, which in itself is ironic, as the first amendment to the U.S. Constitution advocates freedom of speech. The Liberty Institute itself, partly funded by George Soros's Open Society Foundation, had also been the victim of violent attacks when their offices were ransacked and staff members were attacked for their defense of freedom of religion.

Then there is the older generation, who grew up in the "good old days" of the Soviet regime, when health care, education, water, and gas were free; everyone had a job; and life was supposedly good. For them, the new Western-leaning government symbolizes everything that is wrong in Georgia today—high unemployment and low-paying jobs.[3] This is another context for anti-Western sentiment, though these people may forget that the Soviet system had run down the infrastructure of the country, had depleted the government's coffers having used its contents to further their own personal goals, and had allowed the country to be run by local mafia clans.

Finally, I have some preliminary observations. Having moved for a few years in the 2000s between South Africa and Georgia, I find some parallels during these periods between these two emerging democracies. Both countries came out of a very centralized system of government—in the case of Georgia, communist rule, while in the case of South Africa, apartheid. Both countries are involved in nation building, although Georgia's relatively unified cultural character, which goes back centuries before Christ, contrasts with multiethnic and multicultural South Africa, which is in the process of defining its national identity. For this reason, South Africa, which is increasingly defining itself as a leading country in Africa, needs to take a clear, independent stance against the United States in order to help shape its own national identity. Georgia, with its centuries-old cultural heritage, is much more opportunistic. Georgia does not need the United States to set itself against in constructing national identity. Thus, that country uses whatever the United States, or the West, has to offer to its greatest advantage. In the twentieth century it was Russia that provided manna to the Georgians; now it is the United States. What both South Africa and Georgia have in common, though, and I suggest this actually holds for most of the other countries in the world, is that they do have to take a stance vis-à-vis the most powerful nation in the world, be it anti- or pro-American.

Notes

1. This finding did not come as a surprise, as during the time of the anti-apartheid boycott no British programs were shown on South African TV at all due to the British Actors Union ban.

2. The student demonstrations in Yugoslavia/Belgrade (2000), Georgia/Tbilisi (2003), and Ukraine/Kiev (2004) that kick-started the revolutions in these countries were U.S. (Soros) funded.

3. A university professor, for example, earns on average forty dollars per month and even lower pensions of ten dollars per month, whereas to lead a simple but decent life approximately three hundred dollars per month is needed.

Works Cited

BBC World News. "Mandela Condemns US Stance on Iraq." *BBC News World Edition.* Jan. 30, 2003.

———. "US Threatens World Peace, Says Mandela." *BBC News World Edition.* Sept. 11, 2002.

Bush, George W. "Transcript: Bush Addresses Slovak People." *Washington Post.* Feb. 24, 2005.

———. "Transcript of Bush Remarks in Belgium." *Washington Post.* Feb. 21, 2005.

Chivers, C. J. "Bush and Putin Mute Differences, Latching on to the Affirmative." *New York Times.* News Analysis. Feb. 25, 2005. http://www.nytimes.com/2005/02/25/international/europe/25russia.htm.

Civil Georgia. "Putin: No Need to 'Plant Permanent Revolutions.'" *Civil Georgia.* Feb. 23, 2005. http://www.civil.ge/eng/article.php?id=9152.

———. "Saakashvili: Bush's Statement Is a 'New Political Reality' for Georgia." Feb. 22, 2005. http://www.civil.ge/eng/article.php?id=9151.

Democracy Now. "U.S. Psy-Ops Exposed, South Africa Rejects Washington's Claim Aristide Was Denied Asylum." *Democracy Now!* March 2, 2004. http://www.democracynow.org/2004/3/2/exclusive_u_s_psy_ops_exposed.

Fry, Robbie. "The Influences of Nineteenth-Century African American Music on the Popular Music of South Africa." *Black Praxis* 1.1 (2004). http://www.ohio.edu/aas/blackpraxis/articles.html.

Imedi TV. Mikheil Saakashvili comments. Transcript from TV newscast. Feb. 24, 2005.

Masilela, Ntongela. "Black South African Literature from the 'Sophiatown Renaissance' to 'Black Mamba Rising': Transformations and Variations from the 1950s to the 1980s." Lecture presented at the Center for Black Studies at the University of California–Santa Barbara on April 30, 1990. http://pzacad.pitzer.edu/NAM/general/essays/nxumalo.htm.

Rive, Richard. "The Bench." *An African Treasury: Articles, Essays, Stories, and Poems by Black Africans.* Ed. Langston Hughes. New York: Crown, 1960.

Smith, Theresa. "Staggie Keeps Peace at Clash over Murals." *Cape Argus.* Feb. 20, 2004, 6.

Transparency International. http://www.transparency.org/research/cpi/cpi_2003.

Interviews

Burchuladze, Zaza. Author of six novels, including *Mineral Jazz* and *Simpsonebi.* Tbilisi, Feb. 12, 2005.

Cross-Najafi, Rowena. Head of Public Affairs, U.S. Embassy Tbilisi, Feb. 23, 2005.

Kachavara, Vasil. Director American Studies Program, Tbilisi State University, Feb. 24, 2005.

Losaberidze, David. Program Manager. Caucasus Institute for Peace, Democracy, and Development, Tbilisi, Feb. 16, 2005.

Makharadze, Irakli. Film Director. Tbilisi, Feb. 16, 2005

Mamradze, Peter. Chief of Cabinet, State Chancellery, Tbilisi, Feb. 17, 2005.

Tsipuria, Bela. Deputy Minister of Science and Education, Ministry of Education, Tbilisi, Feb. 23, 2005.

Loes Nas on Kate Delaney and Andrzej Antoszek

In the essay "Americanization and Anti-Americanism in Poland: A Case Study, 1945–2006," which I was asked to respond to, I found a lot of echoes, including those of personal experiences having lived off and on in Tbilisi, the capital of Georgia, between 2002 and 2005. Although they are very different countries, Poland and Georgia were nevertheless both subjected to an overlapping Soviet sphere of influence. Some of the trends in Poland can clearly be recognized as having taken place in Georgia as well; for instance, I remember distinctly when teaching postmodern American literature at the state university in Tbilisi how well read the students were in the same modernist, socialist, and proletarian American writers that were read in Poland. However, literary studies seemed to have stagnated in the 1960s, as students appeared not familiar at all with writers from the latter part of the twentieth century.

Delaney and Antoszek argue on the first page of their contribution that Poland has shown itself to be the least anti-American country in Europe—East or West. I would like to nuance this statement by making a distinction here, not only with regard to time and official or unofficial opinion but, more importantly, for both Poland and Georgia, also in terms of whether this anti- or pro-American attitude expressed itself "above" or "under" ground.[1] In Poland, we learn from the article, there were increasing government-sponsored activities to promote U.S. culture, whereas in Georgia, which, unlike Poland, was actually part of the Soviet Union, U.S. culture was primarily enjoyed and promoted subversively underground. I am referring to films, music, and literature especially.

The thaw in U.S.-Polish relations that started toward the end of the 1950s, which led to increased liberalization in Poland and a détente in the 1970s, had no counterpart in U.S.-Georgian relations, as the Soviet Union still had a firm grip on the countries within its sphere of influence, which did not allow for any official ease of restriction. The warming up in official U.S.-Polish political relations could, of course, take place exactly because Poland was not part of the Soviet Union and could therefore more easily be eased away from the Soviet sphere of influence by U.S. interventions.

Curiously enough, I remember when meeting with older members of the Georgian political elite that some of them had been allowed to study in the United

States in the 1970s and '80s, and one of them had even returned as an accomplished amateur jazz pianist. So, unlike Poland, where greater cultural freedom was experienced by the entire population, in Georgia this was reserved aboveground for the *nomenklatura* and underground for others. Only after Georgia had dislodged itself from Soviet grip at the beginning of the 1990s did it more and more openly flirt with things Western. U.S. influence on Georgian politics became increasingly tangible after former Fulbright scholar Mikheil Saakashvili had wrestled power away from old Soviet-style politicians and a special Georgia desk was created in the U.S. Department of State. American advisors were known (and seen in the capital) to have a major influence on internal and external policies of the state just after the so-called Rose Revolution in 2003. One should also not forget the role George Soros's Open Society Foundation, promoting ideals of democracy, played in this.

Like in Poland, a changeover from Russian as a second language to English as a second language took place in the educational system in Georgia the first few years of the twenty-first century, and when the Eastern Bloc was sufficiently "warmed," and new enemies farther east in Afghanistan had started to appear on the horizon, the United States, while reducing activities in Poland, increased activities in Georgia, if only for geopolitical reasons. Geostrategically Georgia was ideally located; not only did U.S. military train the Georgian army, but their airfields were used as stopovers for military planes en route to Afghanistan, and the United States found fertile ground in the country where the underground and later the new regime had fostered warm feelings for the United States. Major aid programs were rolled out—to which if only the sheer size of the staff complement of the U.S. embassy and the United States Agency for International Development, approximately five hundred (whereas, by comparison, embassies from EU countries would have an average of fifteen or so staff members), is testimony.

After having left Georgia in 2005, I returned to Africa and lived in different countries in Southern Africa, primarily Rwanda, South Africa, and Zambia, where U.S. influence and economic imperialism seem to be waning (although since that time Walmart took over a large [South] African store chain in order to get a foothold on the continent), and Chinese influence appears to be on the rise. But that is a completely different story altogether and a topic for another conversation.

Note

1. The Netherlands, my country of origin, was, for instance, pro-American after the Second World War, but due to inter alia U.S. foreign policy, public opinion started to shift in the 1960s and '70s toward anti-Americanism.

Sophia Balakian on Loes Nas

In her essay "Americanization and Anti-American Attitudes in South Africa and Georgia," Loes Nas charts two newly democratic countries' opposing trajectories in their sentiments and policies regarding "the West" and the United States more specifically. Nas envisions these trajectories as two lines forming an "*X*" of pro- and anti-U.S. attitudes as these countries moved from apartheid and Soviet communism, respectively, to democracy. I suggest that there are also other types of parallel and crosscutting vectors operating simultaneously to the temporal axes that Nas follows, which are more implicit in her analysis and which I consider below.

Nas argues that South Africa's black intellectual movements, artistic production, and cultural life in pre-, anti-, and post-apartheid eras found inspiration and solidarity with African American music, literature, and other art forms. From Coca-Cola to blue jeans, South Africa has been "Americanizing" in more mainstream, capitalistic ways as well, at least since the 1950s, Nas points out. However, more recent years have seen a strong critique of U.S. foreign policy by leaders such as Nelson Mandela, as well as South African civil society groups, in their responses to the Iraq War, in particular, and to the United States under President George W. Bush and Vice President Dick Cheney, more generally, in the period under discussion.

Writing on Georgia, Nas charts the anti-Western, anti-U.S. policies of the Soviet era, despite small pockets of cultural and intellectual life that celebrated U.S. music, art, and literature. In the post-Soviet era, by contrast, including and especially under George W. Bush, Georgia's democratic changes and pro-Western administrations have been lauded by the U.S. government, which has positioned Georgia as an important ally in a geopolitically important zone for the United States, including as a troop-sending ally in the Iraq War.

While Nas primarily classifies these changing sentiments chronologically—charting changing attitudes through time—she points to many *different* pro- and anti-American actors, symbols of "America," and types of products of Americanization or anti-Americanism that might also be categorized in alternative ways. Reading her essay, I am struck by other possible categories that we might locate in a broad and eclectic field of "pro-" and "anti-" attitudes and practices that she points to. What kinds of conclusions might we be led to if we further distinguish these trends, types of actors, and institutions from one another?

First, for example, we might think about the kinds of actors that Nas uses as examples and evidence of pro- and anti-American attitudes but who in themselves represent a diverse cast of characters whose pro- or anti-Americanism might seem more complicated than this binary at first suggests if we start to think about how their identities and attitudes may overlap and differ. In her commentary on South Africa, Nas addresses individuals such as the South African musician Robbie Fry; the writers Ezekiel Mphahlele, James Mathews, Richard Rive, and Alex La Guma; the gangster Rashied Staggie; and photographer Cloete Breytenbach. She also addresses U.S.-influenced musical groups—choirs and "coon troupes"; and social and spiritual groups such as gangs and gangsters, the Rasta lobby, black and white gay South Africans, and members of the Metropolitan Church in Cape Town. These figures and collectivities could be broken down further in many ways, but one unifying factor is that they are (historical and contemporary) countercultural figures in South Africa—primarily black and Coloured—who have found inspiration in and solidarity with African American artists and intellectuals from Marcus Garvey to Tupac Shakur. Nas writes that the examples of pro-Americanism in South Africa's past and present indicate "a leaning from marginalized black South Africans (gangsters, Rastafarians, gays) toward perceived American values and ideas of freedom that have thus become instrumental in processes of constructing local identities."

Some of the pro-American or Americanizing processes Nas points to involve mainstream influences such as Coca-Cola and MTV and mainstream visual symbols such as the American flag and the logo of the Chicago Bulls. But more centrally, Nas describes ways in which colonized and marginalized black and Coloured South Africans have drawn upon Pan-African identities and solidarities with African American struggles. As Nas writes, "[African American] spirituals were of special interest to the black population because lyrics usually involved a longing for freedom and justice or dealt with the horror of the black social situation." What is the "America" that Nas is referencing when she draws upon these examples? And is "America" a sufficient label?

Turning to the "anti-American" part of Nas's analysis of South Africa, in what ways does "anti-Americanism" diverge but also overlap with the pro-Americanism of the actors addressed above? Again, Nas addresses several different actors— namely, Mandela and popular groups protesting the war in Iraq. Nas points out their critiques and protests against U.S. foreign policy—specifically U.S. policy in Iraq, Israel/Palestine, and Cuba. If we regard Nas's data from another angle, we might actually see these "anti-American" attitudes and practices—or, more specifically, critiques of U.S. foreign policy—as much as or perhaps even more ideologically connected to the "*pro*-American" or Americanizing artists, gang members, and spiritual leaders.

To clarify this picture, it may be helpful if we address the particular things, actors, and institutions that are "pro-" or "anti-." As noted above, the first group draws inspiration from African American cultural and political movements. The "anti-American" actors in Nas's analysis are not critical, to our knowledge, of the forms of U.S. cultural expression from which these South African groups have drawn inspiration, but of something entirely different that also stands to index—for Nas and many others—"America." These forms of what Nas calls "anti-Americanism" are directed toward the state, specifically its arrogant and violent approaches to other parts of the world. Put this way, we could easily imagine that "Americanization" and "pro-American" sentiments directed toward black American culture and the "anti-American" sentiments directed toward U.S. foreign policy could coexist more or less harmoniously and certainly be held without contradiction for a single individual or group, despite the fact that both African American cultural production and the U.S.-Iraq War widely index "America."

Picking out other patterns that are "latent" in Nas's data can help us to understand issues that are not totally apparent when we engage a "pro-" and "anti-" binary. By looking at different points of intersection, we see, for example, transnational patterns of racial relations (recall Mandela's quote about the U.S. engagement with the United Nations during Kofi Annan's leadership). We also bring into view how ideologically varied are the people, things, ideas, and institutions that are indexed when many people around the world think about "America," as several of this volume's contributors have pointed out.

In her writing on the country of Georgia, Nas focuses more centrally on Georgia's relationship to the U.S. government. She writes about official anti-American policy during the communist period. In the post-socialist era, by contrast, she charts the emergence of democratic reforms and pro-Western leaders, along with Georgia's official role in sending troops to a war that Mandela and many South Africans vehemently opposed. Moreover, she highlights the reciprocal affirmation and approval of Georgia by the United States. Despite the more state-centered focus in this section of the essay, Nas still evokes a range of Georgian actors with diverse interests and concerns vis-à-vis the United States.

On the "pro-American" side, she writes about politically subversive intellectuals of the communist period, the two "pro-American," post–Soviet Georgian presidents—Shevardnadze and Saakashvili. "Anti-American" actors Nas includes are Soviet-era political officials, as well as the contemporary Orthodox Georgian Church, whose anti-West ideological stance is related to its anxieties about losing power to proselytizing churches such as Baptists, Pentecostals, and Jehovah's Witnesses. We again see that "anti-Americanism" and "pro-Americanism" in Soviet and post-Soviet periods encompass a range of sentiments that are directed at a variety of actors, institutions, and events that index "America." Official anti-American and anti-Western policy, coupled with admiration for American cultural life among certain circles during the Soviet period, and pro-U.S. policies, coupled with discourses decrying "Western" and U.S. churches or attacks on U.S. NGO offices during the post-Soviet era, all reflect the multiple meanings of "America" in the context of various competing and converging forces that emanate from the United States.

If South African apartheid-era solidarity with African American artists lacks ideological inconsistency with post-apartheid critique of the military actions of the U.S. state, likewise Soviet-era admiration of U.S. artists and writers among Georgian intellectuals does not meld ideologically with democratic-era Georgian solidarity with Bush's United States. This demonstrates the complexities of the histories that Nas charts, showing "pro-Americanism" as well as "anti-Americanism" to be labels without ideological grounding, as Giorgio Mariani compellingly points out in his essay in this volume.

Nas's comparison offers much food for thought, particularly if we bring into relief the multitude of "Americas"—and how they differ and converge—that she locates in these two national and cultural histories. We find that the "pro-Americans"—or those who find interest, solidarity, and allegiance with various forces that have emerged from the U.S. state and society—may have very little in common ideologically in different historical moments, while actors glossed as "pro-American" in one era may have more in common with "anti-Americans" in another. One possible way of analytically framing the problem of many "Americas" would be to think about the rebels, Rastas, gangsters, artists, and intellectuals in both South Africa and Georgia in terms of what Sabine Broeck calls, in this volume, the "other America." Broeck provocatively asks us if the "other America" might not also be somehow "anti-American." While I hesitate at this suggestion, hoping that instead we could name subversive, counter-hegemonic ideas and movements that poke holes in American exceptionalism as truly *American* (as Broeck also suggests), her question illuminates patterns that rise to the surface in Nas's essay. If Nas presents a binary that packages together dissimilar things in a way that glosses over significant distinctions, by setting such things side by side she provides a space to think through a complicated and always changing kaleidoscope in which the image, or the "dream," of America, as Michael Titlestad writes in this volume, is many things at once and never holds still.

Jane C. Desmond on Nas and Delaney & Antoszek

Reversing the Vectors of Analysis

Calibrating the "Use Value" of Discourses of "Americanism," "Americanization," and "Anti-Americanism"

By this point in the book, it is clear that our objects of investigation are discursive constructs and the conditions of their emergence, sustenance, and overturning, or opposition in particular geopolitical contexts and historical periods. The inadequacy of the terms "Americanization" and "anti-Americanism" has been established, and the capaciousness of their referents has been pointed out.

This capaciousness is not a matter of sloppy intellectual work. To the contrary, it is a constituent part of the mobility of such discourses, and their malleability contributes to their domestic "use value" in multiple times and places. In the end, these processes of naming, and the adoptions and adaptations of discourses, are a political act as well as a conceptual one, drawing on extant discourses that garner political purchase, and can thereby influence material circumstances. In other words, while we analyze discursive acts here, we must always remember that these acts are no less active than physical or material ones and have physical and material consequences on the ground—that is, in terms of individuals' and communities' daily lives, and in terms of access to power and goods that can be necessary for survival or even transformative. Governments and groups know this, and in both Poland and South Africa we see the active manipulation of discourse and actions to yield political effect.

Delaney and Antoszek carefully chart a history of actions that render the relationship between Poland and aspects of the United States over time since World War II up to the mid-2000s. They make clear that "American cultural products" were valued as tools with which to fight the regime as symbols of anticommunism and thus played a different role in Poland than in Western European countries. They note also that at times the primary referent in these politics was "Western" and that U.S. products and ideas were conflated with those from Canada, the United Kingdom, France, or Australia. Thus, they rightfully assert that "Americanization" must be used cautiously as a term of analysis.

This flexibility of referent is part of what this book reveals and documents in great detail, both in historically specific case studies like the two under consideration here and in more broadly sketched theoretical configurations. Not only was "Americanization" sometimes conflated with "modernization" or "Westernization" in certain times and places, but the referent itself—"American"—was flexible. Connotation, and not simply denotation, is a core part of the naming process and must guide our analyses as well. In many cases, a process of affiliation with goods, ideas, or practices associated (accurately or not) with "America" was as much a process of articulating a *disidentification* from something else as it was asserting a friendly feeling for things from the United States.

We must ask in each specific historical and geopolitical case not only if "America" is the actual referent (and not an otherwise generalized "modernity" or "West") but also "whose 'America'" is being invoked and mobilized to do local political work outside of the U.S. context. Just as important is the question: Who is doing that invocation, and with what effects? Is the referent the "America" associated with individual freedoms, with capitalism, or with ethnic and racialized groups and their cultural products? As Nas notes, among the poor black South Africans who name their "gangs" or subcultural communities after U.S. places or hip-hop referents, that "America" is a working-class or poor African America, not a white upper-class America, or a Hispanic middle class, or an Arab American community in Michigan, or Asian Americans on the West Coast, or any other of multiple possibilities.

It becomes clear that while discussions of processes dubbed "Americanization" and "anti-Americanism" seem to be pointed toward the referent of "America," the purpose and effect of such namings are actually directed toward domestic and regional audiences and for local or regional political gain *outside* of the United States. To better understand these processes we *must reverse the vector* of our analysis and trace influence and effects of such namings on the local situations. In the case of the two essays under consideration here, that would guide us to analyze the "use value" of these denotations in the Polish national context, the context of the Cold War in Europe, the context of black and white relations in post-apartheid South Africa, and the emergence of a new government in the country of Georgia as it emerges from the Soviet Bloc.

Delaney and Antoszek's essay is full of invaluable and persuasively specific documentation of how U.S. products and ideas circulated at particular times in Poland during the half century after World War II and how these circulations and their promotion by the United States, or their desirability as seen by the Poles, was directly linked to the broader contours of the Cold War. In a complementary move, in her considerations of South Africa and Georgia, Nas reminds us that our analyses must not homogenize entire "receiving" nations either. In fact, "aboveground" and "underground" assertions of affiliation with ideas, products, or practices denoted as "American" can coexist with different meanings in the same national settings. Or we can analyze these assertions of affiliation or rejection ("anti-Americanism") in broader regional contexts, such as in the aftermath of the 1990s as the Soviet Bloc disintegrated and both Poland and Georgia stressed their affiliation with the United States, often through consumption of its cultural products.

During that time we see the U.S. State Department respond to shifting geopolitics by withdrawing longtime support from American Studies programs and conferences in Western Europe (initiated in the aftermath of World War II), much to the chagrin of a generation of scholars in places like the Netherlands and Germany who had come to rely on such support to build networks of scholars specializing in U.S. literature and other subjects. That monetary support moved, as Nas notes, to places like Georgia and, farther to the east, to nations like Kazakhstan, to begin to build academic community expertise on the United States, funding conferences, study trips to the United States, and so on. This "soft power" diplomacy worked in the academic sphere to foster new knowledge while in the cultural sphere American products like music were featured on arts tours. But whatever is "exported" from the United States is not necessarily what is "received," nor does it determine those uses to which such products or ideas are put in their new national contexts, where affiliation or rejection of affiliation can function in complex ways to gain political currency in the local dynamics of political change.

In these and other essays and commentaries in this book, what becomes increasingly clear is that not only are the terms "Americanization" and "anti-Americanism" discursively constituted and reconstituted, often mutually constitutively, but that they themselves become discursive actors when they are labels applied to actions by groups, states, or individuals. But, even more than that, we must understand that the supposed referent of these terms—the "America" in "Americanization" and "anti-Americanism"—is as much in motion as the other terms. "Whose America?" is a key question when we try to track the implicit referent in these discussions.

For young black South Africans in some of the poorest neighborhoods, "America" is the life on the streets of poor black inner-city neighborhoods depicted in Compton hip-hop, for example. For some in Georgia, it is the vision of a free press and democratic elections or the rise of capitalism in the face of a fading socialist state. At times, merely listening to music like American jazz or wearing Levis was enough to signal a rejection of state policies by a group of "underground" intellectuals or cultural workers. At other times, jazz fests sponsored by the U.S. State Department became part of the promotion of state diplomacy at its most visible.

In each case study in this book, and clearly in the two essays and paired commentaries here, what emerges is the fact that there is no one "America" that is the referent in these discourses, just as there is no simple meaning attached to the naming of discourses as "pro-" or "anti-." Rather, both the discourses and their act of naming are political acts that have specific geo-historical traction and legibility. They do political work in the broadest sense, in terms of framing the terms of debate, delineating the terms of understanding, and naming that which always exceeds our ability to name and tame it—a terrifically diverse set of relations that is called "the United States," and those stances and attitudes toward that imaginary that are termed "Americanization" and "anti-Americanism." Above all, each of these acts of naming or of cultural production in the realms of fashion, music, art, literature, and political structures have a use value that is homegrown and is ultimately domestic, outside of the United States. The reading of works by African American author Toni Morrison in Polish translation has a specific meaning in terms of Poland's relations with the former Soviet Union. The naming of a Cape Flats gang after U.S. hip-hop songs has a specific charge in a Cape Town, South Africa, racial calculus based on the legacies of and challenges to apartheid. From the scale of the individual, to the level of the group, whether aboveground or underground, to the level of the state and region, defining a stance toward a geopolitical entity and imaginary dubbed "the United States" is an act of positioning that can at times do important cultural work at home, wherever home may be.

The current economic, military, and political power of the United States in so many parts of the world means that local and regional actors, as individuals or states, can use public articulations of their relation to the United States (as political entity, actor, and cultural imaginary) to do the political work *at home* that they desire. This applies to actors or subcultures within the United States too. Hence, while the discursive construction of such terms as "Americanization" and "anti-Americanism" seems to point to the United States and its cultural imaginary, in fact, we must remember to reverse the vector analysis to concentrate on the local and regional effects of a declaration of affiliation or of rejection (disidentification as a political act) with an aspect associated with the United States, and to always question as well "Whose 'America'?" is being invoked in the process. When we keep these challenges in mind, we can begin to approach the complexity of these articulations of relations that are so well charted in each set of essays in this book.

PART III

Debating the Terms of Debate

CHAPTER 5

Kefaya and the New Politics of Anti-Americanism

Manar Shorbagy

"What we're seeing here . . . is the birth pangs of a new Middle East," Condoleezza Rice callously said in describing the full-scale attack on Lebanon two days before setting foot in the Middle East. The disproportionate Israeli attack on Lebanon in July 2006, in response to the Hezbollah kidnapping of two Israeli soldiers, killed hundreds of civilians, misplaced hundreds of thousands of others, and destroyed the civilian infrastructure of that defenseless Arab country. Unabashedly, this Israeli onslaught was perceived in Washington as helpful to the reigning illusions of remaking the Middle East.

Arriving in Beirut, the then chief diplomat of the United States made clear that an immediate cease-fire demanded by the Lebanese government—described by the Bush administration as friendly to the United States—was simply not an option. Lebanon must endure the bombardment for yet more weeks until the "new" Middle East is born.[1] "The goal of my trip," Rice explained in 2006, "is to work with our partners to help create conditions that can lead to a lasting and sustainable end to violence," no matter the price, apparently, for Lebanon itself.

Refusing to pressure Israel in any way and with no relations at the time with Iran, Syria, or Hezbollah, the regional "partners" the United States was counting on were the very same tyrannical Arab regimes the Bush administration had earlier criticized as breeding terrorism. "I would just ask you to look back on what is being said by some of these Arab states," Rice noted. "Everybody wants the violence to stop. There is no difference there. But this is different than times in the past, where there has been a reflexive response from the Arab states."

Rice was referring to the official statements made at the time by the governments of Egypt, Saudi Arabia, and Jordan, which put the blame for the war against Lebanon on Hezbollah. The Bush rhetoric on democracy in the Middle East notwithstanding, what the U.S. chief diplomat failed to mention was that the statements of those Arab leaders were extremely unpopular in their own countries and possible only because of the repression of democratic oppositions.

Even before George Bush came to power in 2001, the neoconservatives in Washington had promoted a vision for remaking the Middle East. Regime change in Iraq, as part of an agenda that long predated 9/11, would be "the fulcrum for transforming the broader Middle East" (Phillips 57). According to the plan, an easy regime change in Iraq would help install a secular Iraqi government friendly to the United States. The presence of a threatening U.S. military power in Iraq, at the doorstep of both Iran and Syria, would trigger a domino effect throughout the region (57–58). The goal was a Middle East devoid of any resistance to the United States and Israel, where a "weakened Syria turns away from Iran and enters into an agreement that stabilizes Israel's northern border; where Saddam Hussein's regime has been replaced and where the main strategic force in the region is a Turkish-Israeli alliance" (Abrams 235).

Obviously, the U.S. quagmire in Iraq and its unintended consequences across the region have shackled the U.S. capacity to go ahead with the rest of the plan. However, the ideologues in Washington have refused to abandon their grand schemes and have chosen instead to simply change the means to implement it. As adapted by the Israelis, the military "shock and awe" so brutally displayed against the Lebanese civilians replaced the domino in reshaping a new defanged Middle East.

For all the loss of life and damage to the standing of the United States world-wide, the U.S. policy's colossal failure in the Middle East demonstrates the perils of ignoring the complex realities of that area of the world. In case after case, the U.S. policy in the region produces the very resistance to its policies that it seeks to undermine. By manipulating the autocracies to pass its own Middle East grand strategies, the United States strengthens the disconnect between the Arab people and their own governments that are allied with the United States, thus pushing political action out of the already distorted institutional framework in those countries.

What is striking is that the more violent the shock and awe campaign is, the more resourceful and resilient the Arab societies become in their resistance to such assaults. Not all responses are violent in character, although the armed re-sistances in Palestine, Lebanon, and Iraq have frequently captured the headlines. However, on closer examination it is clear that the U.S. shock and awe in Iraq triggered a new form of resistance in Egypt that has reverberated across the Arab world and beyond. Anti-Americanism played a huge role in fusing the forces that became "Kefaya."

The Kefaya movement has become the first trans-ideological movement in Egypt's modern history and a model for pacific resistance elsewhere in the Arab Islamic world. The movement developed out of an *iftar* of twenty-three people who bitterly asked themselves "Where is Egypt going?" (Abrams 235). "Zionism has ferociously raped the land of Palestine and the American imperialism has occupied Iraq and humiliated its people," commented Ahmed Bahaa El-Din

Shaaban, usefully summarizing the mood. "Threats of aggression were swirling around Syria, Sudan, Egypt and Saudi Arabia as well as other Arab countries. At a time when oppressive political elites control the nation's wealth and fate, in such a way that has turned the whole Arab nation into a large prison degrading the citizens' dignity and thus marginalizing the Arab masses in all power balances in the region, those very same elites bow at the feet of the U.S. and Zionism" (Shaaban, "Kefaya" 73).

By the end of that night, six of the attendants,[2] representing all political trends, were appointed to work on a draft statement that would become the basis for their future political action (73). It took this "group of six" eight full months to develop a consensus statement that brought together the views and approaches of such a diverse group. The statement was later open for signatures by public figures, who quickly reached three hundred signers, leading up to the announcement in September 2004 of the foundation of the Egyptian Movement for Change (EMC)—*Kefaya*. Kefaya's founders came from many different political positions, from the far left to the far right. The movement's importance to Egyptian political life was recognized almost immediately.

This essay argues that Kefaya's significance lies in its transformative potential as a broad political force of a new type that is uniquely suited to the needs of the moment in Egypt. It is at once a cross-ideological force that has the potential, in the long run, of creating a new mainstream and, also, a movement of a new kind that is creating a distinctive and promising form of politics for Egypt. At the same time, it represents an alternative model of resistance to American empire, at once pacific yet adamantly anti-American.

With the seething political discontent on the one hand and the ideologically based mistrust among oppositional political forces on the other, Egypt needs today, more than ever, a new form of politics that pulls together diverse forces from across the political spectrum to forge a new national project. Amid this political disarray, a new generation of Egyptians holds the promise for transforming politics in Egypt. They have found a home and an instrument in Kefaya and, in the process, have invented a new form of politics. Their innovations are historically grounded in the specifics of Egypt's political life in recent decades. Unique Egyptian circumstances have shaped their experiences, aspirations, and vision for the future.

Throughout more than a decade, this group of activists and intellectuals has interacted across ideological lines to reach common ground. Kefaya emerged as one manifestation of these efforts and an important illustration of the possibilities of this new politics. The U.S. invasion of Iraq was a galvanizing event that helped accelerate the fruition of those efforts. While such collaborative work across ideological lines is not unique in democratic experiences around the world, Kefaya represents the first successful effort of that new kind of politics in modern Egyptian history.

Based on primary sources including open-ended interviews, statements, newspaper articles and reports, as well as unpublished documents, this essay illustrates why and how Kefaya represents a new force with the potential of creating a new mainstream politics and explains why a democratic movement like Kefaya strongly opposed the Bush administration's democracy posturing and thus represents a new, alternative form of resistance to American empire.

Overcoming the Ideological Barrier

Although it was announced in 2004, the EMC has been in the making since at least the mid-1990s. The key to understanding the Kefaya movement is to trace it to the political experience of its founders. Belonging to the famously dubbed "1970s generation," the founders of Kefaya are an ideologically diverse group of activists who were all intensely involved under a variety of banners in student movements in Egyptian universities throughout the 1970s.

While they ideologically come from the far right to the far left of Egypt's political spectrum, those leading figures of the "1970s generation" have been keen to extend political bridges among themselves to overcome the ideological battles that have mired Egypt's politics for so long. Through their political action in the 1990s, they have come to realize that the ideologically based mistrust and animosity among Egypt's older generation of political elite only serves to strengthen the ability of those in power to maintain their monopoly of power.

The 1970s generation is in a sense the generation of Nasserism. Born in the late 1940s and early 1950s, this generation's political consciousness was shaped during Nasser's high time. In their teens, they were the most excited about the national dream of that era. They were brought up deeply believing in the promises of achievements, national pride, and Arab unity, all wrapped up in the leadership of a highly charismatic leader. In 1967 this generation was dealt a devastating wake-up blow with the crushing defeat of Egypt at the hands of Israel. Suddenly all the slogans turned out to be shallow and the dreams looked as remote as ever. "The national independence and pride were lost with the occupation of Sinai," explains Shaaban, a key Kefaya founder. "The slogan of the strong army was dashed in the war and the rhetoric of the new political system turned out to be a nightmare of power centers' feuds, police brutality, appalling torture in prisons and a regime eating up even its most loyalists."[3]

Confrontation with this bitter truth is perhaps behind this generation's highly critical approach to national politics ever since. The collapse of their early idealistic image of the Nasser regime left them with a conviction that the key cause to such a resounding collapse of a promising experience was despotism. Even the Nasserists among them have come to realize and admit that reality. Adding to this distinctive experience, the relative political openness of the 1970s allowed the emergence of a highly politicized youth.[4] In their maturity, those activists, whose early political experience was one of direct action, have become highly sensitized in a distinctive way to the public pulse and to the opportunities of public action. While many of them are both intellectuals and activists, it is through their street action that they approach their respective big narratives rather than let such narratives define their political action.

The majority of Kefaya's founders are leaders of the 1970s student movements in both of its key phases, meaning that the founders are either leftists (Nasserists and Marxists) or Islamists. While the two groups disagreed bitterly on many issues, there emerged a clear common ground when it comes to foreign policy—a reality not lost on the part of both sides decades later. At the time, both groups strongly opposed Anwar Sadat's visit to Jerusalem, the U.S.-backed Camp David Accords, and the normalization process with Israel.

The rise of the Islamic movement continued to characterize Egyptian politics in the 1980s. Some of the leaders of the late 1970s student movement later joined the Muslim Brotherhood and became politically active through professional associations. By the end of the decade, they were running a majority of such syndicates through elections.

These Islamist successes generated inevitable tensions. In the early 1990s an increasing Islamist-secularist polarization reached unprecedented levels. Many in the political elite voiced concern and called for putting an end to those fierce battles. Such a call was new in Egypt's politics. During the 1970s there was indeed similar polarization, but no force emerged to articulate such a call for a domestic national dialogue. Ironically, the regime acted to create the basis for a conciliatory trend. In 1981, and just a month before his assassination, Sadat threw into jails intellectuals and activists from all political trends in Egypt, from the far right to the far left. Face-to-face in prison cells, those adversaries found a chance for a dialogue that promised a more conciliatory politics later. However, the path to real dialogue was not a straightforward one. The relative political openness of the early years of the 1980s paradoxically enhanced politics as usual through its promise of political competition, especially for the Islamists.

The early 1990s, however, carried at least a plausible opening for a genuine national dialogue among opposition elements. Winning big in the civil organizations—such as the syndicates and the students' unions—as well as in parliament, it was "politically correct" for members of the Muslim Brotherhood to open a dialogue with the left.[5] The left, on the other hand, faced with one defeat after another, including the collapse of the Soviet Union, found the dialogue with Islamists useful as a way of returning to the public arena more forcefully and with a new contribution.

Those who a decade later founded Kefaya had come to realize by then that the ideologically based mistrust and animosity among Egypt's older generation of political elites served only to strengthen the then ruling party's ability to maintain its monopoly over political power. That insight would prove a galvanizing one.

Kefaya: The Personal Creates the Political

This new generation of activists and intellectuals was determined to open up a genuine national dialogue that would include all political positions, camps, and groups and, for that reason, hold out the promise of reaching a genuine national consensus. Over the next fifteen years, the 1970s generation continued informal dialogues and welcomed diverse participants from older as well as younger generations. Such continuous efforts helped those elements identify shared values and goals and allowed them to create the precondition for reaching a national consensus. For example, the dialogue participants were able to come to terms with the everlasting bitterness of the older generations of both the Islamists and the Marxists toward the Nasserists, a bitterness that stems from the brutality of the Nasser regime toward those imprisoned.[6]

By the end of the 1990s such interactions made it possible for those activists to work together politically on issues of consensus. Foreign policy was an excellent start, since a widely shared platform already existed. The Committee on Supporting the Palestinian Intifada included joint action, not just dialogue. This committee mounted direct action campaigns to resist the process of normalization with Israel. They boycotted Israeli commodities and helped poor Palestinians through fund-raising campaigns.

Such interactions and many others resulted in building a level of trust across ideological lines, unseen among members of the older generations. Trust among those activists reached a striking level by the early 2000s. According to Amin Eskandar, a Nasserist and a founder of both the Karama party and Kefaya, they would, for example, "sign political statements for each other without checking beforehand."[7]

Again, in early 2000 these political forces worked, together with others, on a proposal for constitutional amendments. But that important effort was overshadowed in 2001 when regional events forced themselves onto the agenda.[8] For two years thereafter they were preoccupied with events in the occupied Palestinian territories. The invasion of Iraq then added yet another evocative item to the shared foreign policy agenda. Through their informal interaction, however, consensus emerged that the graver the foreign aggression was, the more important national reform became. To these actors, political freedoms became the key to effective resistance to the occupation of both Palestine and Iraq. The stage was set for the emergence of a new movement that encapsulated the emerging consensus and illustrated the new possibilities it revealed.

The "Present Danger" of the Neoconservatives?

Clearly, the invasion of Iraq aggravated the sense of Egypt's vulnerability in the minds of Kefaya's founders.[9] The founding statement of Kefaya captured the close connection perceived between external forces and domestic forces that led to the movement's emergence. This statement explained that the signatories "came together . . . despite their different intellectual affiliations" to "confront two highly interlinked threats, each of which is a cause and a result of the other"—namely, the foreign threats and political despotism (Kefaya, "Founding Statement"). By placing the foreign threats in the first paragraph, the EMC actually contradicted the wishful thinking of neoconservatives in Washington. To those Egyptians, the "present danger" was in fact U.S. policies in the region under Bush.[10] "The grave dangers and challenges flanking our nation," the statement explained, "repre- sented in the American invasion and occupation of Iraq, the continuous Zionist aggression against the Palestinian people and the projects of redrawing the map of our Arab nation, the latest of which was the Greater Middle East proposal, threaten our nationalism and imperils our identity. They, thus, necessitate the mobilization of all efforts for a comprehensive political, cultural and civilizational confrontation to protect the Arab existence against the Zionist-American proj- ects" (Kefaya, "Founding Statement"). The Bush administration in power at the time, of course, argued that after years of aiding dictatorships, the United States was serious about democratizing the Middle East. The ideologically diverse Egyp- tian Movement for Change, however, did not find that argument credible or help- ful to its cause. Instead, they looked at it as yet another scheme for domination.

Principles: The Art of Creating a Mainstream

Starting with such a strong condemnation of U.S. policies in the region, the statement went to far greater lengths to describe the aggravation of the national calamity by authoritarianism and outlined the reforms necessary to "overcome this overwhelming crisis" (Kefaya, "Founding Statement"). Although Kefaya made clear that foreign domination and political despotism were two faces of the same coin, its approach right from the beginning was that addressing the domestic challenge was key to resisting external threats. This emphasis on political trans- formation showed how working across ideological lines has borne fruit. In the 1990s it was only foreign policy that could bring the diverse currents together. But they then moved beyond this threshold so that they no longer need foreign policy issues to preserve their interactive project intact.

The founders of Kefaya also put forward some guidelines and principles for the movement. The movement, they said, was open to all political trends and ideologies. They added that members of political parties and other movements could be involved provided they took off their party's hat at the door and acted only as individuals. Accusations impugning the patriotism of opponents were disallowed. While the movement was open to civil society activists, its leadership roles were not open to civil society's leaders whose institutions are funded by foreign money (Shaaban, "Kefaya" 76). "Foreign funds that sponsor most of the civil society activities," contends Amin Eskandar, "have corrupted the Egyptian elite and taken them off the track of organized political action. Tuned to a foreign agenda, some in the civil society elite, who were previously Marxists or Nasserist Cadres, have been preoccupied with their numerous travels to the U.S."[11] In other words, receipt of U.S. funding that poured into Egypt's civil society was perceived as a disqualifier for leadership positions. To protect its credibility, Kefaya was to be self-financed by its own members' private money and contributions.

Managing the Conflict with the "Two Dangers"

On May 14, 2005, the semiofficial *al Ahram* newspaper carried an interview given by President Hosni Mubarak to the Kuwait-based *al Siyassa* newspaper. "I know who's behind them. . . . What Kefaya does is paid. . . . I am capable of organizing similar paid demonstrations carrying the slogan 'not enough,'" the president was quoted as saying (*al Ahram* 1). Kefaya responded immediately. In a strong statement issued on the same day, the movement rejected Mubarak's "allegations" and threatened to sue the presidency. "The movement calls on the president of the Republic—out of respect to his office . . . to stick to the facts when he talks to the public. . . . Upon the president's accusations, Kefaya cannot but resort to the courts" (Kefaya, "Statement," May 14). Within hours of the issuance of Kefaya's statement, the spokesman of the Egyptian presidency responded by putting the blame on *al Ahram* for "misquoting the president," referring the public to the "accurate version of the interview" in both *al Siyassa* and *al Akhbar*. In that version of the interview, and responding to a question about Kefaya, the president did say, "I know who are behind them, whether it is Kefaya's or other demonstrations" (El Youm, *al Siyassa*).

A few months earlier, in an interview with the French *Le Figaro* on March 25, 2005, President Mubarak had described Kefaya as a movement "landing on us from abroad and we know such movements very well" (Kefaya, "Statement," March 25). What was retracted by the official statement of the presidential spokesperson, therefore, was that Kefaya was funded by foreign money, not that it was a foreign-made-phenomenon.

In addition to the then president, several others either bluntly accused Kefaya or expressed concerns that the movement might be a foreign agent, implementing a foreign agenda,[12] funded by foreigners or even including foreign members who actually bankrolled the movement's activities.[13] Kefaya's unprecedentedly powerful response to such accusations came from the nonexistence of those links and its systematically uncompromising stance rejecting foreign operational and financial connections.

In a strong statement issued to protest the announcement by the U.S. ambassador about grants for a number of civil society organizations, starting with one million U.S. dollars to six such organizations, Kefaya reiterated its rejection of foreign funds for its activities, stating, "The domestic political tyranny and the foreign colonialist aggression are two faces of the same coin. A struggle against one cannot possibly work without a struggle against the other" (Kefaya, "Statement," March 14). Kefaya had also refused to take part in a conference on democratization organized by Egyptian American Copts and held in Washington, D.C.[14]

Hence, this episode about the president's statement and Kefaya's response is one manifestation of Kefaya's approach to managing conflict with the regime in power in Egypt. Experienced in direct action and in dealing with the Egyptian authorities since the 1970s, Kefaya's leaders developed a sophisticated sense of the politics of brinkmanship: "The worst thing they can do is to throw us into jail. Well, so be it," said Shaaban. Being ready for the worst-case scenario, Kefaya's activists were able to adopt a tough tone that escalated the crisis to the breaking point without fearing the consequences. Promising to confront the "two highly inter-linked threats"—namely, American policies and the regime—Kefaya's strategy shrewdly used the former to face the latter.

Instead of being a product of the Bush democratization domino effect as the neoconservatives argued, or playing into the hands of the U.S. administration, Kefaya understood quite correctly that U.S. pressure for political reform was yet another tool for domination. Skillfully, Kefaya took advantage of that very same U.S. pressure on the government without planning to help the U.S. agenda or allowing themselves to be used in any way by the Bush administration.

Making sure satellite channels knew about their street action in advance, Kefaya used the power of the media to play the Americans against the regime in order to protect their followers. "After a couple of incidents in which we had been brutalized in front of TV cameras, the regime realized that the ensuing international scandal every time we act is too much of a price to pay," explained Shaaban.[15]

Clearly rejecting U.S. policies and any U.S. government role, it was no surprise that when Condoleezza Rice visited Cairo in 2005 and 2006 and made a point of meeting with some civil society and "democracy activists," none of Kefaya's leaders were invited to meet the U.S. Secretary of State—not that they would have agreed to meet with her. In fact, the U.S. embassy sent invitations for some of Kefaya's leaders to join the audience when she lectured at the American University in Cairo in 2005, and deliberately none of them showed up. This mutual snubbing tells volumes about the willful, neoconservative ignorance of political life in Egypt at the time.

Democracy Made in Egypt, Not in America

"Why do they hate us?" Americans innocently asked after the criminal attack of September 11, 2001. While the very formulation of the question speaks volumes about the state of a shocked nation that at best pays little attention to history and its own role abroad, the perverse answer to the question was even more striking. The founders of Kefaya took notice of the way this U.S. public debate had been skewed. "Despite the fact that many Arab and non-Arab academics and politicians . . . pointed out that the anger has to do mainly with the U.S. policy toward the Arab-Israeli conflict and the unlimited support for Israel, the administration insisted that terrorism is simply caused by the lack of democracy" (Mady 70). America's innocence was thus vindicated, thereby justifying the assaults to come.

"The military bombardment was preceded by a theoretical bombardment," says Shaaban. "From Fukuyama's 'end of history' to Huntington's 'clash of civilizations,' those theories that characterized the relationship with this part of the World as hostile and potentially explosive have paved the way for the U.S. military force" (*Butterfly* 22). Right from the beginning, the Kefaya movement did not buy into a U.S. rhetoric of democratization. It was, however, at the forefront addressing both its intellectual and political negative impact.

The American democratic assault has had its shocking waves across the Arab world. Out of despair, democracy from without, at the barrel of the gun, did seem attractive to a few prominent intellectuals and activists. However, resistance to such an idea was far stronger and involved different forces, not just the regimes, with diverse premises for that resistance.

Saad Eddin Ibrahim, the internationally renowned Egyptian sociologist, was first to publicly announce his openness to the idea of democracy from without. Blaming the political leaders for the dismal Arab conditions and deploring their inability to level up with their peoples on the need to reach peaceful compromises to protracted conflicts, Ibrahim saved his harsher critique for Arab intellectuals. Those intellectuals who resist change "under the guise of resisting the Western assault, globalization or in defense of 'Arab Fundamentals' are one of the three angles of the unholy trinity of tyranny, corruption and destruction. It is a vicious triangle composed of complacent intellectuals, tyrannical rulers and knocked out Arab people" (Ibrahim).

Predicting that the U.S. intervention, which has become "a fact" in some Arab countries, "is now expected in others and possible in some more" (Ibrahim), the renowned sociologist introduced the Bush democracy rationale without questioning its premises. Across the political spectrum, however, the resistance to democracy from without was far more prevalent. Some voices even went so far as to demand the suspension of any democratic demands until the U.S. assault dissipated.

The Mubarak regime, on the other hand, exploited the resistance of democratic forces to any U.S. scheme in order to evade any real changes. Flirting with public sentiments against foreign interventions, the regime formulated a discourse paradoxically similar to its opponents in responding to the Bush administration's rhetoric while accusing democratic forces of being agents of U.S. schemes in the region.

Kefaya stood firmly against both the invitation to foreign intervention in the name of democracy and the regime's manipulation of official U.S. rhetoric to crack down on democratic forces. Both positions were dangerous, according to Shaaban. "Our struggle for democracy is an old protracted one that has nothing to do with the U.S. assault against us in the name of democracy" (*Butterfly* 35).

Kefaya's rejection of U.S. rhetoric was grounded in its conception of democracy as well as its reading of the current and historical record of U.S. policies around the world. "Inviting the foreign intervention in the name of democracy negates, with a stroke of a pen, the long hard struggle of several generations for democracy and would end up replacing the current dictatorships that are dependant on the West with puppet dictatorships" (*Butterfly* 24).

Defined as necessarily involving human dignity and self-respect, Kefaya conceived of democracy as the exact opposite of domination and hegemony. "Democracy stands against both occupation and oppression and contradicts with all the false claims that foreign intervention can achieve liberation, for it violates both the national and individual freedoms" (*Butterfly* 28).

At the same time, Kefaya readily admitted that the miserable gap between the national democratic aspirations and the level of achievements in this regard created a vulnerability in the perception of the foreign (indeed in the attraction of the foreign). But for the United States, Shaaban contended, democracy was a means to achieve its own ends: "The U.S. democracy scheme is meant to embarrass the Arab regimes and blackmail them into bowing to the American demands. The sword of smearing under the banners of despotism . . . is in a stand-by mode" (*Butterfly* 36).

In a clear response to the claims of innocence portrayed in the question of "Why do they hate us?" Shaaban pointed out that "the same U.S. that occupies Iraq . . . is, alas deeply troubled by our people's suffering from the lack of democracy. Of course no one believed it nor can we possibly believe it. Facts always expose lies and our memory tells us that the U.S. in particular has been the 'main sponsor' of outright dictatorships that oppressed us but protected themselves—with U.S. backing—by simply protecting the U.S. interests" (*Butterfly* 32).

Had the Bush administration been serious about democracy in Egypt, they would have not adopted a special agenda nor been selective," argued Abul Ela Mady. Although he himself broke up with the Muslim Brotherhood (MB) after a bitter, unrelenting battle in 1996, Mady argues that for the United States to choose to speak out against the imprisonment of (the liberal) Saad Ibrahim and then Ayman Nour, but not (the MB leader) Essam El Eryan, "was a clear case of selectivity that in fact unwarrantly hurt those liberals and exposed the U.S. intentions."[16]

U.S. calls for democracy were "insincere, simply aiming at selecting for us our new leaders," according to Hany Anan, a leading founder of Kefaya. "The fuss over Ayman Nour also illustrates how ignorant this administration is of the Egyptian political arena and who is who in Egypt. . . . It is clear the Americans have no clue and rely on the media to forge easy quick fixes,"[17] added the liberal

Anan. Until he was jailed after his unsuccessful bid for the presidency, Nour was perceived by many intellectuals and activists in Egypt as a politician with a public record that was dubious at best. Since his imprisonment, however, such criticism ceased, being viewed as unseemly for a figure who, whatever his limitations, has been treated unjustly by the country's long-standing authoritarian regime.

Kefaya also stood against some militant nationalists who called for democracy but defended the national regimes against "orders from abroad" and were willing to put off the struggle for democracy, ostensibly to shield Egypt from foreign interferences "as if it was ok to take orders in the economic and security realms but unacceptable only when it is orders to open up politically," Shaaban added satirically (*Butterfly* 35). Regardless of Kefaya's clear rejection of the Bush administration's official rhetoric on democracy, the Mubarak regime accused the movement of being a foreign agent. The self-confident activists were not surprised. The regime regularly and transparently used such baseless accusations against its opponents, they told me in interviews. With gentle sarcasm, Shaaban recalled how three decades ago the student movement, of which he was a leading figure, was accused of acting as an agent for North Korea. "No one understood then why specifically North Korea! Why not the Soviet Union, for instance, which was then the recognized leader of half of the world, or at least China, the major communist power!" (*Butterfly* 156).

Kefaya's path was thus clear. "The sound position is a struggle against both despotism and foreign intervention simultaneously." The only way to do that is "through a broad inclusive national mobilization that brings together all the aggrieved from the left to the right. Those who think they can carry out this difficult responsibility alone are dead wrong" (*Butterfly* 37).

Despite the soundness of these basic responses, it would be a mistake to conclude that the official U.S. rhetoric on democratization has not had deeper negative effects, whether under Bush or even Obama. In particular, the political dynamic of the responses I have just detailed above to the U.S. rhetoric on democratization clearly forced Kefaya to take more radical positions than it otherwise would have, including the ill-advised call for repealing the Egyptian-Israeli Camp David Accords.

The thrust of the Kefaya movement was that Egypt was headed toward a disastrous downfall politically and economically. When the United States invaded Iraq, the activists who had worked for years on foreign policy issues realized that speaking out against the invasion or against the collaborative Egyptian position was futile. This was because they perceived that the national will in Egypt was repressed by a regime that was weak in the face of foreign forces yet not paying much attention to the concerns of its own people. "An inclusive ideologically diverse movement that works as a catalyst for a peaceful democratic change" was key.[18] Kefaya was thus the product of a consensus that democratic change in Egypt had to be the top priority.

The birth of Kefaya, however, coincided with the Bush administration's increasingly loud posture on democratizing the Middle East, a perfect rationale for the

Mubarak regime to discredit the movement and undermine its credibility. And indeed the movement was under constant pressure from the regime and the local media to respond to accusations that they were agents of the United States.

More so, in a cross-ideological movement like Kefaya, the pressure was also from within. Some of the militant nationalists and Islamists were constantly advocating issuing statements against the U.S. and Israeli actions. Those newcomers into the movement have "louder voices," said Hany Anan. "Kefaya has for long resisted such internal calls for distracting the movement from its core goal, namely the democratic change in Egypt,"[19] he added.

But the U.S.-backed all-out war on Lebanon in the summer of 2006 intensified the pressures. "The Israeli barbarism and the blind American support has exposed the weak and clumsy position of the Egyptian regime and made it all the more provocative."[20]

The position of the Egyptian regime on Lebanon "exposed the fact that the Egyptian national will is shackled when it comes to Israel, a fact that goes back to the abnormal bilateral relations that the Camp David Accords created," said M. Said Edris, a leading founder of Kefaya. "What is needed is to turn the Egyptian Israeli relations from an abnormal into a normal relation,"[21] he added. Edris, the Nasserist respected scholar, was in fact at the forefront on the issue of abrogating Camp David. A campaign for a million signatures to repeal Camp David was posted on Kefaya's website and quickly taken down later. Other leaders of Kefaya reported that the campaign was neither discussed nor approved by the two leadership committees of Kefaya.[22] In a decentralized movement with loose internal structure, the movement had gone into several lapses of that kind. "Some colleagues continue to mix up their individual views with the position of Kefaya that must be agreed on by consensus,"[23] Abul Ela Mady argued.

As of this writing, and out of a realization of this major problem, Kefaya's leaders are working out a new structural formula that is "at once flexible and effective."[24] It is important to note, however, that Kefaya is neither anti-American nor anti-West in any sweeping or totalistic way. What they oppose are specific U.S. policies that are considered disastrous for Egypt and the Arab Islamic world. "I have a fully positive view of the [American] people, half positive view of the [American] political elite, yet a totally negative view of the current U.S. administration,"[25] commented the Islamist Abul Ela Mady, recalling his time in the United States in 2004, during which he gave twenty-eight lectures in four different states.

Many of Kefaya's leading figures have an ongoing dialogue with human rights and democracy activists around the world.[26] What they are against is U.S. policies and financial intervention in the name of a democratic ideal that is subverted by these destructive interventions. "The burning of [a] thousand American . . . flags," wrote Shaaban, "will not change what a real nationalist regime in Egypt can change." What is needed, he opined, is "a real democratic change that brings the immense frozen Egyptian will into the heart of the struggle for development, independence and freedom" ("Kefaya" 78).

Conclusion

Kefaya must be understood as a manifestation of a larger, more important phenomenon—namely, the struggle to cross ideological barriers in order to sow the
seeds of a new national mainstream. At this stage of Egypt's political development, the Kefaya movement emerged as the instrument for this larger purpose.

The experience of Kefaya has clearly demonstrated that this emerging mainstream is decisively anti-American. The actual reasons for this strongly held view
have nothing at all to do with the factors usually cited by the Washington think
tanks that advance such explanations as hatred of U.S. democracy, freedoms, or
way of life.[27] Across the Egyptian ideological spectrum, the activists and intellectuals who coalesced under the banner of Kefaya found U.S. policies in the region
no less dangerous to Egypt's future than the authoritarianism of the Mubarak
regime. Democrats across the Egyptian political arena find U.S. policies in the
region destructive and opposition to them both rational and essential. A U.S. sense
of its mission to remake the Middle East along "democratic" lines in the guise of
a benign hegemon (arguments for an Arab Spring with the fall of Mubarak) is
rejected outright by Egyptians.

The Bush administration's crude militarization of foreign policy undoubtedly
heightened the opposition. However, it must be noted that the perception of
the United States as simply the latest in a series of Western imperial powers had
already taken shape earlier. The difference, as the Egyptian political class saw
the matter, was simply a shift by Bush from diplomatic and economic means to
a military means in order to advance the same imperial ends.

Of course, prospects of U.S. change in the Middle East in ways that would lessen
these anti-American sentiments do not appear good. The scope of the current
U.S. debate on Iraq is an excellent example of the limits of potential change in
U.S. foreign policy toward the Middle East. Within the U.S. establishment, even
the Bush critics never questioned the large, imperial paradigm; they remained
preoccupied with tactics and strategies within that same paradigm. The invasion
of Iraq, the managing of the occupation thereafter, and whether and when the
U.S. forces should leave continue to be debated. But the idea that the United States
should remake the Middle East is rarely questioned or challenged. The realists
may reject the use of military force to change regimes, but they would not mind
using other tools to bring about the same kind of changes from without. It has
not gone unnoticed that the U.S. government has reverted to earlier strategies to
foster the desired remaking. For example, many in the political class now recommend that the United States reemphasize its earlier policy of pouring huge sums
of foreign aid into the civil and political arena as a vehicle for democratic change.
Along with such financial support, Egyptian analysts note, comes an unwelcome
pressure to set agendas and even select future leaders for the country.

As I have demonstrated in the case of Kefaya, the political dynamics of how such U.S. policies are received and the politics of its reverberations have been piling up for decades and steadily building the momentum for creating a new mainstream that is clearly anti-American. The American perception that it is the Islamists who represent a threat to U.S. interests in the region is quite clearly false. As is clear from the case of Kefaya, it is the U.S. policies in the Middle East, paradoxically, that represent the real threat to U.S. interests. Those policies have contributed in a major way to mobilizing people from the far left to the far right in what has become a full-fledged national movement with the potential of creating a new anti-American mainstream politics that goes far beyond the Islamists. The emerging mainstream neither hates the United States nor is jealous of its freedoms, as the neoconservatives would like us to believe, but simply find U.S. policies destructive of its dream of a democratic Egypt and a Middle East that creates its own future. The moderate Islamist Abul Ela Mady, a leading figure in Kefaya, responded with no hesitation to a question I posed about his vision of what a constructive U.S. contribution would look like: "The relationship with the U.S. is important to Egypt and I would never dream that the U.S. would support Arab causes," he commented. "But America is capable of building this relationship on a different basis." The United States, he concluded, "needs to consider our interests and respect international law."[28] Without such change, and it does not appear likely, we can expect that the new politics in Egypt will be characterized by an ever more strongly expressed anti-Americanism.

Notes

1. This statement was made in 2006, and the United States is still very entangled in the Middle East a decade later.

2. Those six were George Ishaq, Ahmed Bahaa El-Din Shaaban, M. Said Edris, Sayyid Abdel Sattar, Abul Ela Mady, and Amin Eskandar.

3. Ahmed Bahaa El-Din Shaaban, interview by the author, Cairo, Jan. 18, 2006.

4. Abul Ela Mady, interview by the author, Cairo, Jan. 24, 2006.

5. Essam Sultan, interview by the author, Cairo, Dec. 31, 2005.

6. Amin Eskandar, interview by the author, Cairo, Oct. 19, 2005.

7. Ibid.

8. Abul Ela Mady, interview by the author, Cairo, Oct. 12, 2005.

9. The EMC is a clear example of how the neoconservatives' arguments on "democratizing the Middle East" are irrelevant in the case of Egypt.

10. From the "Committee on the Present Danger" in the 1970s to Bill Kristol's book with the same title in 2000, the neoconservatives have, throughout the years, used the term "present danger." Ironically, it is the neoconservative agenda in the Middle East that is perceived as the present danger by democratic forces in Egypt. See William Kristol and Robert Kagan, eds., *The Present Dangers* (San Francisco: Encounter Books, 2000).

11. Amin Eskandar, interview by the author, Cairo, Oct. 19, 2005.

12. Magdy Mehanna, Al Masri Al Youm, April 2, 2005.

13. *Rose Al Usuf,* Aug. 15, 2005.

14. Nahdet Masr, Oct. 26, 2005.

15. Ahmed Bahaa El-Din Shaaban, interview by the author, Cairo, Jan. 18, 2006.

16. Abul Ela Mady, interview by the author, Cairo, Dec. 4, 2006.

17. Hany 'Anan, interview by the author, Cairo, Dec. 20, 2006.

18. Muhammad Said Edris, interview by the author, Cairo, Dec. 14, 2006.

19. Hany 'Anan, interview by the author, Cairo, Dec. 20, 2006.

20. Abul Ela Mady, interview by the author, Cairo, Dec. 4, 2006.

21. Muhammad Said Edris, interview by the author, Cairo, Dec. 14, 2006.

22. Abul Ela Mady, Ahmed Bahaa El-Din Shaaban, and Hany 'Anan, interviews by the author, Dec. 4, 14, and 20, 2006.

23. Abul Ela Mady, interview by the author, Cairo, Dec. 4, 2006.

24. Ahmed Bahaa El-Din Shaaban, interview by the author, Cairo, Dec. 14, 2006.

25. Abul Ela Mady, interview by the author, Cairo, Dec. 4, 2006.

26. Al Dustur, Aug. 10, 2005.

27. See, for example, Dinesh D'Souza, *What's So Great about America* (Washington DC: Regnery, 2002) 17–23.

28. Abul Ela Mady, interview by the author, Cairo, Dec. 4, 2006.

Works Cited

Abrams, Elliott. "Israel and the 'Peace Process.'" *The Present Dangers*. Eds. William Kristol and Robert Kagan. San Francisco: Encounter Books, 2000. 221–40.

Al Ahram. May 14, 2005. http://english.ahram.org.eg.

Al Siyasssa. May 4, 2005. http://egypty.com/top4/mubarak_seiassa_kuwait.asp.

D'Souza, Dinesh. *What's So Great about America*. Washington, DC: Regnery, 2002.

El Youm, Akhbar. May 14, 2005. http://www.akhbarelyom.com.

Ibrahim, Saad Eddin. "Yes, Democracy from Without, Na'am beyadi Amr." *al Hayat*. August 13, 2003.

Kefaya. "Founding Statement of Kefaya." http://harakamasria.net/informationMOre.asp ?id=803&idd=14, July 13, 2005.

——. Statement. March 14, 2005.

——. Statement. March 25, 2005.

——. Statement. May 14, 2006. https://en.wikipedia.org/wiki/Kefaya; http://www.global security.org/military/world/egypt/kifaya.htm.

Kristol, William, and Robert Kagan, eds. *The Present Dangers*. San Francisco: Encounter Books, 2000.

Mady, Abul Ela. *Al Wassat's Vision for Politics and Society (Ru'uyat al wassat lel seyassa wal mugtama'a)*. Cairo: Al Shorouk Publications, 2005.

Phillips, David L. *Losing Iraq: Inside the Postwar Reconstruction Fiasco*. Boulder, CO: Westview Press, 2005.

Rice, Condoleezza. Special Briefing on Travel to the Middle East and Europe, Washington DC, July 21, 2006. http://2001-2009.state.gov/secretary/rm/2006/69331.htm.

Shaaban, Ahmed Bahaa El-Din. *Butterfly Movement: Kefaya's Past and Future (Rafat al farasha, kefaya al madi wal mustaqbal)*. Cairo: Kefaya Publications, 2006.

——. "Kefaya: Al milad wal maser" (Kefaya: The Birth and the Path). *al Adab* June–July 2005.

CHAPTER 6

Understanding Anti-Americanism in Central Asia

Edward Schatz

> There is a fairly common opinion in Uzbekistan that the government
> is pursuing a policy of consistent corruption of the young people
> with the cult of money and an unbridled desire of carnal pleasures.
> Authorities have issued and are issuing licenses of nightclubs where
> young girls and women are seduced. The public is indignant: in the
> recent past the republic was famous for the chastity of its women.
> —Bahodir Sidikov, "Religious Context in Uzbekistan:
>   Roots and Sources"

To decry the introduction of moral impurities is a strategy that boundary keepers routinely use (Douglas). But how one understands the sources of these impurities is never simple. To whom and to what processes does one assign responsibility for moral degradation? The changes introduced in Uzbekistan that challenged the "chastity of its women" were likely brought about in part by thrill-seekers on business from the Middle East, Turkey, Korea, Russia, France, and Germany. Yet, elsewhere in the paragraph quoted above Sidikov decries these changes as "Americanization without restraints."[1] Why is moral degradation coded as "American"?

We abound in simple answers to this question. In one account, because of prevailing belief systems, certain cultures or population cohorts are understood to be predisposed to anti-Americanism. In this simple view, if we are willing to ignore the variety of Islam as practiced in diverse contexts and code Uzbeks as simply "Muslim,"[2] we might conclude that, by virtue of the central tenets of their faith, Uzbeks are likely to despise rationalism, modernity, tolerance, and liberalism. In this perspective, if America represents everything that Islam holds to be evil, then it is no wonder that Muslims hate the United States; it is axiomatically in their "nature" to do so. The right side of the political spectrum in North America often advances versions of such arguments, positing the inherency of anti-Americanism. In this account, Muslims are "othered," their differences from the West essentialized and rendered in stark relief.

In an account based on the opposite premise, publics are deeply rational. When they oppose the United States, it is because their interests and identities have been trod upon by identifiably injurious U.S. policies. For example, criticizing inherency arguments, Timothy Mitchell comments that "the most surprising thing about anti-Americanism in the Middle East is that there is so little of it" (Mitchell 87). In this view, U.S. policies toward the region are misguided; it is no surprise, therefore, that they generate some anti-Americanism. After all, Muslims are no less and no more reasonable than are non-Muslims.[3] The political left often adopts the Muslims-as-reasonable approach.

In this essay I examine post-Soviet Central Asia and suggest that its example gives the lie to both depictions. Anti-Americanism is not inherent to the region, to the people that inhabit it, or to the belief systems they claim. Nor are Central Asians simply reacting to U.S. policies. The reality of emergent (and still fairly limited) anti-Americanism is more complex and hinges on the particular meanings that Central Asians in the 1990s came to ascribe to the United States as a symbol. More than a focus on U.S. policies or a focus on the properties of a faith system, a focus on the United States as an ambiguous and changeable symbol provides analytic leverage as we seek to understand anti-Americanism in Central Asia.

Central Asia is particularly interesting terrain for thinking about anti-Americanism, since the region experienced almost no direct contact with the United States, its cultural products, or its citizens before the 1990s.[4] The recentness of this contact, coupled with its rapid intensification, makes Central Asia an interesting "laboratory" for dissecting how anti-Americanism emerges. Whereas the perceptions of Middle Eastern or Latin American publics are continually conditioned by centuries-long relations with the United States, the same cannot be said for Central Asia. The story of how it emerges in this region might, therefore, capture a more general dynamic.

In the rest of the essay, I proceed as follows. In the first section, I discuss what inherency and rationalist arguments expect with regard to anti-Americanism in the region and propose an alternative approach based on the United States as a symbolic, *meaningful* actor. In the second section, I provide first a "thin" account and then a "thick" account of changing attitudes about the United States in Central Asia. In the third section, I offer evidence that the United States works as a symbolic, *meaningful* actor in the region, and that its impact on the region must not be reduced to its military, economic, or cultural policies.

Inherency, Rationalism, and Symbolic Politics

Those who argue that there exists an inherent cultural or psychological predisposition to anti-Americanism might not be surprised by the emergence of negative views about the United States in a largely Muslim region. Bernard Lewis speaks for this perspective when he contrasts Islam to Christendom, arguing, "In Islam religion is not, as it is in Christendom, one sector or segment of life regulating some matters and excluding others; it is concerned with the whole of life, not a limited but a total jurisdiction" (Euben 185).[5] Ernest Gellner opens his treatment of Islam by simply stating, "Islam is the blueprint of a social order" (1). Devout Muslims, the thinking goes, hold little autonomy for a religious sphere and find scarce value—or even fundamental danger—in the separation of church and state.

Islam, according to the perspective that Lewis represents, cannot be reconciled with liberalism, because its focus on God-given rules governing society runs up against the autonomous individual of liberal thought. Where Islam is taken seriously, civil society cannot exist as a space protected from political and moral absolutes. To sum it up rather starkly: to be a Muslim means to abhor Enlightenment values of rationality, liberalism, capitalism, and the like.[6] It is also to abhor those world powers—especially the United States—that claim to represent these values.

This line of argument—one that posits a direct causal arrow from the specific theological tenets of a world religion, on the one hand, to patterns of political life and political culture, on the other, is tempting. As Roxanne Euben reminds us, "Perhaps the most common observation in Middle Eastern scholarship concerns the intimacy between religion and politics: the Prophet was both the recipient of the Qur'anic revelation and the founder of the first political community in Islamic history" (Euben 49). To the extent that religious doctrine conflates religious and political community, dissenters and reformists find themselves having to choose, in Daniel Lerner's famous dichotomy, between "Mecca" (embrace of Islam) and "mechanization" (embrace of modernism).

But just as a stopped clock shows the correct time twice daily, this perspective generates a "correct" prediction for Central Asia for the wrong reason. Religion is not a monolith, unchanging and undifferentiated. In the mid-nineteenth century the Catholic Church appeared to be uniquely hostile to liberal notions of civil society;[7] today many observers claim that uniqueness for Islam! But what about a more nuanced view? Could this perspective make sense as a probability, a generality, even if it does not hold in specific cases? The simple answer is that this, too, is doubtful, for the religious practices of "Muslims" vary strongly around the globe. Lewis's view requires that we discount evidence of an emerging reformation of Islamic practice—that is, movements of self-identified Muslims from Jordan to Egypt to Indonesia to Central Asia, women prominent among them, who call for a radical reconfiguration of how Islam should be practiced.[8] Lewis's response might be that these reformists are not practicing *true* Islam.[9] This is to take sides in theological disputes; it is not helpful as a way to understand Islam as a social and political phenomenon.

Citing the variety of Islamic practice is, however, only a starting point. A stronger retort to the inherency argument would not simply paint a more complex picture; it would provide evidence that strongly contradicts this argument, which is indeed what we will find in Central Asian contexts. Central Asian Islamism is better understood as a *consequence* than a *cause* of antiliberal political orientations. In Central Asia, anti-Americanism paved the way for Islamic activism rather than the other way around.

What about the opposite premise—namely, that Muslims in Central Asia who oppose the United States are offering a reasonable and reasoned response to identifiable U.S. policies? This approach is also logically plausible but does little better in contending with available evidence. If there is a strong link between U.S. foreign policies and popular attitudes about the United States, one would expect the pattern of U.S. involvement in the region to mirror the pattern of changing attitudes. As I show below, the major shift in attitudes about the United States occurred in the mid-1990s—well before the United States became a major actor in the region. For the bulk of the 1990s, U.S. foreign policies had limited direct effect on Central Asians. The United States was the world's most powerful political actor, but it was remote. Thus, if Central Asians on the whole shifted their views of the United States during this period, it was in reaction to *something in addition to U.S. policies.*[10]

However distant, the global hegemon nonetheless loomed large in people's imaginations. The United States had become a symbol—ambiguous and open to interpretation as all symbols are, but one that local actors could reference in their attempts at collective mobilization. I propose that we consider the United States as an increasingly meaningful symbol in post-Soviet Central Asia. The importance and intimacy of this symbol, of course, was indirectly related to concrete U.S. policies, but it was diffused and mediated through a variety of local institutions, practices, cultures, and beliefs. This does not necessarily mean that its impact was diluted. Quite to the contrary, its impact could reverberate far beyond its apparent sociological source.[11] It does mean that to depict attitudes about the United States as a linear function of its penetration in any given world region might start but certainly should not end the conversation.

What difference do symbols make? A focus on symbolic politics presents its own set of challenges (Wedeen), among them avoiding reification and insisting on human agency. I find much value in the literature on how social movements "frame," precisely because the literature takes symbols seriously without exaggerating their causal impact or denying space for people to chart their own destinies.[12] Successful social movements provide narratives that resonate not only with local beliefs but also with a "master frame," which is a schema that sorts information at a high level of abstraction; it is a set of meanings/behaviors that enjoys broad, extra-local resonance. Master frames posit concepts that are vague but nonetheless resonant because they enjoy flexible appeal—for example, internationalism, globalization, democracy, human rights, and justice. All of these potentially resonate, and local actors reference master frames to link their local agendas, tactics, and ideologies to issues of more universal concern. Anti-Americanism is one such master frame. What else do Islamists, North American white supremacists,

European pacifists, environmentalists, Russian fascists, economic nationalists, and some ordinary Canadians have in common besides a general belief that the influence of the United States ought to be curbed?

Whether social movement actors can successfully tap the anti-American master frame has much to do with their own rhetorical and organizational skill but also with the changing repertoire of popular attitudes about the United States.

Two Accounts of Change

How did popular attitudes about the United States shift in the 1990s in Central Asia? First, I tell the story in a "thin" way that allows us to view broad patterns and relate them to changes with regard to Islamic activism. Second, I tell the same story in a "thicker," more micro-level way, examining the frames deployed by social mobilizers in their attempt to pursue particular social and political agendas.

Documenting the Shift: A Thin Account

In 2005 the government of Uzbekistan put the U.S. government on notice that it was severing its basing contract and thus evicting U.S. forces from military bases in Uzbekistan.[13] That Uzbekistan could be so bold might be attributed to anti-Americanism. But to a considerable degree popular anti-Americanism had arisen much earlier. In fact, this shift had occurred *before* the United States began to be a major political and military actor in the region.

What happened in Central Asia can be told simply. During the Soviet era, Central Asians experienced the United States distantly and as mediated by Soviet ideological commitments. Soviet state propaganda had focused on capitalism's inequalities, poor race and gender relations, environmental excesses, and foreign policy aggressiveness. But these negative depictions had lost much of their luster by the late 1980s, when ideological and cultural countercurrents had emerged from underground and created a new mainstream. With them, the negative depictions propagated by officialdom gave way to strongly positive portrayals of the United States.

In the early post-Soviet period (through the mid-1990s), Central Asians' expectations for American-style prosperity were elevated. While it might seem natural that the Iraq War in 2003 would sour global views of the United States, it is worth recalling the fundamental optimism about Western and particularly American culture, political institutions, and economic models that engulfed the region in the immediate aftermath of the Soviet collapse. By the middle of the 1990s, across post-Soviet space this initial embrace of the United States gave way to profound ambivalence about its role (and that of other countries perceived to be associated with the United States).

Three reasons stand out for the rising ambivalence. First, the waning years of Soviet rule and early 1990s had fostered broad expectations that post-Soviet states would finally become "normal" states; in some cases, "normal" meant economically prosperous, while in others it meant democratic and free. In either case, the vast majority of post-Soviet publics were disappointed with the lack of progress by the mid-1990s. Second, as domestic manufacturing and distribution channels collapsed throughout the region, foreign-made and especially Western products flooded local markets. In some cases—particularly in the case of cultural products such as American music and Hollywood movies—these products generated resentment. Glorifying sex, drinking, and material decadence, they affronted local values, which were experiencing a revival after Soviet rule.[14] Third, Soviet-era depictions of the United States were still fresh in the public's memory. The image of American capital and products dominating new markets resonated with Soviet propaganda about the United States as the champion of the exploitative classes. The images of poor race relations and crime-ridden inner cities that many low-quality Hollywood films depicted echoed Soviet propaganda about American domestic exploitation. Finally, images of the United States as a global hegemon resonated with Soviet propaganda about American expansionist ambitions. Their accuracy or lack thereof is beside the point; these images were appealing because they were familiar. Crucially, this ambivalence rose well before U.S. troops arrived in the region in late 2001.

How do we know about these changing views? In part, we know from firsthand experience. In 1997 and 1998, Central Asians were increasingly willing to express their concerns about the United States, even to North American researchers.[15] At the elite level, by the middle of the decade many Western scholars and policy advisors spoke of "expert fatigue" that had emerged in the population. Where in the past they had been welcomed warmly, only several years later there was on-the-ground resistance to their work.

How significant and widespread were these changes? In the absence of high-quality public opinion surveys with questions about the United States, I addressed the question indirectly. Together with a research assistant, I coded Radio Free Europe/Radio Liberty (RFE/RL) reports about the region.[16] These are daily news reports that have the best systematic coverage of the former USSR. We coded every news item that appeared in the RFE/RL Newsline on the ex-Soviet states for one weekday from 1991 through 2001. About 7 percent of the more than seventeen thousand news items coded describe an event in which a societal or governmental actor expressed an attitude about the United States. For example, we coded public statements by government officials or societal actors, protest demonstrations, legislation pending or enacted in local parliaments, news conferences, leafleting efforts, and diplomatic negotiations. We judged each relevant news item on a six-point scale; a 6 was strongly pro-U.S., a 1 strongly anti-U.S. The daily scores were averaged and then aggregated into quarters.

The RFE/RL data illustrate three points. First, the mid-1990s witnessed a general decline in attitudes regarding the United States—on the part of both societal and governmental actors. Second, Central Asian governments were generally

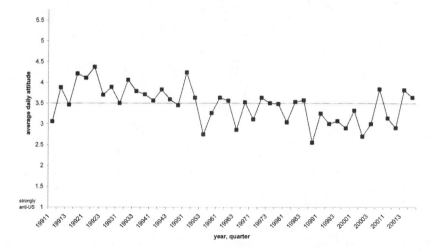

Fig. 1: Behaviorally expressed attitudes about the United States, 1991–2001, total Former Soviet Union (Source: Radio Free Europe/Radio Liberty Newsline daily reports).

pro-American,[17] but the data imply that Central Asian publics were not. Third, the decline in attitudes about the United States occurred in the middle of the 1990s, preceding the rise of Islamic activism, lending plausibility to the notion that the former influenced the latter. Figure 1 depicts the aggregate trend in attitudes toward the United States from 1991 to 2001.

For all the states of the former Soviet Union, attitudes about the United States experienced a decline in the middle of 1995. From that point, the mean attitude scarcely rose above 3.5 (the neutral point) until 2000. Was this a significant change? There are reasons to believe that it was. Most of the actors captured by the data were governmental and tended to use measured language and behaviors with regard to the United States; ruling elites usually try to avoid the political and economic costs of being strongly anti-American. In fact, over the course of the decade, the mean attitude expressed by governmental actors in the region was 3.5; the mean attitude expressed by societal actors was 2.8. This means that any change that lasts (as in that from 1995 to 2000) is likely to underestimate the magnitude of the popular attitude change experienced on the ground.

Figure 2 compares the trend in the total former Soviet Union (FSU) against that of Russia and the Central Asian states.

In the data on Russia, opinions about the United States are generally lower than in Central Asia. The data on the latter endure wide swings in attitude that result from the less thorough RFE/RL coverage of the region. On the surface this paints a picture of Russia as more anti-American and Central Asia as more pro-American. But table 1 helps us to make sense of the patterns.

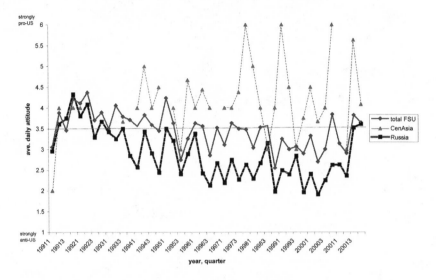

Fig. 2: Behaviorally expressed attitudes about the United States, 1991–2001, comparisons (Source: Radio Free Europe/Radio Liberty Newsline daily reports).

Table 1 shows that, for Central Asia, societal actors were dramatically underrepresented in the RFE/RL coverage. There are two main reasons for this. First, RFE/RL covers events in Russia more thoroughly, in part because Russia is a significant world actor by any measure, and in part because RFE/RL (like other news organizations, government agencies, and academics) largely had ignored the non-Russian republics during the Soviet period. While coverage improved dramatically after the Soviet collapse, Russia still received disproportionate attention. More thorough coverage meant that societal actors' attitudes were more likely to be covered. While government actors and the news they make are easy to cover, societal actors and the news they make require that journalists penetrate society. So less coverage in general of a region usually means a higher proportion of coverage devoted to governmental actors.

A second reason for this underrepresentation of societal actors in reports on Central Asia had to do with the nature of Central Asian political regimes. All of Central Asia's states were authoritarian, varying from the softer version in Kyrgyzstan to the sultanistic regime in Turkmenistan. Since authoritarian regimes monopolize or seek to control the media, these societies are generally less mobilized and therefore less likely to make news than their counterparts in Russia. So when we view the comparison between Russia and Central Asian attitudes (fig. 2), we must keep in mind that we are comparing Central Asian governmental attitudes with a more mixed bag of Russian governmental and societal attitudes.

For these reasons, the RFE/RL data cannot directly speak to Central Asian popular attitudes about the United States. But we can reconstruct the picture

Table 1: RFE/RL Coverage, by Country, with Average Attitude, 1991–2001

Country	Number of Relevant Cases[1]	% Societal Actors	Average Daily Attitude
Belarus	45	20.00	2.36
Russia	707	15.13	2.84
Ukraine	90	13.33	3.87
Turkmenistan	13	0.00	4.00
Kazakhstan	38	13.16	4.20
Georgia	22	13.64	4.20
Armenia	30	3.33	4.28
Kyrgyzstan	12	16.67	4.33
Moldova	39	10.26	4.35
Uzbekistan	17	0.00	4.44
Azerbaijan	33	9.09	4.45
Tajikistan	10	0.00	4.60
Lithuania	68	5.88	4.63
Latvia	40	12.50	4.68
Estonia	49	4.08	5.04

1. Of the more than 17,000 news items that were coded, 1,213 items contained a reference to the United States and an indication of a reaction to the United States on the part of a local actor(s).
Source: Radio Free Europe/Radio Liberty Newsline daily reports.

indirectly. Since we have greater confidence that the data on Russia accurately reflect societal actors' changing views, we can look to the Russian data for the overall pattern that they represent—that is, we can assume that the pattern of change over time is similar in the Central Asian cases, even if the absolute numbers are different. With this analogy as analytic leverage, one might argue that a clear although not overwhelming decline in attitude about the United States began in 1995 and continued at least until the end of the decade.[18] Moreover, if Central Asian politics bears resemblances to Middle Eastern politics, then we have further reason to suspect that pro-U.S. opinions publicly expressed by governments mask underlying anti-U.S. sentiment, both in society and within the state.[19]

I have suggested that this shift was caused in large part by disappointed expectations about political and economic transition. Could rising attention to Islam have played a role? Did Islamic activism dictate a particular ideological response to the United States as an actor? In fact, the sequence of events suggests the reverse—that this shift itself fueled Islamic activism.

The gradual opening of the Soviet polity in the 1980s and the Soviet collapse brought increased popular attention to Islam. Even in the 1970s, Moscow had begun to countenance greater observance of Islamic rites (burials, marriages) and sanctioned construction of prayer houses (Ro'i 60–85). With independent statehood, Central Asian publics turned increasingly to Islam as a source of identity, although claims of being a Muslim were often made simply to distinguish oneself from Russian settlers and to distance oneself from the Soviet experience.

Increased attention to Islam, however, did not bring about much political or social activism in the early part of the decade. Even in the context of the USSR's rapid institutional decay, militant activism—such as that involved in the December 1991 seizure of a building of the Communist Party in Namangan—was particularly unusual. The main Islamist actor, the Islamic Renaissance Party (IRP), which had been created in the city of Astrakhan in 1990, splintered into territory-based parties with the Soviet collapse; it could not sustain widespread support amid fundamentally different conceptions of the party's purpose.[20] The Tajikistan-based party (IRPT) sought to contest parliamentary elections, eschewing the pursuit of other goals before Tajikistan descended into civil war. The IRPT even worked closely with Sufi groups, whom radical Islamists usually oppose on ideological grounds.[21]

The IRPT's agenda shifted during the Tajik civil war (1992–1996), but the testimony of senior IRPT leaders indicates that "the great majority did not favor the establishment of an Islamic state. They had become accustomed to a secular way of life and were in favor of retaining the separation of religion and state" (Akiner 32–33). Moreover, the IRPT remained allied with democratic parties throughout the period—a sign of their pragmatic bent. With the peace accord ending the civil war, the IRPT reasserted itself as an ordinary political party with an Islamic-values agenda, capturing 7.5 percent of the votes in a 2000 parliamentary poll, which translated into two seats. Later, some militant Islamists would became dissatisfied with the IRPT's willingness to compromise, but the point remains that the IRPT's activism was not of a militant sort and that activism had little resonance until the late 1990s.[22]

By the late 1990s some militant Islamic activism had emerged.[23] Most visible was a rise in terrorist acts, such as the attempt on Uzbek president Islam Karimov's life in February 1999, which Uzbek officials attribute to two former members of the Uzbek branch of the IRP, Juma Namangani and Tahir Yoldosh, who had created the Islamic Movement of Uzbekistan (IMU) in 1997 (Roy 24). The IMU staged cross-border armed incursions, taking four Japanese geologists and eight Kyrgyzstani soldiers hostage in 1999 and repeating an incursion in 2000. The IMU had a welcome home in the Karategin valley of Tajikistan, which was dominated by Islamist opposition leaders and—before the fall of the Taliban, at least—had been a hotbed of foreign-born field commanders (Rotar, "Tsentral'naia Aziia").

The U.S. military campaign in Afghanistan disrupted the IMU's operations. Namangani was reported killed in a U.S. attack in November 2001, even while rumors continued to circulate in the region that a close relative of his, rather than Namangani himself, had died. Yoldosh was at large, perhaps in the mountains of eastern Afghanistan or western Pakistan, and later reported killed in 2009. The alleged ability of the IMU to finance operations through drug trafficking was also put to a test. It was the subject of intense speculation whether or not the IMU could successfully regroup in the Garm valley in the mountains of eastern Tajikistan (Institute for War and Peace Reporting). In late March 2004 the government of Uzbekistan was engaged in sporadic armed battles with groups of militants whom it claimed were from the IMU.

Because its activities were militant, the IMU operated deeply underground; this creates difficulties in knowing the number of adherents and the extent of their activities. Groups that professed nonviolence, however, tended to be more visible—even if they are also proscribed by law. Hizb ut-Tahrir (HT), a transnational group that advocates peaceful means of establishing Islamic government, became tremendously active across the region.[24]

In the early 1990s, Islamist activity was limited geographically. In Tajikistan the IRPT was strongly identified with particular regions—a fact that tempered its appeal to other would-be sympathizers (Olimova 179). In Uzbekistan and Kyrgyzstan, activists worked visibly only in the densely settled and economically depressed Ferghana valley. In Uzbekistan they were quickly driven underground by Karimov, who had come to power in 1989 on a strongly anti-Islam platform. In Kyrgyzstan, Islamists were primarily ethnic Uzbeks who felt victimized by the pro-Kyrgyz policies of President Askar Akaev. In Kazakhstan and most of the rest of Kyrgyzstan, such activism was extremely limited.

By the late 1990s the picture had changed. Hizb ut-Tahrir's literature was widely disseminated throughout the region, even though physical possession thereof was a crime.[25] On September 12, 2001, leaflets applauding the 9/11 attacks appeared in Bishkek, Kyrgyzstan—far in both a geographic and a cultural sense from the Kyrgyzstani parts of the Ferghana valley (Rotar, "Tsentral'naia Aziia"). Similar literature was disseminated with increasing frequency throughout all regions of Tajikistan and widely in southern Kazakhstan.

Most activism remained concentrated in areas of traditional activity but no longer exclusively so. Thus, in Kyrgyzstan the Osh and Jalalabad regions were the sites of ongoing HT recruitment (Moldaliev 94). In Tajikistan the inclusion of the IRPT in the ruling coalition after the civil war was an opportunity for Islamist appeals to achieve broader resonance. That is, given the IRPT's close popular identification with the Karategin valley and Badakhshan region of the country, its becoming a "normal" political party in the late 1990s allowed HT activities to spread in the Sughd (former Leninabad) region, where any Islamist appeals would have found little resonance in the past (Olimova 175; International Crisis Group 12). In Kazakhstan, more remote from the regionally destabilizing Afghanistan conflict and relatively more buoyed economically by its wealth of extractive resources, HT found an audience in southern Jambyl and South Kazakhstan regions (Savin) and even became active in the more remote and Russified northern region of Pavlodar. The picture is similar in the Russian Federation, where Islamist activism that had been limited to Chechnya in the early part of the decade began to find resonance in Dagestan by 1997–1998 (Dobaev 76–86).

Foreign funding increased dramatically over the course of the 1990s. Legitimate state aid from Saudi Arabia, Iran, Egypt, Turkey and others aside, much informal assistance began to come from abroad. One critic of HT claims that, given the education levels and relatively privileged socioeconomic positions of many HT members abroad, it overwhelmed alternative messages and even gained the sympathies of foreign think tanks. He argues that in Kyrgyzstan, where the government failed to provide relevant textbooks in Uzbek to its minority Uzbek population, HT provided a wealth of written material to an overwhelmingly literate population (Grebenschikov 2–4). The funding for IMU activism came partly from narcotics trafficking and partly from financial ties to transnational terrorist networks.

In a pattern that resonates with the experience of Deobandi *madrassas* in Pakistan, HT offered not only exposure to religion but also an education about social, political, and economic problems—problems that the Central Asian state often was incapable of addressing. Kyrgyzstan's official religious agency, the spiritual directorate, hired mullahs and imams who often lacked theological education and knowledge of key rites (Grebenschikov 1); the ideas they propagated could ring more hollow than those more "authentic" non-state voices from abroad. A similar situation obtained in 2002 in Kazakhstan, when Nursultan Nazarbaev appointed as the country's official chief mufti Absattar Derbisali, a career academic and Arabist with no religious training, leading many ordinary pious Muslims to deny his legitimacy.[26]

The specific mix of religious ideas prevalent in Central Asia underwent a change. Whereas in the early part of the 1990s, very few proponents of Shariah law, strict interpretations of the Qur'an or Sunnah, or the like were found in the region, by the latter part of the decade a wider range of religious ideas was available. Among the ideas on the "supply side" were those usually lumped together under the label "Wahhabism." While the term has its origins in Soviet-era government efforts to stigmatize devout Muslims, and while it is used imprecisely to cover a range of beliefs, the rise of various puritanical, fundamentalist, and radical currents over the decade was clear.

In short, by the late 1990s Islamic activism had become more widespread, better funded, and occasionally more militant. Attitudes about the United States, on the other hand, largely predated this mobilization. Thus, the macro-level story suggests the possibility that changing attitudes about the United States in some ways fueled changing patterns of social mobilization (rather than social mobilization giving rise to changed attitudes about the United States).

Explaining the Shift: A "Thick" Account

What happened at the micro-level? In this section, I argue that declining attitudes about the United States were not enough to spur Islamic activism. Rather, activists needed to be skilled at using images about the United States as a global hegemon—that is, they needed to tap a "master frame" of anti-Americanism to improve recruitment. By using this resonant master frame, Central Asian mobilizers took advantage of a symbolic resource—a globally resonant idea that helped to crystallize and make sense of ordinary people's emerging grievances.

A comparison of the frames used by the IRPT in the first half of the decade and HT and the IMU in the latter half of the decade illustrates the change. In the early 1990s the IRPT had little to say about the United States. Anti-U.S. rhetoric was all but absent. Roy shows that the party's *Nejat* newspaper (which published from March to September 1992, when the civil war brought it to an end) offered only the mildest reference to the United States, saying that it and the West misunderstood Islamic movements and used double standards with regard to democracy (12–13). He continues:

> No articles appeared condemning the U.S. presence in the Gulf; strangely, the only article on the Gulf dealt with the idea that the participation of women in the armed forces is not against Islamic tradition. . . . One of the few articles mentioning current conflicts where other Muslims have been oppressed . . . placed responsibility on "the communist system," which, although collapsed, was compared to a "scorpion with seven tails." (13)

For its part, HT offered anti-American perspectives well before the end of the decade, but largely through its website. The site offered editorials that lambasted the United States' role in the Middle East, calling it a "state terrorist that must be driven from the Muslim world" (Botobekov). But the anti-Americanism of HT carried little meaning and was hardly accessible to most Central Asians. Even for those with internet access, the events of the so-called Muslim world were too remote to resonate. For much of the 1990s the United States was a familiar actor on the world stage, but a distant one.

By the end of the decade, America as a symbol was difficult to miss. The changes in Islamists' framings that occurred over the decade were the following. First, there were increasing references to the United States and actors (such as Israel, the International Monetary Fund, World Bank) believed to be associated with the United States. Second, claims emerging that Western models of economic relations and governance had failed gave rise to calls for authentic, culturally appropriate alternatives in the latter part of the decade. Third, the United States was depicted as inherently war-seeking, while Islam was painted to be peace-oriented. Fourth, the region's political leaders were depicted as the corrupt puppets of the United States and its economic allies. Indeed, local elites had erected a façade of democracy rooted in deeply flawed or sham elections, had stepped up human rights abuses, and had crafted local economic structures to benefit themselves and their cronies. Fifth, Western (and especially American) values were ruining the local moral fabric, as Sidikov describes in this essay's epigraph.[27]

After the military defeat of the Taliban in the winter of 2001, radical sympathizers dispersed and patterns of recruitment changed. In particular, those who had operated openly in Tajikistan and clandestinely in parts of Uzbekistan now found it difficult to continue their work; many moved elsewhere. There is some evidence that many HT cells moved to more remote Kazakhstan, with its relatively liberal space for religious freedom.[28] In their new locales, they stepped up anti-U.S. and anti-Semitic leafleting efforts.[29] HT printed literature found in April 2002 in economically depressed Kentau city (South Kazakhstan region) began to reflect the messages initially accessible to Central Asians only through its website: "People who abide by the *shariat* of God, restore the religion of Islam and spread it throughout the world will replace the pliant [*poslushnye*] leaders. They will erect a unified caliphate instead of those who helped Jews to assume power" (Savin 8).[30] An observer from the Keston Institute noted that HT "shows signs of taking a more militant stance now. For example, they are regularly calling the president of Uzbekistan, Islam Karimov, a Jew and a Zionist—and this is in the context of the perceived new and unwelcome alliance between Uzbekistan and the United States" (Pannier).

HT's frames were tailored to the circumstances of individual countries. In Uzbekistan the emphasis was on human rights abuses and poor protections for religious freedom. In Kyrgyzstan, with more significant protections for religious freedom, HT focused on the economic crisis and high-level government corruption (Grebenschikov 2). Whatever the particular faults of local regimes, they were linked to the United States and the foreign values and institutions that it propagated, and this link was played up with regularity.[31]

The IMU likewise stepped up its anti-American framing in the late 1990s. In excerpts from undated recruitment literature, authors used seemingly contradictory imagery to depict a threat to authentic Islam. In one hand drawing, the United States, Russia, and Israel, fused together as a venomous-looking snake, are swallowing Tajikistan and are poised to consume Uzbekistan (Babadzhanov). The IMU frequently referred to Uzbekistan's president as a "Jew" and a "Zionist," not to mention a stooge in the U.S.-led military efforts against the Taliban, Al Qaeda, and the Iraqi regime of Saddam Hussein.

This general shift from demonizing the Soviet regime to demonizing U.S. global hegemony is also evident in the willingness of the IMU and HT to embrace Soviet legacies. HT, its radical agenda notwithstanding, accepted many behaviors as long as they could be justified as leading to the creation of the caliphate. For example, HT accepted that women could run for political office. Given the Soviet-era promotion of gender equality, this was a sensible tactical concession to make HT's ideas more palatable locally.

For its part, the IMU used selected Soviet symbols. In internal IMU literature from Uzbekistan, the hammer from the Soviet hammer and sickle was replaced by a sword—a telling appropriation of symbols that would be both familiar and resonant to potential recruits. "Without the sword there is no Islam," claimed the literature (Babadzhanov).[32] Another excerpt offered to potential recruits references Russian and Soviet history that would have been familiar to many:

What did Lenin do? He was always with the people. He who seeks to bring down the government must always be with the people. For example, the Decembrists were all from the intelligentsia. They lost their struggle. The Revolution was committed by Jews in the name of Lenin. But the people do not understand anything. They are like sheep and only know how to eat. (Babadzhanov)

In short, the early 1990s saw the IRPT frame their struggle as anti-atheist and anti-Soviet. The late 1990s saw HT and the IMU frame theirs as anti-American, anti-Israel, critical of local regimes, as well as supporting social and economic justice.

Do Frames Really Matter?

There is much literature from political psychology that broadly suggests that issue framing influences how people imagine political possibilities and how they constitute their own political preferences.[33] But does issue framing make a specific difference for Central Asians who might or might not choose to mobilize? There is little reason to expect that Central Asian patterns differ strongly from those found elsewhere, as some (admittedly limited) data from a survey experiment administered in Kyrgyzstan suggest.

In the survey experiment, ordinary citizens were presented with a variety of survey questions and an embedded, positive depiction of the United States. The idea was to see if this positive depiction might have a positive effect on subsequent expressed attitudes about the United States.[34] Specifically, respondents received the following (in Russian or the titular language), which is a combination of quotations from real U.S. government sources:

America rejects bigotry. We reject every act of hatred against Muslims. America values and welcomes people of all faiths—Christian, Jewish, Muslim, Sikh, Hindu and many others. Every faith is practiced and protected here, because we are one country. Every immigrant can be fully and equally American because we're one country. Freedom of worship is an American value, and more than 2 million American Muslims are associated with more than 1,200 mosques in the United States.

Aside from a control group, which received no information, respondents received the depiction above but with attributions varied. Some were told that George Bush had uttered these words, others that the U.S. ambassador to their country had, others that an ordinary American who had lived in their country since 1994 and was married to a local woman had, and a final group received the depiction with no attribution. A "thermometer" question about whether the United States generally does more harm than good or more good followed.

If framing matters, attitudes expressed about the United States should be more positive among those who read the frame than those who do not. As table 2 shows,

Table 2: Mean Assessment of U.S. as Helpful/Harmful by Treatment, Kyrgyzstan (N = 60)

Control	No Attribution	Bush	Ambassador	Ordinary American
2.9	2.91	3.54	3.33	2.5

1 = U.S. does much more good than harm
2 = U.S. does more good than harm
3 = U.S. does equal amounts of good and harm
4 = U.S. does more harm than good
5 = U.S. does much more harm than good
Source: Radio Free Europe/Radio Liberty Newsline daily reports

they are not. Respondents expressed exactly the same attitude in the "control" group as in the "no attribution" group. At first glance, framing appears not to matter. But once you add the attribution line, the effect of a frame varies by the credibility of the source. Thus, when the words were attributed to George Bush, they were not only discounted, but they had the *opposite* effect. The ambassador's words also produced the opposite effect, though to a lesser degree. On the other hand, the words of the American who was ensconced in the local culture seemed to enjoy credibility, and his framing positively influenced how respondents viewed the United States.

Since in the real world, a *frame* always has a *framer* whose credibility can be assessed by a discerning public, it is fair to conclude that frames do make a difference in affecting Central Asian publics' propensity to mobilize. Like other people, Central Asians are neither purely rational nor purely irrational; their attitudes and actions are the product of a series of inputs that we rarely consider and that normal discussions of anti-Americanism simply cannot capture.

Conclusions and Implications

The dynamic I have identified continued well into the middle of the 2010s. Indeed, frames critical of the United States penetrated the region more and more thoroughly the further that Russia reasserted its power generally in the post-Soviet region (Russia's fighting a proxy war in Ukraine from 2013 was simply the most visible dimension of this resurgent Russian power).

Of course, like all symbols, the United States is open to interpretation—interpretation that occurs in local political and social milieus by local political and social actors. Russia's resurgence was dramatic, but we need not assume that its effect in propagating a particular worldview will prove permanent. Nonetheless, once a symbol is interpreted, especially by actors who enjoy some authority and credibility, it enters the mobilizational repertoire of publics. In 2015 anti-Americanism had become an increasingly common currency among Central Asian publics, prominent societal actors, and government figures; it seemed to be at no risk of abating.

Perhaps because of a perspective on foreign affairs rooted in the "realist" school of thought, which emphasizes narrow pursuit of self-interest, foreign policy actors have been generally unconcerned with the United States' global image. Russia's geopolitical resurgence, and the anti-American views that the Putin regime was entirely willing to profit from and propagate, on first glance seemed evidence enough that the realist school was correct. Yet, such a stance—like the one that views Islam as leading inevitably to anti-Americanism—mistakes cause and effect. Moreover, it falsely renders policy makers as helpless. As challenging as doing so may be once frames have become ensconced in domestic societies, the United States can improve its image abroad (Council on Foreign Relations; Nye). Moreover, the alternative is entirely unappealing: to disengage from image construction as a part of foreign policy is to resign to living with, and contending with, the images that other global and local actors craft.

Notes

1. Bahodir Sidikov, "Religious Context in Uzbekistan: Roots and Sources," *Central Asia and the Caucasus* 9.1 (2000): 57.

2. On the variety of Islam in practice, see Robert W. Hefner, ed. *Remaking Muslim Politics: Pluralism, Contestation, Democratization* (Princeton, NJ: Princeton UP, 2004).

3. Mitchell argues that the United States' "relative weakness, its frequent inability to place client regimes in control, and the long-term failure of many of its efforts to do so" are the main aspects of this failure. See Mitchell 95.

4. I use "Central Asia" to refer to Kazakhstan, Kyrgyzstan, Tajikistan, Turkmenistan, and Uzbekistan.

5. Bernard Lewis, *Islam and the West*, 135–36, as quoted by Roxanne L. Euben, *Enemy in the Mirror: Islamic Fundamentalism and the Limits of Modern Rationalism* (Princeton, NJ: Princeton UP, 1999), 185n1.

6. For the corollary argument, by which the West cannot accept Islam as legitimate because of apparently irreconcilable differences, see Talal Asad, "Muslims and European Identity: Can Europe Represent Islam?" in Anthony Pagden, ed., *The Idea of Europe: From Antiquity to the European Union* (Washington, DC: Woodrow Wilson Center Press, 2002), 209–227.

7. See, for example, Pope Pius IX, *Quanta Cura* (Condemning Current Errors), Papal Encyclical of Dec. 8, 1864, http://www.papalencyclicals.net/Pius09/p9quanta.htm.

8. On political and social movements that pursue reform, see Carrie Rosefsky Wickham, "The Path to Moderation: Strategy and Learning in the Formation of Egypt's *Wasat* Party," *Comparative Politics* 36.2 (2004): 205–228; Mirjam Kunkler, "Advocating Women's Rights in the Language of Islamic Sacred Texts: The Tripartite Struggle for Women's Rights in Iran," Association for the Study of Nationalities, April 15–17, 2004; Max Rodenbeck, "Islam Confronts Its Demons," *New York Review of Books*, April 29, 2004, 14–18.

9. Ironically, advocates of this position seek to inoculate themselves against the variety of Islamic practice by defining Islam as that which is practiced only by the fundamentalists they abhor.

10. I do not deny that U.S. policies have an impact on how people apprehend the United States, but this impact is mediated through local social and political realities and sedimented in various resonant symbols and discursive formations.

11. For a discussion of "reverberation effects," see Anna Seleny, "Tradition, Modernity, and Democracy: The Many Promises of Islam," *Perspectives on Politics* 4.3 (2006): 481–94.

12. See Erving Goffman, *Frame Analysis* (Cambridge, MA: Harvard UP, 1974); and Robert Benford and David Snow, "Framing Processes and Social Movements: An Overview and Assessment," *Annual Review of Sociology* 26 (2000): 611–39.

13. On the politics of U.S. bases in Central Asia, see Alexander Cooley, *Base Politics: Political Change and Security Contracts in the American Periphery* (Ithaca, NY: Cornell UP, 2008), chapter 7.

14. See the vivid illustrations offered by focus groups participants in 1994 Kyrgyzstan in Richard B. Dobson, *Kyrgyzstan and the World: A Report on Ten Focus Groups* (Washington, DC: U.S. Information Agency, October 1995), 11–14.

15. In Kazakhstan, where I conducted the bulk of my field research in 1997 and 1998, this usually took the form of resentment against foreign multinational corporations—perceived to be American—for plundering the region's natural resources. Such sentiments had become even more common by 2002.

16. I devised a coding instrument that took into account challenges highlighted in a pilot coding. Mark Mills used that instrument to code all the data. Tobin Grant was generous with his time and expertise on how to manage and present the data. The data give a glimpse into the changing dynamic, but they must be considered incomplete by themselves. The larger book project of which this essay is a part also examines changing depictions of the United States in Central Asian (Russian- and titular-language) newspapers.

17. The deep surprise that U.S. policy makers and analysts experienced when Islam Karimov, the authoritarian president of Uzbekistan, evicted U.S. forces from its Karshy-Khanabad airbase in 2005 illustrates the general pro-American pattern in government.

18. The upsurge in pro-American attitudes among Russians in late 2001 is attributable to the outpouring of sympathy toward the United States in the immediate aftermath of the September 11, 2001, attacks. More recent events have shown this to be temporary, of course.

19. While governments usually do not assume the costs of alienating or antagonizing the United States, societal actors do not usually feel so constrained. This divergence is the source of tension in many contexts, whereby societal actors question the legitimacy of local governments if they perceive the latter to be too closely allied with the United States. As I address below, a similar process has occurred in Central Asia.

20. The fragmentation of the IRP continued even within some states. In Russia, the All-Russia IRP dissolved by 1993–1994 into regional parties. Some of them had an ethnic tinge; some had a more radical Islamist tinge.

21. Saodat Olimova, "Islam and the Construction of a National State in Central Asia," in Keiko Sakai, ed., *Social Protests and Nation-Building in the Middle East and Central Asia* (Chiba, Japan: Institute of Developing Economies, 2003), 174–75. Igor Rotar suggests that some observers of the IRPT adopt the view that the organization was both fundamentalist (calling for strict implementation of Shariah) and militant (calling for violent struggle as a tactic) even in the Soviet period. This is a minority viewpoint. See his *Pod zelenym znamenem: Islamskie radikaly v Rossii i SNG* (Moscow: Assosiiatsiia Isledovatelei Rossiiskogo Obshchestva XX veka, 2001), 62.

22. Rotar (ibid., 64) reports that in private interviews, IRPT leader Muhammadsharif Khimmatzoda was forthcoming about a desire eventually to create an Islamic state. Nonetheless, the overwhelming public face of the organization was of an ordinary party that played at pragmatic politics.

23. In other parts of the former USSR, the pattern was similar—little Islamic activism of any kind in the early 1990s, more in the late 1990s. In Chechnya an ethnic separatist movement acquired more Islamist militant content after Moscow's first wave of military operations against the republic that began in December 1994. Moscow's brutality toward the region both radicalized indigenous Islamist groups and attracted foreign mercenaries. See Brian Williams, "Unraveling the Links between the Middle East and Islamic Militants in Chechnya," *Central Asia-Caucasus Analyst*, Feb. 12, 2003.

24. HT makes clear its nonviolent tactics, but some analysts believe that membership in HT and that of more militant groups are not mutually exclusive. See, for example, Ahmed Rashid, *Jihad: The Rise of Militant Islam in Central Asia* (New Haven, CT: Yale UP, 2002), 132–36.

25. Kazakhstan was the last of the five states to ban possession of HT literature; it did so in 2005.

26. A prominent local official in the spiritual directorate in the South Kazakhstan region admitted in an interview that this appointment had aroused much controversy. Interview, Suleiman Kadyrbai-uly, deputy to the bas-imam, Spiritual Directorate of Muslims of Kazakhstan, South Kazakhstan branch, June 6, 2002. See also Artur Artem'ev, "Eshche raz k voprosu o svobode sovesti i veroterpimosti," *Saiasat* (March 2001): 44–47.

27. These are some of the tropes that emerge from eighteen focus groups conducted in Kazakhstan, Kyrgyzstan, and Tajikistan in 2006. The larger project of which this is a part will provide greater detail and specific voices from these focus groups.

28. Religious freedom is hardly guaranteed in Kazakhstan.

29. Radio Free Europe/Radio Liberty Newsline, vol. 6, no. 106, part I, June 7, 2002, electronic report; and Radio Free Europe/Radio Liberty Newsline, vol. 6, no. 129, part I, July 12, 2002, electronic report.

30. "Those who helped Jews" is a clear reference to the United States.

31. Their regular use was emphasized by Vladimir Zharinov, specialist on links with religious organizations, South Kazakhstan *akimat*, interview, June 6, 2002.

32. The commingling of a variety of symbols that are noxious to the Western eye may raise suspicions about the authenticity of the excerpts. Following Babadzhanov's presentation, a heated discussion ensued about whether the Uzbek intelligence services had falsified such "literature." Igor Rotar of the Keston Institute, which works to safeguard religious freedom in the region, was particularly suspicious of Babadzhanov's documents. In a private conversation afterward, Rotar pointed out to me elements of the presentation that he found unrealistic from those that he found fully plausible. I have discussed only those that Rotar, a serious critic of Uzbekistan's practices on freedom of religion, found plausible.

33. For example, see James N. Druckman, "On the Limits of Framing Effects: Who Can Frame?" *Journal of Politics* 63.4 (2001): 1041–66.

34. Perhaps a more appropriate test would examine how Central Asians respond to *negative* depictions of the United States. After all, Islamists who sought to recruit would rather use negative than positive images. Unfortunately, however, I was unable to secure

IRB approval for the use of negative frames in this survey experiment. Committee members were concerned that my experiment might "cause" Central Asians to hate the United States. Nonetheless, if frames matter, they ought to matter whether depictions are positive or negative.

Works Cited

Asad, Talal. "Muslims and European Identity: Can Europe Represent Islam?" *The Idea of Europe: From Antiquity to the European Union*. Ed. Anthony Pagden. Washington, DC: Woodrow Wilson Center Press, 2002. 209–227.

Akiner, Shirin. *Tajikistan: Disintegration or Reconciliation*. London: Royal Institute of International Affairs, 2001.

Artem'ev, Artur. "Eshche raz k voprosu o svobode sovesti i veroterpimosti." *Saiasat* (March 2001).

Babadzhanov, Bakhtiar. "Teologicheskoe obosnovanie i etapy dzhikhada v dokladakh Islamskogo dvizheniia Uzbekistana." Paper presented at Organization for Security and Cooperation in Europe conference, "Islam and National Security in Central Asia," Almaty, Kazakhstan, June 24–25, 2002.

Benford, Robert, and David Snow. "Framing Processes and Social Movements: An Overview and Assessment." *Annual Review of Sociology* 26 (2000): 611–39.

Botobekov, Uran. "Vnedrenie idei islamskoi partii 'Hizb at-Takhrir' na iuge Kyrgyzstana." *Islam na postsovetskom prostranstve: vzgliad iznutri*. Ed. Aleksandr Malashenko and Martha Brill Olcott. Moscow: Moskovskii Tsentr Karnegi, 2001.

Cooley, Alexander. *Base Politics: Political Change and Security Contracts in the American Periphery*. Ithaca, NY: Cornell UP, 2008.

Council on Foreign Relations. *Finding America's Voice: A Strategy for Reinvigorating U.S. Public Diplomacy*. New York: Council on Foreign Relations. 2003.

Dobaev, Igor. "Radical Islamism in the Northern Caucasus." *Central Asia and the Caucasus* 11.1 (2000): 76–86.

Dobson, Richard B. *Kyrgyzstan and the World: A Report on Ten Focus Groups*. U.S. Information Agency. October 1995. 11–14.

Douglas, Mary. *Purity and Danger: An Analysis of the Concepts of Pollution and Taboo*. London: Routledge and Kegan Paul, 1966.

Druckman, James N. "On the Limits of Framing Effects: Who Can Frame?" *Journal of Politics* 63.4 (2001): 1041–66.

Euben, Roxanne L. *Enemy in the Mirror: Islamic Fundamentalism and the Limits of Modern Rationalism*. Princeton, NJ: Princeton UP, 1999.

Gellner, Ernest. *Muslim Society*. Cambridge, UK: Cambridge UP, 1981.

Goffman, Erving. *Frame Analysis*. Cambridge, MA: Harvard UP, 1974.

Grebenschikov, Igor. "The Hizb ut-Tahrir through the Eyes of Kyrgyz Journalists." *Media Insight Central Asia* 22 (2002). Available online at https://thehizbuttahrirwatch.files. wordpress.com/2010/12/mica22e-grebenshikov.pdf.

Hefner, Robert W., ed. *Remaking Muslim Politics: Pluralism, Contestation, Democratization*. Princeton, NJ: Princeton UP, 2004.

Institute for War and Peace Reporting Central Asia, No. 130, Part One, July 19, 2002.

International Crisis Group. *The IMU and the Hizb-Ut-Tahrir: Implications of the Afghanistan Campaign*. Brussels: International Crisis Group, 2002.

Kunkler, Mirjam. "Advocating Women's Rights in the Language of Islamic Sacred Texts: The Tripartite Struggle for Women's Rights in Iran." Paper presented at the Association for the Study of Nationalities. April 15–17, 2004.

Lerner, Daniel. *The Passing of Traditional Society: Modernizing the Middle East*. New York: Free Press, 1964 [1958].

Mitchell, Timothy. "American Power and Anti-Americanism in the Middle East." *Anti-Americanism*. Ed. Andrew Ross and Kristen Ross. New York: New York UP, 2004.

Moldaliev, Orozbek. "Islamism and International Terrorism: A Threat of Islam or a Threat to Islam?" *Central Asia and the Caucasus* 5.1 (2002). Available at http://www.ca-c.org/journal/eng-03-2002/10.molprimen.shtml.

Nye, Joseph P. *The Paradox of American Power*. Oxford: Oxford UP, 2002.

Olimova, Saodat. "Islam and the Construction of a National State in Central Asia." *Social Protests and Nation-Building in the Middle East and Central Asia*. Ed. Keiko Sakai. Chiba, Japan: Institute of Developing Economies, 2003: 174–75.

Pannier, Bruce. "Central Asia: Six Months After—Security Still Top Interregional Issue (Part 2)." RFE/RL Central Asia Report, electronic report, March 12, 2002,.

Pope Pius IX. *Quanta Cura* (Condemning Current Errors). Papal Encyclical of 8 December, 1864. http://www.papalencyclicals.net/Pius09/p9quanta.htm.

Radio Free Europe/Radio Liberty Newsline. Vol. 6, no. 106, part I, June 7, 2002, electronic report.

———. Vol. 6, no. 129, part I, July 12, 2002, electronic report.

Rashid, Ahmed. *Jihad: The Rise of Militant Islam in Central Asia*. New Haven, CT: Yale UP, 2002.

Rodenbeck, Max. "Islam Confronts Its Demons." *New York Review of Books*. April 29, 2004, 14–18.

Ro'i, Yaacov. *Islam in the Soviet Union*. New York: Columbia UP, 2000.

Rosefsky Wickham, Carrie. "The Path to Moderation: Strategy and Learning in the Formation of Egypt's *Wasat* Party." *Comparative Politics* 36.2 (2004): 205–228.

Rotar, Igor. *Pod zelenym znamenem: Islamskie radikaly v Rossii i SNG*. Moscow: Assosiiatsiia I'sledovatelei Rossiiskogo Obshchestva XX veka, 2001.

———. "Tsentral'naia Aziia—sleduiushchaia mishen' ekstremistov." *Nezavisimaia gazeta*, Sept. 14, 2001.

Roy, Olivier. *The Foreign Policy of the Central Asian Islamic Renaissance Party*. New York: Council on Foreign Relations, 2000.

Savin, Igor. "'Hizb-ut-takhrir' v Iuzhnom Kazakhstane: sotsial'nyi portret iavleniia." Paper presented at the conference "Globalizatsiia i dialog konfesii v Tsentral'noi Azii," June 21, 2002.

Seleny, Anna. "Tradition, Modernity, and Democracy: The Many Promises of Islam." *Perspectives on Politics* 4.3 (2006): 481–94.

Sidikov, Bahodir. "Religious Context in Uzbekistan: Roots and Sources." *Central Asia and the Caucasus* 9.1 (2000). Available at http://www.ca-c.org/journal/eng-05-2000/07.sidik.shtml.

Wedeen, Lisa. "Conceptualizing Culture: Possibilities for Political Science." *American Political Science Review* 96.4 (2002): 713–28.

Williams, Brian. "Unraveling the Links between the Middle East and Islamic Militants in Chechnya." *Central Asia-Caucasus Analyst*. Feb. 12, 2003. http://old.cacianalyst.org/?q=node/901.

Manar Shorbagy on Edward Schatz

Edward Schatz's essay contributes to our understanding of anti-Americanism, especially in its relationship to Islamist activism. My goal in this commentary is to introduce some points for critical reflection by putting the relationship between anti-Americanism and Islamist activism in a broader context.

Living in Egypt, the birthplace of the Muslim Brothers, the first grassroots Islamist organization with now transnational reach, I was struck by the conclusion of the essay, which suggested that in order to combat Islamist activism, the United States must undermine anti-Americanism. The problem with this statement has to do with both making the combat of "Islamist activism" a legitimate U.S. goal and with the presumed ways in which anti-Americanism can be undermined. The goal of combating all different forms of "Islamic activism" in places like the Middle East is at once counterproductive and futile. In my view, such a policy will stimulate both anti-Americanism and Islamic activism.

In many countries across the Muslim world, Islamic political activism is only part of a broader phenomenon that manifests itself intellectually, culturally, and politically. Moreover, the Islamists who are active politically are highly diverse intellectually, and they do not necessarily have the same goals nor adopt the same tactics and means. In fact, some Islamists, like both the Salafists and the Muslim Brothers of Kuwait and the Justice and Development Party in Morocco are friendly to the United States. At the same time, it is rarely noticed that some of the Islamists in Egypt who use anti-American rhetoric are far less antagonistic to the United States than the left, for example. In many Muslim countries, from Turkey to Morocco, Islamic activism is at the heart of political action, and it is as legitimate in the minds of the average people as the liberal, leftist, and Nasserist political projects. Singling out one of the major trends and working to undermine it will most likely backfire. Just imagine a plan to combat religious activism in the United States, especially if the plan is a foreign one!

In other words, the Islamist trend is here to stay, and for the United States to combat one of the major cultural, intellectual, and political trends is hubris at best. Besides, launching an all-out assault on anything "Islamic," despite the real differences among different kinds of activism, not only generates anti-Americanism but also helps the more fanatic elements at the expense of moderation within the Islamic trend. A better goal for the sole superpower is to respect the phenomenon and learn how to differentiate between the violent and nonviolent elements within the broader transnational Islamic movement.

Schatz rightly argued that Islam is not inherently anti-American nor does Islamic activism necessarily generate anti-Americanism. As he has shown in central Asia, anti-Americanism preceded Islamic activism. The case of Egypt not only supports Schatz's argument but also sharpens it. Just as in central Asia, the United States was demonized during the Nasser socialist era. Sadat's turn to the West by the mid-1970s had the promise of prosperity American-style. Besides, amid the negotiations of the Egyptian-Israeli peace accord, Anwar Sadat had famously argued that 99 percent of the Arab-Israeli conflict is in the hands of the United States. Although anti-Americanism existed as a direct response to Sadat's policies, it had become more intense when none of his promises of peace and prosperity materialized. Anti-Americanism in the late 1970s was by no means a singularly Islamic phenomenon. In the 1970s politicians and activists from the far left to the far right stood out against Sadat's peace accord and the United States' role in concluding it. Those who ended up in prison in Sadat's massive campaign against his opponents, just weeks before his assassination, were Marxists, Nasserists, liberals, and Islamists. In the twenty-first century it is not just the Islamists in Egypt who are against the U.S. invasion and occupation of Iraq, the abuses of Guantanamo, and the infamous U.S. "double standard" when it comes to the Arab-Israeli conflict. Even so, on particular issues like the U.S.-backed neoliberal economic policies, the strongest and most vocal opposition comes from non-Islamist quarters. It is obvious that in the case of Egypt, anti-Americanism goes far beyond the Islamist activism.

While symbolism does matter in analyzing how different political forces in Egypt define, portray, and manipulate the United States in their own discourse, the thesis that argues that U.S. policies are the main source of anti-Americanism may in fact be the most helpful to both understand anti-Americanism in Egypt and to develop strategies to combat it. When different forces interpret the politics of the United States and use these interpretations in Egypt, they more often than not do it on the basis of specific policies. It is striking that in Central Asia, as is clear in Schatz's essay, when the Islamist activists started using anti-American rhetoric it was about U.S. policies, be it the "double standards with regards to democracy" or the "United States' role in the Middle East" as Schatz put it. Besides, in Egypt the American presence is so real and overwhelming and the U.S. policies are so dominant that in order to make up their mind about the United States, Egyptians need neither mobilization nor activists to interpret the country for them. The anti-Americanism in Egypt is not a reflection of America as a society and culture; rather, it is a reflection of the influence of that great power on Egypt's present and future. The current Egyptian discourse about the United

States is highly similar to the discourse against the United Kingdom. In the late nineteenth century and the early twentieth century, the United Kingdom was the colonizing force. Today, the United States is the power that practices hegemony and dominates Egyptian national and international decision making in ways that are perceived to be contrary to the national interest. It is also worth noting that in Egypt, American "social values" hardly appear in the anti-American discourse of mainstream activists, Islamic or otherwise. Moreover, the United States' political values, such as pluralism and term limits, are widely appreciated by the same actors who are vocal against particular U.S. policies.

The main weakness of the symbolism thesis is that it does not help in answering the "how" question when it comes to combating anti-Americanism. The United States' public diplomacy since September 11, 2001, has largely failed in the Muslim world because it focused on initiatives to showcase the American "values," while the reality is that these values are deeply appreciated by the same political forces and even the average people who strongly oppose the U.S. policies. It makes little sense to defend American values when they are not under attack while failing to address the policies that do generate deep resentments.

Edward Schatz on Manar Shorbagy

In her contribution, Manar Shorbagy tells two stories about the Egyptian political movement Kefaya. The first is a story of Kefaya's rise, which weaves together strands of domestic and international politics, emphasizing the generation of leadership that came to political consciousness when Nasserism failed to make good on its promise of defending Egypt against Western encroachments. The second is a story of how U.S. influence in the Middle East proved crucial in helping to forge this new, trans-ideological movement. Although the policies of the Bush administration loom large in this second story, U.S. foreign policy toward the region has a long, and often troubled, history.

Taken together, the Kefaya stories confer upon Egyptians real agency as they navigate the challenges of ongoing political currents and forge their own futures. I applaud Shorbagy for keeping our sights squarely on such agency, for most analyses that consider the U.S. role depict it to be so all-determining that little space is left for much more than pure geopolitics.

Her insights find interesting parallels in the Central Asian cases. As in Central Asia, the rise of political movements cannot and should not be reduced to foreign interference. Yes, Hizb-ut Tahrir in Central Asia and Kefaya in Egypt are in part reacting to perceptions of U.S. influence, but these perceptions are filtered through domestic lenses that themselves are the product of prior imaginings of domestic politics, society, and culture. As a result, U.S. foreign policy does not travel a straight line as it generates its impact on domestic (in this case Egyptian) society and politics.

Of course, even though it is experienced indirectly and in highly mediated fashion, U.S. influence is palpable. Shorbagy is therefore right to aver that "U.S. policy in the region produces the very resistance to its policies that it seeks to undermine." In Central Asia, close ties between a repressive Uzbekistani regime and the Bush administration emboldened Uzbek dictator Islam Karimov to engage in dragnet operations that ensnare ordinary pious Muslims, sending them to long prison terms. In prison they learn the very political ideologies that Karimov and the Bush administration fear most.

Also as in Central Asia, Kefaya goes to great lengths to distance itself from the Bush administration's strategies for promoting democracy. In Kyrgyzstan, for example, human rights activists in the mid-2000s found it increasingly difficult to depict their agendas as being based on universally held human values when the United States had become so discredited as a purveyor and protector of such values.

While Shorbagy's attention to U.S. policy is welcome, we know that ordinary people and political actors form their opinions and pursue their agendas not solely based on policy calculations. Central Asians in the 1990s had begun to question their initially rosy picture of the United States not because of particular policy decisions of the Clinton administration (though the bombing of Kosovo in 1999 did generate some unease across broad swaths of the population), but because of a secular decline in their view of Western (and especially American) cultural products and economic and political models. In fact, U.S. foreign policy was barely visible in the 1990s in Central Asia, and yet Central Asians over the decade became deeply ambivalent about the United States.

If the story of popular support for, or opposition to, the United States is not reducible to concrete and identifiable U.S. foreign policies, then several questions about Kefaya follow. First, is Kefaya as a trans-ideological movement that unites Islamists with secular democrats and others likely to survive the Obama administration, the next U.S. president, their different foreign policy choices, and at times very different rhetoric? Shorbagy writes that "they no longer need foreign policy issues to preserve their interactive project intact." Could one imagine a thoroughly revamped U.S. foreign policy that would, perhaps because of its evenhandedness, serve (though not by design) to drive a wedge among different divisions within the movement?

Second, and related, will Kefaya for its own survival as a movement need to move beyond critiques of "foreign threats and political despotism" and demonstrate its efficacy to the broader public? The Muslim Brotherhood, for example, engages in social service provision and public works projects, creating material change that it can trot out as "evidence" of a superior approach. Kefaya is a young movement, but as it becomes institutionalized in various ways, ordinary Egyptians may start to expect more than a principled and persuasive critique of existing domestic and foreign policies. Of course, in one plausible scenario, Kefaya activists could suffer repression at the hands of an autocratic state; were this to occur, they might continue to enjoy public sympathy.

Finally, Kefaya clearly enjoys Shorbagy's sympathy and U.S. foreign policy does not. But I wonder if Iraq is necessarily a "quagmire" and if U.S. policy is really "crippled" in any long-term sense. Is it possible that the new U.S. administration could creatively engineer new modes of engagement in the region that are much less beholden to old patterns of behavior? To imagine such possibilities is to maintain space for new forms of politics to emerge. What happens to movements like Kefaya in such shifting currents is anybody's guess.

Seyed Mohammad Marandi on Schatz and Shorbagy

What Is Anti-Americanism?

As I was watching the bombing of Baghdad live on television, someone was enthusiastically explaining how "smart bombs" were being used by the Americans for "surgical strikes." I remembered how just over a decade before I heard almost the same words as I listened to the BBC World Service early in 1991. On both occasions I was in shock and awe as I watched, heard, and read American (and British) analysts as well as journalists explain, often with pride, the latest technology in weapons systems and how they were being used to deal with Saddam Hussein. They seemed to be trying to forget, and to help the rest of us forget, what these weapons were doing to countless families and children. Also forgotten was the fact that the Iraqi dictator was for many years their close ally who received weapons of mass destruction from Western countries to use against Iranians as well as his own people.

I remember the picture of a dead Afghan family that I put on the bulletin board in the postgraduate suite at my university in the United Kingdom. American aircraft had bombed an Afghan home, and I vaguely remember the photo showed a man crying beside the bodies of his eight children. A young American student became very angry when she saw the photo. She didn't know that I put it there, but she felt that the photo on the bulletin board was a sign of someone's ignorance and anti-Americanism. A couple of days later a drawing of the United States was posted beside the photo of the dead children. It ridiculed what it saw as an almost complete ignorance on behalf of non-Americans, and more specifically "anti-Americanists," about American culture and society.

The photo of the dead children wasn't taken down, but it was clear that it did not have the desired effect, at least on this tall and blond American PhD student. She saw it in a very different light. For her, it was probably a sign that I wasn't able to grasp the heart of the matter, that the American people are good and decent. Maybe she even thought all of what was happening was imposed upon America and that it had no option but to defend itself. I don't know and I never asked about her politics.

What is anti-Americanism, and am I ideologically bound to anti-Americanism? When I watch CNN sing in praise of the U.S. response to the tragic 2010 earthquake in Haiti and I ask myself, "How responsible is the United States for Haiti's poverty and poor infrastructure, and how many people died as a result?" am I being anti-American? Is this a sign of a systematic opposition to the United States and everything American?

On the other hand, Noam Chomsky provides a significantly different perspective to the term. He states that the counterpart of the term "anti-American"

> is used only in totalitarian states or military dictatorships, something I wrote about many years ago (see my book *Letters from Lexington*). Thus, in the old Soviet Union, dissidents were condemned as "anti-Soviet." That's a natural usage among people with deeply rooted totalitarian instincts, which identify state policy with the society, the people, the culture. In contrast, people with even the slightest concept of democracy treat such notions with ridicule and contempt. Suppose someone in Italy who criticizes Italian state policy were condemned as "anti-Italian." It would be regarded as too ridiculous even to merit laughter. Maybe under Mussolini, but surely not otherwise.

As an American citizen who also views the United States from an Iranian perspective, it does not take much effort for me to see why many in the United States view Iran as systematically and irrationally opposed to anything and everything American. Nevertheless, it also seems clear that Iranian grievances are many and that they are legitimate.

For many the term "anti-Americanism" seems to work like a tool that prevents criticism of the United States from breaking through a glass ceiling. It frames the narrative and helps depict sharp criticism of the United States as irrational and excessive. Its function is viewed as similar to that of the term "anti-Semitism." Those who criticize Israel for its Zionist ideology and compare it to apartheid South Africa are quickly branded as anti-Semites, despite the fact that the displaced and oppressed Palestinian people are Semites themselves. Hence, any sharp criticism of Israeli tribalism, racism, or prejudice against Palestinians can, ironically, lead to the critic being accused of anti-Semitism, thus managing the debate over Palestine.

Hence, when in "Kefaya and the New Politics of Anti-Americanism," Manar Shorbagy states that "anti-Americanism played a huge role in fusing the forces that became 'Kefaya'" and that this Egyptian movement "represents an alternative model of resistance to American empire, at once pacifist, yet adamantly anti-American," one could imagine how differently these statements could be interpreted by different people. Hence, while Shorbagy seems to equate resistance to the American empire with anti-Americanism, in "Understanding Anti-Americanism in Central Asia," Edward Schatz seems to view the term quite differently.

Here Schatz seems to believe that anti-Americanism is irrational and that those who are anti-American actually blame the United States for problems that have little to do with America. He also seems to conclude that anti-Americanism is not very widespread in the Middle East when he states that "inherency arguments predict far greater anti-Americanism than occurs empirically." He presents a number of reasons why the views of Central Asians toward the United States declined in the late 1990s in comparison to what he saw as more favorable perceptions earlier in the decade (whether his methodology for assessing attitudes about the United States is sound or not is another issue). These reasons include the following:

> Soviet-era depictions of the United States were still fresh in the public's memory. The image of American capital and products dominating new markets resonated with Soviet propaganda about the United States as the champion of the exploitative classes. The images of race relations and crime-ridden inner cities that many low-quality Hollywood films depicted echoed Soviet propaganda about American domestic exploitation. Finally, images of the United States as a global hegemon resonated with Soviet propaganda about American expansionist ambitions. Their accuracy or lack thereof is beside the point; these images were appealing because they were familiar.

From his conclusion it seems that Schatz believes that the claims made against the United States are not accurate, and he warns U.S. foreign policy actors that "to disengage from image construction as a part of foreign policy is to resign to living with, and contending with, the images that other global and local actors craft."

Shorbagy, on the other hand, takes a far more critical view of the role played by the United States in Egyptian as well as Middle Eastern politics. She begins her article with the notorious statement made by Condoleezza Rice about "the birth pangs of a new Middle East" during the Israeli onslaught against Lebanese civilians and the country's infrastructure during the 2006 war. Shorbagy then goes on to explain how the U.S. invasion and occupation of Iraq as well as its use of "shock and awe" to intimidate or destroy any opposition to the American takeover of the country actually helped create the Kefaya movement in Egypt as well as resistance and anti-Americanism throughout the world. That is one reason why she views Kefaya's pacific resistance to the "American empire" as being "adamantly anti-American" in nature. She also states that U.S. funding in the civil and political arena as a vehicle for "democratic change" effectively corrupts the political elite and creates "pressure to set agendas and even select future leaders for the country."

While Schatz believes that the fundamental problem for the United States is image construction, Shorbagy believes that the real threat to the interests of the country lies in its foreign policy. She also contradicts Schatz and says that anti-Americanism is widespread and that it is very much a part of mainstream politics in Egypt, both among the religious and the secular.

After reading these two articles, it seems clear that there is a sharp divide over the nature of American hegemony but also that the two scholars have conflicting views regarding the definition of "anti-Americanism." This is a serious problem, because if there is no clear definition of what the term actually means, then using it can only create unnecessary confusion. Therefore, for me the question remains "What is anti-Americanism?"

Works Cited

Chomsky, Noam. "Is Chomsky Anti-American?" Noam Chomsky interview by Jacklyn Martin. *Herald.* Dec. 9, 2002. http://www.chomsky.info/interviews/20021209.htm.

Ira Dworkin on Schatz and Shorbagy

Thinking Outside of America
The State, the Street, and Civil Society

In her essay describing Egypt before the revolution of January–February 2011, Manar Shorbagy writes a rich history of Kefaya, a major activist coalition that came together during the final years of the reign of President Hosni Mubarak. Shorbagy usefully points to some of the political alliances, often unlikely and sometimes fleeting, that resulted in the overthrow of Mubarak. She describes how Kefaya refused foreign funding as a way to maintain its political independence, a decision that has proven both credible and prescient. In his response, Mohammad Marandi, citing Noam Chomsky, correctly points out that this decision should be understood as a matter of anti-imperialism rather than anti-Americanism, since criticism of a state does not make one "anti." The notion that international critics of the United States are motivated by anti-Americanism serves the strategic purpose of diminishing the very substance of their criticisms. At its extreme, as Timothy Mitchell has written, perceived anti-Americanism, "the widely accepted view that Arabs hated America, portraying Iraq as the extreme form of a latent Arab desire to harm the United States," becomes the rationale for war (88). As an American Studies scholar, I take particular interest in the stakes of deploying discourses of Americanism in ways that undermine and overwhelm important conversations inside and outside the field.

This binary system of categorization is often used to shift conversations away from what is most important in the history of organizations like Kefaya in ways that recall Herman Melville's *Benito Cereno*, a text I taught regularly during my six years as a professor in Cairo. The literary work, which recounts the historic rebellion of African captives aboard the *Tryal* slave ship off the coast of Chile, has an American protagonist, while the actual historical narrative is clearly driven by the African rebels. The naïve white American sailor Amassa Delano happens upon the ship (renamed the *San Dominick* by Melville in allusion to the Haitian revolution) and mistakenly believes what he sees—that the now former captives are slaves. The Africans perform their expected roles for the benefit of an American audience that includes the uncritical Delano, who is so blinded by racism and self-interest that he is literally unable to comprehend the possibility of a massive rebellion. Melville's readers, in turn, are misled to share in the character's perspective. Melville dramatizes this myopia—the true protagonist of the rebellion, Babo, refuses to testify in his trial, and after his execution his silenced head is placed on public display as a cautionary reminder. The absence of Babo's voice from the official record in *Benito Cereno* furthers the American's inability to imagine what really matters—the fifty-three days that the people on board the ship experienced freedom and the world historical ways that African rebellion shapes the New and Old Worlds.[1]

American Studies scholars must be careful to not replicate what Greg Grandin describes as "Delano's complete and utter blindness to the social world around him," by seeing anti-Americanism as the heart of activism in the Middle East and North Africa ("Capitalism and Slavery"). Consider, for example, the attention that U.S. ambassador to Egypt Anne Patterson received in the U.S. press as a target of the June 2013 protests that brought down the regime of Muslim Brotherhood president Mohamed Mursi. To focus on Patterson, as the *Washington Post* did, is to miss the larger and more important stakes of political change in Egypt (Fisher). Patterson's insulting and ill-informed comments (not initially covered by the *Washington Post*) arguing against street protests in the days leading up to the huge street protests that brought down Mursi demonstrate a knowledge of Egypt: "I recommend Egyptians get organized. Join or start a political party that reflects your values and aspirations." The new Egyptian regime, installed in part through the "street action" of which she declares the United States "skeptical" (Patterson), responded to the "street action" of others with brutal violence on August 14, 2013, when, after weeks of demonizing pro-Mursi sit-ins as security threats to the electoral and constitutional processes of orderly democracy, government forces killed at least 817 demonstrators at Rab'a and al-Nahda (Human Rights Watch 6).

"Street action" has its own rich tradition in the United States, which my students appreciated as they themselves experienced profoundly new forms of social mobilization after the revolutions of 2011. An American Studies project that is concerned with the functioning of state power takes deep interest in the lessons that groups like Kefaya provide on the importance of strong civil society institutions. Those institutions have been consistently under threat in Egypt, often condemned for their purported pro-Americanism. In 2012, Faiza Abouelnaga, a former Mubarak cabinet minister, famously led the charge against several U.S.-backed NGOs, including some associated with the Democratic and Republican parties, for illegally operating in Egypt (Londoño). While this is especially ironic given the amount of aid that the Egyptian government she represents receives from the United States, this strategy is not new. Mitchell describes how the Mubarak regime sanctioned a Muslim Brotherhood protest against the 2003 U.S.

invasion of Iraq, effectively appropriating "a form of popular anti-Americanism, which operates as a means to circumscribe and weaken the Left" (99). While the influence of the United States in the Middle East and North Africa is real, the caricature of political movements as pro- or anti-American serve to stifle dynamic civil society actors who are important critics of the state.

More recently, Mursi's successor, Abdel Fattah al-Sisi, appointed Abouelnaga as national security advisor as he set a November 2014 deadline requiring NGOs to register under the Mubarak-era Law 84 of 2002, which is purported to curtail the influence of foreign money, including (and especially) American dollars, on Egyptian civil society (*Mada Masr*, "Mubarak-Era Minister"). NGOs have refused and resisted—not because they are under U.S. influence, but because the principles of civil society demand that they remain independent of all state institutions. Many NGOs have responded to the enforcement of these laws by shutting down or otherwise refusing the directive (Farid). The climate is such that international groups like Human Rights Watch and the Carter Center have closed their Cairo offices, and the Cairo Institute for Human Rights Studies moved its regional operations to Tunisia (Kortam). The Egyptian military government's proclamation of itself as the protector of Egypt from outside influence conveniently limits the work of its political opposition.

Among Egyptian NGOs, the Ibn Khaldun Center, where Patterson made her remarks in opposition to public protest, has been at the center of these debates. At the Khaldun Center, the executive director resigned after the founder wrote an article criticizing al-Sisi's crackdown on NGOs receiving foreign funds as hypocritical (Al-Tawy). Fundamentally, the conflict was about whether or not the Khaldun Center should maintain its independence as a critic of the government or whether to back the regime. In July 2014 a coalition of Egyptian human rights organizations wrote a letter opposing "the extent to which the government seeks to impose its complete control over civic groups and subordinate them to security and administrative bodies" ("Proposed Government Law"). Their fears proved correct. Through the first half of 2015, the Ministry of Social Solidarity closed more than four hundred NGOs, mostly on the basis of either their affiliation with the Muslim Brotherhood, a designated terrorist organization, or their receipt of foreign funding (*Mada Masr*, "Social Solidarity Ministry"). In May 2015 another coalition of human rights groups issued a statement decrying the enforcement of registration laws, the reopening of foreign funding cases, the imposition of travel bans on NGO staff, and a series of arrests of activists, including Ahmed Samih, the director of the Andalus Center for Tolerance and Anti-Violence Studies and Radio Horytna. These groups, which experience ongoing harassment by security forces, recognize that the foreign funding investigation, for instance, is "merely a cover for a vicious political-security campaign against rights groups" (Al-Tawy). At a time when progressive human rights organizations and brotherhood-affiliated NGOs are struggling to maintain their autonomy, Shorbagy's report on the pre-2011 history of Kefaya is a timely reminder of the vibrant variety of civil society actors that made the "Arab Spring" possible.

The discourse of anti-Americanism runs the risk of obfuscating some core political issues in Edward Schatz's essay, which compiles rich data from under-studied countries in Central Asia. For Schatz, "image construction" is a desirable tool of foreign policy, and he believes that the United States should "undermine anti-Americanism abroad." Schatz argues that perceptions of the United States do not correlate directly with U.S. policy in Central Asia, which makes sense if "policy" is defined as a series of direct local measures rather than as a longer cu-mulative history of imperial intervention in the region and beyond. Amid bilateral changes in relations, many broader issues that drive supposed "anti-Americanism" remain: its unquestioning support of Israel, its financing of military dictator-ships, its use of drones, its invasions and occupations of countries throughout the world, its increasingly restrictive visa policies, and its own increasingly visible (and for many abroad terrifyingly familiar) forms of domestic police violence. Shorbagy's response to Schatz takes issue "with the presumed ways in which anti-Americanism can be undermined." With Schatz's emphasis on public diplomacy, neither policy change nor social movements seem to register as significant forces capable of transforming international attitudes toward the United States.

These debates about anti-Americanism hold useful lessons for American Stud-ies, which as a discipline must not be confused with public diplomacy, a particular risk on the international stage. The need to maintain its independence from gov-ernment influence is shared with other academic programs in area studies, which must remain vigilant of the ways that, as William G. Martin and Brendan Innis McQuade argue in the case of African Studies centers, U.S. government funding, coupled with a reduction of Title VI funding, has effectively "redirect[ed] aspiring scholars on a career path of service with agencies carrying our national security work" (445). At the American University in Cairo, the Prince Alwaleed Bin Talal Bin Abdul Aziz Alsaud Center for American Studies and Research (CASAR), where I worked as associate director from 2012 to 2014, was conceptualized in a conversation that the prince had with Edward Said following the events of September 11, 2011, when New York mayor Rudolph Giuliani refused to accept a donation to rebuild the city because it came with the modest suggestion that the United States take this opportunity to reflect on its perception and policies in the Middle East, particularly as they relate to unwavering U.S. government support for Israel and its brutal occupation of Palestine (Said; Lubin). While many American Studies centers in the region receive direct support from the U.S. government, Said saw an opening to move beyond government-sponsored neoliberal attempts at mutual understanding. Here, American Studies should take a lesson from Kefaya in recognizing that the support of the U.S. government can only be a corrupting influence and that the challenge for the discipline, shared in some modest sense with activists, is how to build a credible and critical space for our work, which can and should be dynamic enough to contain a full range of discourses from the Middle East rather than only paying attention to what they might be saying about "us."

Notes

The author would like to thank Walid El Hamamsy for providing feedback on an earlier version of this essay.

1. For the definitive historical account of the *Tryal* rebellion, see Greg Grandin, *Empire of Necessity: Slavery, Freedom, and Deception in the New World* (New York: Metropolitan Books, 2014).

Works Cited

Al-Tawy, Ayat. "Egyptian Government Clamps Down on Rights Groups, Seeking their Eradication." *Newstime Africa*. May 5, 2015. http://http://www.newstimeafrica.com/archives/39092.

———. "Egyptian Rights Group Divided over Pro-Regime Support." *Ahram Online*. Nov.16, 2014. http://english.ahram.org.eg/NewsContent/1/64/115654/Egypt/Politics-/Egyptian-rights-group-divided-over-proregime-suppo.aspx.

Farid, Sonia. "Fate of Egyptian NGOs Hangs in the Balance." *Al Arabiya News*. Nov. 14, 2014. http://english.alarabiya.net/en/perspective/analysis/2014/11/14/Fate-of-Egyptian-NGOs-hangs-in-the-balance.html.

Fisher, Max. "Egypt's Protesters Find a New Villain: The U.S. Ambassador." *Washington Post*. July 1, 2013. https://www.washingtonpost.com/news/worldviews/wp/2013/07/01/egypts-protesters-find-a-new-villain-the-u-s-ambassador.

Grandin, Greg. "Capitalism and Slavery." *Nation*. May 1, 2015. https://www.thenation.com/article/capitalism-and-slavery.

———. *Empire of Necessity: Slavery, Freedom, and Deception in the New World*. New York: Metropolitan Books, 2014.

Human Rights Watch. *All According to Plan: The Rab'a Massacre and Mass Killings of Protesters in Egypt*. [New York]: Human Rights Watch, August 2014.

Kortam, Hend. "NGO to Move International Programmes Abroad Due to 'War on Civil Society.'" *Daily News Egypt*. Dec. 9, 2014. http://www.dailynewsegypt.com/2014/12/09/ngo-move-international-programmes-abroad-due-war-civil-society.

Londoño, Ernesto. "Architect of Egypt's NGO Crackdown Is Mubarak Holdover." *Washington Post*. Feb. 7, 2012. https://www.washingtonpost.com/world/middle_east/architect-of-egypts-ngo-crackdown-is-mubarak-holdover/2012/02/07/gIQAk9mgxQ_story.html.

Lubin, Alex. "American Studies, the Middle East, and the Question of Palestine." *American Quarterly* 68.1 (2016): 1–21.

Mada Masr. "Mubarak-Era Minister, Foreign Funding Crusader Breaks into Security Sector." *Mada Masr*. Nov. 7, 2014. http://www.madamasr.com/news/mubarak-era-minister-foreign-funding-crusader-breaks-security-sector.

———. "Social Solidarity Ministry Shutters at Least 39 More NGOs, Over 400 Closed This Year." *Mada Masr*. July 8, 2015. http://www.madamasr.com/news/social-solidarity-ministry-shutters-least-39-more-ngos-over-400-closed-year.

Martin, William G., and Brendan Innis McQuade. "Militarising—and Marginalising?—African Studies USA." *Review of African Political Economy* 41.141 (2014): 441–57.

Mitchell, Timothy. "American Power and Anti-Americanism in the Middle East." *Anti-Americanism*. Eds. Andrew Ross and Kristin Ross. New York: New York University Press, 2004. 87–105.

Patterson, Anne. "Ambassador Anne W. Patterson's Speech at the Ibn Khaldun Center for Development Studies." June 18, 2013. http://egypt.usembassy.gov/pr061813a.html.

"Proposed Government Law Makes NGOs Subordinate to Security and Ministry Control." Joint Press Release. July 9, 2014. http://www.andalusitas.net/News/Details/06d4232b-a445-46db-8e6e-848bd5b772f4.

Said, Edward. "The Other America." *Al Ahram Weekly*. March 20, 2003.

PART IV

Visual Engagements and Their Interpretations

CHAPTER 7

Lost and Found in Translation

Problems of Cultural Translation in Hungary after 1989

Zsófia Bán

Unfamiliar cities make you acutely aware of the advantages or shortcomings of your own. In Boston, whenever I take the subway at Porter Square, the station closest to where I live, I'm always filled with a kind of hopeless longing when I admire the large, playful mobile sculpture standing at the entrance, a complex, colorful structure with paddles seemingly moved by the wind, but in reality, I assume, by electricity. This, I sigh, is what we Hungarians would so badly need: this playfulness, levity, and freedom of spirit—possibly gained by some freedom from the burden of history—to produce public art, as Macbeth would say, *signifying nothing*. Of course, I am not referring to differences between abstract and figurative art but to the lack of purpose or mission other than pure aesthetic pleasure or play. Even though art in public places is, as Sanford Levinson has written, "almost always the product of some instrumental purpose outside the domain of pure aesthetics" and hence art with "political resonance" (39), the greater the number of exceptions to this rule, the greater the cultural difference. Even though Hungarian culture's acute need of such playfulness and levity has often been acknowledged, one of the most enduring stereotypes of American culture in Hungary (and elsewhere in Europe) is precisely its supposed "lack of reflectedness" and "lack of depth," its "childishness" and "unserious" nature. In a country like Hungary, where public art is by definition some kind of monument (either to an event, a person, or a political idea), the attitude toward the uses of public space and toward history, memory, and remembrance is fundamentally different from a culture where this is not the case.

Hungarian intellectuals have deplored the Americanization not only of our culture at large but, more specifically, of our history, primarily via Hollywood. The fierce debates, for example, about Steven Spielberg's *Schindler's List* when it came to Hungary focused on questions of legitimacy—that is, whether Americans had the right to deal with issues relevant to "*our* history," "*our* trauma," given their "lack of direct involvement" and thus "lack of knowledge." There is often a stubborn non-acknowledgment or downright refusal of the notion of *cultural gaze*—namely, that there might possibly be other perspectives, attitudes, and motivations different from the ones "we" have sanctified as legitimate to deal with certain issues relevant to our culture and history. In Hungary a film about the Holocaust—a term itself seen as an Americanized, euphemistic version of the notion of "Auschwitz"—that focuses on survival and victory, as Spielberg's film does, instead of the end, the downfall of European culture as we had known it, is unacceptable. These debates are now being revived with the recent launch of *Fateless*, our own—no less problematic—cinematographic memorial to the Holocaust, based on Imre Kertész's book that earned him the Nobel Prize in Literature in 2002. The film, which received the largest funding from the state in the history of Hungarian cinema, is seen by many as having fallen into the same traps for which Spielberg's film was criticized, and hence as a Hollywoodization or Americanization of our history—this time, however, from within, as an act of "self-colonization."

In 1989, with the advent of political transition, Hungary received a unique opportunity to rewrite and reinterpret its own history and culture. After the initial, euphoric phase, that chance turned out to be a largely unsuccessful attempt at coming to terms with the country's past in the previous sixty years. While we were preparing to join the European Union, a frightening revival of old (pre–World War II) political reflexes, rhetoric, motivations, and partisanship could be witnessed, as if a genie had suddenly been let out of the bottle. While the concept of the European Union stressed unity in *diversity* (a concept that implies assimilation to the norm—that is, the norm of the West), Hungary was striving for an affirmation of *difference*, celebrating this moment as the long awaited opportunity for reconstructing national identity and distinctiveness. These two synchronic but opposing tendencies roughly marked the main lines of political division, where one side was for an opening toward the world and the rejoining of Europe while the other was much more bent on looking inward, at local culture, local traditions, and on reenacting fragments of obsolete national history. At the same time, these tendencies also marked the general attitude toward the United States, toward Americanization, globalization, or postmodernization—these three widely understood as synonymous or congruent terms. In what follows, I focus on examples where this assumed congruence of Americanization and the postmodern can be detected, examples that also offer themselves as problems in cultural translation.

Even though a large part of postmodern, poststructuralist theory has traveled from Europe to the United States and then back again, this original triangulation is largely overlooked and is primarily consumed as "American" due to the vigorous and highly visible ways in which these theories were appropriated and put into practice in American society. This is possibly also because the younger generation reads most of the texts in English translation, which, needless to say, is already an interpretation, in both the linguistic and cultural sense. As Walter Benjamin put it, translation belongs to the *afterlife* of the original, and thus postmodernism comes to us in this doubly removed form (i.e., at a cultural and temporal remove). While the United States has been making significant efforts *not* to universalize its citizens—a policy that has been made visible by the recognition of various identity groups and their related movements based on race, gender, sexual orientation, and ethnicity—Eastern European countries since 1989 have been strongly oriented toward a politics of *national particularism*, national difference, precisely as a result of their having been deprived of the context of their own culture and history during the previous sixty years. However, the homogenizing and bonding concept of "nation" seems to have allowed so far very little room for other kinds of identity politics, which are largely seen as undermining the universally understood notions of nation and culture.

More importantly, conservative theorists and critics (often representatives of a classical, modernist rhetoric) see them as American (and, within that, postmodern) theoretical imports that can and should have no relevance to our own culture. In the field of art, to position yourself as belonging to any other context or frame than that of universal, and within that national art, is still widely understood as placing yourself outside (moreover, beneath) the norm and distancing yourself from it.[1] For instance, if you envision yourself as a woman artist, a queer artist, or a Roma artist, contemporary mainstream criticism in Hungary will predictably put you down for giving preference to such "particular" and "peripheral" viewpoints instead of adhering to universalizing, modernist notions like *quality*, *talent*, or *originality* (regardless of who has the power to set the norm for such notions). A good case in point is that there are quite a few women writers and artists who will not allow their work to be published in women's anthologies or shown at exhibitions for women artists, and similarly, there are Jewish writers and artists who refuse to let their work be thus contextualized, as it were, outside (or, worse, somewhere beneath) the context of Hungarian art, or "art" in general.[2]

Ironically, the practice of constructing multiple identities and multiple narratives, so vigorously present in contemporary American society, used to be a natural and organic part of East Central European history—especially during the time of the Austro-Hungarian monarchy—where multiple ethnic, racial, and cultural adherences were a matter of course. The fact that it is now seen as an "American," intrusive import is the result of the earlier suppression or repression of similar local practices by either nationalist, or later on, communist ideologies. Thus, as I see it, the problem of Americanization in our region goes beyond the simple paradox of "particularism within the US" versus "global Americanization elsewhere." From my point of view, it is precisely *the politics of particularism*, imported via the theory of identity politics (or poststructuralist, postmodern theory), that has been interpreted as the Americanization not just of local academia but of local society as well. Such a form of Americanization is indeed very welcome in a traditionally hierarchical and patriarchal society. Hence, instead of cultural colonization, I like to think of it rather as a form of cultural cross-fertilization.

These are the rough outlines of the context or frame in which I wish to discuss a recent example from Hungarian visual art that seems to carry the burden of many of the problems and issues mentioned above. At the end of 2004, the Stedelijk Museum in Amsterdam organized an exhibition as part of a series whose aim is to represent contemporary art in the countries that recently joined the European Union, an enterprise financed by the Netherlands as then presiding state of the EU. The invited artists (mostly in their thirties, who grew up in the 1960s and '70s) were asked to reflect in their work on important moments of their local history. The answer of the Hungarian art formation known as Kisvarsó (Little Warsaw)[3]—the transplanting of a large bronze statue of nineteenth-century agrarian socialist János Szántó Kovács to the Stedelijk Museum—unexpectedly caused a huge uproar among a large number of artists. The 290 centimeter-high, 600 kilogram statue was created by József Somogyi and originally erected in 1965 in a small town in southeastern Hungary (Hódmezővásárhely) where agrarian movements had taken place. Critics, as well as the otherwise not too active Hungarian Academy of Art, blamed the artists for "making fun" of and "humiliating" a well-known and well respected sculptor,[4] his work, and the historical era in which it was made (see figures 1 and 2).

Part of the uproar was caused by the fact that the piece was automatically interpreted by the Dutch press as a piece of socialist realism, whereas in Hungarian art circles it is a well-known fact that Somogyi's work was highly polemical in its own time (the 1960s) for having made a daring leap from the exigencies of socialist realism toward artistic modernism. Many of the protesters (who formed a uniquely colorful group including artists and art historians from both the political left and right, liberals and conservatives) considered it a scandalous mistreatment to uproot a work of art in such a brutal, radical way and to place it in a context where it would necessarily be misunderstood and misinterpreted. To them it also seemed humiliating to entrap a sizable piece of public art originally made for a large, open-air setting in a room obviously too small for it and thus to make it look like some miserable caged animal.

As it is a part of Little Warsaw's artistic strategy not to offer too much background information, their works start having a life of their own,[5] a situation that indeed does lead to—in their eyes, creative—misreading and misinterpretation that allows the raising of new questions concerning art and makes room for new, alternative perspectives.

The paradox behind the "scandal" is that this kind of radical gesture, familiar from avant-garde art and its postmodern reinterpretations (as, for example, in appropriation art), can also be traced back to practices of conceptual art in

Fig. 1: The sculpture in its original location, 2004. Photo copyright © Little Warsaw Archive.

Fig. 2: The sculpture in the Stedelijk Museum, 2004. Photo copyright © Little Warsaw Archive.

Hungary during the 1960s and '70s (practiced, in fact, by many of those who signed the letter of protest against the Kisvarsó project). There was, however, a fundamental difference between its Eastern European and Western or American variant: while conceptual art in the West raised primarily questions concerning the *system of art and language*, in the East it focused primarily on questions relevant to the *system of contemporary politics* (that is, it was political in a very direct sort of way and was interpreted as such by the audience and critics alike, as well as the censors—the latter two often being the same). Thus instead of the pure, transcendent formalism of Western modernism,[6] Eastern European modernist art was chock-full of direct, local political messages and imbued with a sense of mission. At the same time, it also positioned itself within the context of international modernism, characterized by an open and cosmopolitan "global" attitude as opposed to the claustrophobic confines of the political regime in power. However, after the political transition, as former nonofficial art became canonized and its representatives among artists and critics came into positions of power, their attitudes and reactions to new critical and social theories (transmitted primarily through American channels) became downright hostile as they realized that their modernist positions were being subverted by postmodern theory.

Hence, although earlier representatives of modernism had turned to the West to legitimize their universalist claims about art and culture as an attack against local political authority and communist ideology, now they prefer to stress cultural and regional difference. In this framework it is modernism that becomes tied to the local, while the postmodern discourse on multiple identities, multiple perspectives, languages, and narratives—originally meant to campaign for the local—is seen as a relativizing and globalizing discourse that lacks depth and is full of ideological implications that modernists wanted to avoid like the plague.[7] Hence, a striking reversal of roles can be detected: modernism and modernists go local (and conservative), while postmodernism (as a form of Americanization) is understood as global and colonizing.

Many of those who protested against this radical (or, as they put it, "brutal") uprooting of a Hungarian historical monument did so from the position of the above described, reversed modernism, anchored in local sociopolitical and cultural history. This position prevents them from interpreting the Kisvarsó group's gesture other than politically. By contrast, Kisvarsó's gesture of defamiliarization and decontextualization places the statue in a radically different art-historical perspective and thus focuses primarily on artistic instead of political issues. It offers the statue a new reality, a new existence; it can now be measured again, by new gauges, and found not wanting. This is where the protesters are most mistaken: instead of degrading and humiliating the sculptor and his otherwise long forgotten work, the young artists offered it a new life (an *afterlife*, as it were, a new translation); they made room for new questions and attacked old stereotypes (including the kind that categorizes this work as socialist-realist art, but also the

Fig. 3: The original platform of the sculpture, 2004. Photo copyright © Little Warsaw Archive.

kind that claims this work can be understood only within its own [art] historical context). They removed it from its pedestal, both literally and symbolically (see fig. 3),[8] thereby questioning the authority of anyone who claims to possess the final narrative of the work (including, of course, the authority of the protesters). Besides purely aesthetic questions, their act of appropriation also raises issues related to the use of public spaces for art; questions of history, memory, and remembrance—the topics of lively, current discussions in the West and in the United States surrounding memorials, counter-memorials, and monuments.[9]

One may wonder that after all that happened in avant-garde art, in a world after Duchamp and all of its art-historical consequences, an act of appropriation or recontextualization can still provoke such a surge of intense emotion. But it looks like sixteen years after the fall of the Iron Curtain it is still too difficult to relinquish the exclusive right to one's own cultural-historical past, and this work by Kisvarsó is interpreted precisely as an irresponsible, light-handed endangering of that long lost right. Still, these young artists may have realized that the repetition of a familiar gesture in a different historical-cultural context produces, as postmodernism has taught us, *repetition with a difference* (to quote a proto-postmodernist American, Gertrude Stein).[10] Translation, too, is repetition with a difference, as is cultural translation. I view this project by Kisvarsó as an

interesting experiment in cultural translation (even in the literal sense of translation's etymology—namely, "transferring," "bringing across," "moving to another
place"). Those opposing the project resent what is lost in the process while those
who are in favor prefer to focus on the added value. The reluctance to interpret
culture through loss is, perhaps, in itself, a form of Americanization.

Notes

1. Hungary, as a small nation constantly attacked by larger ones around it, has always
relied heavily on its literature and art as a symbol of national, cultural unity whose importance has always overridden any other type of adherence.

2. Obviously, the historical reasons for such an attitude are different in each of these
cases.

3. Members: Bálint Havas and András Gálik.

4. József Somogyi, besides being an excellent sculptor, was also an important public
figure; he was a member of the Presidential Committee, a member of the Hungarian
parliament, the lay president of the Hungarian Protestant Church, and the rector of the
College of Fine Art.

5. As it also happened with their similarly motivated piece exhibited at the Venice Biennale in 2003, where they presented a sculpted bronze body custom-made to complement
the famous head of Nefertiti, guarded at the Berlin Museum. The head and body were
brought together for a short time at the museum, a performative act filmed by the artists
and also shown at the Biennale.

6. I use the term "modernism" as not inclusive of but distinct from the classical avant-
garde.

7. These ideological implications can be understood in terms of power relations concerning gender, race, and ethnic issues, which in the Soviet era had been repressed by the
concern with the overall political situation, placing everyone on the same side within a
simplified, binary matrix of "us" vs. "them."

8. Even if out of pure necessity, only after the statue had been transported to Amsterdam,
did the curators realize that because of statical problems, the platform could not be exhibited together with the statue. But this suited the improvisatory strategies of Kisvarsó and
proved, once again, that chance circumstances can be incorporated into the work and be
made an organic part of it. Notice the inscription on the pedestal: "Instauration"—offering
a combination of "installation" and "restauration." This combination is actually a perfect
enactment or performance of the central concept and title of the exhibition, "Time and
Again," which can be seen behind the statue on the wall. In other words, time (or history)
requires reinterpretations.

9. These questions are especially acute in a country like Hungary, which had most of
its old, political monuments transported to a park at the edge of the capital, thus making them peripheral and excluded both in an ideological and geographical sense. (For
more information, see http://www.szoborpark.hu/index.php?Lang=en.) The historical and
aesthetic burden carried by traditional monuments in the country makes it very difficult
to construct new *memory sites* instead of traditional monuments—as demonstrated by
a current controversy surrounding the new central monument to the revolution of 1956
erected for the fiftieth anniversary of the revolution.

10. See "The Search for Tradition: Avantgarde and Postmodernism in the 1970s," in Andreas Huyssen's *After the Great Divide: Modernism, Mass Culture, Postmodernism* (Bloomington: Indiana UP, 1986), which deals with the different uses of the tradition of the avant-garde in Europe and the United States.

Works Cited

Huyssen, Andreas. *After the Great Divide: Modernism, Mass Culture, Postmodernism.* Bloomington: Indiana UP, 1986.

Levinson, Stanford. *Written in Stone: Public Monuments in Changing Societies.* Durham, NC: Duke UP, 1998.

Memento Park, Budapest. http://www.mementopark.hu.

CHAPTER 8

Westward Ho with Kholiwood

The Transnational Turn in the Neoliberal Marketplace

Richard Ellis

In 2005, Lonely Planet, the London-based travel guide publishers, published *City Break Secrets*, a section of which endeavored to convey the appeal of the Big Apple. What was slightly surprising was the terms in which it chose to do this: "New York[:] Exploration here can go as deep as you let it. Have a Mexican tamale breakfast, catch a Bollywood flick, or simply grab a pizza" (14). Perhaps this eccentric smorgasbord, fusing America, Asia, and Europe, can convey how, in order to deal with a thoroughly intercalated global economy, U.S. American Studies has necessarily been increasingly compelled to focus on how its field is characterized by complex, fluid interconnections.[1] One of the impressive features of these "New American Studies" is the way they have taken on a number of guises, each of which, by reaching beyond the assumption that the United States is somehow synonymous with the Americas (Rowe, *New American Studies* xvi), twinned in their different ways to postcolonial theory and to cultural, gender, and performance studies. In this sense it was inevitable that the "New American Studies" would jettison "grand narrative" syntheses (like those generated by the myth-symbol-image school that preceded it) in favor of contingent, historically specific analyses of discourse and power, of hybridity, of performativity, of transculturation, of contact zones and interculturality, and of global flows in an increasingly transnational world. Such work is post-Foucault, post-Said, post-Bhabha, post-Pratt, post-Beck, and post-Butler.[2] It rejects the propensity of the "linguistic turn" to privilege indeterminacy over historicization, instead turning resolutely back to history—and almost as often, in the process, it has come to adopt transnational foci.

Setting aside the many intra–USAmerican Studies flowerings that are one key element of this "New American Studies," compelling though these can be, I want to focus on what I see as three of the main trends of *transnational* "New American Studies." These three trends substantially overlap, as will be immediately obvious, but this does not mean that distinguishing between them is pointless.

First, an *intrahemispheric* approach to American Studies can be identified. Within North, Central, and South America, this reemphasis considers the multiple ways in which the United States and the Americas interact and, increasingly, the multiple ways the Americas interact *without* the United States. So, for example, volume 4, number 1 of the journal *Comparative American Studies* considers how it is necessary to attend not only to how Canada and the United States coexist but also to how Canada and the rest of the Americas interact (e.g., concerning issues of migration, refugee flight, asylum, and how these redefine border spatialities—for example, by the way in which, in a sense, South Americans, traveling from Mexico to Canada, experience USAmerica as one huge, often dangerous, border crossing.[3]

Second, *contingent hemispheric studies* have rapidly developed. This is apparent in two aspects above all. First there is the rapid expansion of varieties of Atlantic Studies—including Transatlantic Studies, cis-Atlantic Studies, and circum-Atlantic Studies,[4] which interweave study of black Atlantics, red Atlantics, green Atlantics, Jewish Atlantics, and, of course, white Atlantics—the last, preeminently including white Anglo-Saxon Protestant Atlantics.[5] Second, there is the increasing emphasis on Pacific Studies, specifically Pacific Rim Studies (perhaps these should be called circum-Pacific Studies), examining exchanges between Asia and the United States.[6] Both of these oceanic hemispheres (the Atlantic and the Pacific) possess a long U.S. coastline, and in this sense both oceans are contingent with the United States. Contingent American Studies' reemphases therefore fall upon permeable borders, contact zones, (post)imperial and (post)colonial exchanges, and subaltern resistances.

These hemispheric reorientations have more recently been increasingly accompanied by a *third response*, attending to globalizing changes in the world order, precipitated by the necessary recognition of a new closeness between the postindustrial state and late corporate capitalism, and to the consequent blowbacks that have occurred, faced with multinational corporations' increasingly mobile imperiousness toward the marginalized and dispossessed. Most singularly, this reestimation has been accelerated by 9/11 but also by the events of Lockerbie, Bali, Madrid, Mumbai, and the long history of conflict in Afghanistan (the list ever lengthens).[7] The problems generated by environmental degradations have also been moving back up the scale, subsequent to Hurricane Katrina's impact on New Orleans and other events attendant upon rising sea levels and atmospheric and sea temperatures. All this has thrown emphasis upon a new American Studies that can accommodate the global, as espoused, for example, by Wai-Chee Dimock's and Donald Pease's planetary perspectives, and by Rob Wilson's, Kirstin Greusz's, and Susan Gillman's "worlding" of American Studies. Each of these seeks to respond to an increasingly globalized planet,[8] so inevitably passing beyond what might be called monocular hemispheric studies (be these intra-American Studies, Atlantic

Studies, or Pacific Studies). A common criticism of these approaches is that they somehow rehearse the globalized imperialist pretensions of the U.S. state.

Yet all of these "New American Studies" have at least one thing in common: all have called into question the intellectual foundations embedded in the term "American Studies." Its long assumed clarity of enterprise ("the study of America"), long buttressed by an exceptionalist discourse, is confronted by this transnational turn, threatening its autonomy. In John Carlos Rowe's words, "the 'new' American Studies . . . reconceives its intellectual project as the study of the many different societies of the western hemisphere and of the different border zones that constitute this large region . . . revisi[ing] the traditional interdisciplinary methods of the field to be more comparative in scope" (*New American Studies* xiv, 4). The sheer vigor of the transnational turn, which has seen four new "international journals" starting up in the new millennium in the field of contingent Atlantic hemispheric studies alone (*Atlantic Studies, Atlantic Literary Review, Transatlantica, Transatlantic Studies*), certainly means that the term "American Studies" must now be placed in quotation marks, as the idea of "roots" is more and more often superseded by attention to "routes" (Clifford), in an ever more globalized world of flows and exchanges. As Ulrich Beck reminds us, "Globalization means . . . above all . . . denationalization" (14). If American Studies' theoretical "parasitism" (Wise 315) demands contemporaneity in their methodological approaches, then they must also respond to this shift of global emphasis. And this is what the New American Studies have done.

At stake in these developments are issues of space and spatialization—the way space is conceptualized and acculturated. Static understandings of nation-state are under siege, undermined by Édouard Glissant's identification of how integrated yet boundless political, economic, and cultural convergences of historical trajectories have transversally come about, in spite of the borders that cross through people and places. All confidence in static nation-based definition becomes displaced by new modes of theorizing flows—a focus much better able to accommodate globalizing forces, most visibly those "top-down" ones fostered by international, multinational corporate capitalism; its intergovernmental and NGO free market supports (such as the International Monetary Fund, the World Bank, the World Trade Organization, the General Agreement on Tariffs and Trade, and the transformation of the General Agreement on Trade in Services, the Transatlantic Trade and Investment Partnership, and the Trans-Pacific Partnership); and its multifarious "soft" persuasive powers. These are not uniquely USAmerican, of course, but the USAmerican state and USAmerican corporations' immense economic reach, combined with their market penetration and advertising power, continue to exercise a degree of domination within what are now thoroughly globalized networks. For example, as John Tomlinson points out, however much we may want to emphasize how corporations operate globally, many experiences are permeated by pronounced USAmerican traces. So, although Tomlinson may

also talk about "global capitalist monoculture" (81), he can never escape Ziauddin Sardar and Merryl Wyn Davies's apocalyptic conclusion that "[US]American
consumerist culture assimilates everything, exerting immense, unstoppable pressure on the people of the world to change their lifestyles . . . their values . . . their
identity . . . [their] stable relationships, [and their] attachment to history" (121).
Such an identification of the continuing pressure exerted by the United States
is also reflected upon in the often anticapitalist responses of other, less tangible
bottom-up resistances, which are just as important if less economically powerful—for example, feminist, ethnic, and ecological movements involving varieties
of both productive consumption and antagonistic acculturation.[9]

These latter resistances are encapsulated in Anthony Giddens's definition of
globalization as acting and living (together) over distances, across the apparently
separate worlds of national states, regions, and continents. This acting and living
together may involve and even draw upon technology, commodities, and markets,
but it can also involve migrations, diasporas, and information exchange and collaboration, dissent, and direct opposition (as in green ecologisms). The emphasis
falls firmly upon processes. USAmerican Studies, faced with such transnational,
globalizing complexity, is consequently engaging with deconstructions of the
integrity of globalization, identifying how it is not just a question of the erosion
of national or regional borders in processes of intergovernmental or corporate
co-option and control. Globalization is also a question of transnational capitalist (and often, still, U.S. state) soft-power dominance confronting slippery and
multiple resistances. Conceptualizing the resulting glocal and local interfaces
is by now no longer the preserve of corporate glocalization strategies, as first
developed by SONY, coiner of the term "glocalization" to define the process of
corporate "thinking globally and acting locally" when grooming new markets
for commodified co-option (Robertson 173–74). The New American Studies increasingly identifies how, instead, the global and local may also involve processes
of resistance—the interaction of communities in activities coordinated globally,
exercised locally.

Ulrich Beck promotes this idea when discussing his formulation, "globalization
from below" (68)—a formulation taken up by Elisabeth Gerle when exploring
how "globalization from below" (*In Search of a Global Ethics* 30) interacts with,
counters, or undermines "globalization from above" ("Contemporary Globalization" 158–71).[10] "Globalization from above" can be roughly equated here with what
Beck defines as "globalism," which represents globalization in terms of economic
processes enshrined in the precepts of the free market (as understood by neolib-
erals, first and foremost), producing a world market whose power is superseding
traditional understandings of political action, whether national or international
(Beck 9). By contrast, "globalization from below" subsists in opposition to, critiques of, and alternatives to these economic processes and their consequences.
Gerle's formulation usefully emphasizes the idea that globalization is a question

of not just the processes of global capital and its grand marketing strategies but also of alternative processes routed across borders and contesting their significance. Indeed, Gerle's identification of how there are multifarious participants in global discourses (*In Search of a Global Ethics* 30) ipso facto indicates how these can derive from all world regions.

Yet, when all is said and done, all of these globalizing developments have to be seen as in part subordinate to—and not untypically reacting against—the powerful omnipresence of the U.S. state, U.S. multinationals, and U.S. export culture. What has to be guarded against in advancing this caution is the incidental establishment of a new kind of USAmerican exceptionalism, rooted in a monolithic formulation of both USAmerican dominance and an accompanying indiscriminately monolithic anti-Americanism. To allow such a picture to become established would be to fail to recognize how, in a transnational world of global finance, the "USA" cannot be homogenized in simple binary polarizations, just as "anti-[US]Americanism" is never as simply monolithic as the phrase's formulation suggests, not least because none of the top ten multinational corporations are wholly U.S.-owned; they are indeed multinational. At such a moment, global accommodations need to retain but fundamentally moderate a sense of how global processual routes are still predominantly rooted in nation-states, national economies, and cultural absorption of, resistance to, and adaptation of their "soft-power" interpellative exhortations at various levels (Lenz 5–23).

"American Studies" are consequently both internationalizing themselves more intensely, recognizing their own necessarily transnational makeup, and also harkening to the dialogues that exist in any such an undertaking. Rowe calls this a process of reconceiving "American Studies" as a "comparativist . . . study of . . . many different border zones . . . such as the Pacific Rim and the African and European Atlantics" (Introduction xi-xv). But I add, perhaps more importantly, that this is also a process of reconceiving comparativist studies beyond these contingent hemispheric studies: something always involving both intrahemispheric studies like Mexican or Nicaraguan American Studies and other, wider comparative processes: Indian American Studies, Russian American Studies, Iranian American Studies, Iraqi American Studies—in Rowe's words, a "more internationalist" approach (*New American Studies* 5). Calling for such an adjusted perspective is driven by the pace of changes to the world order following the collapse of the Soviet Empire and the rise of radical Islam, and precipitated by a new closeness between the postindustrial U.S. state and late multinational capitalism—what I call a new USAmerican private-state imperiousness, which has generated increased marginalization, dispossession, and consequent blowbacks to such hard powers and their soft accompaniments. What I want to focus on now is the large gap that has opened up between the kinds of global emphasis these developments have generated on the one hand and the relatively established "new" American intra- and contingent hemispheric studies on the other.

I am aware that in describing this gap I am being somewhat reductive. Contingent American hemispheric studies, for example, inevitably also implicate other hemispheres—and their attendant, globalizing area studies. For example, an increasing stress on the Atlantic as a site of flows and exchanges cannot pass without making an impact on the various European area studies, while analyzing the Pacific Rim similarly has an impact on Australasian Studies, Southeast Asian Studies, Chinese Studies, and Japanese Studies. At its best such work explicitly bridges hemispheres, as when the Caribbeanist Antonio Benítez-Rojo takes Édouard Glissant's analysis of the Caribbean's "originatings" to be inextricably, boundlessly interwoven with Asian as well as African, European, and American histories (Glissant). But what is still less explored presently is how Pacific Rim Studies impact on European Studies, since the emerging world dominance, in economic terms, of the Pacific Rim fundamentally shifts the economic balance away from the old European "West."

What is opening up, I contend, is a chance to address such interhemispheric issues—both their routes and their roots. Such considerations can help prevent too much focus falling on long established and arguably well-rehearsed exchanges— for example, upon the transatlantic or upon US intrahemispheric border studies. What is becoming needed is the identification of a range of interhemispheric American Studies procedures, as USAmerican Studies decenter themselves along a number of intercalated global axes. Groundbreaking work has been emerging in this respect for a while—of an increasingly ambitious nature.[11]

Here is another example of how this might work: a comparative, interhemispheric analysis of two international film coproductions, one Hollywood-style, the other Bollywood-style. Both, much more than incidentally, seek to interrogate their stylistic bases (those of Hollywood and Bombay Film Studios, respectively), but, more importantly, both also overtly cross between hemispheres. The two films are Sofia Coppola's *Lost in Translation* (2003) and Gurinder Chadha's *Bride and Prejudice* (2004). The first traces the midlife crisis of a middle-age, fading Hollywood actor, on a run to Japan to make a substantial sum via a Japanese whiskey commercial film shoot, and his quasi-romantic encounter with a bored and neglected young American woman, trailing along behind her almost continuously absent husband, a celebrity photographer. It is also, quite plainly, a remake of the British film *Brief Encounter* (1945). The second film, *Bride and Prejudice*, as its title makes clear, is a remake of Jane Austen's *Pride and Prejudice*. The Bennet family becomes the Bakshis: Elizabeth Bennet becoming Lalita Bakshi; Jane, Jayta; Lydia, Lakhi; and Mary, Maya. The Reverend Mr. William Collins becomes Mr. Kholi, a nonresident Indian from the States; Fitzwilliam Darcy, Will Darcy, the son of a hotel magnate mother; and George Wickham is recast as Johnny Wickham, an itinerant backpacker known to Darcy because he is the son of a former employee (and the impregnator of Darcy's sister when she was very young). Both films are funded by multinational conglomerates and seek audiences across several overlapping hemispheres.

Lost in Translation at first seems to be a transpacific text amenable to a contingent hemispheric analysis. It depicts the story of a species of brief encounter in Japan between an aging U.S. film star, Bob Harris, played by Bill Murray, and a "recently married" but neglected young woman, Charlotte, played by Scarlett Johansson. However, conspicuously, we are almost immediately forced off-hemisphere, as it were, since the story line largely follows that of David Lean's *Brief Encounter*—the most obvious signal, this, of the film's other and (as we shall come to see) dominant (Atlanticist) hemispheric orientation.

I must immediately declare that I find *Lost in Translation* to be a poor film. One of the causes célèbres of the film became what Bob Harris whispers into the ear of Charlotte at the very end of the film. Deliberately, we are not allowed to hear what is said. And, more pruriently, audience speculation has often focused upon what was actually said by the actors acting the parts, Bill Murray and Scarlett Johansson. My reply is that this moment of unheard exchange is unheard precisely because it is an empty exchange. There is almost nothing to say about the faintly pedophiliac, sub-Lolitan exchange between the two, hence its translation into inaudibility, as the film indulges Bob Harris's midlife crisis.

Yet the title, *Lost in Translation*, referring to the visit of these two Americans to Japan, seems to promise much more. The familiar term "lost in translation" precisely negotiates with the complexity of cultural exchange—the inevitability of some loss, yet, even in that recognition, the paradoxical possibility of some discovery. But is anything being discovered in *Lost in Translation*? The short answer is no. It might be argued that the film self-consciously thematizes the stereotypes produced by people who are both ignorant of and uninterested in the culture within which they temporarily reside. But the film soft-focusedly allows Bob and Charlotte to remain established in our affections and suffer only the most oblique criticism for their Western insularity, into which they keep retreating. So when Bob Harris departs Japan for the United States at the end of the film, and we understand that Charlotte is to return Stateside soon afterward, both remain untouched, unchanged, untranslated. And as in *Brief Encounter*, a Western narrative model that keeps most of its two characters' key exchanges insulated from the world (on a station platform), most of Bob and Charlotte's key exchanges are framed by their near insulation from Tokyo in an international hotel. Ironically, though, where *Brief Encounter* does not allow its two characters a proper final good-bye, Bob is allowed to leap out of his taxi and say his un-overheard good-bye to Charlotte, in one final sentimental softening of the story, insulating it yet further from any cultural engagement. Where *Brief Encounter* has a lot to say about the cultural complexities created by the disruptions of relationships attending a world war, *Lost in Translation* says little meaningful about the impact of globalization, since Bob and Charlotte's relationship, which could well engage with this theme (Bob is, after all, in Tokyo to make a whiskey advertisement), instead segues off into romantic intercontinental travel-book fantasy.

Germanely, in this respect, in the film *Terminal* (2004) Tom Hanks is asked, "Do you ever get the feeling your whole life is being lived in an airport?" Hanks's airport terminal and Charlotte's Tokyo hotel room are both represented in the vein of the hackneyed joke about the globalized replication of "international," denationalized space (albeit with glocalizing touches, such as strategic cultural allusions). But this simplistic joke, insinuated in *Lost in Translation*, is belied even inside the hotel room itself by the existence of glass in the windows and doors in the walls. The experience of any hotel room is much, if not wholly, to do with the expectation of going out. And go out the characters in *Lost in Translation* do. However, the Japan they go out into is a Japan rendered as a disastrous series of clichéd stereotypes. Yes, all the Japanese are of short stature, so that, for example, Bob cannot adjust his showerhead high enough to stand under it. Yes, this "Japan" is inscrutable, as when the Japanese director of the advertising shoot gives long-winded directions to Bob that are translated (in a very well-worn, unamusing joke) into a very few words of USAmerican English that Bob finds incomprehensible. Yes, this "Japan" is framed by constant intimations of the excesses of globalization, particularly towering skyscrapers—perhaps the most decisive intimation of USAmericanization, even after the skyscraper's adoption as the universal symbol of corporate power and potency. And, yes, inevitably, an experience of a species of pole dancing on the Tokyo strip is set against visits to what are represented as the largely deserted legacies of Japanese civilization. *Lost in Translation*'s jokey *reductiveness* is disturbing: the text is replicating the way the stereotype produces frozen representations, relying upon their frozenness to impede any relational ethnic dialogues (Bhabha, "Of Mimicry and Man").

What I suggest is that an interhemispheric analysis reveals just how unwaveringly Atlanticist *Lost in Translation*'s frozen stereotypical representations of the Japanese are. A key scene in this respect is a particularly striking one set in an amusement arcade, where a young Japanese woman stands by distractedly while a person, probably her male partner (for this is left uncertain), plays with "inscrutable" stylishness an arcade game under the static and manipulative gaze established by the eloquent camera-framing's interaction with the mise-en-scène (yes, I do want to praise much of the camera work by Lance Acord and much of Coppola's directing). The "other" produced in this sequence is incomprehensibly alien, a product of the Japanese "inscrutable" interaction with the unseen Western arcade game, in a representation eliding the significance of the global in the development of arcade games, and their pronouncedly Eastern, martial arts debts. Instead, we are firmly stuck in a North Atlantic perspective.

Seemingly more promising, fuller, is the juxtaposition of the meaninglessly vapid karaoke of a touring USAmerican starlet with the karaoke of the rather drunken Charlotte, Bob, and their chance Japanese acquaintances. In the latter scene the performances, as the camera angles and mise-en-scène contrive it, do assume some meaningful dimension of (let us call it) fellow feeling, set in contrast with the starlet's self-absorption. But such a contrast is undercut by the presence of the protagonists' booziness and its attendant, vapid warmth. It becomes another exercise in nostalgia (as the scene itself self-reflexively intimates), devoid of any cultural exchange. The potential for any productive cultural cross-consumption is, at the last, elided.

For, certainly, karaoke, like arcade games, if not reduced to clichéd representations, offers the potential for incisive considerations of complex cultural translation: the adoption and adaptation of Western pop songs in and to karaoke, a complex Japanese tradition of cultural transmission based on careful practice; or U.S. Western shoot-outs within arcade games remodeled and recast as ninja confrontations. It is not enough to represent these as sterile and meaningless cultural losses in the way that they are in Coppola's film, for in their cultural context these losses carry with them some dialogic gains. That is to say, it is possible to represent significantly what is going on in these cultural adaptations, to do with the *relative* cultural status granted to authenticity, originality, and repetition and the *relative* cultural status given to the formulaic. But moving toward such an interhemispheric reading, raising issues concerning the status of individualism, reveals just how much *Lost in Translation* ironically ensures that all of these considerations are lost, washed away in a flood of Western sentimentalism, as the film lamely center-stages instead a highly conventional, faintly pedophilic, deracinated Western romance, valorizing the individual. The film finally becomes mono-hemispherical, another Atlanticist production, for all of its international co-funding. All that is not lost in this translation, one might argue, are fat bottom-line coproduction profits.[12]

Lost in Translation fails to discover any compensatory cultural resources in its international ventures out of the hotel, mostly reduced to ludicrous, cartoon-like, and peremptory visits to tourist sights: Charlotte's visit to a Japanese temple in Tokyo occurs in more or less magnificent isolation. It might be argued that this may offer a sort of stunted, fleeting critique of such Atlantic tourist othering, as (just perhaps) does the nearly sincere karaoke performed by Bob, Charlotte, and their new Japanese acquaintances. But such readings involve an unconvincing stretch of the imagination.

Not least, they are rendered unconvincing because of the filmmakers' disconcerting decision to leave in the scene when Bob waits in the hospital for Charlotte to emerge after her X-ray for a broken toe. This scene was set in an actual hospital in Tokyo, and the sequence results from the actor Bill Murray sitting in one of this hospital's waiting areas and establishing unrehearsed (though, of course, half-staged) exchanges with the Japanese patients who happened to be waiting alongside him. One of these stooges (for want of a better word), having established that Bob Harris/Bill Murray is American, endeavors to indicate that America is a long way away, involving air travel around a large segment of the globe, but Bob, and in this instance, the improvising Murray as well, cannot understand what this Japanese man is trying to convey. Ironically, even when he resorts to perfectly clear hand-signing to explain what he means, his attempt to establish communication is lost on Harris/Murray. Harris/Murray makes no effort to understand the hand signals at all, instead immediately retreating to the safety of clumsy parody, intended to be comical (playing to the gallery as it were—the other Japanese patients and, one suspects, even more to the film crew), even though the hand signals he neglects to try to understand need no translation: they clearly convey an aircraft circling the globe. The minimal cultural engagement, the moment of basic dialogic interhemispheric openness, required by both Bill Murray and behind his character Bob Harris is simply missing. This failure is deeply ironic: an accidental, scathing meta-textual commentary is established, revealing the film as no kind of transpacific text at all, quite unable to engage with the cultural processes with which it treats. All is indeed lost in translation—even the straightforward sign language of the Japanese man. Instead the film retreats into the familiar territory of a Western love-found-love-lost story, full of trans-atlantic cross-references.

Bride and Prejudice does rather better. It, too, has to do with cultural transla-tion—quite literally, since it is loosely based on *Pride and Prejudice*. The most textured debt it owes to its novelistic origins is a pointed one, revolving around how calculations of financial suitability lubricate the wheels of love and mar-riage in both nineteenth-century England and twenty-first-century India and their respective global diasporas—perhaps because India in 2004 was entering upon a phase of rapid industrial and commercial expansion in a way not wholly unanalogous to what happened in late eighteenth-century England (this certainly lies behind its director Gurinder Chadha's claim that "the themes [of *Pride and Prejudice*] are pertinent to India"). *Bride* consequently invites an interhemispheric analysis and, more than incidentally, in this respect it was partly intended to launch the international career of its female lead, the fast-rising Bollywood star Aishwarya Rai.

But what is more striking is the lavishly over-choreographed, over-colored, and clichéd representation of the film's locations: both in Amritsar and when the main Indian female protagonists and their parents travel to the United Kingdom and the United States. Here, the ironic intertextual debt is not to Jane Austen but to the Indian film industry, and particularly to the recent flowering of Bol-lywood that has seen its films penetrate not just the nonresident Indian global community (NRIs) but also a wider audience—so much so that, as we have seen, Lonely Planet has even taken to defining the classic New York experience as one including taking in a "Bollywood movie" (*City Break Secrets* 14). This new, more cosmopolitan Bollywood focuses very much on the experiences of middle-class NRI global travelers.[13] *Bride* consciously echoes this, but Chadha goes beyond the knowing, self-referential, ironic yet celebratory recapitulations of established clichés recurrently found in Bollywood productions. Instead, *Bride* probes into the history of Bollywood film, as its satiric parodies explore the reductive erasures enshrined in the formulations "East" and "West," and so comes to engage with Manoj Kumar's 1970 Bollywood movie, *Purab Aur Paschim*, and a number of intervening turn-of-the-century Bollywood international blockbusters.

To effect this, *Bride* transposes and adapts a crucial strand of Jane Austen's text: its ruthlessly sharp satire upon contemporary mores. The mores satirized by Chadha are those produced in that now dominant Bollywood film culture that strips down to a vapid series of basic clichés the tourist sites of every location in which such Bollywood filmmaking invests. Chadha comically exaggerates this propensity. So London becomes reduced to a string of clichéd depictions of its main tourist sites. Stripped of its guts and deboned, this version of "London" parodically flops before the viewer, ready for easy tourist consumption. Los Angeles, rather more recalcitrant material, is also filleted, in a whirlwind montage juxtaposing the iconic HOLLYWOOD sign, LA's Pacific strip, and fleeting glimpses of LA's signature architecture—all, inevitably, culminating in a helicopter trip to the Grand Canyon, featuring deliberately overfamiliar aerial shots that succeed in containing (by dwarfing) its scale. This satiric cartoon celebration of iconic, bustling tourist sites stands in contrast to the heritage sites in *Lost in Translation*, which, largely empty of tourists and apparently neglected by modern Japan, are lifted out of time into a tourist pastoral of elegiac timelessness. In contrast to such orientalist nostalgia, the depictions of London and LA in *Bride and Prejudice* carefully and deliberately include obviously contemporary icons, featuring, for example, the London Eye (2000) and (pointedly) LA's Walt Disney Concert Hall (2003).

What results is a biting satire of the tourist reflexes of the early twenty-first century transnational upper middle class, represented as the owners of the means of production—including tourist production, since Darcy's family are international hotel magnates. They are exposed as not only conniving in but also fueling the global reduction of locale. London and LA, in these tourist catalogs, are boiled down to a series of invariant visual clichés that, more than incidentally, almost match the stereotypes of provincial India that the film also offers. In India the stereotypical emphases fall upon exoticized depictions of crowded markets and streets, the Golden Temple and Goan beaches, while London is trapped in a near contemporary swinging Cool Britannia mode and LA in lavish consumerism. It is a fiercely satiric critique of mutual othered touristic exoticizations, be they those produced by "Western" or NRI global tourist circulations. In *Bride and Prejudice*, these various European, Indian, or USAmerican tourist otherings are transparently veiled by what is on the surface merely sentimental celebration.

Bride is deliberately drawing upon what has become in Bollywood NRI films a repeated and at times parodic reproduction of the way a set of visual tourist clichés have developed an almost invariable generic formulation to establish the setting and then have this function as "set." This near invariant sequence of establishing shots-cum-sets achieves its almost definitive montage arrangement in one of the first blockbusters to focus on NRI characters—*Dilwale Dulhania Le Jayenge* (1995, dir. Aditya Chopra). In *Bride* such Bollywood tourist otherings are heavily satirized beneath the surface sentimental celebration, both by the perfunctoriness of their appearance and by the way these clichéd establishing shots of tourist venues are not then employed as "sets" within the film. My contention is that *Bride*'s deviant combination of montage and mise-en-scène is rooted in a recognition of the consequences of multinational incorporation of global tourism. The film is parodying the way the often subtly inflected and often self-ironized yet sentimentalized hybridities of NRI blockbusters—the mode in which the films are shot and produced—are inescapably infected with tourist brochure discourses (as when the 2002 hit *Kabhi Khushi Kabhie Gham* features a shot of a Starbucks in London in the middle of the stock sequence of clichéd icons), in a pattern of doubled, comic irony. *Bride*, by contrast, intimates that such commodification is also a cause of bitter anxiety, as culture is reduced to a Disneyfied parody of global commodity exchange, quite opposed to the nostalgic mendacities of *Lost in Translation*, which communicates almost nothing beyond the mere reinforcement of the orientalist othering borne within its stereotypes. *Lost in Translation* has a bittersweetness, but it is a depleted, Atlanticist bittersweetness, rooted in a crudely reductive reworking of the cultural legacies of Henry James and Nabokov concerning innocence and experience.

The bittersweet mood of *Bride and Prejudice*, by contrast, is rooted in a recognition of the consequences of multinational incorporation of global tourism. The film complexly parodies the sweetly sentimental, subtly inflected, and often self-ironized hybridities of Bollywood—the mode in which the film is shot and produced—in a pattern of double irony. *Bride* successfully intimates how such sugared commodification reduces culture to a ghastly Disneyfied parody of cultural exchange.

This is encapsulated in the film in four sharply satiric sequences. First, in a Bollywood dream sequence, Lalita Bakshi's first and unsuccessful suitor, the legal high-flyer Kholi, has transformed the iconic hillside signifier HOLLYWOOD into KHOLIWOOD as a sign of the shift to complex patterns of global financing of world movies (in a moment of exquisite self-reflexivity). Second, as Darcy and Lalita dine in a Mexican restaurant in LA, the musicians in the band playing at their table wear such absurdly large sombreros that these completely dominate their heads, reducing them to ethnic simulacrums, their identities masked behind stereotypical "Hispanic" headgear (while cocktail shakers ironically serve as castanets in the background). Third, Darcy and Lalita, strolling along deserted sands, find themselves suddenly passing a full gospel choir—the African American cultural icon parodically boiled down to its basic signifiers and incongruously placed on a sandy shore. This image not only draws upon Bollywood wish-fulfillment/dream-sequence conventions but also upon that moment of diegetic/non-diegetic fracturing to be found in Mel Brooks's *Blazing Saddles* (1974), which, in anticipation of *Bride*, set out to parodically satirize another stock-ridden movie genre—the Hollywood Western. Finally, *Bride* turns the tables on "Western" propensities for imperial homologization of the "Orient" by cavalierly relocating the fountain in the courtyard of London's Somerset House into Los Angles, with a geographical abandon exactly replicating that found in "Western" views of "the East."

Hence the title change from "*Pride*" to "*Bride*": this film *is* all about marriage—a shotgun neoliberal wedding of East and West, conveyed in terms of an intertextualized exploration of narrative, of form, and of their ideological ramifications, as imposed by the reach of global late capitalism. This redactive global reach has, much more than incidentally, also reified Jane Austen, trapping her writing in the amber of love and marriage adaptations that sideline her fiercely erotic satires. But it has also created a complex series of cultural gains and losses that *Bride* explores. Its syncretistic entwining of Bollywood and Hollywood musical conventions constitutes a generally refreshing culture-lite romp through a narrative long afforded classic status. Yet the film also quite deliberately interrupts this lite-ness, as when Maya Bakshi performs a threatening cobra dance to welcome the family's multinational visitors, to their puzzlement and distaste—and to the surprise of cinema audiences, who sometimes initially laugh at this sudden change of tone: Maya's dance lacks the requisite culture-lite-ness, and its shockingly vital energy suggests that processes of loss attend the process by which the transnational takes hold.[14] This, I think, is the point of the central protagonist's name, Lalita. Her name deliberately sounds very like Lolita's—indeed, someone in the film mishears Lalita's name as Lolita. The seductiveness of such hybridity, offering "young" (yet knowing) independent Indian Bollywood to jaded Humbert Humbert–style Hollywood palates, constitutes a complex, potentially disgraceful trade that Lalita must negotiate (in the way that the Lolita-lite Charlotte in *Lost* does not). Consequently, Chadha's good humor is superseded by something approaching anger over continuing processes of global homologization and market imperialism. As she herself puts it, though "anger might be a bit of a strong word . . . all my films . . . might be dressed up as comedy, but everything I've ever done is always about making whoever's watching [. . .] think differently."[15]

Bride and Prejudice therefore in part satirizes Hollywood's and Bollywood's mutual "KHOLIWOOD-ization," as money's power whisks the NRI protagonists quite literally around the globe. And yet, as Kholi's mispronunciation of America as "Am'rica" makes clear (by making America sound like "Amritsar"), such polarizations are crossed by complex flows of diasporic migration and economic exchange that are impossible to unravel: Am'rica is becoming increasing "Amritsar-nized" (as well as Hispanicized), just as Bollywood increasingly draws on and feeds into Hollywood accommodations, as in recent Bollywood transnational Indian productions, drawing on international conglomerate financing, and so necessarily featuring dialogic exchanges between an Indian middle class and their NRI relatives.

A prime example of this is Karan Johar's 2002 international hit, *Kabhi Khushi Kabhie Gham* (hereafter, *K3G*) (Srinivas 319–44). In this film a key scene features one of two brothers, Rohan Raichand, setting out to bring the other, Rahul, back to India to console his mother. Their meeting in London is choreographed as a particularly lavish, classic song-and-dance routine in which the words of the song, "I bow to thee, Mother," predict that Rahul will accede to returning to his mother while also allowing an ambiguity to develop concerning whether "Mother" solely refers to the brother's mother, or also to Mother India—or even whether, as the reunification unfolds in a London full of clichéd allusions to its tourist attractions (as always), the mother at issue is (also) the Mother of the Commonwealth, the land of Queen Elizabeth and Queen Victoria. *K3G* runs the risk in these ambiguities of losing any political clarity, as the sets become merely settings for the song-and-dance numbers. Indeed, one way of defining the distinction that exists between *Bride* and the NRI Bollywood-derived films it interacts with is to compare the representation of London in *Bride* and *K3G*. In both, London is in retro Cool Britannia mode: the two at first seem closely similar in their representation. But *Bride* does not share *K3G*'s undertone of moral disapprobation, deriving from a constant sense that the Raichand dynastic family's exiled outposts are in danger of succumbing to the turpitudinous fleshpots of London—even if *K3G* conveys this in a slightly tongue-in-cheek and even celebratory way. Nor does *Bride*'s kaleidoscopic montage of London, so close to that found in *K3G*, make any pretense of representing the sites of NRI London life. *Bride*'s London tourist sites are not quite and no more than *K3G*'s fuzzily motivated international stereotypicalities, reductive sets upon which song-and-dance numbers are performed, fusing these sites diegetically with all the film's other song and dance "sets." *Bride* declines to introduce such condensation. Instead, significantly, in *Bride*, the central dramas are mostly set in modest West London suburbs around Southall, where Chadha herself was born and which became in the postwar period a key site for arriving Indian middle-class immigrants to the United Kingdom to congregate—a London suburb where good-quality housing sold cheaply, since the houses lay below the flight paths into Heathrow International Airport. So, although both films are knowingly retro and both films present exaggerated stereotypical portraits, only *Bride* sets up a subtle satiric dialogue between tourist visual excess and suburban mundanity, in sharp contrast to the way London tourist sites are repeatedly condensed into dream-fantasies in *K3G*.

Such complexity has confused moviegoers: Chadha, especially in internet chat rooms,[16] has been regularly slated for what is seen as her clumsy stereotyping. The film's satiric intent can easily be missed. Perhaps this is because the complex interhemispheric translations in *Bride and Prejudice* become deeply disturbing, once brought to the fore. *Bride*, a text apparently avowedly Western in its inspiration, a pastiche of *Pride and Prejudice*, becomes a complex satire upon processes of global homogenization in the cultural marketplaces of India, the United States, and the United Kingdom. *Bride* never offers *Lost in Translation*'s mendacious pretense at sentimentalized realist authenticity, resting on shallow depiction. Rather, its complex parodies expose the blank colorfulness of late-capitalist free-market bourgeois world tourism. By contrast, *Lost in Translation* largely fails to engage with the cultural processes with which it treats. The film does sharply, if all too tritely, and very much in the Romantic tradition, observe how Bob has chosen to sell his integrity to the advertising company, making a Japanese whiskey advertisement for a large paycheck, as part of his midlife crisis (a very familiar Atlanticist theme involving a highly individuated "crisis"). This conceded, *Lost in Translation* otherwise fails to trade effectively between *Brief Encounter* and Japanese transnational postmodernities. It largely remains a dislocated Atlantic text, wrenched from its cultural hemisphere (shot in Japan) to instead engage with a nexus of Western cultural discourses that also fosters a prejudicial misrepresentation of twenty-first-century Southeast Asia.

By contrast a text apparently avowedly Western in its inspiration, a pastiche of *Pride and Prejudice*, becomes a complex interhemispheric satire on the process of global homogenization in the cultural marketplace. *Bride* never offers any mendacious pretense at sentimentalized authenticity, but in its complex parodies it exposes the blank colorfulness of late-capitalist bourgeois world tourism. This is self-reflexively alluded to when, near the film's end, Wickham pulls Lakhi into London's National Film Theater, in the middle of a BFI Bollywood season. As they enter, they pass a poster advertising the classic Bollywood production, Manoj Kumar's *Purab aur Paschim* (1970). The Hindi poster in itself (but only for Hindi speakers) underlines how Western geographical orientations constitute the hegemon's global tradings (the title translates as "East and West"). But, as *Purab aur Paschim* and *Bride* both make clear, underneath this are the quotidian problems of negotiating "mixed relationships," diasporic displacements, and economic realities. *Bride*'s sardonic allusion to how consumerist tradings smooth over such realities in both the East and the West acknowledges the extent to which the pervasiveness of global exchanges across hemispheres renders yearnings for integral cultural authenticity as narrowly nostalgic—vulnerable to contamination by national ersatz myths of origin that have simply lost their viability within rampant interhemispheric exchange—mostly under U.S. suzerainty. Both films carry a central political message. *Purab aur Paschim* advocates "You need India and India needs you. Be proud of India and let India be proud of you" (words spoken by the central protagonist, Bharat, the child of a freedom fighter, played by Manoj and Ashok Kumar, respectively)—a message that in heavily diluted and depoliticized form is adopted as a vague nostrum in many late twentieth-century and early twenty-first-century NRI films. *Bride* offers a politicized consideration of the increasing emphasis upon global interactions. Complex interactions result, involving NRIs, Indians, USAmericans, and forms of empire (including a fading British Empire; a rising consumer-driven, USAmerican corporate-dominated economic postcapitalist "empire"; and an emergent Indian commercial empire, led by corporate giants (like Tata Steel).

Purab aur Paschim and *Bride and Prejudice* in this way critically sandwich internationally financed NRI Bollywood-style films, with their generally depoliticized focus on at best weakly contextualized explorations of love and marriage. So, as Wickham, the would-be seducer of Lakhi, is seen off by Darcy in *Bride and Prejudice,* the fight between them occurs on a stage in front of a scene in *Purab aur Paschim* in which Bharat sees off a would-be rapist of Prithi, who must learn the importance of embracing the culture she has all but lost, just as *Purab*'s NRI rapist needs to rediscover his identity and reject the permissive values of swinging 1960s London.

Having said all this, I have to note that for most audiences *Bride* fails to slough off completely its "international Bollywood" skin. I think this is because of how the film's commercial scale and its interhemispheric spatializations dilute its subtle resistances to global commodification. Internationally oriented NRI blockbusters are big business:

> Among the films reporting a half-to-three-quarters-of-a-million-dollar box office in the U.S. or the U.K. are *Aa Ab Laut Chalen* (1999), *Kaho Naa Pyaar Hai* (2000), *Refugee* (2000), *Lajja* (2001), and *Asoka* (2001). The NRI "million-dollar-box-office club" boasts such films as *Yaadein* (2001) and *Lagaan* (2001) in the U.S. . . . *Taal* (1999), *Hum Saath Saath Hain* (*HSSH*, 1999), and *Mohabbatein* (2000) made the mark or better in the U.K. . . . *Taal* and *HSSH* doubled their U.K. intakes in the U.S. and brought in $2 million each. *Kuch Kuch Hota Hai* (1998) tallied up $2.6 million in the U.K. Most recently, setting a new high-water mark in the overseas box office, *Kabhi Khushi Kabhie Gham* (*K3G*, 2001) grabbed the No. 10 spot its first week of release in the U.S. and earned $2.9 million during its five-week run. In the U.K., *K3G* earned nearly $3.6 million over an 18 week run. (Frederickson)

The film does not always quite stave off the risk of post-national deterritorialization brought by such newfound Kholiwoodization that is so insistently proffered by neoliberal conglomerate international marketing strategies.

Faced with such texts as *Bride and Prejudice* and *Lost in Translation*, and the globalized socioeconomic and cultural processes with which they treat, a new kind of approach to USAmerican Studies is indeed necessary—one fundamentally informed by processes of contact, hybridity, exchange, flow, and migration, and alert to issues of (dis)advantaged exchange and (dis)location. Plainly, in all of this, the bare term "American Studies" (which I have been carefully avoiding whenever "USAmerican Studies" is more accurate) hardly works anymore, its grand narrative projects laid all too bare.[17]

Consequently, American Studies has to recognize that it needs to specify what sort of American Studies it is seeking to be and not leave it to the mendacious operations of implicit ideologies to do (ironically) with the U.S. state's intra-hemispheric (and, indeed, interhemispheric) desire for hegemony-maintenance. The nostalgic term "American Studies" cannot stand alone anymore. We need to specify the kind of American Studies we believe we are undertaking.[18] Some sort of qualification has become essential: USAmerican Studies; intrahemispheric studies; contingent hemispheric studies; global American Studies; interhemispheric American Studies—perhaps these terms can figure in a long list of specific variations that need to be declared or qualified as "American Studies" loses its self-assumed and inherently inaccurate explanatory capacity, faced as it is with a field so saturated with complex, fluid interconnections that draw up where USAmerican Studies ends and other studies begin. Hence my apparently cavalier decision to count *Bride and Prejudice* as an American Studies text. Set partly in LA, featuring an American hotel magnate and her son, and critiquing the slippages between Hollywood and Bollywood—and Kholiwood—*Bride and Prejudice*, in part an internationally co-funded vehicle to launch an Indian Bollywood starlet's world film career, also becomes a complex reflection upon patterns of the cinema industry commercialization that bear down on the issue of interhemispheric East-West globalization in a way that almost entirely eludes *Lost in Translation*.

Notes

1. See, for example, John Carlos Rowe, *The New American Studies* (Minneapolis: U of Minnesota P, 2002); Edward Said, *Orientalism* (London: Routledge and Kegan Paul, 1978), particularly xiv–xv, in which he calls for a "'new' American Studies," working comparatively, over/across/beyond borders. I take the coinage "USAmerican" from Malini Johar Schueller, *U.S. Orientalism: Race, Nation, and Gender in Literature* (Ann Arbor: U of Michigan P, 1998). I find the word an attractive one when seeking to elude the imperialist connotations of "American"—as in the phrase "American Studies." See, for a classic discussion of this issue, Janice Radway, "What's In a Name? Presidential Address to the American Studies Association, 20 November 1998," *American Quarterly* 51.1 (1999): 1–32. See also José Martí, "Our America," rprt. in *"Our America": Writings on Latin America and the Struggle for Cuban Independence*, ed. Philip S. Foner et al. (New York: Monthly Review Press, 1977), 80–99; and Winfried Siemerling, *The New North American Studies: Culture, Writing, and the Politics of Re/cognition* (Abingdon, UK: Routledge, 2005). This article is a reworking of two other articles: R. J. Ellis, "'East Is West': Interhemispheric American Studies and the Transnational Turn," in Winfried Fluck et al., eds., REAL: *Yearbook of Research in English and American Literature* 23: "Transnational American Studies" (Tubingen: Gunter Narr Verlag, 2007), 163–88; and R. J. Ellis, "*Bride and Prejudice*'s Critique of the Interhemispheric Neo-liberal Marketplace," *Dialog* 15 (2007): 1–12.

2. See, for example, Michel Foucault, *L'archéologie du savoir*, rprt., trans. A. M. Sheridan, *The Archaeology of Knowledge* (London: Routledge, 1989); Edward Said, *Orientalism* (London: Routledge); Homi Bhabha, ed. *Nation and Narration* (London: Routledge,

1990); Homi Bhabha, *The Location of Culture* (London: Routledge, 1994); Mary Louise Pratt, *Imperial Eyes: Studies in Travel Writing and Transculturation* (London: Routledge, 1992); Mary Louise Pratt, "Arts of the Contact Zone," in David Bartholomae and Anthony Petrosky, eds., *Ways of Reading: An Anthology for Writers* (New York: Bedford/St. Martin's, 1999), 581–95; Ulrich Beck, *Vad Innebar Globaliseringen? Missupfattningar och Mojliga Politiska Svar* (Gothenberg: Daidalos). Rprt. as *What Is Globalization?*, trans. Patrick Camiller (Cambridge, UK: Polity Press, 2000); Judith Butler, *Bodies That Matter* (New York: Routledge, 1993).

3. See Sarah Phillips Casteel and Rachel Adams, Introduction to *Comparative American Studies*, Special Issue: *Canada and the Americas* 3.1 (2005): 5–13.

4. For a discussion of how these terms can be distinguished, see David Armitage, *Greater Britain, 1516–1776: Essays in Atlantic History* (Aldershot: Ashgate, 2004), 16–21. See also, on the circum-Atlantic, Joseph Roach, *Cities of the Dead: Circum-Atlantic Performance* (New York: Columbia UP, 1996). Armitage has even claimed "we are all Atlanticists now" in "Three Concepts of Atlantic History," in David Armitage and Michael J. Braddick, eds. *The British Atlantic World, 1600–1800* (New York: Macmillan, 2002), 11–30. However, who "we" might be is somewhat opaque. Is he, for example, including my colleagues working in Japan?

5. See Eric Williams, *Capitalism and Slavery* (Chapel Hill: U of North Carolina P, 1944); Walter Rodney, *How Europe Underdeveloped Africa* (London: Bogle-L'Ouverture Publications, 1972; John Carlos Rowe, Introduction to *Post-Nationalist American Studies* (Berkeley: U of California P, 2000), 3–5; Sidney W. Mintz, *Sweetness and Power: The Place of Sugar in Modern History* (New York: Penguin, 1985); Paul Gilroy, *The Black Atlantic: Modernity and Double Consciousness* (London: Verso, 1993); Bernard Bailyn, "The Idea of Atlantic History," *Itinerario: European Journal of Overseas History* 20 (1996): 19–44; Marcus Rediker, "The Red Atlantic; or, 'a terrible blast swept over the heaving sea,'" in Bernhard Klein and Gesa Mackenthun, eds., *Sea Changes: Historicizing the Ocean* (London: Routledge, 2004), 111–30; Nicholas Canny, "Writing Atlantic History; or, Reconfiguring the History of Colonial British America," *Journal of American History* 86 (1999): 1093–1114; David Armitage, "The Red Atlantic," *Reviews in American History* 29 (2001): 479–586; Kevin Whelan, "The Green Atlantic: Radical Reciprocities between Ireland and America in the Long Eighteenth Century," in Kathleen Wilson, ed., *A New Imperial History: Culture and Identity in Britain and the Colonies* (Cambridge, UK: Cambridge UP, 2004), 216–38; and Donna Gabbaccia, "A Long Atlantic in a Wider World," *Atlantic Studies* 1.1 (2004): 1–27. This is not to mention an Atlantic crossed by women's movements. See, for example, Leila J. Rupp, *Worlds of Women: The Making of an International Woman's Movement* (Princeton, NJ: Princeton UP, 1997); Margaret H. McFadden, *Golden Cables of Sympathy: The Transatlantic Sources of Nineteenth-Century Feminism* (Lexington: UP of Kentucky, 1999); Bonnie S. Anderson, *Joyous Greetings: The First International Woman's Movement, 1830–1860* (Oxford: Oxford UP 2000).

6. See, for example, Eric Jones, Lionel Frost, and Colin White, *Coming Full Circle: An Economic History of the Pacific Rim* (Boulder, CO: Westview Press, 1993); Richard Le Heron and Sam Ock Park, eds., *The Asian Pacific Rim and Globalization: Enterprise, Governance, and Territoriality* (Aldershot: Avebury, 1995); Andre Gunder Frank, *ReOrient: Global Economy in the Asian Age* (Berkeley: U of California P, 1998); and Gary Okhiro, *Common Ground: Reimagining American History* (New York: Columbia UP, 2001). Frank's determination to resist the claim to preeminence of the Atlantic is especially germane to my arguments in this essay. See, for example, his exchange with Peter Vries in Peter Vries, "Should We Really

ReORIENT?" *Itinerario: European Journal of Overseas History* 22.4 (1998): 22–38; Andre Gunder Frank, "ReOrient or Not: That IS the Question," *Itinerario: European Journal of Overseas History* 22.4 (1998): 9–22. See also R. Bin Wong, *China Transformed: Historical Exchange and the Limits of the European Experience* (Ithaca, NY: Cornell UP, 1997).

7. The term "blowback" is taken from Chalmers Johnson, *Blowback: The Costs and Consequences of American Empire* (New York: Henry Holt, 2000). I have added Mumbai to the list in a late, limited revision of this essay.

8. See Wai-Chee Dimock, *Through Other Continents: American Literature across Deep Time* (Princeton, NJ: Princeton UP, 2006); Donald Pease proposed his term "Planetary Studies" at a conference in Berlin (February 2005); Rob Wilson, Silva Gruesz, and Susan Gillman proposed their term in *Comparative American Studies* 2.3 (2004), a special issue titled "Worlding American Studies." See, in particular, Susan Gillman, Kirsten Silva Gruesz, and Rob Wilson, "Worlding American Studies," *Comparative American Studies* 2.3 (2004): 259–70.

9. Here I take up a point made by Sabine Broeck at a conference at the International Forum for U.S. Studies, a symposium occurring in March 2005. See also Neil Campbell, George McKay, and Jude Davies, "Globalisation, Americanisation, and the New World Order," in Neil Campbell, Jude Davies, and George McKay, eds., *Issues in Americanisation and Culture* (Edinburgh: Edinburgh UP, 2004), 295–307.

10. See also Jeremy Brecher, Tim Costello, and Brendan Smith, *Globalization from Below: The Power of Solidarity* (Boston: South End Press, 2000).

11. See, for example, Charles A. Price, *The Great White Walls Are Built: Restrictive Immigration to North America and Australasia, 1836–1888* (Canberra: Australian Institute of International Affairs in association with the Australian National UP, 1974); Evelyn Hu-Dehart, "Coolies, Shopkeepers, Pioneers: The Chinese of Mexico and Peru, 1849–1930," *Amerasia Journal* 15 (1989): 91–115; Walton Lock Lai, *Indentured Labor, Caribbean Sugar, Chinese and Indian Migrants to the West Indies, 1838–1918* (Baltimore: Johns Hopkins UP, 1993); Walton Lock Lai, *The Chinese in the West Indies, 1806–1995: A Documentary History* (Kingston, Jamaica: U of West Indies P, 1998); and M. Kale, *Fragments of Empire: Capital, Slavery, and Indian Indentured Labor Migration in the British Caribbean* (Philadelphia: U of Pennsylvania P, 1998).

12. My thanks to Corey Creekmur for his feedback on my original essay, aiding me in developing my argument at this and other points.

13. See Lakshmi Srinivas, "Communicating Globalization in Bombay Cinema: Everyday Life, Imagination, and the Persistence of the Local," *Comparative American Studies* 3.3 (2005). See also Gregory Booth, "Traditional Content and Narrative Structure in the Hindi Commercial Cinema," *Asian Folklore Studies* 54 (1995): 169–90; Rosie Thomas, "Melodrama and the Negotiation of Morality in Mainstream Hindi Film," in Carol A. Breckenridge, *Consuming Modernity: Public Culture in a South Asian World* (Minneapolis: U of Minnesota P, 1995), 157–82; and Wimal Dissanayake, "Globalization and Cultural Narcissism: Note on Bollywood Cinema," *Asian Cinema* 15.1 (2004): 143–50. Srinivas's article, which I first read in the middle of writing this essay, has been very helpful to me.

14. This scene, I think, alludes to *Purab aur Paschim*, in which the Westernized Prithi is shocked by a cobra's striking out at her when she returns to India.

15. See Gurinder Chadha, http://www.imdb.com/title/tt0361411/board/nest/16121321 (accessed April 24, 2005). From my point of view it is pertinent that Paul Giles in his *Virtual America* envisages Lolita as standing not just for the young America, knowingly open to Europe, but also *American Studies*. See Paul Giles, "Virtual Eden: *Lolita*, Pornography,

and the Perversions of American Studies," *Journal of American Studies* 34 (2000): 41–66; and Paul Giles, *Virtual Americas: Transnational Fictions and the Transatlantic Imaginary* (Durham NC: Duke UP, 2002).

16. See, for example, the Internet Movie Database (IMDb), http://www.imdb.com.

17. Of course, it is not only within American Studies that these issues are being debated. See, for example, J. K. Gibson-Graham and Katherine Gibson-Graham, "Area Studies after Poststructuralism," *Environment and Planning* 36 (2004): 405–419. Their analysis emanates primarily from a geographical base (though Katherine Gibson-Graham is based in an "area studies research school").

18. This point is being made with increasing but still often unheeded frequency. See, for example, Sabine Sielke, "Theorizing American Studies: German Interventions into an Ongoing Debate," *Amerikastudien/American Studies* 50.1/2 (2005): 53–98, 90.

Works Cited

Anderson, Bonnie S. *Joyous Greetings: The First International Women's Movement, 1830–1860*. Oxford: Oxford UP, 2000.

Armitage, David. *Greater Britain, 1516–1776: Essays in Atlantic History*. Aldershot: Ashgate, 2004.

———. "The Red Atlantic." *Reviews in American History* 29 (2001): 479–586.

———. "Three Concepts of Atlantic History." *The British Atlantic World, 1600–1800*. Ed. David Armitage and Michael J. Braddick. New York: Macmillan, 2002. 11–30.

Bailyn, Bernard. "The Idea of Atlantic History." *Itinerario: European Journal of Overseas History* 20 (1996): 19–44.

Baker, Houston A. *Blues, Ideology, and Afro-American Literature*. Chicago: U of Chicago P, 1984.

Beck, Ulrich. *Vad Innebar Globaliseringen? Missupfattningar och Mojliga Politiska Svar*. Gothenberg: Daidalos. 1997. Rprt. as *What Is Globalization?* Trans. Patrick Camiller. Cambridge, UK: Polity Press, 2000.

Benítez-Rojo, Antonio. *The Repeating Island: The Caribbean and the Postmodern Perspective*. Trans. James Maraniss. Durham, NC: Duke UP, 1996.

Berkeley, Bishop George. "On the Prospect of Planting Arts and Learning in America." 1726. In *The Works of George Berkeley D.D.: Formerly Bishop of Cloyne Including His Posthumous Works*, Vol. 4. Oxford: Adamant Media Corporation, 2007.

Bhabha, Homi. *The Location of Culture*. London: Routledge, 1994.

———. "Of Mimicry and Man: The Ambivalence of Colonial Displacement," *October* 28 (Spring 1984): 125–33.

Bhabha, Homi, ed. *Nation and Narration*. London: Routledge, 1990.

Booth, Gregory. "Traditional Content and Narrative Structure in the Hindi Commercial Cinema." *Asian Folklore Studies* 54 (1995): 169–90.

Braz, Albert. "North of America: Racial Hybridity and Canada's (Non)place in Inter-American Discourse." *Comparative American Studies* 3.1 (2004): 79–88.

Brecher, Jeremy, Tim Costello, and Brendan Smith. *Globalization from Below: The Power of Solidarity*. Boston: South End Press, 2000.

Butler, Judith. *Bodies That Matter*. New York: Routledge, 1993.

Campbell, Neil, George McKay, and Jude Davies. "Globalisation, Americanisation, and the New World Order." *Issues in Americanisation and Culture*. Ed. Neil Campbell, Jude Davies, and George McKay. Edinburgh: Edinburgh UP, 2004. 295–307.

Canny, Nicholas. "Writing Atlantic History; or, Reconfiguring the History of Colonial British America." *Journal of American History* 86 (1999): 1093–1114.

Casteel, Sarah Phillips, and Rachel Adams. Introduction. *Comparative American Studies*, Special Issue: *Canada and the Americas*. 3.1 (2005): 5–13.

Chadha, Gurinder. 2004. http://www.imdb.com/title/tt0361411/board/nest/16121321 (accessed April 24, 2005).

City Break Secrets. London: Lonely Planet Publications, 2005.

Clifford, James. *Routes: Travel and Translation in the Late Twentieth Century.* Cambridge, MA: Harvard UP, 1997.

Dimock, Wai-Chee (1996) *Through Other Continents: American Literature across Deep Time.* Princeton, NJ: Princeton UP, 2006.

Dissanayake, Wimal. "Globalization and Cultural Narcissism: Note on Bollywood Cinema." *Asian Cinema* 15.1 (2004): 143–50.

Ellis, R. J. "*Bride and Prejudice*'s Critique of the Interhemispheric Neo-liberal Marketplace." *Dialog* 15 (2007): 1–12.

———. "'East Is West': Interhemispheric American Studies and the Transnational Turn." *Yearbook of Research in English and American Literature* 23: "Transnational American Studies." Ed. Winfried Fluck et al. Tubingen: Gunter Narr Verlag, 2007. 163–88.

Evans Braziel, Jana. "'C'est moi, l'Amérique': Canada, Haiti and Dany Laferrière's Port-au-Prince/Montreal/Miami Textual Transmigrations of the Hemisphere." *Comparative American Studies* 3.2 (2005): 29–46.

Fernandez-Arnesto, Felipe. *The Americas: History of a Hemisphere.* London: Weidenfeld and Nicholson, 2003.

Foucault, Michel. *L'archéologie du savoir.* Rprt., trans. A. M. Sheridan, *The Archaeology of Knowledge.* London: Routledge, 1989.

———. "The Order of Discourse." *Untying the Text: A Post-Structuralist Reader.* Ed. Robert Young. London: Routledge and Kegan Paul, 1981. 48–78.

Frank, Andre Gunder. *ReOrient: Global Economy in the Asian Age.* Berkeley: U of California P, 1998.

———. "ReOrient or Not: That IS the Question." *Itinerario: European Journal of Overseas History* 22.4 (1998): 9–22.

Fredrikson, Jeanne. "NRI Number One." *India Currents.* August 2002. https://www.indiacurrents.com/articles/2002/08/17/nri-number-one.

Gabbaccia, Donna. "A Long Atlantic in a Wider World." *Atlantic Studies* 1.1 (2004): 1–27.

Garcia Marquez, Gabriel. "Playboy Interview" (with Claudia Dreifus). *Playboy* (Feb. 1983): 172–78.

Gerle, Elisabeth. "Contemporary Globalization and Its Ethical Challenges." *Ecumenical Review* 52.2 (2000): 158–71.

———. *In Search of a Global Ethics: Theological, Political, and Feminist Perspectives.* Lund, Sweden: Lund UP, 1995.

Gibson-Graham, J. K., and Katherine Gibson-Graham. "Area Studies after Poststructuralism." *Environment and Planning* 36 (2004): 405–419.

Giddens, Anthony. *Beyond Left and Right.* Cambridge, UK: Polity Press, 1994.

Giles, Paul. *Virtual Americas: Transnational Fictions and the Transatlantic Imaginary.* Durham NC: Duke UP, 2002.

———. "Virtual Eden: *Lolita*, Pornography, and the Perversions of American Studies." *Journal of American Studies* 34 (2000): 41–66.

Gillman, Susan, Kirsten Silva Gruesz, and Rob Wilson. "Worlding American Studies." *Comparative American Studies* 2.3 (2004): 259–70.

Gilroy, Paul. *The Black Atlantic: Modernity and Double Consciousness*. London: Verso, 1993.

Glissant, Édouard. *Le Discour Antillais*. Paris: Le Seuil, 1981.

———. *Poetics of Relation*. Trans. Betsy Wing. Ann Arbor: U of Michigan P, 1997.

Hu-Dehart, Evelyn. "Coolies, Shopkeepers, Pioneers: The Chinese of Mexico and Peru, 1849–1930." *Amerasia Journal* 15 (1989): 91–115.

Ickstadt, Heinz. "American Studies in an Age of Globalization." *American Quarterly* 54.4 (2002): 543–62.

Johnson, Chalmers. *Blowback: The Costs and Consequences of American Empire*. New York: Henry Holt, 2000.

Jones, Eric, Lionel Frost, and Colin White. *Coming Full Circle: An Economic History of the Pacific Rim*. Boulder, CO: Westview Press, 1993.

Kale, M. *Fragments of Empire: Capital, Slavery, and Indian Indentured Labor Migration in the British Caribbean*. Philadelphia: U of Pennsylvania P, 1998.

Lai, Walton Lock. *The Chinese in the West Indies, 1806–1995: A Documentary History*. Kingston, Jamaica: U of West Indies P, 1998.

———. *Indentured Labor, Caribbean Sugar, Chinese and Indian Migrants to the West Indies, 1838–1918*. Baltimore: Johns Hopkins UP, 1993.

Lauter, Paul. "The Literatures of America: A Comparative Discipline." *Redefining American Literary History*. Ed. LaVonne Brown and Jerry W. Ward Jr. New York: Modern Language Association of America, 1990. 9–34.

Lefebvre, Henri. "Reflections on the Politics of Space." *Antipode* 8.2 (1976): 30–37.

Le Heron, Richard, and Sam Ock Park, eds. *The Asian Pacific Rim and Globalization: Enterprise, Governance and Territoriality*. Aldershot: Avebury, 1995.

Lenz, Gunther. "Towards a Dialogic of International American Culture Studies: Transnationality, Border Discourses, and Public Cultures." *Amerikastudien/American Studies* 44.1 (1999): 5–23.

Martí, José (1891). "Our America." Rpt. in *"Our America": Writings on Latin America and the Struggle for Cuban Independence*. Ed. Philip S. Foner et al. New York: Monthly Review Press, 1977. 80–99.

McFadden, Margaret H. *Golden Cables of Sympathy: The Transatlantic Sources of Nineteenth-Century Feminism*. Lexington: UP of Kentucky, 1999.

Mintz, Sidney W. *Sweetness and Power: The Place of Sugar in Modern History*. New York: Penguin, 1985.

Okhiro, Gary. *Common Ground: Reimagining American History*. New York: Columbia UP, 2001.

Pease, Donald E. "The Place of Theory in the Future of American Studies." *Hungarian Journal of English and American Studies* 71 (2001): 11–37.

Pratt, Mary Louise. "Arts of the Contact Zone." *Ways of Reading: An Anthology for Writers*. Ed. David Bartholomae and Anthony Petrosky. New York: Bedford/St. Martin's. 581–95.

———. *Imperial Eyes: Studies in Travel Writing and Transculturation*, London: Routledge, 1992.

Price, Charles A. *The Great White Walls Are Built: Restrictive Immigration to North America and Australasia, 1836–1888*. Canberra: Australian Institute of International Affairs, in association with the Australian National UP, 1974.

Radway, Janice. "What's In a Name? Presidential Address to the American Studies As-
    sociation, 20 November 1998." *American Quarterly* 51.1 (1999): 1–32.

Rediker, Marcus. "The Red Atlantic; or, 'a terrible blast swept over the heaving sea.'" *Sea
    Changes: Historicizing the Ocean*. Ed. Bernhard Klein and Gesa Mackenthun. London:
    Routledge, 2004. 111–30.

Roach, Joseph. *Cities of the Dead: Circum-Atlantic Performance*. New York: Columbia
    UP, 1996.

Robertson, Roland. *Social Theory and Global Culture*. London: Sage, 1992.

Rodney, Walter. *How Europe Underdeveloped Africa*. London: Bogle-L'Ouverture Publica-
    tions, 1972.

Rowe, John Carlos. "Introduction." *Post-Nationalist American Studies*. Ed. John Carlos.
    Berkeley: U of California P, 2000. 3–5.

———. *The New American Studies*. Minneapolis: U of Minnesota P, 2002.

Rupp, Leila J. *Worlds of Women: The Making of an International Women's Movement*.
    Princeton, NJ: Princeton UP, 1997.

Said, Edward. *Orientalism*. London: Routledge and Kegan Paul, 1978.

Sardar, Ziauddin, and Merryl Wyn Davies. *Why do People Hate America?* New York: The
    Disinformation Company Ltd., 2002

Schueller, Malini Johar. *U.S. Orientalism: Race, Nation, and Gender in Literature*. Ann
    Arbor: U of Michigan P, 1998.

Sielke, Sabine. "Theorizing American Studies: German Interventions into an Ongoing
    Debate." *Amerikastudien/American Studies* 50.1/2 (2005): 53–98.

Siemerling, Winfried. *The New North American Studies: Culture, Writing, and the Politics
    of Re/cognition*. Abingdon, UK: Routledge, 2005.

Soja, Edward. *Postmodern Geographies: The Reassertion of Space in Critical Social Theory*.
    London: Verso, 1989.

Spillers, Hortense J., ed. *Comparative American Identities: Race, Sex, and Nationality in
    the Modern Text*. New York: Routledge, 1991.

Srinivas, Lakshmi. "Communicating Globalization in Bombay Cinema: Everyday Life,
    Imagination, and the Persistence of the Local." *Comparative American Studies* 3.3 (2005):
    319–44.

Thomas, Rosie. "Melodrama and the Negotiation of Morality in Mainstream Hindi Film."
    Consuming Modernity: Public Culture in a South Asian World. Ed. Carol A. Brecken-
    ridge. Minneapolis: U of Minnesota P, 1995. 157–82.

———. "Popular Hindi Cinema." *The Oxford Guide to Film Studies*. Ed. John Hill et al.
    Oxford: Oxford UP, 1998. 541–42.

Tomlinson, John. *Globalization and Culture*. Cambridge: Polity Press, 1999.

Vries, Peter. "Should We Really ReORIENT?" *Itinerario: European Journal of Overseas
    History* 22.4 (1998): 22–38.

Whelan, Kevin. "The Green Atlantic: Radical Reciprocities between Ireland and America
    in the Long Eighteenth Century." *A New Imperial History: Culture and Identity in Britain
    and the Colonies*. Ed. Kathleen Wilson. Cambridge, UK: Cambridge UP, 2004. 216–38.

Williams, Eric. *Capitalism and Slavery*. Chapel Hill: U of North Carolina P, 1944.

Wise, Gene. "'Paradigm Dramas' in American Studies: A Cultural and Intellectual History
    of the Movement." *American Quarterly* 37 (Sept. 1979): 293–337.

Wong, R. Bin. *China Transformed: Historical Exchange and the Limits of the European
    Experience*. Ithaca, NY: Cornell UP, 1997.

Richard Ellis on Zsófia Bán

On a tourist visit to Turkey, coming over from the Greek island of Lesbos on a day trip to Dikili, while stuck in the port immigration area waiting for the group's visas to be cleared (this delay a product of an enduring antagonistic mistrust between Greece and Turkey that is just one fragment of Europe's convoluted history), I looked through the iron fence of the port holding area onto one of Dikili's main squares. Facing me was a monumentally large statue of a military officer on a horse. Intrigued as to his identity, I began to ask around, but despite my usual obnoxious persistence, I could glean no information. None of the Turks I spoke with knew who he was. This incident called to my mind another monumental statue, this time located in my UK hometown of Derby—on the main road leading toward the station. I recalled how it had taken me considerable time to find out who the statue of an elegantly dressed Victorian woman represented, standing on a pedestal beside this busy street. Again my interlocutors could not shed any light, and it was only by crossing the street at last and examining the pedestal that I discovered she was the famous Crimea nurse, Florence Nightingale, the "lady with the lamp" (Longfellow), whose impact on modern nursing practices is always overstated (the importance to the Crimea of the Jamaican-born, Central American–trained and much overlooked nurse Mary Seacole being substantially greater, with respect to issues of hygiene, at least). It was hard to make out Nightingale's (Derbyshire-derived) last name on this pedestal, begrimed and littered as it was.

How often it is that large, highly visible, public monumental art is also at the same time strangely invisible as well. Such statues are intended to represent the political and cultural identity of a community in any given historical place. But of course they do not and cannot: all monumental art marks an attempt at memorialization that is temporally fragile and ideologically constructed. When "Little Warsaw" (András Gálik and Bálint Havas) noted this, they also noted that this did not mean the complexity of the stories lying behind these productions could not be excavated: "We use information that can only be gained in the local context. This information cannot be viewed from a global point of view or treated with a global attitude. The data we use are informal; they may come from local urban legends and are rooted in the local social space and in how we have been socialized locally . . . these are the most important elements for us" (Silagi).

This approach was crucial to framing what has been described as their post-conceptual work (Tata), "Monument Contra Cathedral—INSTAURATIO!" What intrigues us, as "Lost and Found in Translation" brilliantly points out, is that the further one delves into this complex representation of "legend, social space, [and] locality" (Tata), the more elusive the meanings become. This becomes clear as one unpicks the multiple layering of meanings of the large bronze statue of the late nineteenth-century local hero, the agricultural laborer János Szántó Kovács that Little Warsaw uprooted from its site in the town of Hódmezövásárhely. For one thing, this apparently simple statue was the nub of many conflicts. Szántó Kovács was an early champion of a propertyless population of rural laborers, advocating that "landed property and all means of production should be placed under public ownership," a sentiment reflecting the fact that most farm laborers worked for starvation wages at best, if they could find any job at all, so secure employment on government-owned estates often seemed to them the optimum arrangement (Silagi). Plainly, though Szántó Kovács was far from being exactly a communist, this made him available for post–World War II appropriation and apparently the ideal subject for a socialist realist statue. But this was not what the people of Hódmezövásárhely got. Rather, it was a plainly modernist work that unsettled some of the town's population, many of whom still held Szántó Kovács dearly in their memories and anticipated his representation in the customary statuary mode.

Hungarian television even made a documentary about the resulting furor (Erdosi). Incorporated as part of Little Warsaw's video installation in Apexart, the program reveals the unhappiness of many of the townspeople—including descendants of János Szántó Kovács—and the replies of both the mayor and the sculptor, József Somogyi, to the contention that the statue was insufficiently heroic. In turn, that it was Somogyi who sculpted it was important, for Somogyi was for many years under Hungary's communist regime highly honored, serving as rector of the College of Fine Arts and regarded by the regime as an outstanding postwar artist. His work was never going to be rejected. Over the years this controversy had been largely forgotten, and the statue usually ignored, so that it was only when Little Warsaw uprooted the statue that it was noticed again, and only then was its significance revived. But the controversies surrounding it were misremembered.

As "Lost and Found in Translation" brilliantly notes, mistranslation resulted, with the sculpture retrospectively spoken of by those of both right and left persuasions as being in the mainstream of Hungarian representational art, when it had not been and was not. Though executed by such a prominent sculptor as Somogyi, it was more of an expressionist piece. Herein lies the delightful irony in these mistranslations, for Little Warsaw's András Gálik and Bálint Havas, as they redisplayed the bronze, were to be regarded with suspicion because they apparently departed from the approaches of conceptualism, which had emerged as the dominant type of art production in the soi-disant New Europe, by bringing what are, after all, overt political issues back into art. So the removal of the statue came to be attacked, with Somogyi's daughter denouncing the act and the townspeople complaining over the neglected statue's removal, quite apart from the critical furor. But what they were doing was exposing the political aspect that always invests conceptual art, even from its origins in, say, Dada.

What I like especially about "Lost and Found in Translation" is the recognition that this is a subject suited to study by U.S. Americanists, precisely because it apparently so very much resists all and any attempts to globalize it as an artistic performance. Precisely, it cannot do this, but though it can and in a sense must be viewed miscomprehendingly by its international viewers (it was displayed in Amsterdam's Stedelijk Museum, after all), the puzzlement that it generates also internationalizes its display. The display's puzzlingness precisely demands that the viewer try to make sense of this enigma: a statue on display now no longer as a piece of public statuary but, removed from its public, on display again as an altered piece of public statuary—de-memorialized memorialization, as it were, open to any reading. This can only be seen as a political act, insisting that its conceptualization be recognized as political and globally engaged, by its demand that its audience undertake a reconsideration of the idea of public art and its purposes, redefined as these must be in a world where populations are increasingly transient, displaced, passing through—perhaps like me, only as a tourist, perhaps as a migrant, perhaps an immigrant, perhaps a (very often ignorant) native. How are these now liminalized memorial public artworks to be (re-) appropriated? How are we to understand the selection and mode of display of the memorialized and how that memorialization is carried out? I feel this goes beyond the issue of the disconcertingly hazy interface between modernism and postmodernism into the heart of the politics of art, and this leads us inevitably to think in terms of the resistance Little Warsaw offers to the kinds of global depoliticizations that much U.S. Americanization encourages or even advocates in boosting the preeminence of "the free market." American Studies needs to be capacious in its understanding of what falls within its remit while also ever cautious of imperialistic appropriation.

In this respect I'll end by saying that in "Monument Contra Cathedral—INSTAURATIO!" Little Warsaw originally intended (at least in one account I have read) to juxtapose Somogyi's statue with a small model (a maquette) of the Cathedral of Christ the Saviour in Moscow, one of the finest pieces of nineteenth-century Moscow Russian Orthodox architecture, demolished by Stalin to make room for a Palace of the Soviets that was never built (its foundations becoming a swimming pool), before it was rebuilt in the 1990s, thus erasing a whole passage of history (Fowkes and Fowkes 3). By implication, I would contend, it becomes possible to mentally juxtapose Somogyi's dislocated statue with a whole range of other public memorial works in this manner, internationally, as a way of thinking about the modeling of history and the forgetting of it. So, for example, the statue of Harriet E. Wilson's son, George, clinging to his mother's dress as she looks out across Milford, New Hampshire, a township where she was generally cruelly mistreated, offers a sentimental distortion of the facts of the case, which saw her son left in the care of the Milford guardians of the poor while her mother sought to make a living selling "hair regenerator" in the surrounding towns and writing *Our Nig*. Indeed, it is unclear whether George was ever reunited with Harriet Wilson before he died. He perhaps was, only briefly at best, but he may not have been, though the statue unquestioningly advances this reassuring vision (Gates and Ellis). This statue was erected not at the behest of the town authorities, but through the efforts of New Hampshire black historians and their well-wishers. The statue, then, is far from an uncomplicated tribute. Just so, each public memorial has its history that always extends out beyond its immediate situatedness, just as "Lost and Found in Translation" informs us.

Works Cited

Erdosi, Aniko. "Removed Monuments—Shifted Narratives: The Chances of Reinterpretation." http://www.littlewarsaw.com/displaced_history/sculpturemag.html. 2006.

Fowkes, Maja, and Reuben Fowkes. "Little Warsaw—Displaced Monuments and Deconstructive Strategies." 2003. "Little Warsaw: Selected Works and Projects 2003–2008." http://www.acax.hu/content/_common/attachments/little_warsaw2003-2009.pdf.

Gates, Henry Louis, and R. J. Ellis. Introduction to Harriet E. Wilson, *Our Nig; or, Sketches from the Life of a Free Black*. 1859. New York: Vintage, 2011.

Longfellow, Henry Wadsworth. "Santa Filomena." 1857.

Silagi, Michael. "Henry George and Europe: Hungary Began a Promising Venture in Georgist Tax Reform but Revolutionary Turmoil and Inflation Ended It." *American Journal of Economics and Sociology* 53.1 (1994): 111–27. Published online July 3, 2006. http://onlinelibrary.wiley.com/doi/10.1111/j.1536-7150.1994.tb02682.x/abstract.

Tata, Erzsébet. "From Images to Activism: The Heritage of Conceptualism in the New Millennium in Hungary." *Dailė* 2006/1: 12–15. http://test.svs.lt/?Daile;Number(132);Article(2862).

Zsófia Bán on Richard Ellis

> When the blackbird flew out of sight,
> It marked the edge
> Of one of many circles.
> —Wallace Stevens, *Thirteen Ways of Looking at a Blackbird*

As Richard Ellis aptly points out in the conclusion of his piece in this book: "a new kind of approach to USAmerican studies is indeed necessary—one fundamentally informed by processes of contact, hybridity, exchange, flow, and migration, and alert to issues of (dis)advantaged exchange and (dis)location." Discussing the variants offered by "New American Studies" he mentions, among others, intra-hemispheric as well as contingent hemispheric studies, the latter involving Pacific Rim Studies focused on examining exchanges between Asia and the United States. "Contingent American Studies' reemphases," writes Ellis, "therefore fall upon permeable borders, contact zones, (post-) imperial and (post)colonial exchanges, and subaltern resistances." It is specifically in view of these latter that I would like to offer another interpretation of the film *Lost in Translation*. My take on it is anchored in the very context of post-imperial and postcolonial exchange, as it radically undermines traditional views of America's imperial and colonial power as well as notions of cultural exchange and knowledge, or cultural translation. As I see it, the film is an instance of yet another, and much needed, subspecies of "New American Studies," which would be a combination of intrahemispheric (Atlanticist) and contingent hemispheric studies, by which I mean an Atlanticist perspective *affected by* a (postcolonial) contingent hemispheric perspective—in short, a self-reflexive discussion of America from an othered, alienated position. Instead of dealing with Western views of the East, or with Eastern views of the West, this subgenre offers—to stay within the matrix—Western views of the West from the *East*. While it could be argued that this is only yet another, if slightly different, Atlanticist perspective, I propose it does have quite significant, contingent hemispheric aspects that should not be overlooked and that are anchored in current global cultural-economic reality. Thus in my view, the film's locale, Japan, *is* significant in *Lost in Translation*, and it does have a lot to say about the postmodern contingent global reality the characters (both American and Japanese) live in.

"The film's satiric intent can easily be missed," writes Ellis of the other film, *Bride and Prejudice*, but I suggest the same can be said of *Lost in Translation*. Perhaps this intent could be made more palpable if we imagined the film to have been directed by a Japanese director—a position that cannot, of course, be taken on by Sofia Coppola, but it can be combined with her own, insider, American position. *Lost in Translation*, writes Ellis, "largely remains a dislocated Atlantic text, wrenched from its cultural hemisphere (shot in Japan) to instead engage with a nexus of Western cultural discourses that also fosters a prejudicial mis-representation of twenty-first-century Southeast Asia." I would argue that this "wrenching" is precisely the point: a violent act of dislocation, of decontextualiza-tion and defamiliarization that allows access to knowledge, if only limited, not only of the present other but also of the absent home, or of the (so far absent) self (both the actor and the young girl find themselves in a kind of existential impasse). If we consider the different layers of metaphoricity that the title of the film (as well as the story) carries, we can read it as a loss of *cultural meaning* in translation—in this case, the loss of the cultural meaning of "America" when transplanted, translated to another hemisphere, another culture—hence defying the cliché of American culture's globalizing, colonizing other cultures. It can also be read on an individual level, as the story of the (in this case positive) loss of the *self* in translation (i.e., in being "carried away," translated to another place). The characters are not only in alien space but also in an alien time zone, in a sort of time out of time. Sleepless nights make them move in a kind of daze, jet lag places them in a bubble or a fold in the texture of reality that allows them to deal with existence on a different level.

The plot of *Lost in Translation* works on both levels. I am inclined to see the film as a postmodern discussion of the Jamesian topics of innocence and experience in so far as it avowedly, and I would say honestly, undermines the Occidental-ist, idealist-modernist nostalgia, the expectation of exchange and knowledge in a foreign land and foreign culture. If *Lost in Translation* is a reworking of *Brief Encounter*, it is one with an added postmodern sensibility where the encounter (both on the individual and cultural level) is not only brief but also, you could say, virtual (out of real time and space). This is enhanced by virtual, simulacra spaces like the hotel rooms in which the characters are separated by large glass windows from "reality," located somewhere "out there" from the real city, or spaces like bars, game rooms, and clubs that function here like live chat rooms (not to speak of the virtual, imaginary nature of the "relationship" itself, which nature is momentarily subverted in the end by that private moment not shared with the viewers). No illusion of—touristic—knowledge, exchange, and contact with the foreign other is offered here (the girl's trip to Kyoto also shows her in the detached, forlorn position of someone hopelessly different and distant), no rehearsing of the shallowness of international tourism (itself a well-worn stereotype that *Bride and Prejudice* chooses to play with)—Coppola's film doesn't go there. Where it does go is to the examination of the self, which in this case is both the individual self (the career and marriage of the American actor, himself a symbol of globalizing American pop culture, and the still open future of the young girl) and America as a cultural incorporation of that self (the values it stands for, such as individuality, success, making it, and goal-orientedness). I think it is important to view the Bill Murray character's midlife crisis situation as a kind of national-cultural midlife crisis in which dreams of empire are no longer what they used to be (especially post 9/11—Coppola's film is from 2003). And this is where we turn to what makes this film fundamentally different from others of its kind.

For the question is, Why Japan, then? If the other here simply functions as a mirror to the Atlanticist self, wouldn't any other location have worked just as well? But if we examine the trajectory of the characters in the film, we will see a similarity to the more and more visible (but less and less comfortably acknowledged) trajectory of American culture and economy, that are being undeniably influenced by the culture and economy of the East (i.e., Southeast Asia). In the film, both the iconic American actor, who is no longer so hot at home, and the young photographer (the girl's ever absent, ever working husband) travel to Japan to find work and to make more money than they could at home. Their goal is not to indulge in tourism but to become (literally) engaged by the local market, the local economy, and thus they are in a position to acquire a much more fundamental knowledge of local reality than any tourist could. Instead of a touristic reality (usually an illusion), they acquire experiences of a local, corporate reality (even if this process is shown in a comic, satirical vein). The actor's and the photographer's situation here is no longer that of the colonizers but rather that of elite migrant workers flocking to economically more prosperous areas—certainly an unusual American experience. Thus, the transnational turn in the neoliberal marketplace that the film, in its own satiric and indirect way, does reflect on allows for a different perspective of home (America) *within* the global world, as well as a different view of one's life, the (American) self within that home. As I see it, this no longer insular, isolationist, purely Atlanticist perspective offered by the film is also one of the significant gains that "New American Studies" is able to offer in a post-9/11 era.

Ana Mauad on Bán and Ellis

An Imagined Community for the Twenty-First Century?

In 1991 English historian Benedict Anderson published a revised edition of the book *Imagined Communities: Reflections on the Origin and Spread of Nationalism*. This book was first published in 1983, almost ten years before the revised one, and can be considered an important contribution to the historiography of nationalism and colonialism. In the preface to the new edition, Anderson reflects that somehow the leitmotifs he employed in writing the book in 1983 can themselves be considered part of the same historical process he was actually studying:

> The armed conflicts of 1978–79 in Indochina, which provided the immediate occasion for the original text of *Imagined Communities*, seem already, a mere twelve years later, to belong to another era. Then I was haunted by the prospect of further full-scale wars between the socialist states. Now half these states have joined the debris at the Angel's feet, and the rest are fearful of soon following them. The wars that the survivors face are civil wars. The likelihood is strong that by the opening of the new millennium little will remain of the Union of Soviet Socialist Republics except . . . republics. [. . .] But, having traced the nationalist explosions that destroyed the vast polyglot and polyethnic realms which were ruled from Vienna, London, Constantinople, Paris and Madrid, I could not see that the train was laid at least as far as Moscow. It is melancholy consolation to observe that history seems to be bearing out the "logic" of *Imagined Communities* better than its author managed to do. (xi)

What is clear from these words is the notion that history offers no key for predicting the future, despite the fact that learning from the past can provide us with elements for explaining the present and for understanding future processes. So when Anderson answered the question "What makes people love and die for nations, as well as hate and kill in their name?"—analyzing the sense of nationality, the personal and cultural feeling of belonging to a nation, as "imagined communities"—he was shifting the angle for defining "nation" from a political perspective to a cultural and symbolic one.

In *Imagined Communities* Anderson explores the process that created nations all around the world—not just in Europe. He investigated different aspects of a historical process that can't be wrapped up in a strict period of years but instead deals with continuities, ruptures, and revolutions. The questions related to the creation of these communities are the basis for dealing with the contemporary world: the territorialization of religious faiths, the decline of older models of kinship, the interaction between capitalism and print, the development of vernacular languages-of-state, and changing conceptions of time. He shows how a nationalism originally born in the Americas was adopted by popular movements in Europe, by imperialist powers, and by anti-imperialist resistances in Asia and Africa.

Actually, Anderson's work, along with that of other scholars on nation and nationalism, gave us tools for understanding the impact of a new order in different regions of the world.[1] Nations that were faced with a new symbolic cartography of the world, created by the globalization process, have their own histories as imagined communities. Can the world be an imagined community for the twenty-first century?

Both "Westward Ho with Kholiwood: The Transnational Turn in the Neoliberal Marketplace" and "Lost and Found in Translation: Problems of Cultural Translation in Hungary after 1989" have inspired me to think about how the world can also be seen as an imagined community and have provided a critical perspective for dealing with this cultural, as well as political, challenge.

In Richard Ellis's essay the author focuses upon three of the main trends of *transnational* "New American Studies": (1) "an *intrahemispheric* approach to American Studies . . . considers the multiple ways in which the United States and the Americas interact and, increasingly, the multiple ways the Americas interact *without* the United States"; (2) *contingent hemispheric studies* includes "varieties of Atlantic Studies—including Transatlantic Studies, cis-Atlantic Studies, and circum-Atlantic Studies," and also "Pacific Studies, specifically Pacific Rim Studies (perhaps these should be called circum-Pacific Studies)"; and (3) "*a third response*, attending to globalizing changes in the world order, precipitated by the necessary recognition of a new closeness between the postindustrial state and late corporate capitalism, and to the consequent blowbacks that have occurred, faced with multinational corporations' increasingly mobile imperiousness toward the marginalized and dispossessed."

In Ellis's essay, a "new American Studies that can accommodate the global" is "inevitably passing beyond what might be called monocular hemispheric studies (be these intra-American Studies, Atlantic Studies, or Pacific Studies)." This is a platform from which the author promotes a new perspective for American Studies:

> What I want to focus on now is the large gap that has opened up between the
> kinds of global emphasis these developments have generated on the one hand

and the relatively established "new" American intra- and contingent hemispheric studies on the other. [. . .]

What is opening up, I contend, is a chance to address such interhemispheric issues—both their routes and their roots. Such considerations can help prevent too much focus falling on long established and arguably well-rehearsed exchanges—for example, upon the transatlantic or upon US intrahemispheric border studies. What is becoming needed is the identification of a range of interhemispheric American Studies procedures, as USAmerican Studies decenter themselves along a number of intercalated global axes. Groundbreaking work has been emerging in this respect for a while—of an increasingly ambitious nature.

In order to build an argument for an interhemispheric American Studies that can bear out the planet as a space for concern, the essay analyzes two films: Sofia Coppola's *Lost in Translation* (2003) and Gurinder Chadha's *Bride and Prejudice* (2004). Both films suggest their own ways of dealing with a difficult matter: the close encounter of different cultures. Treating the films as cultural texts, the essay finally concludes that the twenty-first-century world is far from being an "imagined community" and also that "American Studies" is far from being the best platform for envisioning the planet.

Zsófia Bán's essay, "Lost and Found in Translation: Problems of Cultural Translation in Hungary after 1989," suggests how the art world can be a good path for understanding cultural processes. Dealing with the reception of a controversial, avant-garde piece performed by a group of artists in 2004 and examining traditional attitudes toward art in Hungary, the essay reflects upon the impact of postmodern attitudes on cultural expressions.

The polarization of the debate around the 2004 event is explained by the opposition created between modernism and postmodernism:

> In this framework it is *modernism* that becomes tied to the local, while the postmodern discourse on multiple identities, multiple perspectives, languages, and narratives—originally meant to campaign for the local—is seen as a relativizing and globalizing discourse that lacks depth and is full of ideological implications that modernists wanted to avoid like the plague. Hence, a striking reversal of roles can be detected: modernism and modernists go local (and conservative), while postmodernism (as a form of Americanization) is understood as global and colonizing.

Nevertheless, the essay takes a side and contends that cultural translation can play an important role in dealing with the challenges presented by the dissolution of nations as the traditional "imagined communities."

In fact, both of the essays raise the issue of how cultural expression, either popular culture or avant-garde challenges to it, gives us meanings to propose new ways of envisioning the world as a possible imagined community and also reflects the role played by American Studies (especially a new one) in developing a critical approach for the subject. In order to address a new aspect for these polemical debates, I would like to bring into concern the studies developed by Brazilian anthropologist Renato Ortiz about globalization and *mundialização/mundialization*.[2]

In terms of Ortiz's proposal, the globalization of societies is a historical process that began with the development of capitalism between the fifteenth and eighteenth centuries and involved many groups, social classes, nations, and individuals. By the end of the twentieth century, we could recognize a class of economic, political, and cultural phenomena that allows us to talk about the "globalization of societies" and the "mundialization of culture." Ortiz's proposal contends that contemporary society is a new configuration that resulted from this historical process, as a new phase of the "civilizing process."[3]

In this new phase of the civilizing process, modernity became a world phenomenon that blurs the frontiers of the nation-state. In order to understand this new situation, Ortiz demands an updating of the sociological imagination; he argues for a deterritorialized approach for a deterritorialized world; for this, two obstacles must be overcome: one is methodological and the other is ideological.

The methodological obstacle involves two dichotomous ways of understanding contemporary society. The first position posits a one-dimensional world, in which culture is standardized by the use of the same technical system on a planetary scale. The consumption of the same objects, such as blue jeans, credit cards, televisions sets, and so forth, in the world marketplace is the most expressive sign of the one-dimensional face of our contemporary society.

The opposite position exists alongside the first one, as it has to do not with one-dimensionality but with multiplicity. The postmodern, literary keyword for diagnosing the society of the twenty-first century is "fragmentation." Far from being standardized by technology, customs and behaviors have become more and more sophisticated. The niche market and the confirmation of the individuality of groups and people are enhancing the mass culture in a way that merits consideration.

Ortiz suggests that the key to overcoming this deadlock is to understand that world modernity is created and realized through diversity; as modernity, it privileges the individualization of social relations, autonomy, and affirmation of specifics. Modernity is a wholeness in which the totality is expressed through its parts. Diversity and similitude walk together on the same path, expressing the core of world modernity on an enlarged scale; hence, the false problem of culture standardization is avoided (*Um outro território* 19–20).

However, in the field of culture some points must be stressed, and the most important of them, for Ortiz, is the differentiation between "globalization" and "mundialization." When we refer to economy and technique, we are facing processes that are the same in different parts of the planet. There is only one type of world economic system, which is capitalism, and there is only one technical system (faxes, computers, nuclear energy, satellites, etc.), but this reasoning is difficult to sustain for the cultural domain. For this reason, Ortiz proposes the concept of mundialization (*mundialização*).

The idea of a worldwide pattern of culture is the corollary of world modernity; therefore, it is expressed either in terms of a "symbolic universe," where other forms of understanding, such as political or religious, coexist, or in terms of cultural space crossed by different languages and codes of behavior (that sometimes exist together in a conflictive way). A worldwide culture also configures a civilizing pattern, which has different manifestations all around the planet (*Um outro território* 21).

Finally, Ortiz presents the second obstacle to be avoided: the ideological one. Here the fundamental approach is to deny the automatic identification of globalization and modernity, taking them as synonymous. This ideological proposition valorizes the status quo and is linked to the perspective of traditional groups and corporations, which dispute world political hegemony (*Um outro território* 21).

In order to install a critical perspective, Ortiz contends that we have to imagine the world as a public space, as a civil society where different projects and visions, opposite or complementary, are encountered. Therefore, a universe of objects/ signs, such as blue jeans, movie stars, McDonald's, supermarket products, and so on, are no longer seen as alien impositions but as elements of a world collective memory (*Um outro território* 22).

Ortiz's considerations, joined with the previous reflections, provide elements for bringing back the question, Can the world be an imagined community for the twenty- first century? We can desire a world in balance; we can defend a world civil society; we can fight for the plurality of ways of seeing each other; but what we must not forget is that in order to imagine the world, with all its complexity, as a community, we need to put every position into historical perspective, avoiding absolute statements, and to create a unique way of understanding contemporary society.

Notes

1. See, especially, Eric J. Hobsbawm, *Nations and Nationalism since 1780: Programme, Myth, Reality* (Cambridge, UK: Cambridge UP, 1990).

2. Renato Ortiz, *Um outro território: ensaios sobre a mundialização* (São Paulo: Olho d'água, 1999); and Renato Ortiz, *Mundialilização e cultura* (São Paulo: Editora Brasiliense, 1998). The word "mundialisation" or "mundialization" is the English version of the Portuguese "*mundialização*." But the original meaning of *mundialização*/mundialization means the act of a city or a local authority declaring itself a "world citizen" city by voting a charter stating its awareness of global problems and its sense of shared responsibility. The concept was invented by the self-declared first World Citizen, Garry Davis, in 1949, as a logical extension of the idea of individuals declaring themselves world citizens, and

promoted by Robert Sarrazac, a former leader of the French Résistance who created the Human Front of World Citizens in 1945. In this sense, Ortiz's use of the concept *mundialização*/mundialization is related to a world pattern for cultural processes. The word for world in Portuguese is "*mundo*," so this concept defines the idea of a world culture in process.

3. The book *The Civilizing Process* (Oxford: Wiley-Blackwell, 2000), written by German sociologist Norbert Elias, is an influential work in sociology and Elias's most important work. It was first published in 1939 in German as *Über den Prozeß der Zivilisation*. Because of World War II it was virtually ignored; however, it was republished in the 1960s when it was also translated into English. Covering roughly the time span in European history between the ninth and twentieth centuries, Elias's is the first formal analysis and theory of civilization.

Works Cited

Anderson, Benedict. *Imagined Communities: Reflections on the Origin and Spread of Nationalism*. London: Verso, rev. ed., 1991.

Elias, Norbert. *The Civilizing Process*. Oxford: Wiley-Blackwell, 2000.

Hobsbawm, Eric J. *Nations and Nationalism since 1780: Programme, Myth, Reality*. Cambridge, UK: Cambridge UP, 1990.

Ortiz, Renato. *Mundialilização e cultura*. São Paulo: Editora Brasiliense, 1998.

———. *Um outro território: ensaios sobre a mundialização*. São Paulo: Olho d'água, 1999.

PART V

Disrupting Binaries:
Whose "Country Music"
and Whose "Hip-Hop"?

CHAPTER 9

Tales of the West

"Americanization" in an Era of "Europeanization"

Kristin Solli

In the early 2000s, "the West" as a geopolitical unit was under intense pressure. In an article in the *Atlantic Monthly* from 2002 titled "The End of the West," Charles A. Kupchan, an expert on European-U.S. relations, predicted that "the next clash of civilizations will not be between the West and the rest but between the United States and Europe."[1] Although in hindsight this prophecy might seem to have overstated the case, there is no question that at the time, the war in Iraq had strained the relationship between Europe and the United States. "Mistrust of America in Europe ever higher" announced a survey conducted by the Pew Research Center, from March 2004, which featured polls that showed that Europeans were utterly unhappy with U.S. foreign policy (Pew Global Attitudes Project). All over Europe, large-scale protests against the war in Iraq were organized, and critiques of the United States were ubiquitous and passionate. In Oslo, Norway, for example, newspapers reported that Americans in Norway were being verbally and physically attacked because of their nationality (Østli 12–13). While the U.S. embassy advised Americans living in Norway not to fly the American flag in public, angry Norwegian protesters set fire to the flag on the streets of Oslo.

During those turbulent transatlantic times of 2003 and 2004, I was doing fieldwork about country music in Norway. As such, I spent a lot of time with people who had a strong symbolic affinity for "America." Among many country music fans, sporting "American" symbols such as cowboy hats and American flags is common practice. Nowhere were these symbols displayed and celebrated more prominently than at one of the prime sites of my fieldwork: the country music festivals that are held in rural areas of Norway every summer. The contrast, then, between the U.S. skepticism of dominant Norwegian public discourse and the embrace of American symbols at these festivals was stark.

Most Norwegians, however, profess to have a more complex relationship with the United States than this either/or contrast suggests. In editorials and commentaries, many Norwegians were careful to point out that disagreeing with U.S. foreign policy does not translate into a dislike of all things American. Similarly, many of the country music fans I got to know argued that wearing a cowboy hat did not necessarily make them supporters of U.S. foreign policy. On the one hand, such arguments speak to the long-standing European ambivalence about the United States, an ambivalence that has been analyzed extensively by scholars such as Rob Kroes, Richard Pells, and many others.[2] In what follows, however, I use Norway as a case study to suggest that the transatlantic conflict over the Iraq War in the early and mid-2000s speaks to issues that go beyond this "normal" state of ambivalence. More specifically, I argue that Norwegian discourses about "America" and "Americanization" during that time must be understood in relation to the process of "Europeanization" spearheaded by the European Union. This process was of course well under way before the Iraq War, yet the war and the ensuing debates about European responses to it intensified debates about the different "mentalities" and "worldviews" of Europe and the United States, suggesting precisely the "clash of civilizations" scenario that Kupchan evoked in his article in the *Atlantic Monthly*.

More specifically, this essay explores how the increased polarization between Europe and the United States in the post–Cold War era caused grave anxieties among Norwegians about Norway's place in the world at the beginning of the new millennium. Until the early 1990s, "the West" was a geopolitical construct that encompassed Western Europe and the United States. While Norway's position within this constellation was undisputed, the increased distance between the United States and Europe in the 1990s and early 2000s led many Norwegian political analysts and commentators to pose the following ultimatum: Norway must choose between Europe and the United States.[3] In this context, debates about the United States in Norway were implicitly, and often explicitly, about Europe and, more specifically, about the question of Norwegian membership in the European Union. In referendums in 1972 and 1994, Norwegians voted not to join the EU with very narrow margins, and over the last decades, Norway's relationship to Europe has been a consistent point of political and cultural debate.[4] As a country that is geographically located in Europe but has opted not to be part of the EU *twice*, which "West" does, or should, Norway belong to? The discursive and symbolic value of "America" in Norway, in other words, cannot be fully understood without also contextualizing it in relation to the discursive and symbolic value of "Europe."

Although the case study here looks at a historical context that has since changed, the central dynamic of the case highlights a larger analytical point about the discursive and symbolic meanings of "America" outside the United States that still holds true. To understand what sort of work the terms "America" and "Americanization" do in a Norwegian context requires an analytical framework that goes beyond a bilateral conception of U.S.-Norwegian relations. In short, I would like us to consider how the symbolic negotiation of "America" in a given locale and at a given historical moment can be analyzed as a multilateral rather than bilateral process in which meanings of "America" and "Americanization" are inflected and refracted by a host of local and regional power structures and set of relations.

To illustrate this point, I begin by analyzing the embrace of American symbols at Norwegian country music festivals within a larger discourse of the way Norwegian rurality was mobilized in Norwegian EU debates in the early 2000s. I then move on to describe the "culturalization" of the European Union since the early 1990s as a process through which the EU has actively sought to carve out "a European cultural area," in part by relying on the United States as an "other." I conclude by noting how this dynamic shows the persistence of how "culture" is mobilized to produce loyalties and by briefly considering some of the unfortunate implications of this tendency to reduce conflicts and disagreements to questions of "civilizations" and "culture." Events that have passed since the historical moment of this case study suggest the urgency of finding ways to critique and combat such reductionist views and arguments.

The Wild West in Norway: Abject Rurality and the "Norwegian Other"

During my fieldwork, commentaries about the United States and debates about Norway's relationship to the United States seemed endless. In the first few months of 2003, Norwegian newspapers were flooded with editorials, essays, and stories involving the United States in some capacity. Commentaries about Norway's relationship with and attitudes toward the United States were also common. For example, several writers addressed the apparent contradiction between Norway's strong dislike of the Bush administration and the perception that Norway is one of the most "Americanized" countries in the world. "Norwegians have adopted arch-American styles and tastes. Yet our contempt for Americans is increasing," begins a March 2003 feature article that explores Norwegians' conflicted relationship with the United States in *Aftenposten*, one of Norway's largest dailies (Østli 1).

While examples of such "arch-American" tastes are present in many parts of Norwegian society, when Norwegians use the term "Americanization," they tend to refer to a specific subset of American influences or, more precisely, to a subset of Norwegian practices associated with tastes perceived as "American." "When people are afraid of Americanization," comedian and cultural critic Are Kalvø notes, "they are not afraid of Norway becoming a big multiethnic country in North-America. They are afraid of Norway becoming a country of vulgar consumers with simple tastes" (123). Indeed, he points out that in Norwegian the adjective "American" is frequently used as a synonym for "unrefined, loud, [and] narrow-minded" (123). He explains this semantic connection by describing how Norwegians who embrace American cars, country music, fast food, and cowboy boots, are perceived as embodying Norwegian vulgarity and bad taste (123). As such, complaints about "Americanization" are often uttered as a critique of what some Norwegians see as provincial and vulgar aspects of Norwegian culture. In this section, I explain how this sort of Americanness functions discursively within Norway as one element in the construction of a working-class nationalist ethos. From a middle-class point of view, the people who embrace this ethos are frequently perceived as vulgar "others" who embody a kind of abject Norwegianness. In sum, this section analyzes the politics of claiming "America" in light of domestic Norwegian anxieties surrounding the ambiguous status of "the West" as a coherent geopolitical unit.

The association between working-class tastes, rurality, and American symbols can be seen at the dozens of country music festivals held in rural parts of Norway each summer. The festivals, which have been held since the early 1980s, range in size—some attracting a few hundred participants, others attracting several thousand, most of whom are working-class. As I have shown in more detail elsewhere, the musical performances and forms of sociability at the festivals create a fairly coherent world that enacts and celebrates a working-class rural nationalism.[5] The practices and aesthetics of the festivals appear remarkably consistent over time, some of the festivals even have the same line-up of bands today as they did during the time of my field work. The most popular musical acts at these events are bands that merge U.S. country music models with lyrics that describe rural Norwegian life, often sung in Norwegian rural dialects. Similarly, the dominant forms of sociability, such as ways of drinking and dancing, are often perceived as cultural practices that are prevalent in rural areas.

In this context the display of American "country" symbols is another element of this sociability that contributes to the celebration and enactment of this form of rurality. More specifically, these symbols aid in the sort of immersion and participation that is a main part of the appeal of the festivals. The Skjåk Country Music Festival's brochure from 2004, for example, stresses that the festival allows attendees not just to listen to country music but also to "be" country: "The Country Festival Skjåk has found a spectacular setting and we provide quality, distinctiveness (*særpreg*) and a unique atmosphere where we will all enjoy good country music and be Cowgirls & Cowboys for a whole weekend" (Skjåk Country Music Festival). The festival, in other words, is not only a place to *listen* to country music; it also provides festival-goers with an opportunity to "*be* Cowgirls & Cowboys" [my emphasis].

The omnipresence of cowboy hats, boots, western wear, and American flags shows that many of the festival-goers come to the festival seeking more than a musical experience. Festival participants dress up in cowboy and cowgirl outfits and decorate their temporary homes at the festival campgrounds with American and Norwegian flags and "Wild West" decorations such as bales of hay, plastic cacti, and cow skulls. These symbols, then, help construct a festival collective, and for many festival participants being a part of this collective is often more

Fig. 1: Norwegian cowboys and cowgirls at Skjåk Country Music Festival, 2004. Photo: Kristin Solli.

important than knowing the history and background of the symbols. As such, the festivals tend to be centered on evoking a general sense of Americanness rather than on recreating "accurate" representations of U.S. culture. For example, many of the symbols are combined according to principles that might seem odd in a U.S. setting. One such combination is the connection between country music and American cars. At the Seljord Country Music Festival, for instance, what is referred to as the "Country Car Meet" has become an integral part of the festival. This meet is an exhibition of American cars, or *amerikanere* (the English translation of this word is "Americans") as vintage American cars are commonly called. This meet, then, is an extension of the Norwegian Amcar scene, which consists of people with an interest in American cars, predominantly from the 1950s and '60s. Among Amcar enthusiasts, American flags and American music—particularly from the 1950s—are common accessories. Many of the working-class country music fans I spoke with during my fieldwork either owned or expressed admiration for *amerikanere* and saw the "Country Car Meet" as a natural ingredient in the festival.

Another and more contested "country" symbol is the Confederate flag. Along with the American flag, the Lone Star flag, and the Norwegian flag, this flag is a common decoration at the festival grounds. The flag is a point of contention

Fig. 2: Truck with American and Confederate flags, Vinstra, 2004. Photo: Kristin Solli.

between those who know its troubled racial legacy in the United States and those who see it as an "ordinary" festival prop. For example, Hans, a musician who is married to an American and has lived in the United States for several years was very upset at the sight of the flag: "They have no idea what this flag really means. They don't know what they're doing; it's embarrassing!"[6] For Hans, who is well aware of the flag's history and contemporary controversial uses in the United States, the Confederate flag is a symbol of racism, and hence, displaying it is either an act of racism or an act of ignorance.

Fig. 3: Confederate flag at the camp ground, Vinstra, 2004. Photo: Kristin Solli.

For others, however, the flag is an accessory used to enhance the festival atmosphere just like the American flag or the Lone Star flag. Naeem, who moved to Norway from Egypt and who introduced himself to me as "the Egyptian cowboy," owns a stall that sells hats, belts, and belt buckles.[7] At the festivals I attended, his booth was frequently decorated by a Confederate flag. At one festival I noticed that he was replacing a Colorado state flag hanging from his stall with a Confederate flag. When I asked him about the switch, he replied that he liked the colors and design of the Confederate flag better. Naeem's two helpers, an older man from Vietnam and a younger man from Uzbekistan, nodded emphatically in agreement. Naeem and his employees, then, seemed to perceive the flag in terms of aesthetics rather than racial politics.

The Confederate flag, however, remains an ambiguous symbol. Although racism is not the only possible, or even dominant, meaning it has at the festivals, that is not to say that the Confederate flag is never used with explicit racist connotations in Norway. In 2000, for example, the Norwegian neo-Nazi organization Boot Boys used the flag in a public demonstration to commemorate the Nazi leader Rudolf Hess ("Rasistiske Ytringer"). When I asked a woman who has been attending country music festivals since the 1980s what she made of the presence of these flags, she said that she thinks some people do use it as a racist symbol. For some, she explained, "it's supposed to be black and white [svarthvitt]; they're simply racist, some of them." When I talked to people who were using the Confederate flag, however, they talked about it as a symbol of "the land where country music comes from" and said that it helped create "the right atmosphere."[8] I do not know whether such answers were sincere or formulated to not offend my political views, but it would be naïve to conclude that the flag is always devoid of racist undercurrents. Given that overt racism is considered socially unacceptable by most Norwegians, the fact that I never heard comments that explicitly connected the Confederate flag to racial ideologies might reflect that people were reluctant to make such connections in front of me rather than that such connections are never made. As I return to later in this essay, whiteness plays an increasingly important role in Norwegian nationalism, and for some, flying the Confederate flag might be a way of asserting an explicit racialized and racist vision of the nation. Thus, as the Boot Boys incident suggests, the U.S. racist legacy stays with the flag in some circles; in others, however, the flag is predominantly associated with "America" more generally conceived.

In the America evoked at Norwegian country music festivals, then, the frontier of the 1800s and the drive-in restaurants of the 1950s blend seamlessly. A new kind of Norwegian American aesthetic is created from these fragments in which the display of a general kind of Americanness is more important than the individual symbols' original meaning. This symbolic practice focuses on presenting Americanness as a spectacle for public consumption rather than as a realistic representation of U.S. culture. The pleasure involved in enacting this kind of Americanness is rooted in the way it functions as a critique of aspects of

Norwegian modernity, particularly as this modernity is represented by the state. The cowboy and the car, for example, are both icons that center on individuality and independence.

Similarly, for some festival attendees, the Confederate flag is associated with "rebels" even if the historical details surrounding this "rebelliousness" are vague. Many of the working-class festival participants I encountered consider Norway a country with too much bureaucracy, too many rules, with a state that designs laws that unduly meddle in people's private lives. They often cited a law that bans smoking in all bars and restaurants and high taxes on items such as cars, gas, alcohol, and cigarettes as evidence of the intrusive nature of Norway's "nanny state." "You're not allowed to have any fun in this country," an unemployed car mechanic concluded after having explained to me why he "love[s] everything about America." To this car mechanic, who has never been to the United States, an embrace of America as represented by cowboys and the "Wild West" is also a way of critiquing the Norwegian state, which does not allow him to have "fun." These festival symbols, then, evoke the freedom of the open road and the freedom of the frontier and allow an affiliation with rebels and outlaws who refuse to be governed by society's laws and regulations. As such, "being Cowboys & Cowgirls" is not an attempt to become like Americans but an argument for a particular way of being Norwegian.[9]

This way of being Norwegian centers on the mobilization of a working-class rural nationalism that is articulated in opposition to what Barbara Ching and Gerald Creed have called "urban(e) others" (28). These "urban(e) others," however, similarly construct these festivals as sites for "rural others." In Norwegian public discourse, country music festivals have come to represent a rural dystopia of cultural depravity and drunken degeneracy; in short, these events have become associated with a form of abject rurality. For example, over the last twenty years, *Dagbladet,* one of Norway's largest national daily newspapers, has consistently employed a sensationalist preoccupation with excessive drinking and partying in their coverage of country music festivals. Since 1984 these events have made the front page of the newspaper twice. The headline of the first of these front pages reads "Raw Drunkenness in Festival-Norway" and is accompanied by a picture of a man passed out on the ground with people dancing around him. "Many a festival visitor fell asleep from the fun. This year's country festival in Skjåk turned into an orgy of drunkenness," the caption reports ("Rå fyll i festival-Norge"). The headline of the other front page announces "Bit Off and Ate Ear in a Rage" ("Beit av og spiste øret i raseri"). The subheading explains that a young man was attacked by another man at the Vinstra Country Music Festival because he had played hip-hop on his boom box at the festival campground.

These kinds of portrayals in national media outlets have marked country music festivals as spaces of crude and "*vill vest*" ("Wild West") behaviors. As such, dominant national discourse presents country music festivals as events for "vulgar others." Raymond Williams has noted that the tendency to think of rurality and urbanity in terms of dystopian/utopian binaries is a mode of thinking that has a long history and that appears across cultures: "On the country has gathered the idea of a natural way of life: of peace, innocence, and simple virtue. On the city has gathered the idea of an achieved centre: of learning, communication, light. Powerful hostile associations have also developed: on the city as a place of noise, worldliness, and ambition; on the country as a place of backwardness, ignorance, limitation" (1). As such, the Norwegian rural/urban binaries are certainly not exclusively "Norwegian." However, as I explain in the next section, in a Norwegian context this binary has also been constituted along national lines. Rurality has discursively been positioned as "Norwegian," whereas urbanity has been constituted as "cosmopolitan" or "European." The abject rurality of country music festivals thus also amounts to a kind of abject Norwegianness, and the American "country" symbols contribute to this abjectness.

Europe: Norway's Other?

These festivals, then, rely on a dynamic in which rurality is conflated with the nation. This discursive construction draws its power from long-standing divisions within Norwegian culture Since the late 1960s this split has been most vigorously mobilized in the debates over Norwegian membership in the European Union. Norway has turned down EU membership twice. In referendums in 1972 and 1994, the Norwegian population voted not to join.[10] Both times there were clear voting patterns: supporters of EU membership lived in and around Oslo and other urban centers. People living in rural and semirural areas were overwhelmingly against membership.[11] This pattern can be explained by the fact that those who stand to lose economically by joining the EU are farmers who, because of EU regulations, would not be able to maintain the state subsidies that currently keep them in business. However, the agricultural sector currently employs a very small percentage of Norway's labor force. This means that the majority of those who voted against membership did not do so because their personal economic interests were at stake.

Social scientist Iver B. Neumann argues that because previous constructions of Norwegian identity have been so strongly tied to rurality, preserving Norwegian rurality—as represented by farming and fishing—is a question of preserving "the idea of Norway" (176). Hence voting "no" to the EU is not necessarily a question of preserving economic interests, but of preserving a particular national imaginary. This imaginary dates back to the nineteenth-century nation-building efforts. When Norway was let go by Danish colonial rule in 1814, Norwegian political and intellectual elites quickly turned to the culture of rural farmers for symbolic resources in their efforts to build a new independent Norwegian nation-state.[12] The elite presumed that, unlike people in the cities, these farmers had remained uncontaminated by foreign and, particularly, Danish influences. In this decolonization process, the farmers were seen as a link to a Norway of the Middle Ages—a Norway before Danish rule. And as such, these farmers became carriers of a Norwegian essence.

This conflation of rural culture and the nation still figures prominently in Norway's national imaginary. Neumann argues that because EU membership jeopardizes Norwegian agriculture, which again jeopardizes the existence of rural Norwegian culture, the fight against the EU has been inserted into a series of historical struggles for Norwegian independence "against the Danes, against the Swedes, against the Nazis, and now against the European Union" (177). Neumann's analysis identifies a set of binaries that informs the Norwegian EU debate. Those who are against Norwegian membership, he says, tend to define "Norway" and the "EU" as two opposing discursive formations. These formations include the following Norway–EU oppositions: independence–union; people–state; parliament–bureaucracy; sovereignty–supranationality; equality–difference; small–large; country–city; rural–centralized; periphery–center; welfare–competition; anti-colonial–colonial (35).

According to Neumann, in other words, many Norwegians define "Europe" as "non-Norwegian," suggesting that questions of nationalism are at the heart of this binary. Given that almost half the population voted for membership, however, far from all Norwegians understand the EU as a colonial power that will take away Norway's independence as Neumann's binaries suggest. On the contrary, Norwegian political, economic, and intellectual elites are overwhelmingly in favor of EU membership and see the no-voters as impediments to progress. In an era of internationalization and globalization, the fact that so many Norwegians actively reject "joining" Europe irks these EU advocates, who often interpret Norway's "no" as the result of irrational and outdated ideas about the world and Norway's place in it.[13] This polarization between an urban "elite" and a rural "people" means that a positive assertion of a rural identity, such as the one enacted at country music festivals, is not just about asserting rurality but also about asserting a particular vision of the nation. Although I do not mean to say that those who attend country music festivals in the early 2000s or attend them today do so as an explicit political act against EU membership, the Norwegian celebrations of the "Wild West" can be seen as an affirmation of a particular articulation of class, nation, and rurality that gains particular power in light of the Norwegian debates about "Europe."

This articulation should neither be romanticized as an act of progressive local "resistance" nor dismissed as an expression of "fringe" nationalism. At Norwegian country music festivals, the validation of Norway as a rural nation can serve to assert an essentialist and static vision of "Norway for Norwegians" with clear ethnic and racial assumptions that exclude more elastic conceptions of nationhood. The ambiguous use of the Confederate flag, for example, speaks to undercurrents of a racialized articulation of nationalism in which nation, place, and people are imagined as a "natural" and "organic" whole. In addition, given Europe's increasing racial and ethnic diversity, "Europe" might also be associated with racial "others." Even if statistics suggest that there is no correlation between being against EU membership and being for tighter immigration laws, it is becoming increasingly difficult to separate discourses of "Norwegianness" from discourses of skin color and race.[14]

For example, during my fieldwork at the festivals, explicit talk about race was rare. That, however, does not mean race is absent from the nationalism celebrated at the festivals. One of the few direct references to race that I heard was when Hans, the musician who reacted strongly to the way some festival participants use the Confederate flag, quipped that to be black at a country music festival should be considered a new kind of extreme sport. Hans made this comment after having observed a black audience member "with a cowboy hat and everything!" One reason for the relative absence of overt comments about race is probably that an overwhelming majority of festival participants are white. The homogeneity of the festivals hence makes whiteness, and race in general, a nonissue.

In a larger perspective, this resonates with the history of Norwegian nationalism, in which race—or, more precisely, skin color—until quite recently was not a central aspect. In her analysis of Norwegian discourses of immigration, Marianne Gullestad argues that while earlier articulations of Norwegian nationalism did not rely on racial differences, contemporary articulations do: "Previously, Norwegian identity was defined in opposition to Danes and Swedes and other Europeans, and they have all been 'white.' 'Skin color' has thus not been a central element of being Norwegian, *but it has now become important.* 'Whiteness' has emerged as a given dimension of what it means to be 'Norwegian'" (289; emphasis in original). This process, she explains, is closely related to increased immigration to Norway from "non-Western"—that is, nonwhite—countries from the 1970s on. According to Statistics Norway, 1.5 percent of the Norwegian population were categorized as "immigrants" in 1970. Of this group, 16 percent were considered to be of "non-western" origin. In 2004, 7.6 percent of the population were classified as "immigrants," of which 72 percent were considered to come from "non-western" countries. The five largest groups of immigrants were from the following countries: Pakistan, Sweden, Denmark, Vietnam, and Iraq (Forgaard and Dzamarija 18–19). Over the last thirty years, then, Norway has become the home of many people with roots in places outside of Western Europe. This development, Gullestad argues, has contributed to a construction of Norwegian identity that increasingly has come to be defined in opposition to "others" of color. In this context, the opposite of "black," Gullestad explains, is not necessarily "white," but "Norwegian" (208).

It is crucial to understand how pervasive this ideological structure is, Gullestad insists. As both she and Anniken Hagelund have suggested, Norwegian public discourse tends to present racialized and racist ideologies as a feature of "fringe" and "extremist" groups rather than as a deeply ingrained part of Norwegian culture (Gullestad 47–65). These groups are often referred to in such terms as "the dregs of society" ("*grumset i folkedypet*"), indicating that racism is the domain of the "social losers" at "the bottom" of Norwegian society. Gullestad, however, convincingly shows that ideologies and discursive formations that tacitly define Norwegian identity in terms of whiteness are widespread among all groups of Norwegians. The rural nationalism of Norwegian country music festivals— whether explicitly or implicitly coded as "white"—should hence be seen as one articulation of a common way of connecting nation, culture, people, and, increasingly, skin color rather than a particular "extremist" version. This, of course, does not make this articulation of nationalism less problematic; rather, it suggests that racialized nationalism is the norm rather than the exception.

The United States: Europe's Other?

In Norway in the early 2000s, then, debates about the EU mobilized a Norwegian rural identity, and in this mobilization, Europe functioned as an "other," giving this rural identity part of its power. In this section, I suggest that American symbols were particularly potent in the construction of this rurality, particularly in light of the Europeanization efforts spearheaded by the EU that tended to rely on the United States as an "other" to promote a sense of cultural pan-Europeanism. Again, I am not implying that the Norwegians wearing cowboy hats and waving American flags at country music festivals did so as a direct response to these policies. In fact, very few Norwegians knew much about or were interested in these policies. Yet, as I return to in my conclusion, the culturalization of the EU shaped the EU debates in Norway at that time in more indirect ways. Given the increasing centrality of a Pan-European cultural identity in the engineering of a European polity, Norway's outsider status raised questions about the country's allegiances in a time when "the West" was becoming a less clear-cut geopolitical unit. Hence, the promotion of Pan-Europeanism fed into anxieties about Norway's place in the world.

Since the early 1990s, the European Union has paid increasingly more attention to culture. I describe this process as the "culturalization" of Europe, not, of course, because Europe has not "had" culture before, but to highlight that the trend of calling on a Pan-European culture to justify the existence and actions of the European Union has emerged with particular political urgency since the 1990s. EU leaders saw "culture" as a peripheral matter while the alliance was predominantly economic. Although certain symbolic measures were undertaken (such as the creation of a European flag, the adoption of a European anthem, and the institution of a Europe Day), EU technocrats did not see "culture" as the domain of an organization that was first and foremost preoccupied with economy and trade. This changed in the early 1990s when the EU started putting considerable effort into building a "European cultural area."[15] The 1992 Treaty of Maastricht created the legal basis for the establishment of a "European citizenship" and also included a "culture article," which provides the legal grounds for the union's cultural policies.[16] Whereas arguments for a united Europe had previously predominantly centered on strengthening the European economy and creating lasting intra-European peace, since the early 1990s the presumed existence of "European culture" has increasingly been deployed as an argument for why the citizens of European nation-states should embrace the European Union.

An EU informational pamphlet published in 2002 titled "A Community of Cultures" provides an example of a typical rationale that EU officials during this period gave for making "culture" a domain of the EU. "By giving the European Union a say in cultural matters," the pamphlet explains, "the Member States' governments set out to create a 'Europe of the peoples,' the idea being to make people in Europe aware of their shared history and values, to make them more aware of European culture and Europe's heritage" (European Commission 28). The phrase to "make aware" presupposes, then, that a common European culture already exists and that it is simply a matter of making Europeans aware of it. In so doing, "European culture" is posited as a given that is simply awaiting discovery.

An underlying principle for this focus on culture is the belief that "culture" will help legitimize the EU as a polity. In particular, culture was launched as a remedy to fix what is often referred to as the EU's "democratic deficit." This term is used to describe the EU's problems in terms of political legitimacy. The low participation in EU elections is often used as a typical example of this "deficit." In other words, many EU leaders believe that convincing Europeans that they have a cultural stake in the European Union will increase the EU's political legitimacy. Hence, it is important to convince Europeans that a shared European culture exists. For instance, the explicit goal of "Culture 2000," the program that from 2000 to 2007 coordinated all EU cultural initiatives, was "to bring to life the cultural area common to the European people."[17]

A report that evaluated the activities of Culture 2000, tellingly titled "Making Citizenship Work," insists that culture is what will give European citizenship "concrete meaning" and create "a feeling of *belonging* to the Union" (Commission of the European Communities 5). According to this report, culture is what will make Europeans realize their responsibilities and rights as political subjects of the EU and, hence, lend the EU political legitimacy. From this point of view, it is no coincidence that the creation of a "European citizenship" and the inclusion of a "culture article" in the EU legal framework coincided. As Cris Shore points out, despite the fact that the EU likes to present itself as a cosmopolitan postnational improvement on old-school nationalism, "The assumption that cultural and political identities must be congruent if institutions are to have legitimacy echoes a fundamental principle of *nationalist* thinking" ("Governing Europe" 165–92; emphasis in original).

The construction of a European "cultural area" as envisioned in these policies meant that "the rest of the world" needed to be constructed as fundamentally different. "Europeans have a wealth of national and local cultures that distinguish them from one another," argues an official EU pamphlet published in 2004, "but they are united by their common heritage of values that distinguishes Europeans from the rest of the world" (Fontaine 6). The cultural policies rarely name what these distinguishing values are, and when they do, they typically evoke such values as "freedom," "democracy," "tolerance," and "solidarity" (Fontaine). What makes these values uniquely "European," however, is not specified. This lack of specificity is both deliberate and necessary from the point of view of the European Union. Naming values in more detail would risk alienating those Europeans who would not feel that a particular value pertained to them, as well as those whose values might not be specifically listed as "European." Thus, a more effective way of creating a European "us" is to rely on a non-European "them."

A survey titled "Perceptions of the European Union" conducted in 2001 for the European Commission presents a clear example of who a European "us" defined as a non-European "them" in the early 2000s. The report argues that the majority of European citizens "see in Europe first and foremost a historical entity, a land—even *the* land—of culture" (OPTEM 5; emphasis in original). Europeans also, the report says, feel "that this model, built on the foundations of cultural and humanistic values, is unique. It sets Europe in opposition to the United States, whose collective mentality is broadly perceived as very different and which in some of the countries studied, is lampooned as a people without a history, materialist, bereft of these values and which also arouses intense hostility" (OPTEM 5). According to this report, then, when Europeans were asked to define "Europe," they saw it as "the land of culture," most sharply defined when contrasted with its opposite—the United States—a land without culture.

Thus, from the point of view of many Europeans during the early 2000s, the presence of "culture" is what set Europe apart from the United States. European cultural policies, however, frequently posited European culture as something that is fragile and in need of protection from the United States. This rationale was commonly used to argue for the need for specific EU cultural policies. "Making Citizenship Work," the report published in 2004 that I mentioned earlier, presents statistics showing that the average share of European TV and film in European markets is well below 50 percent (Commission of the European Communities 13). The report then goes on to argue that "EU intervention in the audiovisual sector is therefore part of a strategy to give Europeans a choice. Unless Europeans are able to watch stories, drama, documentaries and other works that reflect the reality of their own lives and histories, as well as those of their neighbours, they will cease to recognise and understand them fully" (13).

Although it is never explicitly stated, "giving Europeans a choice" here means providing a European alternative to a market dominated by American products.

Watching U.S.-made audiovisual works, according to this report, risks alienating Europeans from one another, since these works do not depict European realities. Here the argument seems to be that works that do not "reflect" European history and everyday life make up a threat to European integration, hence, the need for a European alternative and, hence, the need for EU audiovisual policies. While this kind of thinking is problematic in that it assumes that European audiences are passive consumers who uncritically accept whatever Hollywood feeds them, the main point here is how the creation of a Pan-European culture at this time relied on the United States as an "other" for self-definition yet was also threatened by U.S. culture as something that would hinder Europeans from understanding and "recognizing" one another. In this way the United States functioned both as an "other" that defined "European culture" and a "threat" that warranted the existence of a "European culture" to protect a European way of life.

Of course, there is absolutely nothing new about this kind of European "othering" of the United States; what was different at the historical juncture of this case study, however, was the political need for such stereotypes.[18] The "unique" European culture that the EU relied on for political legitimacy tended to depend on such stock ideas of American culture as an "other" through which Pan-Europeanism could be discovered. And as this report shows, to many Europeans the most obvious aspect of "being European" in the early 2000s was that it meant "not being American."

By embracing Europe's "other," then, the Norwegian country music festivalgoers I interviewed in 2003 and 2004 asserted a non-European Norwegianness. Again, I do not mean to say that Norwegians attended these festivals primarily as deliberate acts of anti-EU advocacy. But I do want to suggest that the Europeanization of Europe framed the domestic politics and pleasures of the celebration of America at Norwegian country music festivals. Just as the polarized debates over EU membership framed the discursive value of "Europe" in Norway, polarized transatlantic relations framed the discursive value of "America" in Europe. Both of these discourses in turn framed the politics of the flag-waving and revelry in American symbols at Norwegian country music festivals during that time. The embrace of things American was a way of expressing "non-Europeanness" that again was a way of celebrating a rural vision of the Norwegian nation. The celebration of America, in other words, became a way to celebrate Norway. Thus, it is in the discursive triangulation between "America," "Europe," and "Norway" that we can start making sense of the work that the terms "Europeanization" and "Americanization" did in a Norwegian context during the early 2000s.

Conclusion

A lot has happened since Kupchan's prediction of "the end of the west" in 2003. When Barack Obama was elected president in 2008, European mistrust of the

United States subsided radically, particularly in Western Europe (Wike, Poushter, and Zainulbhai). The emergence of ISIS and continued conflicts in the Middle East have in certain ways reconsolidated the West geopolitically, in some ways disproving, or at least complicating, Kupchan's prediction. "Brexit," the UK referendum in 2016 in which a majority of the voters said they wanted the UK to leave the European Union, indicated that European unity is a fragile construction. Despite the efforts described above to mobilize cultural loyalties to Europe, the appeal of nationalism is still very powerful. The rise of Donald Trump as a serious political contender in the United States, however, brings back some of the same rhetoric and discourses about the differences between Europe and the United States that were prevalent in the early 2000s.

In other words, although the case study presented here speaks to a particular historical moment, the lessons of this historical moment still resonate today. To show this, let me first go back to transatlantic relations in the 2000s. Writing in 2003, anthropologist John Borneman argues that transatlantic relations at the time were "no longer triangulated by Communism but by a new configuration of forces, by Europeanization, Americanization, and the Middle East" (487). Much like Kupchan's prediction about "the end of the west," Borneman sees the divisions between the United States and Europe in the early 2000s as ones that were likely to last. In his analysis, he argues that the falling out should be understood in light of two simultaneous processes: what he calls "the Europeanization of Europe" and "the Americanization of the U.S." Europe, he says, is becoming increasingly "cosmopolitan," while the United States is becoming increasingly "provincial" (487). The results of these developments, according to Borneman, were particularly visible in these continents' different approaches to the Middle East. As such, Borneman sees the disagreement over the war in Iraq as a symptom of fundamental social, political, and cultural differences that "widened" "the distance between European and U.S. self-understandings" (487).

Borneman's observations about this widening certainly resonated with Norwegian commentators at the time, many of whom argued that because Norway is closer geographically and culturally to Europe, EU membership should be a "natural" choice for Norway. In a book published in 2003 that discusses the relationship between the United States, Europe, and Norway, Steinar Hansson argued, "Norway is isolating itself from those we should stay the closest to. At the same time, we are farther from the American worldview than ever in the post–[World War II] era" (131). During the time of my fieldwork, what Hansson refers to as Norway's "double no"—Norway's rejection of EU membership and Norway's refusal to support the United States' war in Iraq—was a point of concern for many Norwegian commentators and political analysts. Given the "widened distance" between Europe and the United States, many argued that this double no was untenable and that Norway had to choose which "civilization" with which to affiliate.

While in certain ways Europe and the United States have been each other's "others" for centuries, the emergence of a politically united Europe added an acute political dimension to this othering in the 1990s and 2000s. As such, one of the larger issues at stake at this particular moment in history is how the EU's mobilization of a Pan-European cultural identity since the 1990s is symptomatic of a world in which "culture" is the main site for the production of loyalties (Domínguez 31).[19] "Culture," Virginia Domínguez argues, is "something invoked rather than something that is" (23). She has coined the term "culturalism" to describe how "we think and act in terms of it [culture]" and how "we make strategic social and political interventions by invoking it" (21). The emergence of EU cultural policies can be conceptualized as an invocation of "European culture" to make a political intervention—that is, the creation of a European polity. EU policy makers and administrators see cultural policies and cultural initiatives as necessary steps toward greater European integration, and the EU is presented as a cosmopolitan improvement on old-fashioned nationalism. As Shore argues, however, rallying around "European culture" in the name of European political integration is ultimately a strategy designed according to nationalist rather than cosmopolitan principles ("Governing Europe" 175). This shows not only the persistence of nationalist thinking but also the continued appeal of "culture" in the social engineering of "peoplehoods."

In the 2000s, both the EU's invocations of "European culture" as the basis for European political unity as well as the U.S. administration's invocations of "America's mission in the world" to justify its foreign policy decisions were political interventions that were given cultural rationales.[20] While I am not arguing that culture is an irrelevant factor in such interventions or that there are no cultural differences between the United States and Europe, this case study highlights how international conflicts quite easily seem to be reduced to questions of culture. Robert Cooper, a British foreign policy specialist, for instance, argues that international relations' traditional focus on "interests" and "foreign affairs" is not adequate to understand how decisions are made in "the real world" (83–152). "Identity beats interest, just as domestic beats foreign," he concludes (129). Cooper's call to shift the focus of international relations to questions of cultural values, identity, and domestic affairs is helpful, however, only if culture does not remain a given.

In the time that has passed since the 2000s, the idea of "civilizational clashes" has certainly not subsided. On the contrary, the rise of right-wing nationalism as evidenced by Trump's popularity in the United States, the appeals to nationalist and anti-immigrant rhetoric in the Brexit referendum, the nationalist and xenophobic responses to immigration in European countries, shows that culture continues to be mobilized to do political, strategic, and economic work. Scholars and students of culture should help dispel the idea that cultures "cause" clashes.[21] This is an important task because when international conflicts are understood in terms of non-negotiable cultures rather than as struggles over interests, power, and politics, diplomacy and negotiation are rendered futile. It is also an important task because the notion that cultures "cause" conflicts misses crucial aspects of the interplay between culture and politics. As Fred Halliday has pointed out, the fact that references to culture have become a common way to *justify* political, economic, and foreign policy decisions does not mean that these decisions are determined by culture (64–67). That is, while culture and cultural identities are frequently deployed to explain and rationalize clashes, there is nothing inherent in cultures that make them clash.

"The West" might not be what it used to be. On the one hand, we need to interrogate how the shifts in transatlantic geopolitics shape the meanings and uses of the terms "Europeanization" and "Americanization" in a particular domestic context. On the other, we should be careful to identify the mobilizations of culture in this dynamic rather than positing culture as the cause of this dynamic.

Notes

1. Parts of this text emerge from my PhD dissertation, "North of Nashville: Country Music, National Identity, and Class in Norway," University of Iowa, 2006. All translations from Norwegian to English are by the author. Charles S. Kupchan, "The End of the West," *Atlantic Monthly*, Nov. 2002, http://www.theatlantic.com/doc/prem/200211/kupchan.

2. See, for example, Richard Pells, *Not Like Us: How Europeans Have Loved, Hated, and Transformed American Culture since World War II* (New York: Basic Books, 1997); Rob Kroes, *If You've Seen One, You've Seen the Mall: Europeans and American Mass Culture* (Urbana: U of Illinois P, 1996), and *Us & Them: Questions of Citizenship in a Globalizing World* (Urbana: U of Illinois P, 2000); Richard F. Kuisel, *Seducing the French: The Dilemma of Americanization* (Berkeley: U of California P, 1993); Reinhold Wagnleiter, *Coca-Colonization and the Cold War: The Cultural Mission of the United States in Austria after the Second World War* (Chapel Hill: U of North Carolina P, 1994); and Reinhold Wagnleiter and Elaine Tyler May, eds. *"Here, There, and Everywhere": The Foreign Politics of American Popular Culture* (Hanover, NH: UP of New England, 2000).

3. Many newspaper commentaries could attest to this point, but a longer, more sustained argument can be found in Steinar Hansson, *Vestens fronter: Amerika—Europa—Norge* (Lysaker: Dinamo Forlag, 2003).

4. In 1972, 53.5 percent of the population voted "no" to membership; in 1994 this figure was 52.2 percent. Anders Todal Jenssen, Ola Listhaug, and Per Arnt Pettersen, "Betydningen av gamle og nye skillelinjer," in *Brussel midt imot: Folkeavstemningen om EU*, ed. Anders Todal Jenssen and Henry Valen (Oslo: Gyldendal, 1995), 143–63.

5. See Solli, "North of Nashville."

6. Hans is a pseudonym.

7. Naeem is a pseudonym.

8. Synnøve Riise Bøgeberg comes to a similar conclusion in her interviews with Norwegian country music fans. Her informants say that the Confederate flag symbolizes "the Wild West" and not "the South." See Synnøve Riise Bøgeberg, "Den norske cowboy: en studie av norsk countrykulturs verdier, idealer og ritualer," MA thesis, University of Oslo, 1999, 99.

9. Tom O'Dell makes a similar point in an interesting study of the history of American cars in Sweden. He explains how American cars have gone from being a status symbol among the wealthy and powerful to become a working-class symbol that "challenges the

aesthetics of Swedish modernity." See Tom O'Dell, *Culture Unbound: Americanization and Everyday Life in Sweden* (Lund, Sweden: Nordic Academic Press, 1997), 156.

10. Jenssen, Listhaug, and Pettersen, "Betydningen av gamle og nye skillelinjer."

11. Ibid.

12. Bjarne Hodne, *Norsk nasjonalkultur: En kulturpolitisk oversikt* (Oslo: Universitets-forlaget, 2002).

13. An example of such a view can be found in Hans Fredrik Dahl's preface to Neumann's *Norge—en kritikk* (Neumann's book strongly advocates Norwegian EU membership). Here Dahl, professor of media studies at the University of Oslo, writes: "Everyone who has done some traveling on the continent during the decades that the debates about Europe have been going on at home in Norway has been able to see that the economic integration process has had major consequences, particularly for the European periphery (*utkantene*), for remote areas and local communities that depend on small-scale agrarian production. [. . .] The effect, then, has been precisely the opposite of what the centrist-anticapitalist alliance *SV-SP* in Norway has insistently argued—that the EU robs the periphery. But as we all know: The visible observable reality has no effect on a believer" ("Norge på en ny måte" 12). Here, then, those who argue against Norwegian membership in the EU are cast as irrational "believers." (*SV* and *SP* are acronyms for two Norwegian political parties, the Socialist Left Party and the Centre Party, that have been vocally against EU membership.) See "Norge på en ny måte," in Neumann, *Norge*, 9–12.

14. Surveys conducted in 1994, for example, suggest that there is no clear correlation between being against Norwegian EU membership and being for stricter immigration laws or against immigration altogether. Bernt Aardal, "Ideologi på tvers?" in *Brussel midt imot: Folkeavstemningen om EU*, ed. Anders Todal Jenssen and Henry Valen (Oslo: Gyldendal, 1995), 171–72.

15. See for example, Cris Shore, *Building Europe*, for a thorough analysis of this move.

16. The "culture article," or article 151, reads:

1. The Community shall contribute to the flowering of the cultures of the Member States, while respecting their national and regional diversity and at the same time bringing the common cultural heritage to the fore.

2. Action by the Community shall be aimed at encouraging cooperation between Member States and, if necessary, supporting and supplementing their action in the following areas:
   - improvement of the knowledge and dissemination of the culture and history of the European peoples;
   - conservation and safeguarding of cultural heritage of European significance;
   - non-commercial cultural exchanges;
   - artistic and literary creation, including in the audiovisual sector.

3. The Community and the Member States shall foster cooperation with third countries and the competent international organisations in the sphere of culture, in particular the Council of Europe.

4. The Community shall take cultural aspects into account in its action under other provisions of this Treaty, in particular in order to respect and to promote the diversity of its cultures.

5. In order to contribute to the achievement of the objectives referred to in this Article, the Council:
   - acting in accordance with the procedure referred to in Article 251 and after consulting the Committee of the Regions, shall adopt incentive measures, excluding

any harmonisation of the laws and regulations of the Member States. The Council shall act unanimously throughout the procedure referred to in Article 251;

- acting unanimously on a proposal from the Commission, shall adopt recommendations.

17. "Decision No 508/2000/EC of the European Parliament and of the Council of 14 February 2000 establishing the Culture 2000 programme." *Official Journal L 063*, March 10, 2000, 0001–0009. http://eur-lex.europa.eu/LexUriServ/LexUriServ.do?uri=CELEX: 32000D0508:EN:HTML.

18. See note 2 for some examples of studies that have analyzed such forms of othering.

19. As Virginia R. Domínguez has pointed out, the tendency to place "culture" at the heart of group formation is a relatively recent phenomenon. She writes that "[a] culturalist form of legitimation (or means of attempted unification) takes over in the late twentieth century—the contemporary counterpart of 'racial' theories, spiritual theories, economic/ class theories, and naturalist theories that dominated previous centuries." "Invoking Culture: The Messy Side of 'Cultural Politics,'" *South Atlantic Quarterly* 91.1 (1992): 31.

20. A typical example can be found in President George W. Bush's State of the Union Address in January 2004: "America is a nation with a mission, and that mission comes from our most basic beliefs. We have no desire to dominate, no ambitions of empire. Our aim is a democratic peace—a peace founded upon the dignity and rights of every man and woman. America acts in this cause with friends and allies at our side, yet we understand our special calling: This great republic will lead the cause of freedom." George W. Bush, "State of the Union Address," Washington, D.C., January 20, 2004. http://georgewbush-whitehouse.archives.gov/stateoftheunion/2004/text.

21. Samuel P. Huntington's famous "clash of civilizations" thesis was originally published in the article "The Clash of Civilizations?" in *Foreign Affairs* 72.3 (1993): 22–49. An expanded version of this argument appeared in the book *The Clash of Civilizations and the Remaking of World Order* (New York: Simon and Schuster, 1996). Very briefly summarized, Huntington's main hypothesis is that the kinds of conflicts that will emerge after the end of the Cold War will be "civilizational"—that is, conflicts rooted in culture, values, traditions, and beliefs—rather than ideological or economic. For an insightful analysis of how his "clash of civilizations" theory has become a standard framework within which to contextualize international conflicts, see Ervand Abrahamian, "The U.S. Media, Huntington, and September 11," *Third World Quarterly* 24.3 (2003): 529–44.

Works Cited

Abrahamian, Ervand. "The U.S. Media, Huntington, and September 11." *Third World Quarterly* 24.3 (2003): 529–44.

"Beit av og spiste øret i raseri." *Dagbladet.* July 9, 1995, 1.

Borneman, John. "Is the United States Europe's Other?" *American Ethnologist* 30.4 (2003): 487–92.

Bush, George W. "State of the Union Address." Washington, D.C., January 20, 2004. http://georgewbush-whitehouse.archives.gov/stateoftheunion/2004/text.

Bøgeberg, Synnøve Riise. "Den norske cowboy: en studie av norsk countrykulturs verdier, idealer og ritualer." MA thesis, University of Oslo, 1999.

Ching, Barbara, and Gerald Creed. "Recognizing Rusticity: Identity and the Power of Place." *Knowing Your Place: Rural Identity and Cultural Hierarchy.* Ed. Barbara Ching and Gerald Creed. New York: Routledge, 1997. 1–38.

Commission of the European Communities. "Making Citizenship Work: Fostering European Culture and Diversity through Programmes for Youth, Culture, Audiovisual, and Civic Participation." COM (2004) 154. Brussels, 2004. http://eur-lex.europa.eu/legal-content/RO/ALL/?uri=uriserv:l29013.

Cooper, Robert. *The Breaking of Nations: Order and Chaos in the Twenty-First Century.* London: Atlantic Books, 2003. 83–152.

Dahl, Hans Fredrik. "Norge på en ny måte." Forord. *Norge—en kritikk: Begrepsmakt i Europa-debatten*, by Iver B. Neumann. Oslo: Pax Forlag, 2001. 9–12.

Decision No 508/2000/EC of the European Parliament and of the Council of 14 February 2000 establishing the Culture 2000 programme. *Official Journal L 063*, March 10, 2000, 0001–0009. http://eur-lex.europa.eu/LexUriServ/LexUriServ.do?uri=CELEX:3 2000D0508:EN:HTML.

Domínguez, Virginia R. "Invoking Culture: The Messy Side of 'Cultural Politics.'" *South Atlantic Quarterly* 91.1 (1992): 19–42.

European Commission. *A Community of Cultures: The European Union and the Arts.* Luxembourg: Office for Official Publications of the European Communities, 2002.

European Union. "Panorama of the European Union." http://europa.eu/abc/panorama/index_en.htm#.

Fontaine, Pascal. *Europe in 12 Lessons.* Luxembourg: Office for Official Publications of the European Communities, 2004.

Forgaard, T.S., and M.T. Dzamarija. "Immigrant Population." In "Immigration and Immigrants," *Statistical Analyses* 87 (2007).

Gullestad, Marianne. *Det norske sett med nye øyne: Kritisk analyse av norsk innvandringsdebatt.* Oslo: Universitetsforlaget, 2002.

Hagelund, Anniken. "A Matter of Decency? The Progress Party in Norwegian Immigration Politics." *Journal of Ethnic and Migration Studies* 29.1 (2003): 47–65.

Halliday, Fred. "Culture and International Relations: A New Reductionism?" *Confronting the Political in International Relations.* Ed. Michi Ebata and Beverly Neufeld. New York: St. Martin's, 2000. 64–67.

Hansson, Steinar. *Vestens fronter: Amerika—Europa—Norge.* Lysaker: Dinamo Forlag, 2003.

Hodne, Bjarne. *Norsk nasjonalkultur: En kulturpolitisk oversikt.* Oslo: Universitetsforlaget, 2002

Huntington, Samuel P. "The Clash of Civilizations?" *Foreign Affairs* 72.3 (1993): 22–49.

———. *The Clash of Civilizations and the Remaking of World Order.* New York: Simon and Schuster, 1996.

Jenssen, Anders Todal, Ola Listhaug, and Per Arnt Pettersen. "Betydningen av gamle og nye skillelinjer." *Brussel midt imot: Folkeavstemningen om EU.* Eds. Anders Todal Jenssen and Henry Valen. Oslo: Gyldendal, 1995. 143–63.

Kalvø, Are. *Harry.* Oslo: Det norske samlaget, 1999.

Kroes, Rob. *If You've Seen One, You've Seen the Mall: Europeans and American Mass Culture.* Urbana: U of Illinois P, 1996.

———. *Us & Them: Questions of Citizenship in a Globalizing World.* Urbana: U of Illinois P, 2000.

Kuisel, Richard F. *Seducing the French: The Dilemma of Americanization.* Berkeley: U of California P, 1993.

Kupchan, Charles S. "The End of the West." *Atlantic Monthly.* November 2002. http://www.theatlantic.com/doc/prem/200211/kupchan.

Neumann, Iver B. *Norge—en kritikk: Begrepsmakt i Europa-debatten*. Oslo: Pax Forlag, 2001.

O'Dell, Tom. *Culture Unbound: Americanization and Everyday Life in Sweden*. Lund, Sweden: Nordic Academic Press, 1997.

OPTEM S.A.R.L for the European Commission. *Perceptions of the European Union: A Qualitative Study of the Public's Attitudes to and Expectations of the European Union in the 15 Member States and 9 Candidate Countries*. June 2001, 5.

Østli, Kjetil S. "Amerikanere—våre nye landsmenn." *Aftenposten Aften*. March 13, 2003.

Pells, Richard. *Not Like Us: How Europeans Have Loved, Hated, and Transformed American Culture since World War II*. New York: Basic Books, 1997.

The Pew Global Attitudes Project. *A Year after Iraq War: Mistrust of America in Europe Ever Higher, Muslim Anger Persists*. New York: Pew Research Center, 2004. http://www.pewglobal.org/files/pdf/206.pdf.

"Rasistiske Ytringer." *Norges Høyesterett*. December 17, 2002. http://www.hoyesterett.no/news/5004.asp.

"Rå fyll i festival–Norge." *Dagbladet*. July 13, 1987, 1.

Forgaard, Tanja Seland, and Minja Tea Dzamarija. "Innvandrerbefolkningen." *Innvandring og innvandrere 2004*. Ed. Kristian Rose Tronstad. Oslo: Statistisk sentralbyrå, 2004. 17–54.

Shore, Cris. *Building Europe: The Cultural Politics of European Integration*. London: Routledge, 2000.

———. "Governing Europe: European Union Audiovisual Policy and the Politics of Identity." *Anthropology of Policy: Critical Perspectives on Governance and Power*. Ed. Cris Shore and Susan Wright. London: Routledge, 1997. 165–92.

Skjåk Country Music Festival brochure, 2004.

Solli, Kristin. "North of Nashville: Country Music, National Identity and Class in Norway." PhD dissertation. University of Iowa, 2006.

Wagnleiter, Reinhold. *Coca-Colonization and the Cold War: The Cultural Mission of the United States in Austria after the Second World War*. Chapel Hill: U of North Carolina P, 1994.

Wagnleiter, Reinhold, and Elaine Tyler May, eds. *"Here, There, and Everywhere": The Foreign Politics of American Popular Culture*. Hanover, NH: UP of New England, 2000.

Wike, Richard, Jacob Poushter, and Hani Zainulbhai. *As Obama Years Draw to Close, President and U.S. Seen Favorably in Europe and Asia*. New York: Pew Research Center, 2016. http://www.pewglobal.org/2016/06/29/as-obama-years-draw-to-close-president-and-u-s-seen-favorably-in-europe-and-asia.

Williams, Raymond. *The Country and the City*. New York: Oxford UP, 1973.

CHAPTER 10

Japanese Rappers, 9/11, and Soft Power

Anti-American Sentiments in "American" Popular Culture

Ian Condry

What do the terms "pro-American" and "anti-American" mean in today's globalizing world? Is it pro-American to argue that prisoners should not be held without a fair trial? Is it pro-American when we are talking about journalists held in Beijing prisons but anti-American if we are referring to "enemy combatants" held in Guantanamo Bay by the U.S. military? Did protests against the U.S. military's actions in Iraq constitute an anti-American sentiment, or do we need to know the nationality of the protester to decide? In the 1950s quite a few Americans were famously designated "un-American," but does it make sense to say that Americans today can be called "anti-American"? If young people in Japan expressed devotion to hip-hop music, in part because it represents the vitality of African American creativity, and then used hip-hop style to criticize President Bush's policies in the Middle East, was this pro-American or anti-American? Such conundrums are symbolic of the current reconfiguration of American power in the twenty-first century, and they speak to the importance, and the challenges, of cultural analysis in an age of globalization. Japanese rapper Libro, for example, used hip-hop music to say "that president [Bush] needs a psychiatric exam" for his response to September 11, and he asks whether the Bush-led war in Iraq was just a veiled attempt at spreading American corporate control. Is he, to paraphrase Bush himself, with us or against us?

Early on, the post–Cold War era seemed to pave the way for American leadership as "the world's only superpower." But since 9/11 and in the context of ongoing troubles in Iraq and elsewhere in the Middle East, we see a widening recognition that power in world politics depends not only on military might and economic pressure but also on the more intangible, yet vitally important, elements of "soft power." Political scientist Joseph Nye defines soft power as "the ability to get what you want through attraction rather than coercion or payments. It arises from the attractiveness of a country's culture, political ideals, and policies" (x). Nye rightly views popular culture as a vehicle for soft power—for example, in the ways U.S. television courtroom dramas can help convey the workings of the American legal system. But it would be a mistake to view the spread of American popular culture styles in itself as an effective national tool in world politics. Examples from Japanese rap musicians, portrayals of 9/11 and the Iraq War are cases in point. While Japanese rap artists express love for hip-hop music and culture, which they understand emerged from largely African American communities in New York, they also view American government policies with skepticism. This points to the importance of developing a more nuanced understanding of the relationship between global popular culture, national identity, and political messaging. In particular, it illustrates the need to conceive of culture, and cultural flows, not in terms of "values and ideals" but rather in terms of how values and ideals are put into practice. In other words, we require a means to recognize culture not as a static menu of ideals but as something brought to life through performance in particular contexts.

We can learn from some of the parallels between identifying "American soft power" with questions of "Japanese hip-hop." Consider, for example, what happens when an "American" popular culture form—namely, hip-hop music—is performed by Japanese artists in their language for a local audience. Does this hip-hop become Japanese? Is hip-hop always and forever "American" because it was largely invented in New York City in the 1970s? If so, does that mean "democracy" and "human rights" cannot be American ideals because we can trace their origins to settings that predate the birth of the United States? How can we understand the relationship between values, cultural styles, and national identity? The analytical puzzle of how to associate popular culture with national identity can also help us understand the shifting nature of national politics and global media in terms of soft power.

One doesn't have to look far to see how global media is producing a wider awareness of world events while also revealing that responses to those events follow unpredictable, and at times explosive, paths to expanding influence. As culture and politics transcend national borders, national frames of analysis seem ill-suited to coping with the challenge. Danish cartoons featuring Mohammad, global responses to the tsunami disaster of December 2004, and, of course, the shifting sands of reactions to 9/11 and the Iraq War, all highlight flashpoints in the workings of media and culture in the contemporary world.

To explore these relationships, I have selected musical examples that suggest ways of thinking about national boundaries and transnational politics, particularly as related to war, militarism, and globalization. Since the mid-1990s I have been following the development of Japanese rap music, a perfect example of the attractiveness of American—or, really, African American—culture overseas. I detail my findings in my book *Hip-Hop Japan* (Condry 2006). In this essay I return to some of the examples discussed there but take a new look at how they can be applied to issues of soft power and discourses of anti-Americanism. Many people, both in Japan and the United States, regard it as paradoxical that Japanese musicians would adopt an American cultural form—rap music—to express "anti-American" sentiments. I would argue instead that the cultural logic of hip-hop in Japan encourages Japanese rap artists to take a critical view of U.S. militarism at the same time that they express their admiration for a variety of Americans, none of whom, however, worked for the Bush administration. Moreover, because Japanese rappers think of hip-hop as a "global culture," albeit with origins in largely African American communities in the United States, they have struggled with precisely the kinds of media and globalization questions that open this section of the book. The conundrums can be reformulated, however, by drawing on discourses of cultural production common among hip-hop artists in Japan—namely, their focus on the *genba*, or "actual sites" of performance, primarily nightclubs and recording studios. They use the term "*genba*" to draw attention not to the "Japaneseness" or the "foreignness" of hip-hop in Japan but rather to the ways that the power of Japanese hip-hop arises from its *performance* in *particular locations*. I suggest that hearing what some rappers say about war and the media can tell us something about contemporary youth culture in Japan, and in particular, about attitudes toward the United States. As we will see, "anti-American" or "pro-American" are too blunt as analytical concepts; instead, a focus on performance in particular locations can help us better understand their attitudes and the workings of world politics.

Rhymester "911 Everyday"

Let's begin with a musical example by the group Rhymester that addresses the media response to 9/11. In a song called "911 Everyday," the emcees Mummy-D and Utamaru rap about media distortions surrounding depictions of the 9/11 bombings and the Iraq War that followed. The song begins with Utamaru rapping about watching daily disasters on television yet feeling helpless to do anything about it. To me this captures one of the peculiar aspects of the development of global media. In the 1960s Marshall McLuhan argued that the spread of electronic media would create a kind of "global village" whereby the sufferings of distant others would increasingly engage our sympathies and promote a sense of international responsibility. Today we can see that the opposite has happened. The vastness and ubiquity of global suffering can encourage a feeling of helplessness, and ultimately *disconnection* as we become overwhelmed by the images of bombings, genocide, natural disaster, and so on. The chorus of Rhymester's song introduces this theme with the idea that 9/11-type disasters seem to happen every day now, and it leads to a kind of moral fatigue. The rappers also take a nuanced look at the shift in world opinion after the 9/11 attacks. Mummy-D says in the first verse that although people around the world were shocked and sympathetic after the

9/11 attacks, many people later saw America as ignoring its own commitment to solving problems without violence. This draws attention to the challenge of viewing critiques of the Iraq War as "anti-American." At times, for some people the U.S. government calls for nonviolent solutions. But when America's new priority became "stopping terrorism," this "just cause" led to cluster bombs and bunker busters that kill civilians. Mummy-D is in effect asking, Which is the real America? Is it necessarily anti-American to criticize U.S. military policies? As an American who is similarly horrified by what has happened in Iraq, I am loathe to call Mummy-D's lyrics anti-American. Rather, the lyrics raise the question, How can we conceive of this use of expressing transnational values—avoiding war at all costs—that were once associated with the United States yet recently have been seemingly repudiated through recent U.S. policies (such as its strategies for fighting terrorism)?

Other lyrics in the song point to another layer of complexity. Mummy-D suggests, albeit implausibly, that the United States invaded Iraq in order to set up more McDonald's and 7-Eleven stores. Interestingly, because these words are trademarks, the record company, presumably with the rapper's assent, removed the words from the CD recording, replacing them with the sound of a machine gun. I have attended more than fifty recording sessions in Japan, and one of the first steps before recording involves the record company's A&R (artists and repertoire) representative checking the lyrics for discriminatory words (*sabetsu yôgo*), references to the Japanese emperor (all of which are forbidden due to fears of right-wing extremists' violent retaliation), and commercial words (*shôhin yôgo*). In my experience in Japan, the lyrics most often policed are commercial words. Usually the record company prefers rewrites on the spot, removing words like "Coca-Cola," or the name of a popular brand of pudding, or "Nippon Airways." The perceived importance of censoring commercial words points to the creeping hegemony of capitalist notions of intellectual property. Mummy-D can criticize the U.S. military, but he cannot name McDonald's and 7-Eleven outright. Notably, the global 7-Eleven chain is now owned by a Japanese corporation. What links McDonald's and 7-Eleven, then, is their ownership of transnationally recognized brand names, names that are protected by globally enforced trademark laws, even in basement recording studios.

Rhymester's other rapper, Utamaru, takes up the themes of capitalism, military violence, and world affairs from another angle. He asks,

How much is the value of a person's life? shouldn't everyone's be worth the same?	How much *hito no inochi no kachi kimochi wa tashika hitoshiku onaji hazu da ga*
yet a child dead of starvation is given less concern than a heavy gun	*uete shinda kodomo no taijû yori mo zutto zusshiri jûtai jû*

He continues the verse with the idea that this distortion of value—the attention given to a gun being much greater than the attention given to a starving child—is just "prices, adjusting upwards," while, he adds, most people can only hope to catch the crumbs that fall off America's table. Notably, Utamaru in this verse directs his anger not at the United States, per se, but at the larger capitalist political economy that accords more weight to guns than starving children. The impetus of economic growth is taken as an unquestioned path to progress ("prices up, the world marches ahead"). Indeed, he sees in this the logic of Japan's response; as "yellow Uncle Sam," the Japanese government hopes to profit from the war, as it had done in the Korean War and the Vietnam War. But Utamaru also emphasizes the importance of developing new kinds of "reconnection," by drawing attention to the importance of respecting life across national boundaries.

Implications for Soft Power

Why is the power of a gun given so much more weight in the media than a child dead of starvation? Why is it that human beings' lives are valued differently depending on their nationality, race, ethnicity, and age? For me, this is one of the most pressing issues for the study of media and globalization—namely, coming to a deeper understanding of the distortions caused by contemporary media. Why is it that we live in a time of peak media saturation historically and yet the information traveling through the media seems ill-suited to addressing the common needs of humanity? Of course, this is too big a question to be solved by a study of Japanese hip-hop alone, but in the back of my mind, this is one of the issues that drives my research. Similarly, concerns with how media representations feed back into political power is one of the driving concerns of studies surrounding soft power.

Joseph Nye points to the centrality of the information revolution in making soft power more pivotal in world politics, in part because it is creating virtual communities and networks that cut across national borders. The following quotation shows how Nye argues in terms of broadly defined norms and values as key factors in the workings of soft power:

> The countries that are likely to be more attractive and gain soft power in the information age are those with multiple channels of communication that help to frame the issues; whose dominant culture and ideas are closer to prevailing norms (which now emphasize liberalism, pluralism, and autonomy); and whose credibility is enhanced by their domestic and international policies. . . . To the extent that official policies at home and abroad are consistent with democracy, human rights, openness, and respect for the opinions of others, America will benefit from the trends of this global information age. But there is a danger that the United States may obscure the deeper message of its values through arrogance. (32–33)

Indeed, the mixed messages of American policies that Rhymester highlighted in their song can also be seen in issues related to prison abuses by the U.S. military. One of the striking findings of the Pew Global Attitudes Project, based on a spring 2006 survey, is that around 90 percent of the people of Western European countries and of Japan have heard about the Abu Ghraib and Guantanamo abuses, but only 76 percent of Americans had heard of them (Pew Research Center 6). This disjuncture illustrates the importance of analyzing soft power not only in terms of "attractive" political actions but also in terms of "repulsive" ones.

By considering how popular culture flows around the world, we can come to a deeper understanding of some of the mechanisms of media influence. In my research on hip-hop in Japan I found that local musicians relied heavily on live performance spaces—namely, all-night hip-hop clubs—to build up fan bases, networks of like-minded groups, and business and media connections. Although artists and fans would describe their love of hip-hop in terms of ideals—speaking out, being socially oppositional, keeping it real—in practice, it was the networked, live events that built the scene. These events were initially centered in Tokyo through the mid-1990s, but over the past two decades they have spread throughout Japan. As mentioned above, Japanese rappers use the term "*genba*," or "actual site," to refer to these clubs, because it is there that the scene is made real in the sense of provoking excitement and commitment among Japan's hip-hoppers. Although Japanese rap fans express an admiration for the values emphasized in hip-hop, they became committed to hip-hop through a long process of engagement. In this sense the key to hip-hop's power abroad has been not so much "its appeal to universal values," as Nye would put it, than a willingness of local actors to put the ideals into performances that speak directly, and engagingly, to a youthful Japanese audience in their terms. As I argue in my book, hip-hop does not so much "flow" from the United States to Japan. Rather, the repeated performances of hip-hop and its circulation in Japan produced an emergent community of devotees. Through this process, the "Americanness," or rather African Americanness, of hip-hop became attenuated and associated instead with a more transnational history. Hip-hop fans nowadays get nostalgic hearing Japanese rap songs, not just American rap songs, of the past. This too brings into focus how discussions of soft power must increasingly consider transnational imagined communities rather than trying to reduce soft power to national frames of reference.

My analysis relates to broader trends within anthropology to rethink the relationship between culture and place. Akhil Gupta and James Ferguson have proposed moving beyond common assumptions of thinking about the link between culture and place by focusing on "location." They argue that it is important to see anthropology's distinctive trademark not as a commitment to "the local," as in the people of some local community but rather to emphasize anthropology's "attentiveness to epistemological and political issues of location" (39). "Ethnography's great strength has always been the explicit and well-developed sense of location, of being set here-and-not-elsewhere. This strength becomes a liability when notions of 'here' and 'elsewhere' are assumed to be features of geography, rather than sites constructed in fields of unequal power relations" (35). Gupta and Ferguson stress the importance of foregrounding questions of "location, intervention, and the construction of situated knowledges" and focusing on "shifting locations" rather than "bounded fields" (5, 39). This approach offers a way of focusing cultural research across and through transnational connections. Hip-hop offers an intriguing case study in part because of its ontological questioning of its own rankings of artists, fans, and media networks.

I would also argue that the "actual site" of nightclubs in Japan provides a way of thinking about the intersections between the different groups that drive the music scene. Much of the analysis of popular culture's political power hinges on an opposition between producers and consumers—for example, in highlighting either the production-oriented analyses that grew out of the Frankfurt School or the consumer-centered analyses commonly associated with Daniel Miller (Adorno and Horkheimer, "Culture Industry"; Miller, "Consumption Studies"). In my fieldwork in Tokyo nightclubs and recording studios, however, I found that this opposition captured only some of the dynamics of the scene. A more important factor was how the synergies among participants in the scene competed for attention and built particular audiences over time. What this means for our understanding of soft power is that audiences, or global citizens, may care less about points of origins (e.g., whether democracy is "American" or not) than in the practical instantiation of these values. We can see that as well in a Japanese rap song that would seem to reinforce Japan's nationalists but on closer examination produces a more subtle and more transnational perspective on the violence of war.

Hannya "Oretachi no *Yamato*"

Another song worth considering was written for a Japanese film released in December 2005. The film is called *Otokotachi no* Yamato (Men's *Yamato*) and is an action film that dramatizes the sinking of Japan's largest battleship near the end of World War II. The battleship takes its name from the imperial clan that has ruled Japan since the 700s, and thus the term "*Yamato*" itself evokes an ethnic nationalism that was used to devastating effect by Japanese militarists in the first half of the twentieth century. Although the film signifies to some Japanese citizens a worrisome, rising nationalism, Hannya's song attempts to capture an ambivalent nationalism—that is, a love for country combined with a desire for international peace. Thanks, in part, to the celebrity actors of the film, and its widespread media coverage, the rap song for the film achieved much wider recognition than Rhymester's song. Hannya, in his lyrics, emphasizes a profound ambivalence and uncertainty about war. If he had been of fighting age in the 1940s, would he have gone to war? Would he have resisted? He also criticizes as "idiots" (*baka*) those who created atomic bombs and those who still have them. But above all, he criticizes the unfairness of an older generation sending a younger generation to fight.

| you big men of the countries over there | *otaku no kuni no oerai san to* |
| should get with big men of other countries | *otaku no kuni no oerai san de* |

| and why don't you fight by yourselves? | *sashi de kenka shite kuremasen ka* |
| all I really hope for is peace | *kocchi wa honki de negau yo heiwa* |

Because, as Hannya notes, any fighting will lead to the loss of loved ones, of family members and friends. In this example we can hear a certain take on the war by today's generation of youth in Japan. This reminds us that in addition to considering national understandings of war history (and war's future) we must also consider generational differences within given societies. Hannya's song is inspired by a film with strongly nationalist overtones, linked more broadly to the current conservative government's efforts to encourage the teaching of patriotism in schools and to revise what neo-nationalists view as a "masochistic" view of history, highlighting instead the honor and courage of Japanese soldiers during World War II. What Hannya demonstrates, however, is that youth in Japan, when they think about the bravery of Japan's World War II soldiers, also see an unfortunate loss of life on both sides of the battlefield. Hannya argues that it is the "great men" who, rather than using youth as pawns, should be fighting it out among themselves, leaving a younger generation to live in peace.

There is also a lesson here for analyzing why some stories get wider play than others. Hannya's song reached a wider audience, compared to Rhymester's "911 Everyday," in part because it was carried on the winds of the film's popularity. Indeed, it was in some ways the popularity of the film, perhaps more than the talent of the rapper, that conveyed this song to a broader audience. This helps illustrate the dynamics of the interaction between artists, fans, record companies, and media: what drove the circulation was the film, but it still depended on all the actors working in tandem. The contrast between the success of Hannya's song and the relative lack of circulation for Rhymester's songs demonstrates, I suggest, that the audience for political message rap exists in Japan but that reaching that audience depends on navigating media gatekeepers who tend to be obsessed with celebrity over message. Nevertheless, when the two combine, messages of peace can reach large audiences.

King Giddra "911"

A final musical example comes from the group King Giddra. Their song "911" looks at New York City's "ground zero" from the ashes of Hiroshima. This extends the theme of thinking about popular culture and politics being mediated through particular locations. In a 2002 music video the group King Giddra rapped about the aftermath of 9/11 using images of Hiroshima after the atomic bombing. The linkage of images shows how world politics can be reimagined through the lenses of different, specific locations that teach us about the intersections of wider forces. As Zeebra intones at the opening the song, "It is time to rethink world peace," and his group does so by thinking about civilians caught in wars' firestorms. Each of the three artists who make up King Giddra (Zeebra, K Dub Shine, DJ Oasis) offers a particular take on "nine-one-one" as they call it. Zeebra's lyrics express sympathy for New Yorkers, describe the shock of watching "live on CNN," witnessing "a wound in world history." But he also questions the response of the U.S. government and media.

is this terrorists against a nation? No,	*kore wa terorisuto tai kokka? iya, chigau*
that's mistaking one part for the whole	*ichibu no hôdô dake de mimachigau*
the media's strategy: push good and evil	*sonna media senryaku yuragu zen'aku*
and I see an atom bomb that fell in the past	*ukabu genkaku wa ochita genbaku*

Although television networks broadcast the tragedy of September 11 worldwide, viewers responded and interpreted it differently depending on their location. For example, some American commentators likened 9/11 to Pearl Harbor in the sense that both events were surprise attacks. Some Japanese bristle at the suggestion, pointing out that Pearl Harbor was an attack on the U.S. military and not civilians. Moreover, while American commentators called the site of the World Trade Center towers "ground zero," Japan has two locations known as ground zero: Hiroshima and Nagasaki.

The music video created for King Giddra's "911" track opens with an image of "ground zero" Hiroshima. At the center of the picture, the government building now known as the "Peace Dome" figures prominently. Although it is located close to the epicenter of the blast, the building remained standing while everything around was flattened and incinerated. It stands as a testimony to the destructive power of technology and the resilience of the Japanese people in the face of adversity. At the start of the video, the image of the destruction of the building and the surrounding area of Hiroshima is doubled so that the two images of the Peace Dome side by side recall the look of the Twin Towers after they fell. From this Hiroshima ground-zero location, we see how a Japanese response to 9/11 carries special weight.

In his verse, K Dub Shine addresses civilian casualties and political infrastructures. He notes that "civilization and justice" get mixed with hypocrisy in that it is usually "the civilians who get sacrificed." He raps that a cold wind blows on Afghan refugees while President Bush sleeps comfortably in bed. Shine's emphasis on the civilian tragedies points to a consonance between ground-zero Hiroshima,

New York, Afghan refugees, and the countless others caught in the crossfire of larger political and military conflicts. In addition, King Giddra's rap underscores an affinity between African Americans as disenfranchised in the United States and Japanese youth unable to see their concerns adequately addressed in their own political system. They also are involved in the work of imagining new transnational connections through vehicles of popular culture. In this regard, the "ephemeral" side of popular culture may be better viewed in terms of its immediacy in responding to world events.

One lesson for soft power is that the efforts of Japan's nationalists, who dominate in positions of power in the national government, must also contend with the transnational movements that see Hiroshima and Nagasaki as locations that vividly emphasize the importance of peace and nuclear nonproliferation. How would the analysis of soft power be transformed if, instead of asking how American or Japanese soft power can be heightened, we asked instead, How can transnational goals of human rights, environmental protection, fair trade, and so forth, be made to seem "more attractive" to the world as a whole? From the perspective of Japanese hip-hop, this has always been part of the challenge—that is, linking a transnational style with very local concerns while also understanding that these local concerns, such as the memory of Hiroshima, speak back to a global anxiety. The reflexivity of performances like this, from America through Japanese live music stages, and back to America highlights the more poignant aspects of soft power, but is difficult to analyze if questions remain focused on national coherence. From this perspective, it makes perfect sense for hip-hop in Japan to have both "pro-American" and "anti-American" elements, sometimes even within a single song. By the same token, making hip-hop Japanese (in the Japanese language, by Japanese, for a Japanese audience) does not necessarily entail a pro-Japan, nationalist message.

Conclusion

In the songs discussed here, my intent has been to show how some of today's youth are using hip-hop, an ostensibly "American" popular culture, in a distinctively "Japanese" way. Yet what is interesting to me is how each of the songs challenges a simplistic national orientation while also challenging other nations for their inability to stop warring practices. As Gupta and Ferguson suggest, the key to understanding the political potential of their popular culture expressions depends on *not* returning to a simply "Japanese" (or "foreign") interpretation of their interventions. To some extent, this may be the key to developing coalitions across national boundaries to resist the impetus to fight. In addition, the idea of the actual sites (*genba*) also suggests a way of seeing where and how such goals can develop. The inability of Rhymester to reach a large audience may be less related to the political message of their song and a presumed lack of politics on the part of Japanese youth. Of course, one cannot make assumptions about the political aims of an entire generation of young Japanese based on a few songs, but the relative hit status of Hannya, and lack of hit status on the others, shows primarily that the limitations on the spread of such messages should not be attributed solely to political apathy. Rather, perhaps it is the need to see the potential for political activism in unexpected and underexplored places.

In this regard we can gain a new perspective on discourses of anti-Americanism and the uses of Japanese hip-hop. First, as these hip-hop artists are showing, the national frame of reference for analyzing political statements is too broad a category to describe accurately the connections they are proposing. Rhymester's song "911 Everyday" criticized both the American military in Iraq and the Japanese government's willing acquiescence in the interest of improving the economy. In turn, Mummy-D calls for the younger generation to rethink politics beyond "United Nations and media agitation." Hannya, in contrast, presents a new reading of the sinking of the *Yamato* battleship at the end of World War II. Although treading close to a kind of Japanese nationalism, he brings the focus back on the need to work for peace, to reject nuclear weapons as a tool of politics, and to acknowledge the shared humanity of war victims. The fact that Hannya's song achieved a wider circulation than Rhymester's song is evidence of the forces driving the spread of popular culture messages, in this case, traveling on the winds of the success of the blockbuster action film. Overall, I propose that considering whether hip-hop in Japan is ultimately "pro-American" or "anti-American" misses the larger point that future politics depend in part upon getting beyond the analytical frame of the nation-state. King Giddra's reframing of 9/11 and the U.S. military response in Afghanistan in terms of Hiroshima and Nagasaki again draws attention to war's victims, wherever they may reside.

How does this help us answer the question I posed at the beginning? If one opposes holding prisoners without trial, it shouldn't matter whether those prisoners are being held by authorities in Beijing or Guantanamo Bay. I believe there is an emerging sense of the necessity of such transnational politics and that we can see it in some aspects of popular culture. Questions of "Japaneseness" or "Americanness" of hip-hop music can be effectively reframed through consideration of ideas, of locations, and of performance as a way of thinking about media power and cultural influence. By rethinking national politics in terms of particular sites of performance and production, I believe we may also be able to imagine new kinds of relationships between transnational movements and national politics. I hope through these examples that we can get a sense of how some young people in Japan are approaching these issues. What makes their political statements so provocative is the way they cannot be so easily categorized as "pro-Japanese" or "anti-American" but instead struggle to define ethical politics across national boundaries.

Works Cited

Adorno, Theodor, and Max Horkheimer. "The Culture Industry: Enlightenment as Mass Deception." *Cultural Studies Reader*, 2nd ed. Ed. S. During. London: Routledge, 1999. 31–41.

Condry, Ian. *Hip-Hop Japan: Rap and the Paths of Cultural Globalization*. Durham, NC: Duke UP, 2006.

Gupta, Akhil, and James Ferguson. "Discipline and Practice: 'The Field' as Site, Method, and Location in Anthropology." *Anthropological Locations: Boundaries and Grounds of a Field Science*. Ed. A. Gupta and J. Ferguson. Berkeley: U of California P, 1997. 1–46.

Hannya. "Oretachi no *Yamato*." *Naikoku Kokuhatsu*. Avex Rush, AVCF-22605. 2006.

King Giddra. "911." *Saishû Heiki* (video). Defstar, Japan, DFVL-8052. 2002.

Libro. "Michigusa." *Sanmai*. Unlimited Group. 2003.

McLuhan, Marshall. *The Gutenberg Galaxy: The Making of Typographic Man*. Toronto: U of Toronto P, 1962.

Miller, Daniel. "Consumption Studies as the Transformation of Anthropology." *Acknowledging Consumption: A Review of New Studies*. Ed. D. Miller. London: Routledge, 1995. 264–95.

Nye, Joseph. *Soft Power: The Means to Success in World Politics*. Cambridge, MA: Public Affairs/Perseus Books, 2004.

Pew Research Center. *Conflicting Views in a Divided World 2006*. Washington, DC: Pew Research Center, 2006.

Rhymester. "911 Everyday." *Grey Zone*. Sony Ki/oon. 2003.

Ian Condry on Kristin Solli

In the summer of 1993, I had the opportunity to attend a Lakota Sioux powwow on Pine Ridge Reservation in South Dakota. As I read Kristin Solli's fascinating essay, I was reminded of the multiple levels of "Americanization" that I witnessed at this summer festival for Native Americans. Solli shows us that the meanings of America at Norwegian country music festivals are shaped by the history of Norway, its independence vis-à-vis the European Union (rejecting membership twice), and the divide between rural and urban Norwegians in imagining what's best for their future. Despite a widening distaste in Europe generally for American foreign policy, especially the wars in Iraq and Afghanistan started by the Bush administration, the country music festivals in rural Norway were a chance for many Norwegians to express cultural affinity with the United States, especially through the prominence of American flags, American cars, cowboy hats, boots, and belt buckles. Solli shows us that this affinity for American country music also functions as a celebration of rural Norwegian lifestyles, highlighting the disjuncture between rural Norway attitudes and those of cosmopolitan elites, who were more likely to view the events as "a rural dystopia of cultural depravity and drunken degeneracy." The Pine Ridge powwow also encapsulated a kind of fundamental ambivalence that reflects not only America's fraught history but also the difficulties we have in understanding the role of culture in the context of today's political economic realities.

At one point the Lakota Sioux now based in Pine Ridge were a people "more American" than the invading newcomers from Europe, and yet, after generations of genocide, racism, and neglect, they now reside in one of the most poverty-stricken areas of the United States. My wife, who spent a summer working as a midwife on the reservation, told of more than once seeing cars driving long distances backward down dusty roads, because the transmissions of those decrepit cars would only work in reverse. Cars that only drive backward seem a sad commentary on a process of Americanization that clearly left many behind. This too seems to be a lesson of Solli's essay—namely, that the forces of "Americanization" and "Europeanization" can be understood only by attending to the specific localities of interest and desire, a reminder that local particulars make all the difference in interpreting the power of culture, not as a thing, but as something invoked in an effort to do something.

But to do what? When EU elites point to America as a "land without culture," they refer vaguely to the image of Americans as "unrefined, loud, and narrow-minded," yet when they lament the relative absence of European media on television, they fear the crass abundance of U.S. media culture. American culture here is constituted by brutish tourists and vapid, if addictive, television shows. For those of us interested in analyzing the complexities of contemporary cultural formations, we should be delighted to hear governmental elites turn their attention to "culture"—for example, by the bureaucrats of the European Union who seek to unify the diverse peoples of Europe through assertions of shared values and histories. But these abstractions of America and Europe necessarily have less force, it seems to me, than the engaged uses of country music by Norwegian festival-goers. What makes the difference, perhaps, is not just who does the invoking of culture but how the integration of such cultural affinities happens in everyday lives. Rather than abstractions about values, especially when these abstractions seem little more than cynical attempts to bolster political legitimacy, Solli shows us that we need a sense of how these "values" are embodied and lived.

So too at Pine Ridge, symbols depended on context. At one level, the pow-wow was clearly a chance to celebrate the cultures of Native Americans through expressions of their history, language, music, and dance. Yet the powwow also operated at multiple levels, with diverse cultural connections made among different groups of Lakota, and other tribes, in attendance. Most striking for me were the singing and dancing contests, because they represented what I saw as authentic Native American culture. Groups of men would sit around a microphone and screech-scream-sing while beating a large drum in the middle. The musician groups were arrayed around a circular field in which dancers, who wore paper numbers like marathon runners, performed in their elaborate handmade costumes as judges walked among them and scored their prowess. The singing and dancing was mesmerizing, and it evoked a history of struggle to retain one's language and community stories in the face of "Americanization" that wiped out the bulk of First Nation peoples.

Yet to see the powwow merely in terms of this historical struggle is to see only part of the interactions, because next to the dance circle was a rodeo stadium where the traditional Native American costumes were exchanged for cowboy hats, boots, and belt buckles. In the dance ring there was no alcohol, but in the rodeo stands, longneck Budweisers were in the hands of many, and some of these sadly drunken "Indian Cowboys" stumbled down the steps in fits of dangerous inebriation. But one also could sense the pride in the audience members at a few of the Lakota professional riders, whose accomplishments on the rodeo circuit were announced over the loudspeakers. These rodeo stars were welcomed as local heroes by the Lakota audience, because they had made it, a couple of them winning national competitions, in mainstream America. They had achieved an American dream through skill and had overcome racism through their hard work, even though it meant leaving the drum and dance circles behind.

The rodeo and the dance circle folks operated like separate cultural worlds, but it was not a simple binary. The powwow also had carnival rides (Ferris wheel, salt and pepper shakers) that fed the dreams of children. And then, perhaps most surprising to me, as I walked around the merchandise stalls that sold fried dough, dream catchers, and leather goods, I felt I recognized the hormone-charged circulation of teenagers remembered from the shopping malls and weekend summer carnivals of my youth, or the hip-hop clubs in Tokyo where I did my research, and where gossip, hookups, and week-to-week drama operated in a world removed from adults. Which was the real representative of Lakota culture? Was it the jingle dancers or the professional bull riders who had best achieved a (Native) American success? The uses of culture are complex, and it is difficult to second-guess meanings that operate on many levels and through a complicated negotiation of outer and inner cultures, not to mention one's own personal desires and ambitions.

Kristin Solli shows us that "Americanization" is a process that is not in the hands of Americans but is operated by others who are caught in their own complicated circumstances. We can also see, however, that the decline of American dominance in world affairs opens possibilities for imagining alternative touchstones for freedom and independence. For those who see "civilization clashes" on the horizon, perhaps it would be helpful to remind ourselves that day-to-day life is a matter of "clash" all the time and that an openness to diverse cultural formations can equally be a source of inspiration and not just conflict. I see in the Norwegian country music fans a vision of America that is not "less authentic," even for the mixing of the Wild West frontier of the 1800s with the drive-ins of the 1950s, as Solli points out, but a desire to make more out of one's life through participation in a community of peers that cares about something together. For those who want to define for others what "their culture" should be, Solli's essay reminds us of the importance of fieldwork among a people and an openness to seeing what "American culture" means to them, in their worlds. Only then, it seems to me, can we talk about what the invocation of culture can mean.

Kristin Solli on Ian Condry

Ian Condry's analysis of hip-hop in Japan shows how the Japanese hip-hop scene infuses the genre with local concerns, politics, and histories. More specifically, Condry introduces us to the Japanese concept *genba* as an analytical tool that captures how music becomes meaningful at very specific moments, times, and places. "*Genba*," Condry explains, is a way to talk about how "the power of Japanese hip-hop arises from its *performance* in *particular locations*" (emphasis in original). Condry illustrates the usefulness of this approach by showing how Japanese rappers alternately distance and affiliate themselves with various aspects of the United States in ways that might not seem apparent for an outsider to the scene. Condry's example also points out how the pervasiveness of U.S. popular culture abroad is not always a means for U.S. political dominance. As the Japanese hip-hoppers in Condry's study demonstrate, liking hip-hop does not necessarily mean liking the United States.

In the brief commentary that follows I extend Condry's ideas about music, location, and power by discussing an example that, like Condry's case, suggests the intricacies and paradoxes that follow in the wake of the global dissemination of U.S. popular culture. More specifically, I look at jazz, a genre that has received considerable attention by scholars interested in the local/global dynamic that Condry addresses.[1] In one sense the case I describe below is another illustration of how local meanings emerge through local practices. This focus on the particularities of "local variants" of various cultural products and practices is common in both scholarship and popular discourse about the global spread of U.S. culture. Indeed, my own work very much falls into this category. I use this example in order to ask a question that I have not quite resolved about this approach. Does the emphasis on identifying and detailing "the local" implicitly position the United States at the center even as we try to show how people in other places are not necessarily dominated by U.S. power? That is, does this approach tend to position the United States as the "original" to which "the local" must be compared? If so, do we risk reproducing the center-periphery power dynamic that we often seek to problematize? I ask larger questions than this short piece can answer. In fact, I do not know that I have any answers. But I do think these are questions that this volume as a whole can help us consider.

Jazz, an early U.S. musical export, has a long history as an international genre, and many jazz scenes outside the United States have developed quite independently from those within the United States. Inside the United States, jazz is often perceived as uniquely "American," but elsewhere this is not necessarily the case. In fact, in Norway, from which my example is drawn, jazz has become "Norwegian" to the extent that it is now used as a part of Norwegian cultural diplomacy.[2] Between 2002 and 2016, the Norwegian Ministry of Foreign Affairs (MFA) has sponsored CD box sets with Norwegian jazz artists that are aimed at foreign markets. The projects, called *JazzCD.no: Jazz from Norway*, have been put together by the Norwegian Jazz Federation, an organization for Norwegian jazz musicians. The CDs work as a marketing tool for the federation's members. The MFA's choice to sponsor the CDs and to be actively affiliated with jazz, however, might require additional explanation.

What, then, is going on when the Norwegian Ministry of Foreign Affairs uses jazz in an effort to portray Norway as an attractive and appealing country to the rest of world? The reasons that the genre occupies this position in a Norwegian context are complex and have to do with shifting constructions of national identities, developments within the area of cultural policy, and with the history of jazz in Norway. There is not room to further explore those reasons here, but despite the fact that jazz has emerged as a kind of new national music in Norway, American jazz is still frequently evoked as the center that gives the Norwegian "periphery" meaning. That is, despite the way the genre in Norway has developed somewhat independently from jazz in the United States, "Norwegian jazz" acquires a specific discursive meaning in contrast to "jazz proper"—that is, American jazz.

The liner notes that accompany the 2010 edition of the CD box sets illustrate this dynamic. They are written by British jazz critic Stuart Nicholson, who has published extensively on the difference between jazz in the United States and jazz elsewhere. For example, his book *Is Jazz Dead? (Or Has It Moved to a Different Address?)* consistently contrasts a "dying" American scene with a thriving European scene. Indeed, in the book as well as in his other writing, Nicholson has pointed several times to Norway's scene as an example of a place where jazz is particularly alive. The choice of Nicholson as the spokesperson for the CD box set is therefore not surprising, and in this role he continues to praise the vitality of jazz in Norway by contrasting it with a U.S. jazz scene in decline.

The liner notes begin by referencing a 2005 article in the *Guardian* that declared "Oslo and not New Orleans, Chicago or New York" "the jazz capital of the world." (Nicholson, "Liner notes"). "Of course," Nicholson explains, "many countries boast about their own local jazz scenes, but in Norway there is a real sense of what jazz can become, not what it was. [. . .] Norway is a country where the genie has well and truly escaped from the bottle marked 'tradition'" (ibid.). Norway, according to Nicholson, is the home of a jazz scene that is particularly innovative and cutting-edge. "But why should this be?" he asks and continues by answering: "Perhaps one reason is that in Europe in general, and Norway in particular, the language of jazz is neither mother tongue nor sacred text. Musicians are not constrained by notions of a 'jazz tradition' so that elements as diverse as classical, pop, folk, rock, free and electronics are used to enrich the basic jazz ingredient" (ibid.). Interestingly, Nicholson's answer does not mention the United States or America by name. Yet when Nicholson refers to how, in Norway, the "language of jazz is neither mother tongue nor sacred text," the United States is evoked as a place where jazz *is* "mother tongue" and "sacred text." Americans, Nicholson implies, revere the genre too much to be able to push it forward and are thus trapped in "the bottle marked 'tradition.'" In Norway, however, jazz has escaped this fate and lives on as a dynamic, inventive musical form. One reason, then, why the Norwegian foreign ministry might consider jazz a suitable element in their cultural diplomacy efforts is that this kind of critical recognition of the Norwegian jazz scene helps the nation appear modern, dynamic, and creative. And in the way Nicholson's liner notes contextualize this CD box set, Norway emerges in this light in contrast to the United States, which is associated with tradition and stagnation.

In a larger sense this is a reversal of an old trope within European discourses about "America." As Rob Kroes has argued, Europeans have frequently cast the United States as a country without tradition and history, as opposed to a Europe that "has" history. Nicholson instead sees Europe as the continent that is not hampered by tradition, while the United States is bogged down by it. It should be noted that Nicholson is a contentious figure within jazz circles, where many think that he overgeneralizes the differences between U.S. and European jazz. However, the point here is that it is this kind of rhetoric that casts Norwegians as particularly forward-looking and modern by positioning the United States as old-fashioned and stagnant.

Whether or not the discursive tropes about America are shifting, what is clear is that discourses "about America" often rely on dichotomies in which "local" practices gain meaning in relation to that which is not "local"—that is, the United States. Even in an example in which non-U.S. musicians are perceived to have created a new center for a genre that is now as Norwegian as it is American, this can only be done in relation to the original center—the United States. In this sense, then, American jazz still defines Norwegian jazz.

Hip-hop in Japan and jazz in Norway are very different cases. Yet the dynamic whereby the music in part gains meaning from being positioned in relation to a perceived U.S. center seems to be working in both instances. Often both academic and popular discourses tend to focus on how U.S. cultural products and practices are changed and reworked by people in other places. Does this move risk recentering the United States even if the goal is often the opposite? Does focusing on "the local" put the United States at the center in ways that reproduce rather than challenge U.S. power?

In the end, I do think it is important to show how hip-hop in Japan, jazz in Norway, or country music in Brazil, for that matter, complicate simplistic models of U.S. cultural imperialism. Yet, after all the work that has been done to show processes of localization, has the time now come to examine what does not "localize"? What, in other words, stays the same and why? If we wish to discuss issues of power, disempowerment, and empowerment, these might be questions that are also worth considering.

Notes

1. There is a large body of scholarship about jazz outside the United States. For some central studies, see Taylor Atkins, ed., *Jazz Planet* (Jackson: U of Mississippi P, 2003); E. Taylor Atkins, *Blue Nippon: Authenticating Jazz in Japan* (Durham, NC: Duke UP, 2001); Christopher Ballantine, *Marabi Nights: Early South African Jazz and Vaudeville* (Johannesburg: Ravan Press, 1993); and George McKay, *Circular Breathing: The Cultural Politics of Jazz in Britain* (Durham, NC: Duke UP, 2005).

2. For an interesting study of how the U.S. State Department used jazz as part of their Cold War cultural diplomacy, see Penny von Eschen, *Satchmo Blows Up the World: Jazz Ambassadors Play the Cold War* (Cambridge, MA: Harvard UP, 2004).

Works Cited

Atkins, E. Taylor. *Blue Nippon: Authenticating Jazz in Japan*. Durham, NC: Duke UP, 2001.

Atkins, Taylor, ed. *Jazz Planet*. Jackson: U of Mississippi P, 2003.

Ballantine, Christopher. *Marabi Nights: Early South African Jazz and Vaudeville*. Johannesburg: Ravan Press, 1993.

Kroes, Rob. *If You've Seen One, You've Seen the Mall: Europeans and American Mass Culture*. Urbana: U of Illinois P, 1996.

McKay, George. *Circular Breathing: The Cultural Politics of Jazz in Britain*. Durham, NC: Duke UP, 2005.

Nicholson, Stuart. *Is Jazz Dead? (Or Has It Moved to a Different Address?)*. New York: Routledge, 2005.

———. Liner notes to *JazzCD.no 4th Set*. http://www.jazzcd.no.

von Eschen, Penny. *Satchmo Blows Up the World: Jazz Ambassadors Play the Cold War* Cambridge, MA: Harvard UP, 2004.

Michael Titlestad on Solli and Condry

Dreaming America

For all the efforts of (postmodern, poststructuralist, postcolonial, and post-Marxist) theorists at describing transnational histories, epistemologies, and processes of identification, and their attempts to complicate hydraulic notions of resistance to hegemony, much analysis remains trapped in an anachronistic understanding of the dynamics of culture. The nationalist imaginary has proved remarkably tenacious, as have Enlightenment notions of power and its contestation. We continue to think dialectically about seemingly bilateral relations in spite of the contemporary theoretical emphasis on rhizomatic cultural formations, liminality, the (global) circulation of texts, and translation and transculturation.

If we refuse the dialectical turn and renounce bilateralism as a way of understanding how cultures and (imagined) nations relate to one another in the modern world, we are better placed to conceive of the passages, circulation, and tactical deployment of cultural practices. The two essays comprising this section are refined instances of this refusal and renunciation: both describe the use of aspects of "American" culture (country and rap music, respectively, as well as their social-symbolic architecture) in dynamic processes of triangulation that link their origins (in the United States), their destinations (Norway and Japan, respectively), and third terms demarcated by the context and political priorities of performers and their publics (the "abject rural" Norwegian constituency's opposition to the European Union and Japanese rap performers' sense of the invidious spread of Euro-American military power and the technologies of global capital).

Kristin Solli and Ian Condry each trace a (dis- and re-)location of culture, a journey of cultural practice that exists beneath the sign of the verb: how, they ask, do particular communities put aspects of American culture to work? In both arguments—given the complicating effects of the triangulation they describe—this work entails a redefinition, a resetting, indeed a *productive consumption*, of cultural practice. It is a reworking (I would be tempted to use the trope of *improvisation* to describe this practice of manipulation, redefinition, recombination, and the insinuation of local priorities) that complicates any sense of a bilateral relationship, just as it challenges the idea of nations inscribed in any bilateral model of analysis.

This complication is evident at three levels. First, neither of the two musical subcultures described by the authors can be identified with *the* United States in any uncomplicated singular sense (both country and rap speak to particular American histories, priorities, and ideologies and cannot themselves be generalized as just "American"). Second, the contexts of their reception (Norway and Japan) are, of course, socially, politically, and economically variegated and dynamic societies that comprise a number of constituencies with different histories, cultural priorities and fears, and political commitments and aspirations. Finally, the particular Norwegian and Japanese communities and subcultures described are embroiled in transnational imaginaries in which "America" already circulates as shorthand for a number of contemporary ideological proclivities and global dispositions (among others, it is simultaneously synonymous with opportunity, democracy, late capitalism, globalization, neoliberalism, unchecked consumption, rampant militarization, neocolonialism, and so on). Further, U.S. history, from its origins to the invasions of Iraq, which is so widely and continuously circulated in our mediated CNN-Macworld, provides correlates for the understanding and formulation of local concerns and positions. The United States is inevitably a compelling resource for understanding and describing the world and the place of various collectives (nations, cultures, and subcultures) within it.

It is this *use* of aspects of "American" culture and history—this endless reworking—that (in many contexts and situations) gives the lie to any clear sense of "Americanization" and "anti-Americanism." As Solli and Condry point out, these turn out to be blunt terms—endlessly rehearsed rhetorical formations rather than useful descriptions—when we admit the complex triangulation entailed in transnational cultural flows and circulations. We are, both of their arguments suggest, in a territory of both/and, not either/or: of mimicry, emulation, imitation, use, manipulation, recombination, improvisation, but also of rejection, denunciation, judgment, disparagement, and occasionally even militant hostility. It's all "Yankee go/come home!" This doubling should not take us by surprise; in very different ways, postcolonial theory, transnational cultural studies, and even psychoanalysis have made it legible.

I would like to conclude with an oblique digression. Unbeknownst to many Americans, Richard Widmark became South African. He is probably best remembered for the moment in *Kiss of Death*, released in 1947, when, playing the villainous Tommy Udo, giggling maniacally, he pushes a woman in a wheelchair (played by Mildred Dunnock) down a flight of stairs to her death. He won a Golden Globe for his role and was nominated for the Best Supporting Actor Academy Award. Widmark went on to star in several more films noir, dozens of westerns, and a few popular thrillers, amassing an impressive filmography of seventy-three titles. In the 1950s he was much beloved—as the short stories of

Can Themba (1985), Bloke Modisane's memoir (1986), Lewis Nkosi's essays (1983), a social history by Mike Nicol (1991), and Rob Nixon's (1994) academic study attest—of South African township gangsters and toughs, particularly members of a flamboyant gang called "the Americans," who emulated not just his style of clothing but also his characteristic drawl. It was from among the twenty-six films that Widmark made during the 1950s that many township favorites were chosen, and it was these that apparently led to the most cacophonous audience participation—much of which seems to have amounted to cheering the villains and ridiculing the police.

Widmark "became" South African to the extent that his rugged individualism and defiant demeanor provided a section of the black South African urban community with a style for expressing both a version of modernity (in the face of the apartheid state's efforts to reify "African tradition") and a politics of defiance. There is little to be gained by making the obvious point that this entails a politics of *style*, not political content as such, or that it decontextualizes and fetishizes one figure in a system of meaning. The point is that Widmark—the South African Widmark—came to mean something particularly significant for disenfranchised, impoverished, and oppressed black South Africans.

This is another instance of the triangulation indentified by Solli and Condry, but that is not my point here. I wish to dwell, albeit briefly, on the figure of the metonym. In his theorization of the rhetorical construction of subalterneity, Homi K. Bhabha explores Jacques Derrida's understanding of the metonymic process. A metonym, of course, is that figure of contiguity in which a part circulates for a whole—the example Bhabha uses is "eye for an I" (54). In *Of Grammatology*, Derrida understands this substitution as participating in the logic or play of the supplement: the metonym is premised on presence (it can stand for something other than itself), but it simultaneously circulates as an empty sign that "allows itself to be filled through sign or proxy" (Derrida, in Bhabha 55). In Bhabha's reading, the metonym provides a rhetorical lens for understanding the process through which subaltern identities are erased and persist only as faint traces of elided presence that we should endeavor to recover. It is not this precise sense of the metonym that concerns me here, although Bhabha's interpretation of the cultural construction and destruction of identities resonates with my suggestion.

I would like to propose that understanding the logic of the metonym is essential in conceiving how cultural meanings and practices circulate transnationally. For increasingly defiant young black South Africans during the 1950s, Richard Widmark came to embody an entire block of affect and a range of meanings that relate to, but are also independent of, the films in which he appears. He functions as a metonym (as, in turn, do his Florsheim shoes, his coat, hat, and gun): a sign of simultaneous absence and presence that permits a local ownership and reworking of meaning. Through the logic of the Derridean supplement, Widmark—in this local appropriation—emerges as both himself and not, as a vehicle of existing meaning (for which he always stands) and a cipher that lends itself to the flood of an urgent, tactical investment of significance in the communal, subaltern constructions of Sophiatown, New Brighton, and Fordsburg.

It may be useful to recall that the logic of the metonym is intrinsic to dreaming. In contemporary psychoanalysis, dreams are generally held to be excessive, ambiguous texts that relate, in often elusive ways, to our other modes of thought. Since the work of Freud and his commentators, one might take any one of a number of positions on the nature of this relation: dreams are the "condensed and dramatized" expression of a precipitating cause (Freud 50); they encode generally repressed desires and fears in a language that simultaneously exposes and conceals them; they arise within the discursive and narrative logic of the unconscious; they exemplify the dynamics of an anarchic play of meaning that disrupts the syntax of more public forms of speech; they are inexhaustible and suggestive texts that pry open the clumps of generally unexamined meaning that we use to manage the real; they represent the multiplicity of dissenting voices comprising the self; and so on. In each of these versions of dreaming, meaning is concentrated in symbols that indicate swaths of meaning and feeling, and the syntax of the dream—the plot that unfolds—commonly has a perverse relation among its metonyms (characters can shift roles, objects can mean different things in every instance, the meaning of signs can remain elusive even as we sense their profound significance, things can mean at once themselves and their opposite, and so on).

It should by now be apparent that I am not concerned with dreams in their aspirational sense—not "the American Dream," for instance—but the processes and practices of meaning that render transnational flows of discourse *dreamlike*. Dreaming, that is, of Richard Widmark. Elements of meaning flow along pathways, increasingly detached from their contexts—but dragging with them traces of those contexts in which they originate. They float free in some regards, steadily decontextualized as they travel and, on occasion, dramatically (even discordantly) recontextualized. They become more versatile, less confined and structured by the networks of meaning from which they derived. They decompress certain meanings and compress others. In their dislocation and relocation of cultural practice, this opening up through the logic of the metonym, they become not only elements in ways of dreaming up selves and others but also versions of community and sometimes even nations.

Perhaps if we think more in terms of the metonymic illogic of dreams (their anarchy of signification, their fluid substitutions, their insistent figuration), we might be less taken by surprise by the contradictions that are generated when meaning travels from one context to another. There is no reason to assume that flows of cultural practice and meaning—in this case of "American" cultures—should conform to the hypostasized (rational and fully conscious) categories of nationalism nor to the binary logics of endorsement or opposition. We all, at whatever remove, only dream America.

Works Cited

Bhabha, Homi, K. *The Location of Culture*. London: Routledge, 1994.

Freud, Sigmund. *Psychological Writings and Letters* (Vol. 59 of *The German Library*). Ed. Sander L. Gilman. New York: Continuum, 1995.

Modisane, Bloke. *Blame Me on History*. Johannesburg: Donker, 1986.

Nicol, Mike. *A Good-Looking Corpse: The World of DRUM—Jazz and Gangsters, Hope and Defiance in the Townships of South Africa*. London: Secker and Warburg, 1991.

Nixon, Rob. *Homelands, Harlem, and Hollywood: South African Culture and the World Beyond*. New York: Routledge, 1994.

Nkosi, Lewis. *Home and Exile and Other Selections*. London: Longman, 1983.

Themba, Can. *The World of Can Themba*. Ed. Essop Patel. Johannesburg: Ravan, 1985.

PART VI

Is It "Americanization"
or "Pro-Americanism"?
The Americas, Pan-Americanism,
and Immigration

CHAPTER 11

"Making Pals in Panama"

U.S.–Latin American Relations and the Trope of the Good Neighbor in Coca-Cola Advertising during the 1940s

Amy Spellacy

> Since the Yankees came to Trinidad,
> They have the young girls going mad,
>
> . . .
>
> They buy rum and Coca-Cola . . .
> Working for the Yankee dollar.
> —"Rum and Coca-Cola," Lord Invader, 1943

On the back cover of the April 1944 issue of *National Geographic*, an ad for Coca-Cola promoted inter-American friendship and cooperation with an image of U.S. servicemen sharing Coca-Cola with a Panamanian man and his son. Ships pass peacefully through the Panama Canal in the background while the servicemen and the Panamanians share a moment of camaraderie and enjoy Coca-Cola provided by the soldiers. The text of the ad links the image to the Good Neighbor policy, suggesting that "Down Panama way, American ideas of friendliness and good neighborliness are nothing new" (fig. 1).

In this essay I examine a series of Coca-Cola ads that offer insight into the relationship between domestic notions of neighborhood and community in the United States and U.S. foreign policy during the 1940s, focusing in particular on the relationship between the 1944 ad set in Panama and the Good Neighbor policy.[1] I juxtapose Coca-Cola ads featuring international settings with ads that rely on domestic imagery to argue that a significant relationship existed between U.S. imperialism and domestic racial anxieties. In these ads the domestic tropes of the soda fountain and the neighborhood, used to promote an association between the soft drink and an American way of life, reflect racially limited, exclusionary ideas of community that operated domestically and were exported to other parts of the world through U.S. imperial practices. Local iconography is complicit in producing a vision of the United States that serves domestic and international political ends. The racially divided social structures and built spaces in the Panama Canal Zone during this period offer a particularly pointed example of the ways that U.S. international imperialism echoed and built on U.S. domestic principles and practices. While these processes were more pronounced in Panama, a space that might be understood as both domestic and foreign because of the presence of a U.S. colony in the Canal Zone, I suggest that an interdependent relationship between the domestic and the foreign is at the heart of the U.S. Good Neighbor policy.

This essay works from a broad understanding of imperialism that emphasizes its economic and political components as well as its cultural and ideological aspects, informed by the work of Edward Said, Michael Doyle, and Amy Kaplan.[2] Although Panama was an exceptional case that involved direct U.S. colonialism of Panamanian territory, it is most useful to think of how the United States established and maintained an "informal empire" in Latin America during the period of the Good Neighbor policy.[3] While the policy reduced direct political intervention in the region, it encouraged the establishment of economic and cultural ties between the United States and Latin America, contributing to the strengthening of an informal U.S. empire.

I begin by providing an overview of the ways U.S. ideas of race shaped the physical and social landscape in Panama during the early decades of the twentieth century, exploring the realities of continued U.S. imperialism in Panama as a counterpoint to the rhetoric of inter-American friendship at the heart of the Good Neighbor policy. During World War II, Coca-Cola's relationship with the U.S. government helped the corporation to forge a connection between the soft drink and an idea of America. I offer detailed analysis of the 1944 Coca-Cola ad set in Panama, placing the ad within the context of the "Coke = Friendship" advertising campaign. Finally, I conclude by looking at a series of postwar Coca-Cola ads and considering the implications of these ads for understanding the Good Neighbor policy and postwar U.S. culture.

U.S. Imperialism and the Panama Canal Zone

During the early decades of the twentieth century, the United States imposed a system of informal colonialism in Panama, maintained through military intervention, supervision of elections, domination of the Panamanian economy, and control over foreign policy (LaFeber 70). The imperial policies and practices of the United States shaped the physical and social landscapes of the Panama Canal Zone, particularly evident in the unequal, racially determined pay structure that favored U.S. employees of the Canal Company, and the disparities between the living conditions for white residents of the U.S.-controlled Canal Zone, West Indian laborers, and Panamanians.

During the construction of the canal, both Ferdinand de Lesseps, the French engineer who first attempted a canal in Panama, and later American engineers imported laborers from the British West Indies who spoke English and were largely of African descent. Because these laborers were given preference for jobs also coveted by Panamanians, their presence further complicated racial tensions between the U.S. administrators and Panamanians. While the majority of mestizo Panamanians separated themselves from the black West Indian workers, the unequal wage system implemented by the Americans who managed the construction of the canal grouped the two populations together as second-class workers. Historian Walter LaFeber explains that "while the Canal was being built, some 5,300 United States citizens and a few Panamanians received wages in gold coin. The remaining 31,000 laborers, including most Panamanians and all the blacks, were paid in lesser silver coin" (LaFeber 65). This racially based, unequal payroll system attests to the extent to which West Indians were seen as a dispensable labor source and Panamanians as subservient workers rather than partners in the construction and management of the canal and the society that developed to maintain it.

The social and physical architecture of neighborhoods in the Canal Zone also reflected the intense racial and cultural divisions in the zone and transferred U.S. notions of race and class to Panama. When the canal administrators designed the residential areas of the U.S.-controlled Canal Zone in 1912, the area was declared a "sanitized zone" within which workers could be protected from diseases and health risks associated with living in the tropics. The 450-square-mile Canal Zone was systematically cleared of "non-official inhabitants" in order to make way for the planned communities where administrators and laborers were to live (Frenkel 91). As residential communities were designed, the terms used to designate the unequal system of pay were adopted as euphemistic descriptions for the strictly segregated settlements in the Canal Zone: white residents lived in "gold towns" while West Indian residents lived in "silver towns." Housing conditions in the West Indian towns were markedly worse than in the white towns. A visiting official from the U.S. National Housing Administration commented in 1944 that the housing for West Indian laborers was "generally crowded, shabby, and barracks-like . . . creating an impression which registers most unfavorably with visitors" (quoted in Frenkel 93). As residents of the zone, West Indian laborers represented the margins of Zonian society and lived with a system of segregation that replicated the Jim Crow United States. Segregated drinking fountains and toilets reflected the extension of the labels of "silver" and "gold" to public facilities in white towns (LaFeber 65).

Because they were perceived as unfit to work for the Canal Organization, Panamanians were largely excluded from life and work in the zone. U.S. administrators preferred West Indian laborers because they spoke English and made possible a racial hierarchy understood by Americans. Frenkel comments that the absence of Panamanians was "so complete during the early years that they might not even be encountered during the course of a normal day; they were likely to be seen only on trips outside the protective Zone. Panamanians garnered scant mention by Americans in the daily Canal records; removed geographically, socially, and linguistically, they became a silent majority" (LaFeber 89). The presence of Panamanians, it seems, would have complicated the divided society that planners envisioned. U.S. exclusion of Panamanians from jobs and housing in the zone fostered Panamanian resentment of both West Indian workers and U.S. administrators. Panamanian cities outside of the limits of the U.S.-controlled zone also suffered from neglect. Resources and development initiatives focused on the zone while the Panamanian cities, including Panama City and Colon, continued to be associated with slums, overcrowding, and disease. The United States essentially cut Panamanians out of their own space in order to create a community that relied on U.S. models of racially divided labor and segregated housing.

In the "gold towns," every effort was made to transplant the comforts of life in the United States to the settlements in Panama. The hyper-Americanization of these spaces reflects both the desire of white residents to separate themselves from Panamanians and West Indians and the need to sustain the U.S. colony with tangible structures and institutions. Much of the Americanization of the zone was facilitated through the direct involvement of the Canal Company, which provided familiar foods as well as American-style recreational and entertainment facilities. Recreation was centralized in social clubs, such as the Cocoli Clubhouse, which had a movie theater, bowling alley, tailor, barber, shoe repair, soda fountain, bingo hall, and dining area. One former Zonian recalls visiting the American-style soda fountain at the Balboa Clubhouse during his high school years: "The Balboa Clubhouse like others in the Canal Zone had an honest to goodness soda fountain. It was super! My favorite drink was Cherry Coke. Of course, there was also banana splits, chocolate malts, hot fudge sundaes, and so on" (Barbier). The Canal Company promoted Elks and Moose lodges and even arranged visits from American baseball teams (Frankel 96). These transplanted aspects of American life created a separate, privileged world in the Canal Zone for U.S. employees and their families. It was also extremely important to canal authorities that the white towns appear safe, tidy, and clean. To maintain this image, the zone's health department devoted a great deal of its resources to beautification and sanitation projects, including lawn maintenance, garbage collection, and street cleaning (95). Canal authorities even sponsored gardening contests to encourage Zonians to beautify their homes by domesticating jungle plants in their gardens (93).

While the Canal Zone served as an inspiration to U.S. corporations with colonial aspirations, it also fueled resentment among Latin Americans who opposed U.S. domination in the region. The situation in Panama offered a glimpse into just how far the United States would go in extending its control and influence in the region if left unchecked and was therefore a rallying point for anti-imperialists throughout Latin America, who were terrified by the possibilities represented by U.S. colonization of Panama. At the crossroads of the Americas, Panama was watched carefully by both those who promoted U.S. interests in Latin America and those who resented U.S. hegemony in the hemisphere.

Panama and the Good Neighbor Policy

The Good Neighbor policy was a U.S. plan to improve its image in Latin America and repair relationships damaged by a long history of U.S. interventionism. Herbert Hoover first articulated the rhetoric of inter-American friendship and cooperation on which the policy was based by deploying the metaphor of the good neighbor during his 1928–1929 Goodwill Tour of Latin America. In the opening speech of the tour, given at Ampala, Honduras, Hoover presented himself as a neighbor paying a friendly visit: "I come to pay a call of friendship. In a sense I represent on this occasion the people of the United States extending a friendly greeting to our fellow democracies on the American continent. I would wish to symbolize the friendly visit of one good neighbor to another" (Hoover 3).

In spite of Hoover's earlier use of the metaphor of the good neighbor, Franklin D. Roosevelt is often credited with launching the policy in his 1933 inaugural address, in which he implies a covenant of obligation between members of the hemispheric neighborhood: "In the field of world policy I would dedicate this Nation to the policy of the good neighbor—the neighbor who resolutely respects himself and, because he does so, respects the rights of others—the neighbor who respects his obligations and respects the sanctity of his agreements in and with a world of neighbors" (Nixon 20).

Between Hoover's first declaration of goodwill and neighborliness in 1928 and the end of the policy in 1947, the Good Neighbor policy evolved from a plan initially designed to forge economic ties to a wartime political strategy also focused on countering Nazi influence in the hemisphere. While the desire to eradicate Axis networks and prevent subversive activity in Latin America was a central motivation for the policy as a whole, the strategic importance of the Panama Canal made the United States particularly watchful in Panama. During the 1930s U.S. officials became anxious about the vulnerability of the canal because of the perception of a substantial Axis presence in Panama.

In 1938 Nelson Rockefeller advised Roosevelt on the need to reassert control over Latin America with a U.S.-led propaganda campaign (Schoultz 308). Soon after, Rockefeller was appointed to head the newly formed Office of the Coordinator of Inter-American Affairs (OCIAA), the U.S. government agency concerned with promoting the ideals of the policy, largely through the production and distribution of cultural products. Because of their ability to reach mass audiences, Hollywood films were considered particularly important in achieving this goal.

In films such as *Down Argentine Way* (1940) and *Weekend in Havana* (1941), Brazilian star Carmen Miranda emerged as a cultural icon and contributed to the cause as a goodwill ambassador. The OCIAA also promoted the policy through educational films, shortwave radio broadcasts, magazines and pamphlets, public lectures, and special events, including annual Pan-American Day celebrations.

With the implementation of the Good Neighbor policy, the United States sought to temper its more outwardly colonialist policies and made a few gestures toward forging a more egalitarian relationship with Panama. However, Panama presented the Roosevelt administration with a dilemma. On the one hand, the United States was eager to appear to be a good neighbor in Panama, where U.S. presence was especially visible. On the other hand, concern over the canal made the United States particularly anxious about relinquishing control over Panamanian affairs. The issue of radio communications, for example, was a continued point of contention between the United States and Panama during the period of the Good Neighbor policy. While Panamanians sought to break the U.S. monopoly of Panamanian wireless stations and develop a Panamanian broadcasting system, the United States refused to compromise, arguing that maintaining control over radio communications, particularly transmissions between ships and shore stations, was necessary to protect the canal (LaFeber 73–74; Major 357–77). The U.S. response to Panamanian concerns over this issue suggests that the United States continued to prioritize control of the canal over improvement of relations with Panamanians.

Additionally, Roosevelt failed to take steps toward eliminating the gold and silver payroll system, in spite of his professed interest in using Panama as a showcase to demonstrate the Good Neighbor policy. In December 1944 Panamanian foreign minister Samuel Lewis paid a visit to Washington to advocate for the dismantling of the silver and gold system. Roosevelt's assistant Jonathan Daniels commented after Lewis's visit that the president was "'cool on abolishing the gold and silver roll system'"(Major 374). Certainly, Roosevelt's disinterest in taking on this fundamental issue reveals a great deal about the president's true views on Panama and suggests that racist and colonialist principles continued to guide U.S. policy with Panama during the 1940s. While the "gold" and "silver" terminology gradually faded from use, the racialized distinctions tied to these terms continued to structure life in the Canal Zone, even after organized opposition to Jim Crow laws began to dismantle the system in the United States (LaFeber 65).

Coca-Cola's Wartime Strategy

The Good Neighbor policy goal of promoting a positive image of the United States as an international good neighbor was echoed by a wartime Coca-Cola advertising campaign that featured U.S. military personnel sharing Coca-Cola with allies around the world. During World War II, Coca-Cola and the U.S.

government developed a symbiotic relationship that both facilitated the global spread of Coca-Cola and supported U.S. cultural imperialism, in Latin America and in other parts of the world. On the ground level, Coca-Cola and the U.S. government worked together to pave the way for the establishment of bottling plants around the world. On an ideological level, they cooperatively promoted an association between Coke and an American way of life. In this mutually beneficial relationship, boundaries between Coca-Cola and the U.S. government were purposefully blurred as Coca-Cola was enlisted to spread American culture at the same time that the U.S. government was used to spread Coke.

After the bombing of Pearl Harbor, Coca-Cola executive Bob Woodruff made a pledge that every man in uniform would have access to Coca-Cola for a nickel a bottle, a brilliant public relations move that launched the wartime partnership between Coca-Cola and the U.S. government (Louis and Yazijian 56–57). The Coca-Cola corporation was spared the burden of financing this project when a War Department circular, signed by General George C. Marshall, "informed theater commanders that they could order entire bottling plants directly to the front lines with the food and munitions" (56). This decision not only facilitated the worldwide spread of Coca-Cola and the construction of bottling plants in more than eighty countries around the world; it also elevated Coca-Cola to a wartime priority item, protecting the company from the sugar shortages and rationing it had battled during World War I (56). Bottling plants followed the battlefronts, and the U.S. government assigned officer status to the "Coca-Cola Colonels" who were dispatched to oversee the plants (57).

Coca-Cola's desire to penetrate new markets around the world coincided with the U.S. government's goal of spreading American influence in Europe and Latin America. The company's ties to the U.S. government were strengthened by their decision to hire James Aloysius Farley, former chairman of the Democratic National Committee and advisor to Franklin Roosevelt, as chairman of Coca-Cola Export in 1940. Hired to this position with the goal of increasing Coca-Cola's foreign revenues, Farley was sent on an eighteen-nation tour of Latin America in 1941 (Louis and Yazijian 63). While he was officially attending to the business of Coca-Cola on this tour, Farley's travels in Latin America were facilitated by letters of introduction that failed to distinguish between his role as a representative of the U.S. government and his role as a Coca-Cola executive. Franklin D. Roosevelt's presidential papers contain both a general letter introducing Farley to the "American Diplomatic and Consular Officers in the American Republics" as well as a letter from Roosevelt to Brazilian president Getulio Vargas, dated January 4, 1941, in which Roosevelt describes Farley as an "old friend" and presents him as a representative of the United States (Roosevelt).

The alliance between Coca-Cola and the U.S. government was bolstered by a wartime Coca-Cola ad campaign that promoted the idea that Coca-Cola is fundamentally linked with an American way of life, prompting people around the world to identify the soft drink with the United States.[4] Coca-Cola's ads during the early years of the war emphasize that U.S. servicemen have access to Coca-Cola wherever they are around the world and establish a link between Coca-Cola and "home." A 1942 ad depicts a soldier who encounters a sign for Coca-Cola, presumably while walking along a road or path in a foreign land. The text of the ad suggests that Coca-Cola is ubiquitous in all parts of the world: "No matter where you go, somewhere near you is a big, friendly red sign with the trade-mark 'Coca-Cola'" (Coca-Cola, "Howdy Friend"). A 1943 ad in the "That Extra Something" series features a smiling armed soldier in camouflage and a small inset of three American soldiers in dress uniform drinking Coca-Cola at a canteen. The text of this ad suggests that Coca-Cola is a coveted treat for American servicemen abroad, who equate the soft drink with home. The ad copy relates anecdotes told by war correspondents about American soldiers abroad who enjoy Coca-Cola: "One tells how a Ranger, returned from Dieppe, asked for Coca-Cola in preference to anything. Another cables that the main event of the week for the doughboys at a desolate South Pacific outpost was 12 bottles of Coke" (Coca-Cola, "That Extra Something!").

One particular way that this ad series links Coca-Cola with an idea of "home" is by connecting Coke with the local soda fountain and by establishing the soda fountain as an important community gathering place. These ads draw on the idea of the soda fountain as a quintessentially American institution. Because carbonated soda water was first promoted for its health benefits, the first soda fountains in the United States were located in drugstores. Gradually, soda fountain proprietors began to experiment with adding flavored syrups to soda water, resulting in the development of a variety of soft drinks, including Coca-Cola, which was a popular staple at soda fountains by 1902 (Schwartz 124). The emergence of the soda fountain as a social gathering place was bolstered by Prohibition, which forced Americans to find nonalcoholic social venues. According to David Schwartz, "When the Eighteenth Amendment took effect in 1919, many a cocktail lounge traded its bar for a soda fountain" (124). During the 1920s the development of mechanical refrigeration simplified the work of operating a soda fountain by eliminating the need to use large blocks of ice to cool the soda water and also allowed soda fountains to expand their menu offerings to include more substantial food, resulting in the emergence of the soda fountain luncheonette. While the soda fountain was a popular American institution during the early 1940s, during World War II many of the soda jerks were drafted, sugar was rationed, and the manufacturers of fountain equipment shifted to the production of airplane parts, contributing to a slowdown for the fountain industry (124).

In wartime Coca-Cola ads the connections between Coke and the soda fountain, and between the soda fountain and the community, position the soft drink as a fundamental part of the neighborhood community and therefore an essential component of life in the United States. A 1942 ad featuring a marine in his dress uniform suggests that he associates the soda fountain with the happy days of

childhood in his hometown: "On furlough and headed home! Everybody's hometown has an extra something no other place possesses. Family ties . . . familiar
things . . . familiar scenes and places. A place like the old neighborhood soda
fountain, for instance. And the happy times of youth spent there" (Coca-Cola,
"On furlough and headed home"). A 1943 ad that highlights the roles that women
played in the war effort suggests that it is "the custom in every neighborhood . . .
to enjoy delicious ice-cold Coca-Cola at the soda fountain" (Coca-Cola, "On the
campus or off "). These ads in the "Extra Something" series solidify the association between Coca-Cola and the United States by using the neighborhood soda
fountain, a place inextricably linked with Coca-Cola, as a signifier that represents
community and home.

"The Global High-Sign": Making Imperialism Go Down Easy

In mid-1943 Coca-Cola introduced a new ad campaign that reinforced the links
between Coca-Cola and the United States while extending the notion of neighborhood from the earlier ads to include a larger world community. While the earlier
ads established that Coca-Cola was a basic component of any U.S. neighborhood
and therefore an integral part of an American way of life, these later ads use the
expanded notion of a global neighborhood to naturalize U.S. imperialism and
facilitate the international spread of Coca-Cola.

This new series of ads, centered on the theme "Coke = Friendship," depicts
U.S. servicemen interacting with allies around the world. Created by D'Arcy
Advertising, Coca-Cola's advertising agency from 1907 to 1955, these ads feature
U.S. soldiers sharing Coca-Cola with people in international settings, ranging
from exotic tropical outposts to charming old-world European cities. In the open
spaces and natural settings of these ads, the social conventions used to structure
interactions in public spaces in the United States, such as the soda fountain, are
temporarily suspended. The text of the ads continues to emphasize that U.S.
servicemen have access to Coca-Cola wherever they are stationed. More importantly, however, the ads equate sharing Coke with spreading American culture,
encouraging the diffusion of the soft drink while also endorsing the creation of a
global community dominated by the United States. Each of the ads in this series
features the Coca-Cola logo and the phrase "the global high-sign" superimposed
onto a red image of the globe, oriented so that the location featured in the ad is
visible. This fusion of the globe and the Coca-Cola logo suggests internationalism
while also implying domination and homogenization. The phrase "global high-
sign" works as a pun on "high" and "hi," suggesting that Coca-Cola functions as
an international form of greeting that bridges linguistic and cultural differences
while also emphasizing the stimulating effects of the soft drink.

Like the other ads in the series, the 1944 Panama ad simultaneously endorses
American culture and Coca-Cola. While the ad superficially uses the metaphor

of the good neighbor to evoke a cosmopolitan international community and promote interhemispheric friendship in the spirit of the Good Neighbor policy, it also works to endorse U.S. hegemony in the region by allowing U.S. readers to vicariously participate in the dominance of the hemisphere by identifying with the U.S. soldiers drinking "Coke" and spreading American influence (fig. 1). The text that accompanies the image in the 1944 Coca-Cola ad proclaims, "Folks there

Fig. 1: Coca-Cola, "Have a Coca-Cola = ¿Qué Hay, Amigo?" *National Geographic*, April 1944.

[in Panama] understand and like our love of sports, our humor, and our everyday customs. Have a 'Coke,' says the American soldier, and the natives know he is saying We are friends" (Coca-Cola, "Have a Coca-Cola = ¿Qué Hay, Amigo?"). The ad suggests that the people in Latin America welcome the presence of "our" culture in "their" lives and are eager to have U.S. culture imposed upon them.

The setting of the ad in Panama ignores the history of conflict between Panamanians and U.S. Zonians living in the Canal Zone, presenting an image of harmony and camaraderie that misrepresents the tensions that continued in Panama during the 1940s. Given that mestizo Panamanians would have had very little contact with U.S. military personnel, the encounter between the soldiers and the Panamanians depicted in the 1944 Coca-Cola ad seems extremely improbable. While on the surface the image suggests a friendly meeting between the Panamanians and the U.S. soldiers, it also reinforces the idea that Panamanians were ultimately unfit as workers. The U.S. soldiers are taking a break from their work to enjoy a Coke, but the Panamanian man has no clear occupation and is represented as a simple peasant who makes his living off of the land, as implied by the roosters hanging from the saddle and the machete he carries.

By setting up a contrast between American and Panamanian forms of transportation and technology, the ad associates the Americans with modernity and progress and the Panamanians with backwardness and inefficiency. While the Americans are unloading more crates of Coca-Cola and other supplies from a speedboat, the Panamanian and his son rely on an overloaded burro for their transportation. The Americans are also presumably responsible for the construction of the radio tower and the communication station in their camp. Not only have the Americans brought Coca-Cola to Panama, but they have also brought communications technology to protect the canal. The triangular shape of the roof of the hut that houses the communications equipment reflects the shape of the mountain in the background, evoking the "naturalness" of the presence of the soldiers in Panama. The material of the hut is also clearly linked to the natural environment by the palm leaves on the roof, which match the leaves in the bottom right corner.

The fact that the issue of radio communications was an unresolved source of tension between the United States and Panama adds another layer of meaning to the ad. The image makes clear that the U.S. military personnel are responsible for the radio communications and that the Panamanians would be incapable of managing this technology on their own. Even though the U.S. audience for whom this ad was intended was probably not familiar with the intricacies of the debate over radio communications in Panama, the ad draws attention to an issue that would have been extremely sensitive for Panamanians, reinforcing U.S. control through the image of the soldiers managing the communications station.

The image in the Panama ad also establishes U.S. superiority by marking physical differences between the bodies of the Panamanians and the Americans that reinforce long-standing stereotypes of Latin Americans as racially inferior and untrustworthy. First of all, the Americans are soldiers and the Panamanians civilians, immediately suggesting that the Americans are in control. Not only do the American soldiers outnumber the Panamanians (there are five soldiers and two Panamanians), but they also appear healthier and stronger. Several of the soldiers are shown with their shirts off, their bodies displayed to highlight their strength and good health, including the soldier with the muscular arm in the lower left-hand corner and the soldier unloading the boat. The bodies of the soldiers contrast with the overweight Panamanian, whose protruding stomach occupies the center of the image. The visual parallels between the son and his father imply that the boy will someday be just like his father, suggesting a narrative of cultural or political stagnation and lack of progress. The position of the son's head on the burro echoes exactly the position of his father's head, and their identical dark hair is covered by matching hats. Given the links between father and son, it is especially noteworthy that while the father appears friendly in this ad, he is not necessarily trustworthy. He holds the Coke in his right hand, but his left hand rests on what appears to be a sword or machete in a scabbard. If the son is to be like his father, then continued American presence will undoubtedly be required after the war in order to secure the canal. The image ultimately condones U.S. imperialism by suggesting that the Panamanians need and want U.S. help and intervention. By separating the Panamanians from the Americans in ways that ultimately reaffirm U.S. superiority, this 1944 ad exposes U.S. anxieties about Latin American racial and cultural difference that persisted during the period of the Good Neighbor policy.

Other ads in the "Coke = Friendship" series reinforce the racial boundaries established in the Panama ad. The most striking example of this tendency is a 1945 ad depicting an encounter between a U.S. Navy construction battalion and a group of native men in the Admiralty Islands (fig. 2).[5] The scene shows one of the "Seabees" holding a military radio up to the ear of a native man who is dressed in an elaborate headdress and a loin cloth. The wide-eyed native man looks skeptically at the foreign technology while the other U.S. Seabees look on with interest and amusement. The image itself clearly pokes fun at the bewildered natives, who curiously are not mentioned at all in the text, which focuses instead on describing the "refreshment counter" where weary soldiers can enjoy Coca-Cola.

Significantly, this ad is also distinguished from the others in the series by the fact that the soldiers in this ad do not offer to share their Coke with the natives. While the other ads in the series show U.S. soldiers sharing their Coke with people in other countries, including Belgium, France, England, and Ireland, the most prominent bottle of Coke in this image is in the hand of an American soldier who has his back turned as he watches the natives. The native language of the local people, a feature of the other ads in the series, is also conspicuously absent.

Now you're talking... Have a Coca-Cola

...or tuning in refreshment on the Admiralty Isles

When battle-seasoned Seabees pile ashore in the Admiralty's, the world's longest refreshment counter is there to serve them at the P.X. Up they come tired and thirsty, and *Have a Coke* is the phrase that says *That's for me*—meaning friendly relaxation and refreshment. Coca-Cola is a bit of America that has travelled 'round the globe, catching up with our fighting men in so many far away places— reminding them of home—bringing them *the pause that refreshes*— the happy symbol of a friendly way of life.

＊　　＊　　＊

Our fighting men meet up with Coca-Cola many places overseas, where it's bottled on the spot. Coca-Cola has been a globe-trotter "since way back when".

Coca-Cola
-the global
high-sign

You naturally hear Coca-Cola called by its friendly abbreviation "Coke". Both mean the quality product of The Coca-Cola Company.

Fig. 2: Coca-Cola, "Now You're Talking . . . Have a Coca-Cola," *National Geographic*, October 1945.

While other ads include the language or dialect of the country featured, the text of the ad in the Admiralty Islands is written in standard American English. The fact that these ads offer different levels of friendship to white and nonwhite allies suggests that the international neighborliness promoted by this series of ads and by the Good Neighbor policy was limited by racist U.S. assumptions about who could participate fully in the world community. Reflecting and echoing racial divisions in U.S. neighborhoods during this period, these ads set limits meant to keep people of color in the international community at a safe distance.

Good Neighbors Are Local Neighbors: Refocusing the Neighbor in Postwar Coca-Cola

The end of World War II signaled the end of the period of U.S. enthusiasm for Latin America, a shift that was reflected in American culture as well as foreign policy. When the war ended in 1945 and people in the United States turned inward to focus on domestic matters, even Carmen Miranda's appeal as an entertainer waned. While Miranda was interested in advancing her career with more substantial acting roles, she was not taken seriously as an actress and seemed to have no place in postwar Hollywood ("Carmen Miranda"). The decline of Miranda's popularity can be linked with what Allen Woll refers to as "the public weariness with South American music" during the postwar period (291). Woll notes that "In *Call Me Mister* (1946), Betty Garrett sang 'South America, Take it Away,' urging the Latins to 'take back the rhumba, mambo, and samba' because 'her back was aching from all that shaking'" (291).

This reaction against the cosmopolitanism represented by the Good Neighbor policy and retreat to domestic culture was reflected in postwar Coca-Cola advertising, which shifted its focus from the international scene to the domestic scene.[6] Images of soldiers abroad were replaced by images of soldiers returning home, and the rhetoric of neighborliness in the ads adjusted to accommodate this change. While the earlier ads that were international in scope implied that people around the world were "neighbors" to U.S. soldiers, and therefore to citizens of the United States, the later ads refocus the concept of neighbor to include only those who live in the same neighborhood or town, reinforcing a racially and culturally limited sense of neighborliness. The prevalence of this more local concept of neighbor and neighborliness in the later years of the Good Neighbor policy speaks to the tendency toward isolationism in the United States during this period and suggests that the rhetoric of tolerance and international community was limited and temporary.

In order to think about this shift from the international to the domestic, it is helpful to consider two final Coca-Cola ads that are a part of the same series as the international wartime ads. The layout of these ads is consistent with the earlier ads, but instead of emphasizing intercultural contact in foreign locations, the later ads feature local soda fountains in the United States where friends and acquaintances gather to visit and drink Coca-Cola. The soda fountain functions as a strategic space that is closed, domestic, and white. In contrast to the open-air encounters between people represented in the international ads, the domestic ads call attention to the soda fountain as an exclusive, enclosed space to which only certain members of the community have access. The soda fountain is represented as a space reserved for white, middle-class people and as a fundamental component of American neighborhoods, which replaces the inclusive idea of neighbor with an exclusive concept of neighbor and neighborhood.

An ad depicting a soldier in uniform at the local soda fountain bridges the gap between the international and the domestic, marking the transition to nostalgic representations of local communities in Coca-Cola ads. The headline text stresses that the soldier has returned home to his "neighbors" by suggesting that "Have a Coca-Cola = Howdy, Neighbor" (fig. 3). In the ad, which appeared in June 1944, a young soldier who has recently returned from the war appears to be telling a war story to an audience that includes a mother with her two children as well as the fountain attendant. In this domestic scene of innocence and experience, the young boy looks up to the soldier with admiration while the mother and the girl look on. The people depicted in the ad are all unquestionably part of the same white, small-town American community. The text of the ad describes the local soda fountain as one of the first places that servicemen visit when they return home to the United States. While the ad is focused on the process of reintegrating veterans into domestic life, it reminds people of the important role that Coca-Cola played during the war in the lives of soldiers, who were able to find their "old friend" Coca-Cola in "many places overseas." The ad suggests that Coca-Cola is an international "symbol of our way of living," but the overriding message of the ad is that Coca-Cola unites people in the United States with their neighbors at home.

An ad from 1946 takes this emphasis on the local neighborhood even further. By 1946 it appears that the interest in international community so prevalent in wartime Coca-Cola ads had completely disappeared. In this ad, also set in a local soda fountain, a farmer in overalls displays his blue-ribbon ear of corn while two other men congratulate him (fig. 4). Here and in the June 1944 ad featuring the returning soldier at the local soda fountain, the viewer is positioned behind the soda fountain with the attendant. This perspective includes and interpolates the viewer of the ad in the neighborhood community that is represented in the soda fountain. This ad makes no mention of Coca-Cola as an international symbol, instead describing the soda fountain as "America's friendliest club." In fact, the phrase "the global high-sign," which appears in the other ads in the series, is no longer included. These domestic ads also replace the bottle of Coke (which appeared along with the logo in the international ads) with a glass of Coke, further

Fig. 3: Coca-Cola, "Have a Coca-Cola = Howdy, Neighbor," *National Geographic,* June 1944.

emphasizing the domestic context with a form of the soft drink available only in a soda fountain. The use of both "neighborhood" and "club" in the ad suggests a limited, local community that is not open to outsiders. While the soda fountain is a place for local folks to get to know each other, it is an isolated, insular community that does not reach across racial or cultural borders.

America's Friendliest Neighborhood Club ... Admission 5¢

Not far from you right now is a neighborhood branch of America's friendliest club—the soda fountain. There folks get to know each other better. There's always something going on in the friendly exchange at the soda fountain. Over an ice-cold Coca-Cola you'll hear ball games won by proxy, elections fought in chummy booths. It's the place where everybody can good-naturedly air their opinions, parade their pet peeves, and tell their favorite stories. Drop in and enjoy *the pause that refreshes* with ice-cold Coke. A nickel will let you in on the proceedings.

Coke = Coca-Cola

"Coca-Cola" and its abbreviation "Coke" are the registered trade-marks which distinguish the product of The Coca-Cola Company.

Fig. 4: Coca-Cola, "America's Friendliest Neighborhood Club," *National Geographic,* August 1946.

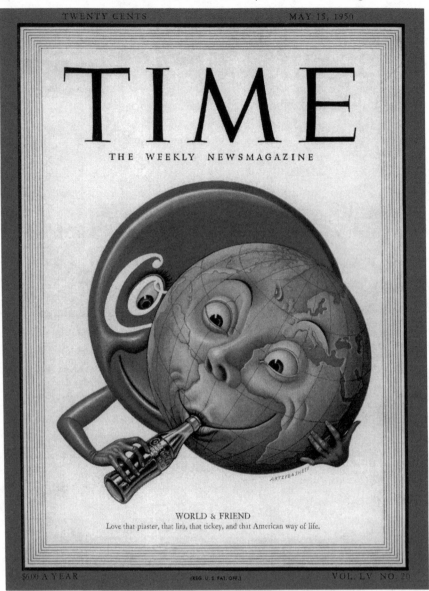

Fig. 5: *Time*, May 15, 1950.

The emphasis on neighbors and neighborhoods in these two final ads is especially interesting when viewed in light of the Good Neighbor policy. Because of their concern with reestablishing and reinforcing white communities in the postwar period, these ads can be understood as a response to the changes brought about in American cities during the war, when African Americans and Latinos made their way into previously white-dominated jobs and neighborhoods.[7] Given that Anglo-American domination was being challenged on the domestic front, the border-crossing rhetoric of the Good Neighbor policy would have been seen as especially threatening.

White women, who also entered the public world of work during the war, are also excluded from full participation in the "neighborhood club" represented in these postwar ads. In the June 1944 ad, the soldier's narrative is directed at the young boy and the soda jerk. The mother and the sister of the boy stand on the margins, watching the boy listening to the story rather than the soldier telling the story. In the ad from August 1946, a woman passes by the window of the soda fountain while the men inside admire the phallic ear of corn displayed by the farmer. The presence of the woman on the other side of the window reinforces the masculine nature of the conversation taking place between the men.

During the postwar period the connection between the global spread of Coca-Cola and the red circle logo that developed during the 1940s continued to resonate. An image that appeared on the cover of *Time* magazine on May 15, 1950, features the red Coca-Cola logo cradling the globe, which drinks from a bottle of Coca-Cola (fig. 5). This image of Coca-Cola nourishing a thirsty globe reflects the international reach of the soft drink during the postwar period.[8] The caption under the image reads "WORLD & FRIEND: Love that piaster, that lira, that tickey, and that American way of life."

The Soda Fountain and Civil Rights

While the soda fountain is often associated with innocence and nostalgic ideas of small-town life, the fact that early civil rights battles were fought around this space suggests that it also operated as a space of public recognition and community that symbolically and physically excluded people of color. The soda fountain was used in Coca-Cola advertisements because it was a powerful image of a communal space into which one could gain entry by purchasing a Coke. Early civil rights protesters understood that being refused service at the counter of the soda fountain meant they were being excluded from the community represented by this space. The segregated space of the soda fountain in postwar American culture was directly challenged in the Midwest by Edna Griffin, a civil rights advocate who took on the mission of ending discrimination in Iowa after being refused service at the Katz Drug Store in Des Moines.[9] On July 7, 1948, Edna Griffin; her one-year-old daughter, Phyllis; and friends John Bibbs and Leonard Hudson entered Katz Drug Store on the corner of Locust and Seventh streets and ordered ice cream at the lunch counter. A waitress took their order, but after someone whispered to her, she informed the group, "We don't serve colored." When they asked to see the fountain manager, he told them, "It is the policy of our store that we don't serve colored; we don't have the proper equipment" (Salemy). On July 10, criminal charges were filed by the Polk County Attorney's Office and the Iowa Attorney General's Office against Maurice Katz and Katz Drug Store for violation of the 1884 Iowa statute that prohibited discrimination in public accommodations.

Griffin and her companions targeted the Katz Drug Store because it was in a highly visible downtown location, was part of a national chain, and because charges had been brought against Katz on three separate occasions between 1943 and 1947 for refusing to serve African American customers. The Des Moines Katz Drug Store, which opened in 1930, was one location in the multistate chain of stores founded by brothers Isaac and Mike Katz, whose family had emigrated from Poland to St. Paul, Minnesota. They opened the first Katz Drug Store in Kansas City in 1914, later expanding their business to include stores in St. Louis, Oklahoma City, Des Moines, St. Joseph, Memphis, and Sioux City. The Katz stores later became known as Skaggs Drug Centers, and then Osco Drug Stores, which are still in operation. Griffin suggested that the store's connection with a larger chain of stores was a motivating factor for the protests. She commented, "We had a firm understanding that the reason we were picketing Katz Drug Store was not because he was Jewish but because it was a chain. I think it was the only or certainly the largest chain drug store in the state" (Williams 6–7). A photograph of the store shows that it occupied a prominent corner in Des Moines and that the main marquee sign featured large Coca-Cola logos, further evidence of the connection between Coca-Cola and the drugstore soda fountain (Iowa Civil Rights Commission).

During August and September 1948, Griffin organized a coordinated campaign against Katz that included pickets in front of the store and sit-ins at the lunch counter. She recalled that there were eighteen stools at the counter and that sometimes they had fifteen to twenty people there, and other times there were not enough people to fill the stools (Williams 7). Protesters were supported by Henry Wallace's Progressive Party of Iowa and by students from Drake University.[10] Katz was convicted on October 6, 1948, but even after the decision against the store, owners and management continued to refuse service to black customers and appealed the ruling. The Iowa Supreme Court upheld the ruling in 1949, making it the first successful enforcement of the 1884 Iowa Civil Rights Act and resulting in the desegregation of lunch counters and restaurants in Des Moines.

The persistence of the protesters and the recalcitrance of the store owners suggests that both sides realized the potential significance of the Katz Drug Store case for debates over civil rights on the state and national levels. The Des Moines protests reveal the pervasive nature of racial segregation throughout the United States during this period and demonstrate the centrality of the soda fountain and of the Midwest in early civil rights battles. While the Midwest may have been tied to images of idyllic relations at the neighborhood soda fountain, this case illustrates that Jim Crow practices extended into America's heartland to divide communities over issues of race. Griffin's case was a clear victory for civil rights in that the Iowa Supreme Court ruled in her favor and the ruling paved the way for more complete access to public accommodations for African Americans in Iowa. However, it is clear that this case did not settle the issue of the soda fountain as a segregated space on a national level, an issue that reemerged with the now famous 1960 Woolworth lunch counter sit-ins in Greensboro, North Carolina.

Fifteen years after Coca-Cola ads used the image of the soda fountain to re-claim white neighborhoods and public spaces in postwar America, the soda fountain continued to function as a site for the negotiation of U.S. racial anxieties and tensions. On February 1, 1960, four African American students from North Carolina A&T State University began their now famous sit-in at the Woolworth's lunch counter in Greensboro, an event that inaugurated an unprecedented period of black activism in the United States. During the days of the sit-ins, African American students occupied the seats at the lunch counter, ignored by the wait staff and taunted by white patrons. As the protests continued, young white men began to come to the store early in the day in an effort to get to the seats before the black students.

After successfully solidifying its association with the American soda fountain during the 1920s–1940s, Coca-Cola was a visible presence in the lunch counter protests. A photograph of the lunch counter taken in April 1960 shows a large Coca-Cola sign displayed above the back counter of the luncheonette (Wolff 129). Additionally, a police report notes that on the morning of Thursday, February 4, 1960, one of the white men opposing the protesters dumped a Coke on the head of one of the African American students:

> The police report for that morning read: "The tension at that time was already running high. . . . We maneuvered into several potential dangerous situations and broke up the gathers [*sic*]. During the mid-morning, a white boy spilled a glass of coke on the head of a colored student. We are unable to say whether it was accidental or intentionally." Two white youths were escorted out of the store after yelling and swearing. "Nigger" and "burr-head" were favorite epithets. The students ignored the taunts. (Wolff 42)

These reminders of the place of Coca-Cola in the Greensboro sit-ins suggest that Coca-Cola continued to function as a symbol of an American way of life that was inaccessible to people of color within and outside of the United States.

Conclusion: "Working for the Yankee Dollar"

As a representation of Latin America that circulated during the Good Neighbor policy, the 1944 Coca-Cola advertisement set in Panama reveals the persistence of imperialistic designs on Latin America and the tenuous sincerity of the rhetoric of friendship at the heart of the policy. The reluctance and hesitancy represented by this ad suggest that the policy temporarily shifted the rhetoric used to describe and direct U.S.–Latin American relations but failed to dislodge longstanding stereotypes, defuse political tensions, or alter economic disparities.

On October 18, 1944, just months after the Panama ad appeared in *National Geographic*, the Andrews Sisters recorded the song "Rum and Coca-Cola," which was an immediate success and eventually sold three hundred thousand records (Holden and Zolov 170). Like the 1944 Coca-Cola advertisement, the song reflects the interdependence of domestic culture and international relations, providing further evidence of the conflict between professions of good neighborliness and the realities of U.S. presence in the hemisphere. Although some U.S. radio stations refused to play the song because they felt it was essentially an unpaid promotional jingle for the soft drink, the song's lyrics actually connect Coca-Cola with the damaging effects of the U.S. presence in Trinidad. While this message seems to have gone largely unnoticed, Coca-Cola ironically served as a conduit for bringing a critique of American imperialism in the hemisphere to a wider U.S. audience.

The song's history points to a process of cultural appropriation whereby the Andrews Sisters and the American composers of the song profited from the labor and artistic production of black calypso singers from the Caribbean. After "Rum and Coca-Cola" was popularized by the Andrews Sisters in the United States, a U.S. District Court judge ruled that its American composers, Morey Amsterdam, Jeri Sullavan, and Paul Baron, had plagiarized the music from "L'Année Passée," a 1906 song written by Lionel Belasco of Trinidad (Holden and Zolov 170). Additionally, Rupert Grant, a Trinidadian calypso singer who performed as "Lord Invader," brought a separate successful suit against the publisher in 1950, charging that the words and the title of the song had been taken from him (170).

Lord Invader first performed his version of the song, which offers a pointed critique of the impact of the U.S. presence in Trinidad, for the 1943 carnival in his home country.[11] Although Trinidad was a part of the British Empire, the increased U.S. presence there during World War II was motivated by its strategic importance to the United States. Not only was Trinidad a key oil- and pitch-producing region, but it also had air bases in close proximity to the Panama Canal and Venezuelan oil fields (Von Eschen 36). Because calypso singers typically base their songs on contemporary events, Lord Invader explained, he had the idea of writing about the American soldiers and sailors in Trinidad who "have been taking the girls down to Point Cumana, a bathing beach, where they can rent houses and have their favorite drink, rum and Coca-Cola" (Lowe). As historian Penny Von Eschen has suggested, the song is about "the impact of American money as Yankee occupation disrupted familial, gender, and sexual relationships" (37). While many of the lyrics of the version of the song sung by the Andrews Sisters were altered, the refrain that referred to "both mother and daughter, working for the Yankee dollar" remained the same, a reference to prostitution that apparently escaped notice of the American singing group.

Both Lord Invader's version of the song and the Andrews Sisters' version draw attention to the international ubiquity of Coca-Cola and its connection with the U.S. military. The song provides further evidence of how Coca-Cola began to be seen as a symbol of America that was also linked with the emergence of the United States as a dominant presence in the hemisphere and the world. The song might be read as a commentary on the cultural contact and collision between the American military personnel, represented metaphorically by the Coca-Cola, and the people of Trinidad, represented by the rum. But while this combination resulted in a new cocktail for U.S. soldiers, Lord Invader's lyrics suggest that it also led to the destruction of social order for the people of Trinidad.

In a 1945 article in the *Chicago Defender*, Ramona Lowe reported on the controversy surrounding the song and connected the song with U.S. imperialism in the hemisphere, commenting that the lyrics drew attention to "the complications Americans have invariably left after their occupation of Caribbean islands." On the one hand, the song's history suggests that, like the Coca-Cola that greeted soldiers in foreign lands, U.S. ideas about race were also omnipresent, following U.S. imperialism throughout the hemisphere. However, Lowe's response to the song in the *Chicago Defender* provides evidence that the actions of the United States abroad facilitated the development of a new kind of international anti-imperialist solidarity based on race. Penny Von Eschen has suggested that "anticolonial solidarities and identities were necessarily racial because activists understood race to be a product of the global processes that had shaped the modern world: slavery, exploitation, racial capitalism." The development of solidarity among people of color throughout the hemisphere was certainly an unanticipated side effect of a U.S. foreign policy that in many ways reinforced racial boundaries within the Americas.

Notes

1. The 1944 ad set in Panama is part of a series of ads that promote international friendship with scenes of U.S. soldiers sharing Coca-Cola with allies around the world. The ads were printed in U.S. magazines, most notably featured on the back covers of *National Geographic* and *Life*. Although I have not encountered any evidence that the Panama ad was created with the explicit intention of promoting the Good Neighbor policy, the links between Coca-Cola and the U.S. government during World War II suggest the possibility of this kind of direct collaboration. This ad has also been mentioned by George Black in *The Good Neighbor: How the United States Wrote the History of Central America and the Caribbean* (New York: Pantheon Books, 1988) and by María del Carmen Suescun Pozas in "From Reading to Seeing: Doing and Undoing Imperialism in the Visual Arts," in *Close Encounters of Empire: Writing the Cultural History of U.S.–Latin American Relations*, ed. Gilbert M. Joseph, Catherine LeGrand, and Ricardo D. Salvatore (Durham, NC: Duke UP, 1998). Black does not comment directly on the ad. Suescun Pozas briefly comments on the ad as an instrument of homogenization and Americanization of the continent.

2. See Edward W. Said, *Culture and Imperialism* (New York: Vintage Books, 1994); Michael W. Doyle, *Empires* (Ithaca, NY: Cornell UP, 1986); and Amy Kaplan, *The Anarchy of Empire in the Making of U.S. Culture* (Cambridge, MA: Harvard UP, 2002).

3. Ricardo D. Salvatore has examined the development of an informal U.S. empire in Latin America between 1890–1930 in "The Enterprise of Knowledge: Representational Machines of Informal Empire," in Joseph et al., *Close Encounters of Empire*.

4. Although the explicit connection between Coca-Cola and the U.S. military was not forged until World War II, the global spread of Coca-Cola was linked to the U.S. military prior to that war. Cuba was the first targeted market for international expansion. J. C. Louis and Harvey Yazijian point out that the first bottling plant was constructed in Havana in 1906 to cater to American tourists, and the second was constructed in Santiago in 1913

to supply the American military base at Guantánamo, which had been acquired in the Spanish American War in 1898 (29).

5. The Admiralty Islands are a group of small islands in the Southwest Pacific that are a part of Papua New Guinea. During World War II the islands were a key strategic point for patrolling the Pacific and staging invasions. The islands were occupied by the Japanese starting in April 1942 but were recaptured by U.S. troops in March 1944.

6. While not all of the wartime Coca-Cola ads were international in focus, it is striking that as the war came to an end these international ads were replaced by ads featuring soldiers and citizens in domestic settings, with a particular emphasis on images of small towns.

7. For more on this, see Rodolfo Acuña, *Occupied America: A History of Chicanos* (New York: Longman, 2000); and George Lipsitz, *Rainbow at Midnight: Labor and Culture in the 1940s* (Urbana: U of Illinois P, 1994).

8. The cover story, "The Sun Never Sets on Cacoola," *Time,* May 15, 1950, 28–32, suggests that the international spread of the soft drink was facilitated by World War II.

9. I would like to thank Jeffrey Charis-Carlson for bringing to my attention Edna Griffin's 1948 case against Katz Drug Store.

10. A photograph taken in front of the store features Griffin and three other protesters holding picket signs that point to their connection with the Progressive Party of Iowa. The photo was printed in Jason J. Clayworth, "Civil Rights Trailblazer," *Cedar Rapids Gazette,* June 18, 1998, sec. B.

11. References to Lord Invader's version of "Rum and Coca-Cola" are from the lyrics reprinted by Ramona Lowe, "Rum and Coke Author Sings Woes of Trinidad after Invasion by GIs," *Chicago Defender,* March 31, 1945.

Works Cited

Acuña, Rodolfo. *Occupied America: A History of Chicanos.* 4th ed. New York: Longman, 2000.

Barbier, Louis J. "My Reflections of Canal Zone Clubhouses." *Panama Canal Society.* https://www.pancanalsociety.org/articles/MyReflectionsOfCanalZoneClubhouses.html.

Black, George. *The Good Neighbor: How the United States Wrote the History of Central America and the Caribbean.* New York: Pantheon Books, 1988.

"Carmen Miranda: The South American Way." *Biography.* A&E Television Network, 1996. Videocassette.

Clayworth, Jason J. "Civil Rights Trailblazer." *Cedar Rapids Gazette,* June 18, 1998, sec. B.

Coca-Cola. "America's Friendliest Neighborhood Club" (Advertisement). *National Geographic,* August 1946.

———. "Have a Coca-Cola = Howdy, Neighbor" (Advertisement). *National Geographic,* June 1944.

———. "Have a Coca-Cola = ¿Qué Hay, Amigo?" (Advertisement). *National Geographic,* April 1944.

———. "Howdy, Friend" (Advertisement). *National Geographic,* August 1942.

———. "Now You're Talking . . . Have a Coca-Cola" (Advertisement). *National Geographic,* October 1945.

———. "On furlough and headed home" (Advertisement). 1942. Rprt. in Dennis V. Wrynn, *Coke Goes to War.* Missoula, MT: Pictorial Histories Publishing, 1996.

———. "On the campus or off" (Advertisement). 1943. Rprt. in Dennis V. Wrynn, *Coke Goes to War.* Missoula, MT: Pictorial Histories Publishing, 1996.

———. "That Extra Something!" (Advertisement). *National Geographic*, August 1943.

Doyle, Michael W. *Empires*. Ithaca, NY: Cornell UP, 1986.

Frenkel, Stephen. "Geographical Representations of the 'Other': The Landscape of the Panama Canal Zone." *Journal of Historical Geography* 28.1 (2002): 85–99.

Holden, Robert H., and Eric Zolov, eds. "Rum and Coca-Cola." *Latin America and the United States: A Documentary History*. New York: Oxford UP, 2000. 170–73.

Hoover, Herbert. *Addresses Delivered during the Visit of Herbert Hoover to Central and South America*. Washington, DC: Pan American Union, 1929.

Iowa Civil Rights Commission. *Communicator* 16.2 (998).

Kaplan, Amy. *The Anarchy of Empire in the Making of U.S. Culture*. Cambridge, MA: Harvard UP, 2002.

LaFeber, Walter. *The Panama Canal: The Crisis in Historical Perspective*. Oxford: Oxford UP, 1978.

Lipsitz, George. *Rainbow at Midnight: Labor and Culture in the 1940s*. Urbana: U of Illinois P, 1994.

Louis, J. C., and Harvey Z. Yazijian. *The Cola Wars*. New York: Everest House, 1980.

Lowe, Ramona. "Rum and Coke Author Sings Woes of Trinidad after Invasion by GIs." *Chicago Defender*, March 31, 1945.

Major, John. "F.D.R. and Panama." *Historical Journal* 28 (Jan. 1985): 357–77.

Nixon, Edgar B., ed. *Franklin D. Roosevelt and Foreign Affairs*. 3 vols. Cambridge, MA: Harvard UP, 1969.

Roosevelt, Franklin D. Letter from FDR to Getulio Vargas, January 4, 1941. Farley, James A.; President's Personal File. Papers of Franklin D. Roosevelt. Franklin D. Roosevelt Library, Hyde Park, New York.

Said, Edward W. *Culture and Imperialism*. New York: Vintage Books, 1994.

Salemy, Shirley. "Activists Keep Alive Memory of Iowa's Civil Rights Pioneers." *Des Moines Register*, June 21, 1998, sec. Metro Iowa.

Salvatore, Ricardo D. "The Enterprise of Knowledge: Representational Machines of Informal Empire." *Close Encounters of Empire: Writing the Cultural History of U.S.–Latin American Relations*. Ed. Gilbert M. Joseph, Catherine LeGrand, and Ricardo D. Salvatore. Durham, NC: Duke UP, 1998.

Schoultz, Lars. *Beneath the United States: A History of U.S. Policy toward Latin America*. Cambridge, MA: Harvard UP, 1998.

Schwartz, David M. "The Appeal of Soda Fountains." *Smithsonian* 17.4 (1986): 114–24.

Suescun Pozas, Maria del Carmen. "From Reading to Seeing: Doing and Undoing Imperialism in the Visual Arts." *Close Encounters of Empire: Writing the Cultural History of U.S.–Latin American Relations*. Ed. Gilbert M. Joseph, Catherine LeGrand, and Ricardo D. Salvatore. Durham, NC: Duke UP, 1998.

"The Sun Never Sets on Cacoola." *Time*. May 15, 1950: 28–32.

Von Eschen, Penny M. *Race against Empire: Black Americans and Anticolonialism, 1937–1957*. Ithaca, NY: Cornell UP, 1997.

Williams, Verda. "Interview with Edna Griffin." Box 1, Tape 13, Verda Williams Papers, Iowa Women's Archives. University of Iowa Libraries, Iowa City, Iowa.

Woll, Allen L. "Hollywood's Good Neighbor Policy: The Latin Image in American Film, 1939–1946." *Journal of Popular Film and Television* 3.4 (1974): 278–93.

Wolff, Miles. *Lunch at the 5 & 10*. 1970. Rev. and exp. ed. Chicago: Ivan R. Dee, 1990.

Wrynn, V. Dennis. *Coke Goes to War*. Missoula, MT: Pictorial Histories, 1996.

CHAPTER 12

Americanism and Anti-Americanism
of Mexican Immigrants in Los Angeles

Guillermo Ibarra

> We must Americanize them (the newcomers to our shores) in every
> way, in speech, in political ideas and principles, and in their way
> of looking at the relations between Church and State. We welcome
> the German or the Irishman who becomes an American. We have
> no use for the German or Irishman who remains such. We do not
> wish German-Americans and Irish-Americans who figure as such in
> our social and political life; we want only Americans, and, provided
> they are such, we do not care whether they are of native or of Irish
> or of German ancestry. We have no room in any healthy American
> community for a German-American vote or an Irish-American
> vote, and it is contemptible demagogy to put planks into any party
> platform with the purpose of catching such a vote. We have no room
> for any people who do not act and vote simply as Americans, and as
> nothing else.
> —Theodore Roosevelt (1894), *True Americanism*

In the book *Anti-Americanism in the Islamic World*, Sigrid Faath points out that after 9/11 the term "anti-Americanism" has been used as a synonym for negative opinion or sentiment regarding the foreign policy of the United States in another country. Based on the definition of the term by Alvin Z. Rubinstein and Donald B. Smith, Faath recalls four types of anti-Americanism: *issue oriented* (spontaneous, tied to U.S. policy measures), *ideological* (inspired by Marxism or fundamentalist Islam), *revolutionary* (such as Castro and Chavez in Latin America), and *instrumental* (stimulated by some governments to attain domestic goals, or used for legitimating purposes).

U.S.-Mexico relations are paradoxical, unstable, sensitive, so it is difficult to determine whether or not Mexican people have anti-American sentiments. It could be an *issue oriented* or an *instrumental* issue, but in general the Mexican population is becoming more empathetic toward Americans. Regarding geography, the neighbors' ties are deep and diverse, 60 percent of the Mexican people have a relative living in the United States. The troubling historical background of these two nations has produced a kind of reluctant partnership.

In March 2006 CIDAC-Zogby International's first survey on Perceptions between Mexico and United States revealed that only 47 percent of the Mexican people have a favorable opinion of Americans, 66 percent have a negative opinion of the U.S. government, and 73 percent consider Americans to be racist. Yet, Mexicans are not anti-American in a broad sense. Only 2.9 percent believe that Mexico is a poor country as a consequence of U.S. policies, 88 percent think that English is the most convenient second language for their children, 52.3 percent would approve of a son, daughter, or brother marrying an American (CIDAC).

The perception of the United States in Mexico is multidimensional. In 2004, in a survey of the Centro de Investigación y Docencia Económica (CIDE), Mexican perceptions of Americans were 68 percent positive. It was the country with the highest sympathetic perception, in comparison to 46 percent of Cubans. In the same survey, 63 percent found favorable the incursion of U.S. agents into Mexican territory to fight terrorism (CIDE). However, in the Centro de Investigación para el Desarrollo (CIDAC) survey of 2006, in the context of immigration reform in the United States and U.S. plans to build a wall along the U.S.-Mexico border, positive opinion about Americans decreased. Only 17.8 percent approved of U.S. police agents working in Mexico for security reasons, and 90.4 percent were against building the wall.

In this essay I use the term "anti-Americanism" in a different sense. By "anti-American" I am pointing to the sentiment of American people toward immigrants who have not become completely assimilated—in other words, those who do not participate in mainstream U.S. culture—in its uniqueness and particularity. By contrast, according to Theodore Roosevelt, an immigrant who voted as an ethnic minority in a U.S. election was anti-American. Today many U.S. citizens perceive immigrants to be eroding U.S. culture and institutions, particularly undocumented immigrants. For Samuel Huntington, Latinos/Hispanics are a serious threat to an Americanism that reaches back to the eighteenth century.

I point out that current immigrants who protest in U.S. cities for immigration reform are constructing a new kind of citizenship that challenges a hegemonic, nativist concept of citizenship. Based on what is arguably a postmodernist approach, I argue that through the social fragmentation of American society—more precisely, of American cities—multiple identities emerge, constructing new patterns of citizenship, opposed to a modernist and universalistic notion of national belonging. Using the results of a survey of Mexican immigrants in Los Angeles in 2004, I argue that these immigrants' political sentiments and perceptions demonstrate a new kind of pro-American attitude.

The construction of citizenship and national belonging is also a process of producing the outside of belonging—images of aliens, strangers, and barbarians. The citizen becomes "naturally superior" to the others. In the process of social interaction, individuals distinguish themselves as part of socially dominant groups. The logic of alterity implies strategies for exclusion, incorporation, and congregation. The formation of social groups requires solidarity, agonistic relations, recognition, and alienation, simultaneously.

Citizenship as a social, political, and legal category produces otherness and "outsiderness," relations of power, and multiple political projects. As a political space, the city is a fabric composed of difference. It structures multiple social identities and engenders legal institutions, rights, rituals, cults, festivals, and so on. Urban histories show hegemonic groups constructing an image of themselves as morally upright and as natural members of the polis, in contrast to other social groups cast outside of it. The Greek polis, the *civitas romana*, the medieval Christianopolis, the capitalist metropolis, and the global post-metropolis have all entailed recognition of different groups and their virtues and defects and have included agonistic strategies and various forms of alienation.

In modern cities, undocumented immigrants are the "others," the postmodern "barbarians." Americans fear new waves of immigration, believing that "aliens" could substantially change the United States, therefore making it imperative to Americanize immigrants. The new immigrants become political when they challenge the "universal" concept of citizenship and belonging that predominates in the United States.

To U.S. conservatives, the new generation of immigrants represents a kind of Trojan horse that threatens to penetrate the physical and cultural gates of the U.S. city. The same prejudice expressed by Samuel Huntington regarding the dangers posed by the cultural influence of immigrants—especially Latinos/Hispanics—to U.S. cultural particularity is present in public opinion in the United States; it is more so as immigrants fill the streets and demand immigration reform.

According to a survey from the Pew Research Center, in March 2006 more than 50 percent of Americans considered immigrants a burden because they consume scarce jobs and housing. However, in September 2000 this same sentiment was shared only by 38 percent. Those who considered immigrants' work and talent to benefit the United States in 2006 were only 41 percent as compared to 50 percent in 2000 (Pew Center). In this essay, I am arguing that immigrants are social actors who struggle for political citizenship and defy hegemonic and legal frameworks. Additionally, based on the results of a survey I conducted in a Mexican community in Los Angeles, I argue that, despite their legal status or their lack of fluency in English, these individuals are pro-American, believers in and producers of a new Americanism yet to be decoded.

Migration in the United States is becoming more urban, making cities more cosmopolitan, multiethnic, multicultural, flexible, fragmented, and simulated. Within cities, immigrants create social worlds that defy conventional visions of city life. The creation of deterritorialized global production chains based on subcontracting nets allows the entrance of millions of immigrants from all over the world into urban social and economic agglomerations. These immigrants come primarily from poor countries, without the necessary papers, and therefore come to constitute cheap labor targets of exploitation that enable the maintenance of highly competitive levels of profit making for U.S. businesses.

Immigrants not only replace U.S.-born laborers in high-risk, low-pay activities such as the lumber, textile, and metallurgical industries. They also engage in high-tech production chains, as well as in the service industry meeting the demands of the middle and upper classes; the services they provide are janitorial, retail, landscaping, construction, and home services, among others. Another section of the immigrant population is self-employed, working as day laborers, for example, offering the kinds of services mentioned above on the streets. Others become small entrepreneurs catering to the immigrant population, or they engage in illicit activities with economic aspirations.

When immigrants arrive in U.S. cities without citizenship or residency rights, they integrate themselves into channels of people with the same national background who are located in areas with available housing. This is largely due to the flight of middle and upper classes from city centers of old industrial areas. This allows immigrants to participate in the reconfiguration of the urban form. Immigrants consume common urban spaces and at the same time develop their own ideologies, cultural practices, and modus vivendi, where many of their cultural features are produced and reproduced. As urban actors they experience, perceive, and imagine the city in their own ways, facing their exclusion from democracy as well as facing multiple forms of social and political injustice.

Wondering about immigrant Americanism or anti-Americanism in 2006 from an assimilation approach is of little use. If there is any meaning to the globalization the United States has promoted since World War II, it is the production of new political identities and actors, particular and regional, that go beyond the nation, even if this nation is the United States. In U.S. nativist conservative thought, the United States has common values that immigrants should adhere to and share, leaving their old prejudices and cultural heritages behind, particularly those that go against U.S. interests and sensibilities. The social and political movement advocating immigrants' political rights and the regularization of their immigration status, which has emerged in major multicultural U.S. cities, goes beyond a legislative conjuncture or a movement in response to the initiative that criminalizes those who entered the United States illegally. These peaceful protests, contrary to the violent urban movements in Paris, have meaning as deep as the Vietnam War protests of the 1960s and early 1970s, which also occurred within a global context of geo-economic, political, and cultural reconfiguration. What is common about the current urban movements is that they are reactions to injustices produced by the new, flexible world labor markets.

The majority of the international immigrant laborers compose what Karl Marx called a new industrial army reserve that has neither welfare conditions nor personal security (that social liberalism claims for all individuals). The immigrant laborers' presence within other nations and urban regions presents a citizenship conflict left to federal jurisdictions of the nation-state, with the subordinate apparatuses located on other levels (states, counties, or cities) lacking the power to confer political rights.

This does not mean that in the urban political game different political actors do not develop strategies and social movements to construct identities that are able to enhance possibilities for achieving citizenship. Let us recall Aristotle's definition of the individual as a *zoon politikon*, a city-space animal, with all the economic, political, ideological, and cultural implications this has. This is the reason that being a citizen means having a right to the city or a right to be in the city just as the rest. It means being political.

The issue of citizenship within global cities, which are multicultural and inhabited by millions of new illegal immigrants, forces us to reconsider the frameworks of analyses we use to determine their rights as "animals" of the global city. When analyzing the issue of social cohesion and governance, Emile Durkheim argued that the nation-state has difficulties establishing a single relation with each citizen; hence this relation was mediated by lesser entities, such as municipalities. Other authors stress that corporations or professional associations were also constituted as intermediaries that create a relationship of rights and obligations and produce a common project between the individual and the state.

Engin F. Isin considers guilds and professional associations located in cities as the intermediaries that construct norms of citizenship that over time become economically, politically, and culturally hegemonic. In the nineteenth century, professions began to consolidate and, along with the institutionalization of higher education, created elites who successfully established norms of professional performance and personal behavior and defined dominant and acceptable values, attitudes, and desirable ideas.

With the restructuring of capitalism that began after World War II, labor markets have influenced new patterns of professional formations within institutions as well as in daily life, creating a turn toward an entrepreneurial professionalism that left behind more humanistic values. The hegemony of the new waves of professionals established paradigmatic patterns and values of what it means to be a normal, desirable citizen.

Isin argues that within current postmodern city-spaces, professionals spatialize their hegemony; they contribute to the physical and social fragmentation of the city, where they secure the viability of the hegemonic urban project, establishing a set of rules and governance patterns to which those who are not citizens are subject. Immigrants are going out to U.S. streets. They are springing from grassroots movements that construct an alternative citizenship, which cannot be comprehended by received notions of Americanism or anti-Americanism. They cannot be understood in terms of assimilation into mainstream U.S. culture or whether or not they will share mainstream U.S. values once they take part in U.S. citizenship rights.

To say there will be a favorable solution to the demands of millions of protesters who have gathered in the streets and carried out boycotts throughout the country simply because the United States has been a country of immigrants puts us on dangerous ground. Whether or not the United States was composed of immigrants (which indeed it was), its global cities are multiethnic and are inhabited by new urban actors. These urban actors are denied the possibility of universally accepted standards of human development because of juridical structures, institutions, and ideologies that the new hegemonic professional entities have imposed. This means that a U.S. citizen must speak educated, standard U.S. English and share mainstream U.S. cultural ideologies, political liberalist values, and a "proper moral code."

What is new about the current historical conjuncture is that the U.S. city-space is exploding with new grassroots movements that locate immigrants, Hispanics/Latinos in particular, as actors who claim spaces arguably redefining urban citizenship. David Harvey uses "militant particularism" to denote action from below by particular urban actors with particular interests who are in pursuit of particular goals within a particular time and space. All urban actors immerse themselves, to different degrees, in militant particularisms related to their cartographic identities. When they acquire coherence they can impose their goals, interests, and perceptions onto other actors. The militant particularism's cartographic identity is overwhelming in its formation of the global city-space in the United States, hegemonized by the new professionals who consider homeless people, the working poor, and low-qualified immigrants as undesirable elements of the civic space.

On the other hand, immigrants' militant particularism within U.S. cities is achieving a coherence that is able to shake up the U.S. political system, forcing it toward legal reforms and establishing new patterns of citizenship that could overcome desires for immigrant assimilation. This movement is rooted in telluric movements of a geographic, economic, and political globalization promoted by the United States, generating transnational and transregional solidarities that will feed an anti-Americanism on an international level.

In the past five years my research team and I have done exhaustive research on Mexican immigrant communities in Los Angeles and their insertion into labor markets as well as into urban spaces, business communities, and social networks.[1] We have focused on the spatialization of their economic and social activities to understand their militant particularisms.

A random survey we conducted in 2004 with foreign-born Mexicans from Sinaloa in Los Angeles County included questions about their attitudes and values. The answers revealed a growing adhesion of these immigrants to an American way of life but in a transformed fashion, keeping their ethno-national identities and forming transnational multicultural identities that cannot be labeled as anti-American. These Sinaloans in LA came to the United States with the hope of a better life and see the United States as a positive place full of opportunities that they cannot find in their places of origin. Do they not bring more competitiveness to U.S. business abroad through their exploitation? Does this not facilitate an economic edge for the United States? Surely being part of the strength of U.S. global capitalism is not anti-American.

Moreover, they largely expressed overwhelmingly positive sentiments toward U.S. society. One section of the survey dealt with perceptions of the survey participants' lives in the United States. The results were unexpected: 96 percent answered that it was fortunate that they were able to come to the States; 92 percent thought that they would soon improve their economic status (32 percent very soon and 46 percent in the short run); 69 percent found a job "very easily"; 69 percent considered themselves to have a good job; 83 percent answered that they have a better life than in Mexico; 75 percent said they have never encountered discrimination; 76 percent enjoyed a "good social life"; 67 percent have better health services than in their home country; and only 18.4 percent said they would like to return to Mexico.

The community surveyed can be considered "working poor," where 49 percent have earnings of fourteen hundred dollars (U.S.) per month or less, only 18.3 percent speak English, 58 percent are undocumented immigrants, and only 38 percent have a high school education or higher. In contrast to the data that convey an overwhelmingly positive perception of life in the United States, 60 percent also consider the U.S. legal system to be "unjust."

Is it possible to imagine that these poor populations with low levels of English proficiency, limited schooling, and undocumented legal status could be experimenting with and producing a new form of Americanism? Is it possible that the ten million Mexicans living in the United States will assimilate into mainstream culture with no trace of their origins? This is an authoritarian and conservative fantasy. American particularity is a historical process; it did not have a definitive moment of creation and does not have a defined trajectory. Current immigrants' fight for political citizenship is redefining what it means to be American, and the social sciences have the challenge of building new conceptual frameworks to address this new sociopolitical landscape. The Sinaloans in Los Angeles who took part in my survey likely appear to many U.S. conservatives as a threat. Yet, they are the new Americans; they are building a citizenry and in the process redefining what it means to be an American.

Notes

I acknowledge the support of the Grant CONACYT 41446-S.

1. Guillermo Ibarra, *Migrantes en Mercados de Trabajo Globales. Mexicanos y Sinaloenses en Los Angeles* (Culiacán, México: Universidad Autónoma de Sinaloa, 2006); and Guillermo Ibarra and Ana L. Ruelas, *Inmigrantes y Economía Informal en Los Angeles.* Dirección de Fomento de la Cultura Regional del gobierno de Sinaloa (México D.F.: Casa Juan Pablos, 2006).

Works Cited

Centro de Investigacion para el Desarrollo (CIDAC). http://cidac.org/eng.

Centro de Investigación y Docencia Económica (CIDE). http://www.cide.edu.

Faath, Sigrid. *Anti-Americanism in the Islamic World.* Princeton, NJ: Markus Wiener, 2006.

Harvey, David. *The Condition of Postmodernity: An Enquiry into the Origins of Cultural Change.* Oxford: Blackwell, 1990.

Huntington, Samuel. *Who Are We: The Challenges to American National Identity.* New York: Simon and Schuster, 2005.

Ibarra, Guillermo. *Migrantes en Mercados de Trabajo Globales. Mexicanos y Sinaloenses en Los Angeles.* Culiacán, México: Universidad Autónoma de Sinaloa, 2006.

Ibarra, Guillermo, and Ana L. Ruelas. *Inmigrantes y Economía Informal en Los Angeles.* Dirección de Fomento de la Cultura Regional del gobierno de Sinaloa. México D.F.: Casa Juan Pablos, 2006.

Isin, Engin F. *Being Political. Genealogies of Citizenship.* Minneapolis: University of Minnesota Press, 2002.

Pew Center. 2006 Immigration Survey. March 30, 2006. http://www.people-press.org/2006/03/30/2006-immigration-survey.

Roosevelt, Theodore. "True Americanism." *Forum.* April 1894.

Rubinstein, Alvin, and Donald Smith. *Anti-Americanism in the Third World.* Greenwood, CT: Greenwood Publishing Group, 1985.

Guillermo Ibarra on Amy Spellacy

In her essay on Coca-Cola and the creation of social and racial boundaries in U.S.–Latin America relations, Amy Spellacy connects the Good Neighbor policy in Panama to inequality in U.S. society during and after World War II. She considers neighborhood soda fountains, which were configured as sites of racial exclusion in the postwar period, and reveals how the Coca-Cola iconography produced a racial vision of the United States on both the international and domestic stages. From a cultural geography approach, Spellacy explains how racial ideas contained in this commercial imagery were linked to the formation of an unjust socio-spatial landscape. Following the same theoretical framework, here I make some conjectures related to the persistence of Coca-Cola as an iconic American product in the ongoing growth of global capitalism in recent decades, noting how Coca-Cola ads, slogans, and images still play a central role in the production of U.S. cultural hegemony. If Spellacy's analysis is focused on how U.S. ideas about race and gender shaped the physical and social landscape in both Panama and in the domestic field, we can formulate some hypotheses about the new ways that Coca-Cola ads have contributed to developing a new U.S. cultural hegemony through global capitalism. We assume that there is continuity in the cultural role of Coca-Cola in the newer form of U.S. imperialism we have today (Harvey, *New Imperialism*). The Coca-Cola Company is very conscious of this. It recognizes that in its history as a company, "Advertising for Coca-Cola has changed in many ways, but the message of its trademark has remained the same [. . .] Coca-Cola remains a timeless symbol of quality refreshing [people . . .] from Boston to Beijing, from Montreal to Moscow, Coca-Cola, [and] more than any consumer product, [it] has brought pleasure to thirsty consumers around the globe. For more than 120 years, Coca-Cola has created a special moment of pleasure for hundreds of millions of people every day" (Coca-Cola). Its slogans and iconography try to attach its consumption to the "American way of life"; to emotions such as happiness and love; and to positive symbols and actions such as family ties, friendship, relaxation, spiritual improvement, success, and good taste. In the new neoliberal society, social equality and attainment of comfort and happiness for all are promised to come through market freedom. In the free market, people can presumably decide as individuals what goods or services to consume in order to gain satisfaction and emotional contentment. In the totalitarian society of Aldous Huxley's *Brave New World*, the consumption of "Soma" was the way to feel that effect.[1] In late capitalism, characterized by rapid and ephemeral production and consumption (Harvey, *Condition of Postmodernity*), the plethora of goods and services available in the market precludes the possibility for a single product to perform as Soma does in Huxley's world. Nevertheless, for all kinds of market products there is the challenge of being sought after as a magical object of desire. Therefore, the advertising of commercial products refers to the effect of producing happiness by eating or drinking them. And Coca-Cola has been a paradigm of how to accomplish this. Its ads promote the drink as a sort of benign Soma for achieving happiness.

This characterization of the bottled and canned drink is what Karl Marx called the fetishism of the commodity. Like any other good produced in a regime governed by a capitalist division of labor, Coke requires explanation—that is, explaining the value beneath it, because its use value is not a mere metaphysical thing, but rather reifies social relations of production and the cultural contexts in which it is produced. This fetishism attached to commodities is important in comprehending how they perform as a channel of communication among individuals and explaining the articulation between consumption rituals and community life. The consumption rituals represent different forms of belonging to, or exclusion from, a specific community or social group. These rituals mark the proximity or remoteness of those consumers to the social group.[2] From this perspective, the ability of an individual to consume a good or service defines how much he or she is included in a given society or how much he or she aspires to be included.[3]

With recent developments in globalization, the advance of a capitalist "democracy of consumption" presumably makes available all different kinds of goods previously considered exotic or extravagant. The globalization of the market seemingly plays the role of integrating all inhabitants of the planet into a new cosmopolitan society that promotes the values of neoliberalism as well as U.S. notions of equality, freedom, democracy, tolerance, competition, and respect for human rights. This "democracy of consumption" creates, through the market, a new form of social inclusion into the new global society shaped by U.S. culture. Therefore, the possibility that anyone in 240 countries could have unlimited consumption of Coca-Cola might indicate unrestricted forms of social inclusion in a global community. Thus, Coca-Cola reifies values, traditions, feelings, and emotions that define "America" as a civilization.

From a cultural geography perspective, the production and consumption of goods also entails the production of spatiality.[4] As human beings, we not only produce ourselves and an artificial world of artifacts, places, regions, cities, and nations; we also produce symbols for them. That means that products index place.

For Harvey Molotch the product contains the "character of the place" in which it was created, and it subsumes local traditions, values, and artisan sensibilities, social relations, local tastes, and features of its physical form. Thus, consuming a product means not only the physical appropriation of it but also a parallel and symbolic consumption of the place and its cultural meanings: "People desire goods associated with a specific place because they want, at a distance, the place itself. We cannibalize a place—take in some of its social and cultural power, its cachets—by consuming the objects from it. The human relations that adhere in its products can be appropriated through the material acquisitions" (Molotch, "Los Angeles" 229).

The symbolic consumption of a place, a bottled and canned beverage in this case, is the material base for imagining an adherence to a common world or, one might say, to develop an emotional attachment as part of a real or imagined community.[5] As an example, while drinking Coca-Cola abroad, a veteran felt as if he were consuming "America": "I've served in the Army for 30 years . . . peace and war . . . around the world and when things were at their worst in jungle or desert, Coke brought me home to family and memories. Coke made a difference!! It's America in a bottle" (Coca-Cola).

If the consumer "cannibalizes" the place and its cultural meanings, likewise we could assume that drinking Coca-Cola is a peculiar way of sharing U.S. society, its territory, values, and social systems. The supposed pleasure a person gets when drinking Coca-Cola is akin to "cannibalizing" America; it is a ritual entailed in becoming part of a society of liberty, openness, solidarity, family, responsibility, straightforwardness, idealism, and honesty. It occurs supposedly through moments of pleasure: "to experience a delicious refreshing moment" (Coca-Cola). The official website of the Coca-Cola Company has a "Heritage" section with different stories about feelings and thoughts associated with drinking Coca-Cola: romance, military, childhood, and family memories. In different ways and in different contexts, those stories describe the inherent appropriation of "America" as a place and culture through the consumption of Coca-Cola. The narrators are Americans and foreigners sharing beliefs about the meanings of Coca-Cola that purport to bridge barriers of gender and class, creating as a result fresh modes of interpersonal communication and empathy. A Latino man realizes that different "countries have in common Coca-Cola"; an army officer says that "Coke has bridged the gap of culture" and is "like a friend of a piece of home"; a woman realizes that "Coca-Cola would be the universal symbol for people who did not speak the same language":

> I am of Latin background. I am privileged to have parents who are both Latin but from different countries. It has given me the opportunity to learn about two diverse cultures. My mother is from El Salvador and my father is from Dominican Republic. Despite the fact that both are Latin, the cultures are very different. When I visited my mother's country for the first time and then my father's, the one thing I realized that the countries had in common was Coca-Cola.

As an officer in the military (U.S. Army), I have had the opportunity to travel to 17 (+) countries worldwide. In each country from Belgium to Rwanda, Coca-Cola is there. From the capital city to the smallest village in central Africa, even in the Sahara Desert, Coke was there. It is like a friend or a piece of "home" that puts a smile on your face when deployed far from home on difficult missions! "Have a Coke and a Smile" is not just a jingle; it is the truth! Coke has bridged the gap of culture. I have seen it place a smile on a child who suffers as a refugee in war-torn Africa and Eastern Europe. This is a blessing for those who serve to ease suffering.

These narratives, along with many others, reveal the moral and aesthetic values that Americans have peddled globally. The stories refer to attitudes toward life, death, romance, love, and personal loyalty, attitudes that spread throughout the world via Hollywood films and television series:

My father would always tell me fond stories of his childhood, although he was very poor growing up in Tulsa, OK. So last year we took a trip back there, now that I am a grown man and I wanted to see where he grew up. He took me around the town and we stopped at a park when he began to tear up. I asked what was wrong. He explained that as a boy, although he was dirt poor, his mom would bring him to this park with bologna sandwiches and buy him a Coke, and he would feel like the luckiest boy in the world. My father was 77 years old and a proud father of 11 children. He was a gentle old man who drank Coca-Cola since he was a young boy. In September 2003 he was diagnosed with prostate cancer and a month later his cancer had completely spread. On October 23, 2003, I was at the hospital by my father's side; we laughed and he told me stories like he always did. That afternoon he was in bed; suddenly he lifted his head from the pillow and said, "You know what I would drink? A little Coke." [...] I got up and called my mother at home and let her know that I had a special request. She laughed and said she would come to the hospital shortly. That afternoon, my father died of heart failure. My mother had a wake at the house in memory of my father. I purchased 24 small glass bottles of Coke. That night we each took a small Coke and raised it in his memory.

Current Coca-Cola messages embrace the new plurality of the globalized market, the diversity of national and ethnic groups. The Coca-Cola ads during the soccer World Cup held in South Africa in 2010 revealed this new ethos. This new iconography displays less marked racial and social differentiation than Spellacy found in the ads displayed in Panama in the 1940s and the soda fountain ads in the United States in the 1950s. The contemporary images are more visually egalitarian. They now include as iconic Coca-Cola consumers people of different races, ages, and gender, though seemingly successful individuals predominate—athletes, celebrities, the young, and the rich. Nevertheless, Coca-Cola continues to impose mainstream U.S. cultural values.

Currently a range of beverages rival Coca-Cola, such as Pepsi. Some of them pretend to represent other countries like the recent "Coca Colla" in Bolivia or

"Inca Cola" in Peru. They attempt to break into the symbol of cola that Coke has created—a bottled taste of America. As in the 1940–1960 period when Coke emerged as a symbol of "American" supremacy in the free world, currently Coca-Cola is a product that is shaping a new cultural global community. While other products, such as McDonald's hamburgers or Levi Strauss jeans, hold a similar position, only Coca-Cola can be found and consumed everywhere on the planet—immediately, easily, quickly, and cheaply.

We could conclude from this brief analysis that as a consequence of its ads and traditions Coca-Cola is omnipresent in the globalized world and that it functions as a cultural product available to all epitomizing an instantaneous link to the "American community" and its values. The consumption of Coca-Cola thereby materially contributes profoundly to the rise of a new United States around the planet.

Notes

1. "There is always soma, delicious *soma*, half a gramme for a half-holiday, a gramme for a week-end, two grammes for a trip to the gorgeous East, three for a dark eternity on the moon. [. . .] And if ever, by some unlucky chance, anything unpleasant should somehow happen, why, there's always *soma* to give you a holiday from the facts. And there's always *soma* to calm your anger, to reconcile you to your enemies, to make you patient and long-suffering. In the past you could only accomplish these things by making a great effort and after years of hard moral training. Now, you swallow two or three half-gramme tablets, and there you are. Anybody can be virtuous now. You can carry at least half your morality about in a bottle. Christianity without tears—that's what *soma* is" (Huxley, 2006 rprt. ed., 53).

2. "We must be interested in the myriad ways in which the consumer can taste goods to create fences against unwanted others. This is culture, essentially a set of justifying principles for mustering support and solidarity, and a set of keep out signs. Culture does not just depend on organization, it is part of organization, it provides the justification for boundaries and control" (Douglas and Isherwood xxiv).

3. "In displaying their consumption aspirations and accomplishments, individuals exhibit to one another and confirm for themselves that they belong to particular groups" (Molotch, *Where Stuff Comes From* 10).

4. "[The] process of producing spatiality or 'making geographies' begins with the body, with the construction and performance of the self, the human subject, as a distinctively spatial entity involved in a complex relation with our surroundings. On the one hand, our actions and thoughts shapes the spaces around us, but at the same time the larger collectively or social produced spaces and places within which we live also shape our actions and thoughts in ways we are only beginning to understand. Using familiar terms from social theory, human spatiality is the product of both human agency and environmental or contextual structuring. Moreover, our 'performance' as spatial beings takes place at many different scales, from the body, or what the poet Adrianne Rich once called 'the geography closest in,' to a whole series of more distant geographies ranging from rooms and buildings, home and neighborhoods, to cities and regions, states and nations, and ultimately the whole earth—the human geography furthest out" (Soja 9).

5. "At most profound level, artifacts do not just give off social signification but make meanings of any sort possible. [. . .] They form the tangible basis of a world that people can take to be a world in common, things to be taken as 'real' in an agreed upon working consensus against the social vertigo of living in a world of random and dreadfully unsteady meanings" (Molotch, *Where Stuff Comes From* 11).

Works Cited

Coca-Cola Company Inc. http://www.coca-colacompany.com/stories/coke-lore-slogans.

Douglas, Mary, and Baron Isherwood. *The World of Goods: Towards an Anthropology of Consumption*. London: Routledge, 1996.

Harvey, David. *The Condition of Postmodernity*. Cambridge, UK: Blackwell, 1990.

———. *The New Imperialism*. Oxford: Oxford University Press, 2003.

Huxley, Aldous. 1932. *Brave New World*. (October 17, 2006) rprt. ed. New York: Harper Perennial Modern Classics.

Lefebvre, Henri. *The Production of Space*. 1974. Oxford: Basil Blackwell, 1991.

Marx, Karl. *Capital*. Vol. 1: *A Critique of Political Economy*. 1867. New York: Penguin, 1990.

Molotch, Harvey. "Los Angeles as a Design Product: How Art Works in a Regional Economy." *The City: Los Angeles and Urban Theory at the End of the Twentieth Century*. Ed. Allan Scott and Edward Soja. Berkeley: University of California Press, 1996.

———. *Where Stuff Comes From: How Toasters, Toilets, Cars, Computers, and Many Other Things Come to Be as They Are*. New York: Routledge, 2006.

Molotch, Harvey, William Freudenburg, and Krista E. Paulsen. "History Repeats Itself, but How? City Character, Urban Tradition, and the Accomplishment of Place." *American Sociological Review* 65 (1997): 791–823.

Soja, Edward. *Postmetropolis: Critical Studies of Cities and Regions*. Malden, MA: Blackwell, 2000.

Veblen, Thorsten. *The Theory of the Leisure Class*. 1899. New York: Penguin, 1994.

Amy Spellacy on Guillermo Ibarra

In his essay "Americanism and Anti-Americanism of Mexican Immigrants in Los Angeles," Guillermo Ibarra examines the ways that Mexican immigrants in the United States enact a new form of citizenship and reshape the American cities in which they live. He is interested in tensions between Mexican immigrants and other Americans and in how these two populations view each other. One of the central questions that Ibarra considers in this essay is whether Mexican immigrants should be considered anti-American. He explores this question in relation to a 2004 survey of Mexican immigrants from Sinaloa living in Los Angeles County, evaluating responses to questions about political sentiments and perceptions of the United States to argue that Mexican Americans are in many ways pro-American rather than anti-American. Ibarra also points to the political role of immigrants in the United States and how they are active participants in shaping understandings of citizenship, even though they do not share in the benefits of citizenship. He argues that immigrants are actually pro-American in the sense that they believe in "a new Americanism yet to be decoded" and suggests that these immigrants model a new way of being American, embracing "transnational multicultural identities." According to Ibarra, Mexican immigrants participate in a process of revitalizing American cities by contributing to the economies of these cities and by living in areas that have been vacated by other populations. Ibarra views immigrants as "urban actors" who revitalize the global and multiethnic American cities in which they live, in spite of the fact that institutional and legal barriers prevent them from having full access to the rights enjoyed by other citizens. Ibarra is especially interested in how participants in the pro-immigrant demonstrations staged across the country in May 2006 constructed "a new kind of citizenship that challenges the nativist and hegemonic concept of citizenship." After laying out some of the debates surrounding citizenship and examining results from the 2004 survey of Mexican American immigrants, Ibarra suggests that the academics and social scientists need to conceptualize new ways of understanding citizenship and American identity.

Ibarra might have strengthened his argument about citizenship by expanding on the relationship between the different forms of citizenship that interest him in this essay. At one point he refers to citizenship as a "social construct," which leads me to wonder about the relationship between legal citizenship and other forms of citizenship. If the immigrants described in this essay are not legal U.S. citizens, to what extent does the language of citizenship help to explain their status? Can one enact or perform certain aspects of citizenship without being a citizen? Ibarra might have placed himself in dialogue with other scholars who have considered these issues. For example, in *Latinos and Citizenship: The Dilemma of Belonging*, Suzanne Oboler comments on scholarly debates surrounding the concept of citizenship: "Defined variously as a legal status, a political activity, a set of rights, and a collective identity the concept has been debated with an urgency matched only by a simultaneous awareness of the unabated changes wrought by an evermore rampant globalization process on the autonomy of the nation-state throughout the world" (3). Which of these understandings of citizenship are important for Ibarra? Oboler raises the possibility of seeing citizenship as "a process that is inclusive and ongoing and one that is neither imposed nor dictated by the state alone" (5). She views citizenship as "a lived experience, grounded in the negotiated participation of all groups, of all sectors and individuals within the community" (5). This idea of citizenship as "lived experience" resonates with the processes described by Ibarra and draws attention to how individuals might enact a form of citizenship that does not correspond to their legal status.

Ibarra's essay serves as a reminder of the many ways that the United States and Latin America are connected through networks of contact and exchange. He highlights the transnational nature of U.S. cities and how Mexican immigrants in the United States remain tied to communities in their home country even as they embrace positive views of the United States. I would like to think about situating Ibarra's project in relation to scholarly and artistic works that conceive of the Americas as a space joined by historical ties and by the continued traffic of people, ideas, commodities, and culture across national borders. How does a hemispheric understanding of the Americas help us comprehend the new form of citizenship embraced by the Mexican immigrants whom Ibarra considers in his essay? Perhaps it could be fruitful to think across disciplinary divides and consider these questions in relation to the work of scholars who work on hemispheric cultural studies. If citizenship is performed rather than granted, then what role does culture play in this process?

Scholars and artists who are invested in examining cultural connections across the U.S.-Mexico border might inform conversations about transnational citizenship in the United States by shedding light on the ways that cultural texts represent the dynamics of belonging, exclusion, and identity. For example, in *American Encounters: Greater Mexico, the United States, and the Erotics of Culture*, José E. Limón examines the love-hate relationship between Anglo America and the culture and people of "Greater Mexico," a term he uses to describe the border-crossing culture of "all Mexicans, beyond Laredo and from either side, with all their commonalities and differences" (3). Limón explores the evolving relationship between Greater

Mexico and the United States by looking at a range of popular and high culture texts produced by Anglos and Latinos in the United States and by Mexicans and Americans in Mexico. Limón's analysis focuses on the complex ways that love and hate, opposing but linked emotional responses, appear side by side in these cultural texts.

We might also consider how Gloria Anzaldúa's influential work *Borderlands/ La Frontera: The New Mestiza* celebrates border-crossing identities in a way that challenges exclusionary models of American citizenship or identity. Rejecting assimilation and homogenization, she emphasizes a model of *mestizaje* that incorporates and acknowledges difference rather than one that seeks to melt different components into one homogenous culture. Anzaldúa describes her life in the physical borderlands and uses the space of the borderland—a "vague and unde-termined place created by the emotional residue of an unnatural boundary"—as a metaphor for other kinds of psychological, sexual, and spiritual borderlands (3). Anzaldúa rejects binary divisions and argues that the new *mestiza* consciousness involves a tolerance for ambiguity and contradiction (79).

Performance artist and cultural critic Guillermo Gomez Peña is interested in forms of transnational solidarity that exist outside of or reject official government initiatives or legal structures. In *The New World Border* Gomez Peña envisions new ways of establishing alliances between people, across and in spite of national boundaries, not necessarily based on race or ethnicity. For Gomez Peña, art plays a vital part in the creation of a borderless society in the Americas. However, he is careful to distinguish his work from what he calls the "official transculture" or "transculture imposed from above" (11). Instead, he foregrounds the importance of *mestizaje* in understanding the post-NAFTA (North American Free Trade Agreement) Americas: "But there is a better alternative to the obvious choice between ultranationalisms and a homogenized global culture: a grassroots cul-tural response that understands the contextual and strategic value of nationalism, as well as the importance of crossing borders and establishing cross-cultural alliances" (11). Because of his emphasis on unofficial or resistant ways to unite people who have been separated or split by national borders, it could be useful to think about how his work informs discussions of alternate forms of citizenship. Gomez Peña suggests that in this newly envisioned "trans- and intercontinental border zone," the only "others" will be those "who resist fusion, *mestizaje*, and cross-cultural dialogue" (7).

Scholars such as José Limón and authors and artists such as Gloria Anzaldúa and Guillermo Gomez Peña could contribute to conversations about transnational citizenship in the Americas in important ways. By claiming a space for hyphen-ated and hybrid identities within the United States and across the Americas, they point to the importance of letting go of exclusionary models of what it means to be American and therefore support an expanded notion of citizenship in the Americas.

Works Cited

Anzaldúa, Gloria. *Borderlands/La Frontera: The New Mestiza*. San Francisco: Aunt Lute Books, 1987.

Gomez Peña, Guillermo. *The New World Border*. San Francisco: City Lights, 1996.

Limón, José E. *American Encounters: Greater Mexico, the United States, and the Erotics of Culture*. Boston: Beacon Press, 1998.

Oboler, Suzanne. "Redefining Citizenship as a Lived Experience." *Latinos and Citizenship: The Dilemma of Belonging*. Ed. Suzanne Oboler. New York: Palgrave, 2006.

Virginia R. Domínguez on Spellacy and Ibarra

"Not Just for Latin Americanists"

Clearly of interest to Latin Americanists, hemispheric studies scholars, Latina/o studies scholars, and U.S. American Studies scholars with a special interest in the U.S.–Latin America relationship, this section should intrigue all of us engaging with the United States, especially in its various twentieth- and twenty-first-century incarnations. We have paired an essay by Amy Spellacy thinking with, and about, Coca-Cola and the U.S. government's Good Neighbor policy with an essay by Guillermo Ibarra thinking with, and about, Mexican immigrants to the United States in the early twenty-first century.

There are many ways to compare and contrast these essays and their authors but also to tease out their shared concerns. For one, Spellacy is more concerned with the first half of the twentieth century and Ibarra with the latter part of the same century and even into the twenty-first century. And Spellacy is a humanities scholar with strong literary, visual, and historical training and interests, while Ibarra is a sociologist with strong grounding in economics, labor studies, and sociology of the state. There is also the matter of citizenship, residence, and national affiliation. Ibarra is Mexican by birth, residence, citizenship, and usual institutional location, but he is also a specialist on Mexican migration to the United States. Spellacy is U.S.-born and raised, a U.S. citizen, a resident of the United States, and a specialist on the United States in its relation to Latin America. Ibarra tends to look north, Spellacy tends to look south, and both do so with full awareness of the histories and complexities of the countries in which they live and the countries they study.

The mix is provocative. Little is predictable here, and little should be assumed by the simple fact of the usual institutional location and residence of each author. Separately these essays raise questions about what is assumed (and perhaps shouldn't be assumed) about U.S. interest in Latin Americans and the consequences of that interest for those who live in one or another country in the Western Hemisphere. Together they compel me to think about "pro-Americanism" (or, better put, positive attitudes, values, thoughts, and orientation toward the United

States in various mixes and forms) much more than its presumed opposite—
"anti-Americanism"—whether as a label or as a set of attitudes critical of the
U.S. government, U.S. economic or military institutions, U.S. culture or cultures,
or the U.S. legal system. That this should come from my reading of two essays
largely dealing with U.S. relations with Latin America and Latin Americans is
surprising, to say the least. Had I thought about it ahead of time—had any of
us thought about it ahead of time—I am convinced that I (or we) would have
guessed the opposite.

Many of us know of U.S. military and political interventions in the Caribbean,
Central America, and South America since the late nineteenth century, and perhaps
even more know of frequent debates, actions, exclusions, and practices framing "illegal" or "undocumented" immigration as a serious problem for the United States
and as heavily indexing those who cross into the States across the Rio Grande (or
Rio Bravo, as it is called in Mexico). And many also know of the long-standing
U.S. boycott of Castro's Cuba (lasting deep into the Obama presidency) and, if
old enough, remember the 1961 Bay of Pigs invasion and the 1962 Cuban Missile
Crisis. All of this leads to a logical expectation that reading two essays centered on
the U.S.–Latin America relationship would compel a respondent to criticize the
United States, come across as critical of the United States, and highlight the logic
and rationale of Latin American criticisms of the United States. Yet that is not what
Spellacy and Ibarra lead me to explore. As I said above, they make me contemplate
"pro-Americanism(s)" much more, perhaps because those discourses and attitudes
exist and were not all induced through advertising and governmental manipulation
and perhaps because they are harder to understand or, if I am truly honest, harder
to "swallow" given everything else intellectuals know and critique.

I realize that I come to this topic wondering how anyone in the Western Hemisphere would not be suspicious of the United States given the history of U.S.
government action in relation to Latin America and the Caribbean since at least
the Monroe Doctrine. I also realize that I am very aware of the large number of
people from many Latin American and Caribbean countries trying to move to
the United States or succeeding in moving to the States over more than a century.
That there is an apparent contradiction here does not escape me. That some of it
is explained by the class hierarchy of Latin American countries is true but war-
rants commentary because it often remains unremarked. Yet it is also very clear
that it is not just the very poor who dream about migrating to the United States,
nor is it necessarily the poorest who do, nor do all the poor in Latin America
hold positive attitudes about the United States. The United States has clearly been
used by political exiles at various points over the past two centuries as a location
in which to live, a relatively safe place in which to design political or economic
change for their original home or homeland, a site in which they and their families
can physically survive, perhaps also wait for structural or political change "back

home," and even as a country from which to launch raids or seek U.S. support for their cause. Most notably in recent years it is the anti-Castro Cubans who have garnered the lion's share of attention as Latin American–origin political exiles in the United States and who benefited extensively from the Cuban Refugee Act of the 1960s. But southern Florida is also home to many who fled Nicaragua when the Somoza family lost power in Nicaragua, and the New York area is home to many who see themselves now as Haitian exiles or saw themselves as Dominican exiles in the 1960s and '70s, and, even further back in time, Cubans and Puerto Ricans who lived in New York while organizing themselves to try to topple the Spanish colonial government in the latter years of the nineteenth century. The United States is definitely on the radar of many Latin Americans, especially (but not limited to) those from the northern parts of the region.

But of equal interest is the question of whether Latin America is on the radar of most U.S. residents, businessmen, and politicians, whether it has long been, and what that level of interest and orientation has been over the years. If I admit that I come to the topic of this section wondering how anyone in the Western Hemisphere would not be suspicious of the United States given the history of U.S. government action in many places in Latin America and the Caribbean since at least the Monroe Doctrine, I also want to admit that I come with ambivalence about U.S. attention to Latin Americans and Latin America. For one thing, that attention often seems tainted by a kind of "hispanicism" that assumes all Latin Americans are poor, racially different from people in the United States, and desperate to get into the United States even if it means doing so illegally. But my ambivalence also comes from a sense that U.S. children and adults should know much more about Latin America than they do, should want to know much more about Latin America than they do, and should at least understand something of the similarity in European history that shaped both the United States and the rest of the Americas (including Canada)—our shared history of European conquest, colonization, exploitation of labor (both native and forced), export-crop orientation, racial stratification, and early declaration of independence from European powers as republics.

That there is some sense among many U.S. residents that it would be useful to learn Spanish would be much more gratifying if it were not accompanied by the utter dismay I frequently experience upon hearing that someone who has had quite a few years of Spanish in school can do practically nothing in Spanish. Jane Hill has written aptly about "mock Spanish" and the mocking of Spanish in the southwestern part of the United States, and I think she is exactly right, painful though it is, especially to someone born and largely raised in Latin American countries. But does that mean the United States has *always* had little interest in Latin America and Latin Americans except when the U.S. government worried that a powerful enemy—a "real" world power—was intruding, inserting itself, or taking advantage of weak Latin American governments and widespread revolutionary zeal? I am thinking of the many decades of the Cold War with the Soviet Union and, prior to that, fear of the big Western European imperial powers, especially France and England.

I remain struck by Amy Spellacy's phrase "making U.S. imperialism go down easy"—the heading, in fact, of one of her essay's sections. Joseph Nye might prefer to phrase this as U.S. "soft power" and others of us as the production, distribution, and consumption of U.S. hegemony, but I prefer Spellacy's seemingly simpler formulation. When and how has U.S. imperialism been noticed and by whom? It hasn't always been the case, as is obvious reading Amy Spellacy's essay. And when and how has it mattered—and not mattered—to U.S. residents, residents of other countries in the Western Hemisphere, and even those elsewhere? Is it possible that Sinaloans (and many other Mexicans who migrate to the United States with and without proper U.S. papers) do not care about U.S. imperialism or are even tacit (or vocal) if unacknowledged supporters of U.S. imperialism? And is it possible that the vast majority of U.S. residents also do not care, or perhaps do not know, do not believe, or do not have the information that would enable them to see what so many Latin American intellectuals and university students see as U.S. imperialism?

When we see the results of Ibarra's 2004 survey of Sinaloans in Los Angeles County, it is hard to know what to do with seemingly strongly positive views these migrants have of much of the United States. He reports that 96 percent of their respondents said it was good to have come to the United States, that 92 percent thought their circumstances would soon improve, that 69 percent found a job "very easily," that 75 percent had never encountered any discrimination since moving to the United States, and that only 18.4 percent would like to return to Mexico. Ibarra does report 60 percent of his Sinaloa respondents considering the U.S. legal system unjust, but the rest of his statistics were quite unexpected. One could explore Sinaloans more, especially in relation to other areas of Mexico, or wonder about the representativity of Ibarra's sample, but I suspect we would be doing that because we expect Latin Americans moving to the United States to develop (if they did not already have) negative views of the States. Yet Ibarra's data command contemplation. I am not sure I see enough evidence for what he argues—namely, that Mexicans are becoming more empathetic vis-à-vis Americans—but it is important food for thought. If he is right, what in the world would explain it? And if he is not right, how can the variance (or variety or diversity of opinion, position, and affect) be explained? Ibarra does include mention of the statistical results of a 2006 survey he did not conduct, and that 2006 survey reported that only 47 percent of Mexicans have a favorable opinion of the United States, that 66 percent have a negative opinion of the U.S. government, and that 73 percent of those Mexican respondents consider "Americans to be racist."

I wonder how all of this would have looked fifty years ago, eighty years ago, or one hundred years ago. After all, Spellacy tells us something I find deeply interesting and intriguing—namely, that the end of World War II was the end of the period of "U.S. enthusiasm for Latin America." She has much more data than most of us, and the period of the Good Neighbor policy has always struck me as odd and mysterious precisely because it implies much greater interest in Latin American countries than I have experienced during the decades I have been based in the United States. But I realize now that the mystery should be both about the rise of "U.S. enthusiasm" and its disappearance. Proximity does not explain it either, and neither does mass media or popular culture. Coca-Cola made huge inroads there but also elsewhere in the world, and Coca-Cola continues its presence in multiple regions and social classes now. Can it all be explained by looking at the changing U.S. economy? Would that not be too lopsided, since there are quite a few other economies to consider and quite a few other factors to take into account?

Works Cited

Hill, Jane H. *The Everyday Language of White Racism*. Malden, MA: Wiley-Blackwell, 2008.
Nye, Joseph S., Jr. *Soft Power: The Means to Success in World Politics*. New York: Public Affairs, 2004.

CONTRIBUTORS

ANDRZEJ ANTOSZEK (1971–2013) taught English and American Studies at the Catholic University of Lublin, Poland, where he completed his doctoral dissertation on *Don DeLillo's Evolving Picture of Contemporary America*. He was co-author of "Poland: Transmissions and Translations" in *The Americanization of Europe: Culture, Diplomacy, and Anti-Americanization* (Berghahn Books, 2006). He was also the co-editor of a 2009 volume, *Black on White: African Americans Who Challenged America*, which scholar Marek Paryz called "the most comprehensive presentation of African American culture, literature, and history in the Polish language" in an online appreciation of Antoszek's work. Along with his Polish colleagues, we mourn Antoszek's all too early passing.

SOPHIA BALAKIAN is a PhD candidate in the Department of Anthropology at the University of Illinois at Urbana–Champaign. She is completing a dissertation about ways that Somali and Congolese refugees navigate the bureaucracy of refugee resettlement processes between Kenya and North America. She conducted fieldwork for this project in Nairobi, Kenya, and Columbus, Ohio, from 2013 to 2015. Her research was funded by the Wenner-Gren Foundation and the Social Science Research Council. She is currently a Mellon/ACLS Dissertation Completion Fellow.

ZSÓFIA BÁN is associate professor in the Department of American Studies, Eötvös Loránd University, Budapest, where she teaches courses on American literature, literary and critical theory, and American art and visual culture. She is author of *Desire and De-Scription: Problems of Word and Image in the Late Poetry of W. C. Williams* (Rodopi, 1999) and co-author of *Exposed Memory: Family Pictures in Private and Collective Memory* (Central European University Press, 2010). Her three volumes of essays are *Amerikáner* (2000), *Próbacsomagolás* (Test Packing, 2008), and *Turul és dínó* (The Turul Bird and the Dinosaur, 2016). She made her fiction debut in 2007 with *Esti iskola* (Night School: A Reader for Adults), followed by *Amikor még csak az állatok éltek* (When There Were Only Animals, 2012). Her short stories have been widely anthologized in a number of languages, and her two books of fiction have come out in German and Spanish. She is currently DAAD writer-in-residence in Berlin.

SABINE BROECK is Professor of Literature and Cultural Studies and teaches American Studies with a strong emphasis on gender and race from a post-slavery perspective at the University of Bremen, Germany. From 2002 to 2005 she served as vice president for International Relations at the university. She is author of *White Amnesia—Black Memory? American Women's Writing and History* (Lang, 1999) and *The Decolonized Body: Female Protagonists in the African-American Narrative Tradition from the 1930s to the 1980s* (in German, Campus Verlag, 1988). From 2007 to 2015 she also served as president of CAAR, the Collegium for African American Research, centered in Europe, and was the director of the University of Bremen's Institute for Postcolonial and Transcultural Studies (INPUTS) from 2004 to 2015. Currently Broeck is at work on *Gender and Anti-Blackness*, contracted with SUNY Press.

IAN CONDRY is Professor of Japanese Culture and Media Studies at the Massachusetts Institute of Technology in Global Studies and Languages. Dr. Condry is a cultural anthropologist who uses fieldwork and ethnography to study media, popular culture, and globalization from below. He is the author of *Hip-Hop Japan: Rap and the Paths of Cultural Globalization* (2006) and *The Soul of Anime: Collaborative Creativity and Japan's Media Success Story* (2013), both from Duke University Press. In 2012 he founded the Creative Communities Initiative at MIT, which explores ethnographically the connections between online and offline worlds and their potential to offer new solutions to old problems.

KATE DELANEY had an extensive career in the U.S. Foreign Service and among other postings served as cultural attaché at the U.S. embassy in The Hague and from 1996 to 2000 as U.S. cultural attaché in Warsaw. After her work in the Foreign Service, she taught literature courses at MIT and served as a housemaster there with her husband, Thomas Delaney, retiring from MIT in 2014. As a specialist in American Studies, she served for many years on the editorial board of the *Journal of American Studies*, and her current research interests include international American Studies, American cultural influence abroad, and post–Cold War culture. Many of her publications deal with the "transmission and translation" of American culture into other contexts.

JANE DESMOND is Professor of Anthropology and Gender/Women's Studies at the University of Illinois at Urbana–Champaign, where she also directs the International Forum for U.S. Studies: A Center for the Transnational Study of the United States, which she co-founded with Virginia Domínguez in 1995. A specialist in American Studies, performance studies, and human–animal studies, she holds a PhD in American Studies from Yale and is the author or editor of several books, including *Staging Tourism: Bodies on Display from Waikiki to Sea World* (University of Chicago Press, 1999) and of *Meaning in Motion: New Cultural Studies of Dance* (Duke University Press, 1997), among others. She is a past president of the International American Studies Association (2007–2011) and co-editor of the Global Studies of the United States book series at the University of Illinois Press. Her most recent book is *Displaying Death/Animating Life: Essays on Human-Animal Relations in Art, Science, and Everyday Life* (University of Chicago Press, 2016).

VIRGINIA R. DOMÍNGUEZ is the Edward William and Jane Marr Gutgsell Professor of Anthropology (and member of the Jewish Studies, Middle Eastern Studies, and Caribbean Studies faculty) at the University of Illinois at Urbana–Champaign. She is also co-founder and consulting director of the International Forum for U.S. Studies (established in 1995) and co-editor of its book series, Global Studies of the United States. A political and legal anthropologist, she was president of the American Anthropological Association from 2009 to 2011, editor of *American Ethnologist* from 2002 to 2007, and president of the AAA's Society for Cultural Anthropology from 1999 to 2001. Author, co-author, editor, and co-editor of multiple books, she is perhaps best known for her work on the United States (especially in *White by Definition: Social Classification in Creole Louisiana* [Rutgers University Press, 1986]) and her work on Israel (especially in *People as Subject, People as Object: Selfhood and Peoplehood in Contemporary Israel* [University of Wisconsin Press, 1989]). Prior to joining the University of Illinois faculty in 2007, she taught at Duke University, the Hebrew University of Jerusalem, the University of California at Santa Cruz, the University of Iowa, and Eotvos Lorand University in Budapest.

IRA DWORKIN is Assistant Professor of English at Texas A&M University and previously taught at the American University in Cairo. He is the editor of *Daughter of the Revolution: The Major Nonfiction Works of Pauline E. Hopkins* (Rutgers University Press, 2007) and *Narrative of the Life of Frederick Douglass, An American Slave* (Penguin Classics, 2014). A 2005–2006 Fulbright Professor in the Democratic Republic of the Congo, he is the author of the forthcoming book *Congo Love Song: African American Culture and the Crisis of the Colonial State* (University of North Carolina Press, 2017).

RICHARD J. ELLIS is Professor of American Studies at the University of Birmingham, Emeritus. In the summer of 2010 he was a visiting fellow at the W.E.B. Du Bois Institute at Harvard University and in the spring of 2011 a visiting fellow at IFUSS at the University of Illinois at Urbana–Champaign. He is author of *Liar, Liar! Jack Kerouac, Novelist* (Greenwich Exchange, 1999) and *Harriet Wilson's Our Nig: A Cultural Biography* (Rodopi, 2003). He has edited editions of *Our Nig* (the latest with Henry Louis Gates, published by Vintage Books in 2011), as well as Charles Chesnutt's *The Colonel's Dream* (West Virginia University Press, 2014) and Harriet Jacobs's *Incidents in the Life of a Slave Girl* (Oxford University Press, 2015). From 2012 to 2015 he was president of the Society for the Study of American Women Writers.

GUILLERMO IBARRA has a PhD in economics from the National Autonomous University of Mexico (UNAM). He was founder and dean of the School of International Studies and Public Affairs at the Autonomous University of Sinaloa (UAS) and president of the Mexican Association for Canadian Studies. His latest published books are *Reurbanización Neoliberal: Atlanta y el megaproyecto del Betline* (2014); *Trabajar en tierras lejanas: Vidas mexicanas en Los Angeles* (2013); and *Santa Monica: La construcción de una ciudad sustentable* (2012). He is currently professor of Regional and Urban Studies at UAS.

SEYED MOHAMMAD MARANDI is Associate Professor in the Faculty of World Studies at the University of Tehran. He writes on American literature and on colonial and postcolonial studies. He is author of "The Oriental World of Lord Byron and the Orientalism of Literary Scholars," *Middle East Critique* (2006); and "Reading Azar Nafisi in Tehran," *Comparative American Studies* (2008).

GIORGIO MARIANI is Professor of American Literature at the "Sapienza" University of Rome and one of the editors of *Ácoma*, an Italian journal of American Studies. He has written, edited, and co-edited several books, including *Spectacular Narratives: Representations of Class and War in Stephen Crane and the American 1890s* (P. Lang, 1992), *Post-tribal Epics: The Native American Novel between Tradition and Modernity* (E. Mellen Press, 1996), *Le parole e le armi* [Words and Arms: Essays on War and Violence in American Literature and Culture] (Marcos y Marcos, 1996), *La penna e il tamburo* [The Pen and the Drum] (Ombre Corte, 2003), *Emerson at 200* (Aracne, 2004), and *America at Large* (Shake, 2004). His latest book is titled *Waging War on War: Peacefighting in American Literature* and was published in 2015 in the same Global Studies of the United States series of the University of Illinois Press in which the present volume appears. From 2011 to 2015 he served as president of the International American Studies Association.

ANA MAUAD is Associate Professor at Universidade Federal Fluminense, Rio de Janeiro, Brazil. Her interests include the theory and methodology of history, cultural history, the history of images and memory, oral history, photography, and film studies. Her current research project analyzes the relationship between twentieth-century photographic experience and historical narrative both in Brazil and abroad, focusing on Brazilian, U.S., and European photojournalists, the images they have produced, and their impact in producing historical meanings.

LOES NAS is Extraordinary Associate Professor in the Department of English at the University of the Western Cape, South Africa. Her research and teaching interests are in literary theory, contemporary American literature and film, media studies, and journalism. She has published research articles in the *Journal of Literary Studies, Literator, Semiotica, English Academy Review*, and *Imprimatur*, and has translated books and manuscripts from Dutch to English for the past thirty years. After living in Kuala Lumpur, Malaysia, for three years, from 2013 to

2016, she returned to Cape Town and moves in snowbird fashion between Cape Town and The Hague.

EDWARD SCHATZ is Associate Professor of Political Science at the University of Toronto, Canada. He is interested in identity politics, social transformations, social movements, anti-Americanism, and authoritarianism with a focus on the former USSR, particularly Central Asia. His publications include an edited volume, *Political Ethnography* (University of Chicago Press, 2009), and *Modern Clan Politics* (University of Washington Press, 2004), as well as articles with journals such as *Comparative Politics, Europe-Asia Studies*, and *International Studies Quarterly*. He is currently completing a book on the politics of America's changing image in Central Asia.

MANAR SHORBAGY is currently Associate Professor of Political Science at the American University in Cairo, where she also served as the academic director of the American Studies Center from 2003 to 2006. Her scholarly interests revolve around U.S. and Egyptian politics. She has scholarly publications in both Arabic and English. Her most recent Arabic book appeared in 2009, titled *Aswat Obama al thalatha* (The Three Voices of Obama). And her most recent publication is a book chapter titled "Egyptian Women in Revolt: Ordinary Women, Extraordinary Roles" in *Egypt's Tahrir Revolution* (Lynne Rienner, 2013). She contributes weekly political commentaries to both the Egyptian *Al Masry Al Youm* newspaper and the UAE-based *Al Bayan* newspaper.

KRISTIN SOLLI has served as Head of Studies for masters' programs and Head of Research in the Faculty of Education at Ostfold University College in Norway and is currently Associate Professor in English for Academic Purposes at Oslo and Akershus University College of Applied Sciences in Norway. Solli holds a PhD in American Studies from the University of Iowa and held a postdoctoral appointment at Duke University in Durham, North Carolina. Her work has centered on issues of music and identity, especially country music as a global genre. She is also interested in the linguistic politics of academic writing, especially the increasing dominance of English as the language of the academy.

AMY SPELLACY is Assistant Dean of Advising and Associate Faculty at the Gallatin School at New York University. Her teaching and research interests include nineteenth- and twentieth-century American literature, literature of the Americas, U.S. Latino/a literature, and transnational literary and cultural studies. Prior to Gallatin, she was a lecturer and assistant director of studies in the history and literature program at Harvard. She holds a PhD in English from the University of Iowa and is author of "Mapping the Metaphor of the Good Neighbor: Geography, Globalism, and Pan-Americanism during the 1940s," *American Studies* (2006).

MICHAEL TITLESTAD is a Personal Professor in the Department of English at the University of the Witwatersrand, Johannesburg. He is widely published in two fields: South African literary and cultural studies and maritime literature. For the last several years he has been engaged in a project concerning the prevalence and history of apocalyptic ideology, rhetoric, and intimation in South African literature. He is also an academic and literary editor, a book and music critic, and the author of a monograph concerning jazz in South African literature and reportage.

INDEX

Page numbers ending in an f or a t indicate a figure or table, respectively.

AARP magazine, 12–13
Abouelnaga, Faiza, 162
Acoma, 14, 22
Admiralty Islands, 277f, 278, 288n5
advertising. *See* Coca-Cola
Afghanistan, 22, 104, 140, 179
African Americans: academic studies about in Europe, 33–35, 65, 66; centrality of the soda fountain in the civil rights movement, 283–85; cultural influence in Poland, 84, 89n13; cultural influence in South Africa, 93; German magazine's depiction of an African American woman, 41–42; German progressives' interest in the plight of, 36–37, 42; impact of the U.S. civil rights movement in Europe, 45; interaction between white Germans and, 35–36; police killings of in the U.S., 31
African American Studies, 33
African Image, The (Mphahlele), 93
AIESEC, 85
Akaev, Askar, 141
Ali, Muhammad (Cassius Clay), 40
Al Jazeera, 95
"America": cultural meaning when transplanted abroad, 206, 218, 220, 231, 300; multiple meanings of, 1, 23, 47, 58n14, 70, 108, 218–19, 223; as a referent, 109, 110, 111–12; use as a symbol, 11, 87, 259, 299
"'America' in the World" (conference), 31
"America and Its Critics" (Fabbrini), 49; failure to allow for a variety of opinions about America, 52–53; presentation of anti-Americanism, 50–51; rejection of anti-Americanism as an analytical category, 50; review of

Italian forms of anti-Americanism, 52, 58n9. *See also* Italy
America Embattled (Crockatt), 49; depiction of America as always under siege, 51–52; presentation of anti-Americanism, 50–51; rejection of anti-Americanism as an analytical category, 50. *See also* Italy
America in the Eyes of the Germans (Diner), 58n17
American culture: African American culture in Poland, 84, 89n13; African American culture in South Africa, 93; American films and literature in Poland, 78–79, 82, 84, 89n9, 112; appropriation of country music in Norway (*see* Norway); Coca-Cola ads and (*see* Coca-Cola); commentary on the trajectory of, 207; complexities in transnational appropriations of, 258–61; dissemination through international broadcasting, 74–75; examples of Americanization in South Africa, 94–95; exploration of in Georgia, 97, 103; Hollywood and, 34, 35, 36, 136, 231, 269, 278, 301; Japanese embrace of hip-hop (*see* Japanese rappers); jazz music in Norway, 254–57; jazz music in Poland, 75, 76, 77, 81, 83–84, 89n13; political dimensions of, 233, 236n20; soda fountains and, 272–73, 279, 283–85; triangulation with other cultures, 11, 170, 231, 258, 259, 260
American Encounters (Limón), 305–6
Americanization: adoption of American culture in Poland (*see* Poland); embracing of country music in Norway (*see* Norway); examples of in South Africa, 94–95; of Hungary's culture and history, 169–70; during the Panama Canal build, 268; subversive, 34, 62, 64

GLOBAL STUDIES OF THE UNITED STATES

The University of Illinois Press
is a founding member of the
Association of American University Presses.

———————————————————————

University of Illinois Press
1325 South Oak Street
Champaign, IL 61820-6903
www.press.uillinois.edu